Nationalism, Labour and ethnicity

MANCHESTER
UNIVERSITY PRESS

For Eric Hobsbawm

Nationalism, Labour and ethnicity
1870–1939

edited by
Stefan Berger and Angel Smith

Manchester University Press
Manchester and New York

distributed exclusively in the USA by St. Martin's Press

Published by Manchester University Press
Oxford Road, Manchester M13 9NR, UK
and Room 400, 175 Fifth Avenue, New York, NY 10010, USA
http://www.man.ac.uk/mup

Distributed exclusively in the USA by
St. Martin's Press, Inc., 175 Fifth Avenue, New York,
NY 10010, USA

Distributed exclusively in Canada by
UBC Press, University of British Columbia, 6344 Memorial Road,
Vancouver, BC, Canada V6T 1Z2

British Library Cataloguing-in-Publication Data
A catalogue record for this book is available from the British Library

Library of Congress Cataloguing-in-Publication Data applied for

ISBN 0 7190 5052-9 *hardback*

First published 1999

05 04 03 02 01 99   10 9 8 7 6 5 4 3 2 1

Typeset in 10.5/12.5 pt Baskerville
by Servis Filmsetting Ltd, Manchester
Printed in Great Britain
by Bookcraft (Bath) Ltd, Midsomer Norton

Contents

Notes on the contributors   *page* vii
Preface   ix
List of abbreviations   xi

1 Between Scylla and Charybdis: nationalism, Labour
   and ethnicity across five continents, 1870–1939
   Stefan Berger and Angel Smith   1

2 British and German Socialists between class and
   national solidarity
   Stefan Berger   31

3 Spaniards, Catalans and Basques: Labour and the
   challenge of nationalism in Spain
   Angel Smith   64

4 Appropriating the symbols of the *patrie*? Jacobin
   nationalism and its rivals in the French Third Republic
   Roger Magraw   93

5 Labour and the national question in Poland
   Jie-Hyun Lim   121

6 Stalin's victory over Lenin: Russian Social Democrats
   and the nationality problem
   Geoffrey Swain   145

7 The working class in the United States: between
   radical republicanism and the 'American standard'
   Neville Kirk   164

8 Labour, state and nation building in Australia
   Terry Irving   193

9 Treading the diverse paths of modernity: Labour, ethnicity
   and nationalism in South Africa
   Tim Moldram   215

10 Nationalism, ethnicity and the working classes in India,
   1870–1947
   Rajnarayan Chandavarkar   242

   Select bibliography   270
   Index   276

Notes on the contributors

Stefan Berger is a Senior Lecturer in German history at the School of European Studies, University of Wales, Cardiff. His most recent book is *The Search for Normality. National Identity and Historical Consciousness in Germany since 1800* (Berghahn Books, 1997). He is working on a general history of German Social Democracy from 1800 to the present (Longman, forthcoming 1999).

Rajnarayan Chandavarkar is a Fellow of Trinity College, Cambridge and University Lecturer in History. His most recent publications are *The Origins of Industrial Capitalism in India: Business Strategies and the Working Classes in Bombay, 1900–1940* (Cambridge University Press, 1994) and *Imperial Power and Popular Politics: Class, Resistance and the State in India, 1850–1950* (Cambridge University Press, 1998).

Terry Irving is an Associate Professor in the Department of Government, University of Sydney. He is the editor of the Australian journal *Labour History* and his most recent book is *Youth Policy in Australia since 1945* (with David Maunders and Geoffrey Sherington, Macmillan, 1995). He is currently working on Labor intellectuals in Australia.

Neville Kirk is Professor of Social and Labour History at Manchester Metropolitan University. His most recent book is *Change, Continuity and Class: Labour in British Society, 1850–1920* (Manchester University Press, 1998). He is researching labour, politics and ideology in Britain, the United States and Australia between the 1880s and 1930s.

Jie-Hyun Lim is an Associate Professor in the Department of History at Hanyang University, Seoul. He has published widely on modern European intellectual history, nationalism and Marxism. He is working on Polish Socialist irredentism.

Roger Magraw is a Senior Lecturer in the History Department of the University of Warwick. He has recently published *The History of the French Working Class* (Blackwell, 1992), and is working on *A Social History of France in the Nineteenth Century* (Longman, forthcoming).

Tim Moldram completed his Ph.D. in history at the University of Bristol. The thesis is an explicit attempt at a comparative and theoretical analysis of ethnicity in relation to the emerging twentieth-century nationalisms of South Africa and, to a lesser extent, Zimbabwe.

Angel Smith is Lecturer in Modern Spanish History at the University of Leeds. He has published *An Historical Dictionary of Spain* (Scarecrow Press, 1996), and co-edited *Nationalism and the Nation in the Iberian Peninsula: Competing and Conflicting Identities* (Berg, 1996) (with Clare Mar-Molinero), and *The Crisis of 1898: Colonial Redistribution and Nationalist Mobilization* (Macmillan, 1999) (with Emma Dávila-Cox). He is working on the crisis of the Spanish nation state between 1898 and 1939.

Geoffrey Swain is a Professor of European History at the University of the West of England, Bristol. His most recent book is *The Origins of the Russian Civil War* (Longman, 1996), and he is studying the role of the Latvian Riflemen in that conflict.

Preface

Two of the central debates in the contemporary world focus around the issues of the decline of working-class parties, and in particular the decline of socialism and Communism as ideologies, and the rise of nationalism and ethnic identities. Often these debates are interconnected, for it is argued that nationalism as an ideology of the right has taken over from the bankrupt socialist utopias of the left. Furthermore, Labour, the argument goes, as an essentially internationalist movement has never been able to understand properly the power of nationalism and ethnic belonging over people's minds.

In the light of such contemporary debates this volume intends to take a look at the relationship between Labour and nationalism so as give some historical depth to the current arguments. The nine countries represented here provide the reader with an in-depth insight into a variety of very different experiences with class, national and ethnic identities across five continents.

Apart from core Western European countries such as France, Britain and Spain, there is a key Central European nation, Germany, and two East European nations, Poland and Russia. Furthermore we also wanted to look outside Europe at the United States, where exceptionalist arguments in terms of its labour history have recently come under sustained attack. Finally, the experiences of Labour in Australia, South Africa and India should serve to counteract a Eurocentricism which has become very prevalent in university courses as well as within the general discourse on Labour and nationalism. The strong home-grown nationalism of the Labor Party in Australia, the interconnection between nationalism and freedom from colonial rule in India and the struggle against all-pervasive racism in South Africa should make for interesting comparisons with the European experiences.

For the coherence and success of the volume it was vital, the editors felt, that all contributors addressed themselves to a common set of questions tackling the specific relationship between nationalism, Labour and ethnicity. First, we asked for the impact of politics on that relationship: to what extent was the state able to integrate Labour into the 'national community'? What was the role of the military, the Churches and the educational systems in this respect? How important was social reform or the absence of it for the processes of (non-) integration which were taking place? What was the relationship between progressive left and populist right-wing movements and Labour? Was Labour able to find party-political allies among non-working-class parties? What effect did such parliamentary cooperation or its absence have on the perspective of Labour regarding the nation state and nationalism?

Secondly, we shifted the focus to the impact of economic pressures. How far was labour divided in its attitude to nationalism according to skill and position in the labour market and at the workplace? What was the relationship between labour and ethnic minorities at the workplace? What effect did social and economic upheaval and change have on Labour's relationship to nationalism? What was the relationship between unemployment and racism/nationalism? What impact did racism have on labour? What attitude did labour take towards immigration?

Thirdly, we asked for the impact of cultural factors. In what sense did populist nationalist cultures impinge on working-class/labour movement cultures? What was the impact of a homogenising popular culture on labour?

Finally, we came up with a set of general questions which seemed of particular relevance to our topic. What definitions of the nation were adopted by Labour and what definitions were rejected (political, voluntarist, democratic *v.* ethnic, xenophobic, cultural?)? Can a dividing line been drawn between 'good left patriotism' and 'bad right nationalism'? What was the impact of imperialism on Labour's attitude towards the nation state? What was the response of labour to nationalism in multi-national and multi-ethnic states? How did class loyalties develop in relation to national loyalties? Where and why did they clash? To what degree were they compatible? What was the impact of war? Can one describe nationalism as an 'ideology of integration'?

Obviously, not all the questions raised were of equal importance to each of the countries discussed in this volume. Yet we feel that the above list provided useful guidance for authors and has contributed to a remarkable homogeneity which has allowed us to draw out some comparative observations in the introduction. The only exception is the chapter on Russia, which deals mostly with Lenin's and Stalin's differing views on nationalism and how to deal with the diverse nationalism within the Soviet Union. Although it does not quite fit the above outline, as editors we have decided to include this contribution because it clearly deals with a very important aspect of our overall question on the relationship between three key identities which have shaped people's self-perception around the world.

Finally, it is a pleasure to express our thanks to all our contributors for their patience and willingness to cooperate in our requests for yet further revisions and extra information. In the course of planning, developing, writing, rewriting and editing this book, a number of other individuals played important roles. We would like to thank Vanessa Graham of Manchester University Press for her support and encouragement. Anett Pförtner's help with the conversion of disks and the general layout of the manuscript was also greatly appreciated. Rick Halpern invited the editors to present a paper on this project to the 'Comparative Labour and Working Class History Seminar' at the Institute of Historical Research in London and we are grateful to him and all those who asked pertinent questions and made critical comments. Although we have never personally met Eric Hobsbawm, this book is dedicated to him. We could not think of any other scholar whose work on both labour and nationalism has rivalled his own in influence and importance. Like many other younger historians across the world, we therefore feel endebted to Eric Hobsbawm, whose histories on class and nation have been an important inspiration to us.

S. B., Cardiff
A.S., Leeds

List of abbreviations:

ADGB	General German Trade Union Confederation
AITUC	All India Trades Union Congress
AFL	American Federation of Labor
ALF	Australian Labour Federation
ALP	Australian Labor Party
AMWU	African Mineworkers' Union
ANC	African National Congress
BNP	British National Party
BOC	[Catalan] Workers' and Peasants' Bloc
CADCI	[Catalan] Autonomous Centre of Industrial and Commercial Clerks and Shop Assistants
CFTC	French Catholic Union Confederation
CGT	[French] Trade Union Confederation
CGTU	[French] Communist Trade Union Confederation
CNT	[Spanish] National Confederation of Labour
CIO	Congress of Industrial Organisation
CPGB	Communist Party of Great Britain
CPSA	Communist Party of South Africa
CPSU	Communist Party of the Soviet Union
CRT	[Catalan] Regional Confederation of Labour
ERC	Catalan Republican Left
FAI	Anarchist Iberian Federation
GDP	Gross Domestic Product
ILP	[British] Independent Labour Party
IWW	[US] International Workers of the World
KPD	Communist Party of Germany
KPP	Polish Communist Party (previously KPRP)
KPRP	Communist Workers' Party of Poland (later KPP)
KPU	Communist Party of Ukraine
ICU	Industrial and Commercial Workers' Union
LSD	Latvian Social Democratic Party
MSPD	Majority Social Democratic Party of Germany
NPR	[Polish] National Workers' Party
NUS	National Union of Seamen
NZR	[Polish] National Workers' Union
PCE	Spanish Communist Party
PCF	French Communist Party
PNV	Basque Nationalist Party
POF	[Marxist] French Workers' Party
POUM	[Spanish] Workers' Party of Marxist Unification
PPS	Polish Socialist Party
PRC	Catalan Republican Party
PSF	[quasi-fascist French] Parti Social Français
PSOE	Spanish Socialist Workers' Party
PSUC	Catalan Unified Socialist Party
PZPR	Polish United Workers' Party
RKP	Russian Communist Party

RSDLP	Russian Social Democratic Labour Party
RSFSR	Russian Socialist Federative Soviet Republic
SDF	[British] Social Democratic Federation
SDKPiL	Social Democracy of the Kingdom of Poland and Lithuania
SFIO	French Socialist Party
SOV	Solidarity of Basque Workers [Union]
SPD	Social Democratic Party of Germany
SRs	Ukranian Socialist Revolutionary Party
TUC	[British] Trades Union Congress
UGT	[Spanish] General Workers' Union
UNC	[French] Catholic Trade Union Federation
URP	Union of Russian People
USC	Catalan Socialist Union
USPD	Independent Social Democratic Party of Germany
ZRP	Union of Polish Workers

Between Scylla and Charybdis: nationalism, Labour and ethnicity across five continents, 1870–1939

Nationalism, Labour and ethnicity: the challenge of new times

The breach of the Berlin wall on 9 November 1989 marked the surprising collapse of Communist regimes across Eastern Europe accompanied by the even less expected renaissance of deadly nationalisms and ethnic strife. As official Communist ideologies of class were increasingly destabilised and challenged from below, many people turned to alternative identity discourses, thereby re-discovering and often reappropriating the languages of nation and ethnicity. In multinational countries such as Yugoslavia, Russia and Czechoslovakia, Communist dictatorships had been able if not to overcome then at least to freeze the disastrous effects of nationalism which had ravaged large parts of Eastern Europe in the nineteenth and the first half of the twentieth centuries. Yet the diverse cultural, religious and in particular ethnic forms of nationalism predominant in Central and Eastern Europe before 1945 returned with a vengeance once Comintern Marxism, with its peculiar mix of championing both working-class internationalism and struggles for national liberation, was dislodged from its position as prescribed truth handed down from the olympian heights of Communist Party Political Bureaus and Central Committees.

By comparison, the dominant Social Democratic variant of the labour movement in Western Europe was more successful in adopting and reformulating civic and political forms of national identity. The Social Democratisation of Western European nation states after 1945 was possible only on the basis of shedding much of labour's traditional class discourse and instead opting for appeals to citizenship and social justice. At the same time, however, Social Democracy retained its earlier internationalist outlook and channelled it into support for transnational regionalisms such as the European Union. Yet the Europeanisation of the Western European nation states together with the increasing globalisation of the capitalist economy has produced considerable anxieties among wide sections of the Western European populace. Far right-wing neo-nationalist movements in France, Austria and Germany have prospered on anti-European sentiments in their countries, testifying to the continued strength of national feeling even in Western Europe. They have been particularly successful in winning converts among Europe's working classes. In multinational countries like Spain and Britain, the nationalisms of Catalan, Basque, Scottish and Welsh minorities have increased substantially since the 1960s, and even in a country like France the regional movement of the Bretons has won an increasing number of supporters. On the other hand, in January 1999 Social Democratic parties were in government in thirteen of the fifteen member states of the European Union. Recent election victories of the left in Germany, Britain and France have raised hopes of a renaissance of the Social Democratic age of the post-Second World War era, even though sceptical observers may well point out that Britain's 'New Labour' has cut all ties even with the most right-wing versions of the Social Democratic tradition, whilst the victory of the more traditionalist French Socialists had more to do with short-term dissatisfaction with the austerity policies of the previous centre-right government.[1]

The relationship between labour, nationalism and ethnicity is not only of great contemporary relevance. Within the organised labour movement both nationalism and internationalism have a long history, and a wide variety of social scientists have spent much time and ink trying to come to terms with the question of multiple identities and the competing pull of national and class identities. The debates of the past, as well as the social history reflecting and inspiring those debates, will hopefully shed some light on the contemporary discussions and the urgent need for the left to find some appropriate answers to the crisis of socialism and the revival of nationalisms at the end of the twentieth century. As any comparative historical investigation will soon reveal, the relationship between labour, nationalism and ethnicity was never a stable and coherent one, but, quite to the contrary, one which was for ever fluctuating and dependent on historical circumstances. At the present time, when political commentators are debating the revival of

---

1 Note that thoughout this book the term 'socialist' is used to refer to all sections of the organised labour movement, whilst the term 'Socialist' (with a capital) refers only to parties which were close to the Second International. In some countries these Second International parties are more commonly referred to as Social Democratic. Hence, for example, we talk about the French and Spanish Socialists but the German Social Democrats.

2 S. Hall, 'Ethnicity: Identity and Difference', *Radical America* 23:4 (1989), pp. 9–20.

nationalisms, whilst the supposed 'end of class'[3] or the 'end of the Social Democratic project'[4] was already diagnosed more than ten years ago, it seems appropriate to pause and reflect on the past relationship between the narratives of these grand social identities: nation, class and ethnicity.

The obvious fragmentation and dispersal of social and cultural identities have led some thinkers on the wilder shores of postmodernism to reject any identity politics. Instead, all we are left with are monadic existences wandering about aimlessly in a vast nothingness faced with equally endless and meaningless choices. Such conceptual attempts to do away with the concept of identity altogether leave no basis for any kind of political action. In a world which is still rife with social injustice, political discrimination, racial hatred and exclusionary practices of various kinds, this surely must be termed either unrealistic or reactionary. Hence what is really at stake is to reconceptualise past (and present) class, national and ethnic identities so as to allow for heterogeneity, historical contingency, plurality and ambivalence. The past may always be a linguistic construct but it is not an arbitrary one. The central point of disagreement with extreme postmodernists has to be over the issue of the alleged complete autonomy of discourses. Most historical work (including the chapters in this book) tend to indicate the significance of a given social context in which any discourse takes place. Here Neville Kirk has rightly argued that postmodernist historiography tends to conflate language and reality, thereby leading to renewed forms of idealism and subjectivism.[5] Similarly the editors of this volume would tend to agree with the late Raphael Samuel, who found in postmodernism traces of 'symbolic overloading' and insisted that 'the historical record cannot be read only as a system of signs'.[6]

The liberal nationalist heritage

Between roughly the 1780s and the 1840s a generation of founding fathers of the national idea such as, for example, Johann Gottfried von Herder and Johann Gottlieb von Fichte for Germany and Guiseppe

---

3 A. Gorz, *Farewell to the Working Class. An Essay on Postindustrial Socialism* (London, Pluto, 1982); A. Touraine, M. Wieviorka and F. Dubet, *The Workers' Movement* (Cambridge, Cambridge University Press, 1987).

4 R. Dahrendorf, 'Das Elend der Sozialdemokratie', *Merkur* 41:12 (1987), pp. 1,021–38.

5 N. Kirk, 'History, Language, Ideas and Postmodernism: a Materialist View', *Social History* 19 (1994), pp. 221–38.

6 R. Samuel, 'Reading the Signs', *History Workshop Journal* 33 (1992), p. 245.

Mazzini for Italy were engaged in a kind of folkloristic rediscovery of 'the people', who were often portrayed as pure, simple and uncorrupted in comparison with the allegedly decadent aristocratic ruling classes in Europe. Hence the national idea was linked from early on with notions of freedom, citizenship and mass political participation. It could be used as an anti-absolutist weapon in the American and French revolutions of the 1770s and 1780s, and in the smaller irredentist 'nations', such as Poland and the Czech lands, liberal nationalist movements also grew up in response to linguistic and cultural oppression by reactionary multinational empires. Their points of reference were the Greek struggle against Ottoman rule and the unification of Italy.[7]

Liberal nationalist ideologies, moreover, did not remain the preserve of the more industrial world for long. Together with investment, merchandise, armies and slaves, European and US ideologies also travelled to the colonial world, and liberal nationalism was quickly used by (often Western mission-educated) indigenous elites, to demand independence against perceived foreign oppression. The United States was, indeed, the original example, and, from its territory and from Europe, liberal nationalist movements were to extend to the rest of the Americas (where ironically in the twentieth century powerful movements would grow against US imperialism) and to the British dominions.

As a result, during the nineteenth and twentieth centuries, in much of the world, popular liberal nationalism was consolidated as the major vehicle of political and social reform. As such, in Europe and the United States, it came to represent the frustrations and hopes of wide sections of the middle and working classes, who saw themselves as marginalised from the centres of political and economic power, and in the colonial world natives equally excluded from power and privilege. It was increasingly undercut by class-based movements and ideologies from the 1870s onwards, but this could be a slow and uneven process, with some workers on the European continent still voting republican or liberal in the 1930s. Furthermore, it was able to adapt to new times quite effectively. In some of the major industrial states there tended to emerge a 'classed' republican left which overlaid its language of people and nation with a greater attention to the problems of labour. This was of fundamental importance in Australia, where, as Terry Irving explains, labour was, in the early twentieth century, to play a key role in the construction of the nation. In the United States entrenched con-

7 We should, however, be careful not to take nationalist claims at face value. After Greek and Italian independence it was clear that most of the population, made up of illiterate peasants, had little or no concept of nationality.

servative interests were from the start more powerful. Nevertheless, as Neville Kirk has pointed out, there grew up in the nineteenth century a labour republicanism which combined democratic principles with criticisms of monopoly power and 'classist' legislation, and demands for trade union rights and the regulation of the free market. This was to be the dominant idiom through which US labour spoke right through to the 1930s. Left-wing 'classed' republican movements were also to be found in Western Europe. In Britain, the second half of the nineteenth century was characterised by the links between labour and Liberalism. In France, the Third Republic was proclaimed in 1871 but there remained a leftist, populist republicanism which was critical of the new republic's reconciliation with elite society. And in Spain from the 1890s, a republican left also emerged, which adopted a socialistic, even pseudo-anarchist rhetoric.

In the 'dominated nations', within multinational empires and colonies, liberal nationalist movements were often to maintain a particularly strong position. This was a two-way process, with workers, on the one hand, continuing to vote for nationalist parties, while socialist politics was directly infused with nationalism. This could be seen in such diverse settings as the Austro-Hungarian Empire, South Africa, Australia and India. Nevertheless, as the chapters in this book indicate, such mobilisation should not be seen as a simple instrumentalist process. Nationalist ideologues had to elaborate policies with a definite appeal to the working-class constituency. For example, in India various labour organisations used the nationalist campaigns of the 1920s and 1930s as a cover to ensure the achievement of their own sectionalist aims, such as higher wages or better working conditions. The aura of having conducted a successful national liberation campaign could also give new nationalist governments broad support, at least for a time. This was, for example, the case of Poland after independence in the aftermath of the First World War, where, as we learn from Jie-Hyun Lim's chapter, the Socialist PPS gave the regime of Piłsudski qualified support despite its increasingly authoritarian policies.

The impact of 'official' state and right-wing nationalisms

Yet, despite such revolutionary-democratic origins of the national idea, the practice of most aspiring and existing nation states was in fact exclusionary. Communities of the educated *de facto* excluded an uneducated and sometimes half literate underclass from political participation in the nation state./Ethnic, linguistic, cultural and political boundaries were erected which left some groups outside the shelter provided by the nation state. Hence one of the basic paradoxes of liberal nationalism was that it emphasised the unity of one people and aimed at overcoming all internal divisions, but in reality it was based right from the very start on a wide range of horizontal and vertical divisions. Nationalism as an inter-cultural, inter-ethnic or inter-class movement was often little more than wishful thinking by its largely middle-class advocates. The nation, in the words of the famous French declaration of human rights 'one and indivisible', was soon to reveal itself as extremely divided.

Thus nationalism was from the first Janus-faced, and in subsequent sections we shall briefly review the divisions which it was to bring in its wake. Furthermore, towards the end of the nineteenth century, the liberal nationalist discourse increasingly shed its emancipatory potential. In Europe, as Hans Kohn in his classical studies of the national idea has pointed out, nationalism began to change its political affiliation with the emergence of both conservative 'official' state nationalisms and militant, right-wing, ethnic and racial nationalist movements, the latter reaching their apogee in National Socialist Germany.[8] As a result nationalism ceased being the sole property of liberalism. Instead liberal, labour and conservative forms of nationalism coexisted (rather uneasily for the most part) and competed with alternative identities – not least the inter-nationalism espoused by the socialist labour movement.

'Official' state nationalism was quite different from its liberal counterpart. Rather than emphasising the revolutionary potential of 'the people' it aimed at stabilising the nation state and attempted to create a loyal citizenry proud of their country – and government – and its achievements, while also combating what were seen as subversive leftist currents. At the same time, in the Age of Imperialism states also turned to nationalist rhetoric to try and mobilise citizens behind dreams of great-power status and colonial expansion. This process took several forms. Most prominently, the educational system and military recruitment were used, reinforced by nationalist rhetoric in press and pulpit, and mobilisation on the streets in times of crisis. This occurred within a context in which economic development and the growth of a transport system were breaking down the isolation of rural areas and starting to create a unified national market.[9]

8 Hans Kohn, *The Idea of Nationalism* (London, Macmillan, 1967).
9 M. Hroch, *Social Preconditions of National Revival in Europe. A Comparative Analysis of the Social Composition of Patriotic Groups among the Smaller European Nations* (Cambridge, Cambridge University Press, 1985), is one of the most interesting attempts to develop a model for the emergence of irredentist nationalisms in East Central Europe. Hroch identifies three different phases of the evolution of the

The chapters in the book indicate that the period between roughly the 1890s and 1920s did, in general, witness an 'incorporation' of sections of labour into the national state. However, this was a more complex and difficult process than has often been assumed. It involved negotiation and compromise and was predicated upon the state making real concessions to the interests of labour. As the case of late nineteenth-century Germany, for example, makes clear, the hostility of the Protestant Church, the military and education establishment to the SPD was as likely to drive workers away as create converts.

Overall, the greater the reforming impetus of the ruling regime the more likely it was to mute a working-class and leftist challenge. For this to be possible it was necessary for labour to identify at least partially with the state. In part, as we shall see, this was a question of image. But it also required state institutions, the Church and the middle classes to show a genuine concern for the problems of labour. The key elements here were the willingness of the state to carry out a vigorous programme of social reforms, to democratise, and for employers and the middle classes to accept labour's representatives as bargaining agents. Imperial expansion could also, it seems, inspire sections of labour, though it did have to appear a success, bringing glory to the nation and, equally, export markets to industry.

/Four states which, in their different ways, had considerable success in this respect were Australia, France, the United States and Britain. In all four cases the regimes were to a degree able to connect with labour's liberal nationalist heritage/Australia was, in a way, exceptional. Because it was colonised by large numbers of Europeans only in the nineteenth century, labour was from the first able to play a key role in national construction. Hence to an important degree nation building was a democratic and labour-friendly process. It was only after the onset of the First World War that more conservative forces would strike back, adopt forms of integral nationalism, and put labour on the defensive.

In France, the Third Republic, set up in 1871, was able to link up with the traditions of the French revolution. From the 1880s, as Roger Magraw describes in his chapter, it set up a system of lay schools (thereby appropriating anticlerical traditions on the left), and instituted universal

---

national idea. Phase A was characterised by the attempt of a cultural intelligentsia to propagate a populist cultural renaissance. In phase B a movement of activists emerged who were largely drawn from the lower middle classes. Phase B also saw the extension of state educational systems, widely spreading the idea of national sentiment. Mass support, often inter-class in character, emerged only subsequently in phase C.

military conscription (again connecting with French revolutionary ideas of the 'nation in arms'). The result was that though, in terms of 'objective' criteria for integration, France occupied, in European terms, according to Marcel van der Linden, only a 'middling position', worker acceptance of the regime was rather greater than such criteria would suggest.[10]

Another republican regime which was able to connect with labour's past and present hopes was that of the United States. For much of the period under consideration it, in fact, encouraged anti-union policies and left much welfare provision to the big business corporations. However, labour's critique was framed in terms of a return to the original republic, which had, supposedly, championed the 'American standard' of personal liberty and independence for the producer. And, indeed, the pro-labour policies of the New Deal in the 1930s could be seen as approximating to this ideal.

The aristocratising British monarchical regime could never hope to appropriate 'progressive' imagery in this way. Nevertheless, through its programme of gradual but substantial reform it could create a broad consensus in favour of the 'parliamentary road' to social and political reform, and of acceptance of the institution of the monarchy. In Germany under the semi-authoritarian Bismarckian and Wilhelmine regimes this issue was, as Stefan Berger demonstrates in his comparison of Britain and Germany, more contested. In a way the German state found itself in the contrary position to France; advanced social reform had obviously been instituted to counter the socialist threat, and the regime was still viewed as the enemy of labour. Yet it was the case that in the Reichstag, and the areas of local government and union bargaining, arenas were being built in which Social Democrats could pursue reform without stepping outside the bounds of legality.

In other European countries, the left's aim centred more on overthrow than reform. This was the case in out-and-out autocracies like the Russian Empire, and oligarchic regimes like the Spanish Restoration (1875–1923) which, as Angel Smith explains, though theoretically accepting a liberal system of government, in reality retained power through electoral manipulation. In both cases little effort was made to pursue active policies of nationalist mobilisation. Rather it was seen as sufficient for the majority of the population to live outside the realm of politics. The one attempt made by the Russian regime to sponsor a populist nationalist movement, the URP, represented an anti-labour front

---

10 See M. van der Linden, 'The National Integration of the European Working Classes, 1871–1914', *International Review of Social History* 33 (1988), pp. 285–311.

rather than any serious attempt to appeal to sectors of the left. Nevertheless, there were fundamental differences between the two regimes, for the liberal legislation (including universal manhood suffrage) introduced in Spain between 1883 and 1890 did provide a space for political and economic action within the bounds of legality which would hardly exist in Russia.

/In the colonial regimes of the early twentieth century the great powers were finding increasing difficulties in securing allegiance. In particular, they failed to create national symbols with which the colonised could identify. As a result, nationalist movements grew up which challenged the colonial powers' hegemony. As has been suggested, they could develop alliances with socialist and labour movements, but social division and, in some cases, the existence of competing nationalist discourses would mean they were uneasy and fragmented/ Australia represented a case of relatively strong cooperation. Here, as Terry Irving shows, an alliance grew up between the urban middle classes and organised workers which managed to frame the outlook of the Australian states from the second half of the nineteenth century to the outbreak of the First World War. In a very different institutional context, the Indian National Congress in its struggle against colonialism forged a broad-based alliance including many workers and peasants. Yet, as Rajnarayan Chandavarkar argues, nationalists and socialists often had very different ideas and aspirations as far as the outcome of the national struggle was concerned. Hence, the moment Congress found itself in government, it often confronted its erstwhile working-class allies with stark anti-labour legislation and outright repression. Even more problematic was the case of South Africa. Afrikaner nationalists were able to use the hardening of the colour bar against blacks in the 1930s and 1940s to gain support among the wider Afrikaner working-class community. Yet not only were non-whites excluded, the Afrikaners also found it very difficult to forge alliances with British workers and their organisations./

Nationalism, socialism, and the organised labour movement

The complex relationship between nationalism, socialism and labour was reflected both at a theoretical level and in the development of socialist parties and unions./Despite the fact that socialism and nationalism have been widely perceived as standing on opposite ends of the ideological spectrum, socialist thinking on the nation undoubtedly had much in common with liberal nationalism. At a most basic level both nationalism and socialism are both ultimately rooted in the post-Enlightenment discourse centred on 'progress'. In the one case, it is the nation which pushes history forward to new and brighter shores, and, on the other, it is the working class. Certainly most liberals tended to think about nations as 'natural' and 'objective' entities, based on a unique 'spirit' (*Volksgeist* – Herder's term), a peculiar ethnic or political 'essence', or a specific cultural way of life. Not all socialists totally disagreed. During the nineteenth century the anarchists' stress on federalism produced considerable support for the plight of 'oppressed nations'. Most notably, Michael Bakunin began his conspiratorial career as a revolutionary pan-Slavist, and never abandoned his sympathy for peoples he viewed as struggling for freedom from multinational empires. Thus in his blueprint for a future United States of Europe (eventually united states of the entire world) he emphasised 'natural' nations had the right to secede from a state whenever they wished, and (decoupled from the state) had a role to play in the future organisation of society.[11] By contrast, Marxists in particular stressed the material, economic foundations of nation states. Nations had been founded because large internally unified units had fostered the development of capitalism. They made sense economically, not because they embodied a particular set of ideas. In advancing the contradictions inherent in the development of capitalism, the creation of nation states, as in the Germany or Italy, would either set the stage for the social revolution or, as in the case of Austria-Hungary or Russia, hasten the demise of multinational, dynastic empires, widely regarded as anachronisms at the beginning of the twentieth century. However, in a sense a liberal nationalist spiritual essentialism was simply replaced by an economic essentialism.

Both liberals and socialists maintained that the nation state was a necessary stage in the evolution of humankind towards its final destination – be this the confirmation of nations (in their plurality) as the apogee of world history, the struggle for the survival of the fittest nation, international cosmopolitanism or the classless world society. The socialist teleology of a one-world nation state, brought about by economic globalisation and cultural symbiosis, was reflected in anarchist dreams of a future bottom-up worldwide federation, in which Esperanto could become a new universal language, and in Karl Kautsky's belief that

---

11 M. Bakunin, 'Federalism, Socialism, Anti-theologism', reproduced in S. Dolgoff (ed.), *Bakunin on Anarchism*, 2nd edn (Montreal, Black Rose Books, 1980), pp. 102–47.

national languages would eventually deteriorate into dialects and give way to one world language. Liberals and Marxists not only believed that nation building was necessary, they also found common ground in the belief that it was necessary only for some. Like the economic nationalist Friedrich List, Marxists tended to agree that there were only some 'viable' nations which were characterised by a sufficiently large population, extensive territory and considerable natural resources.[12] On that basis Friedrich Engels could borrow the categories of 'historical' and 'ahistorical' nations from Hegel and pontificate on the eventual disappearance of the Czechs or describe the Balkan Slavs as 'another bunch of terrible cattle thieves'.[13]

Yet another similarity between socialists and nationalists can be identified in the attempt to resurrect a utopian past. Both ideologies harboured ideas of a 'Golden Age' which had much to do with folk tradition and an imperial legacy in the case of nationalists, and with primitive communism and eras allegedly free of forms of capitalist alienation in the case of socialists. Furthermore, both socialists and nationalists shared a similar kind of paradox: they extensively used the universalist rhetoric of rights and emancipation yet often were quite willing to violate the rights of others. Notions of cultural or racial superiority of one nation over the other and the idea of class revolution – and in the case of Marxists the dictatorship of the proletariat – signify the oppressive potential of both nationalism and socialism. Last but not least, both ideologies have been described as representing the rebellion of 'marginal men', i.e. intellectuals who were overproduced by the educational systems in Europe in the nineteenth century and who were dissatisfied with their social position in society.[14]

Yet, for socialists, horizontal affiliations of class had to be regarded as more important than vertical affiliations of national identity. The Communist Manifesto contains one of the most widely quoted passages regarding the allegedly antagonistic relationship between nationalism and socialism:

the workers have no fatherland. One cannot take from them what they have not got . . . national differences and antagonisms between peoples are vanishing more and more . . . The rule of the proletariat will make them vanish even more.

12 On variables which furthered or hindered nation-state building in Western Europe see also C. Tilly (ed.), *The Formation of National States in Western Europe* (Princeton, N.J., Princeton University Press, 1975).
13 Cited in Eric Hobsbawm, *Nations and Nationalism since 1780* (Cambridge, Cambridge University Press, 1990), p. 41.
14 The point was made some time ago by E. Kedourie, *Nationalism*, 4th edn (London, Blackwell, 1993), pp. 43 ff.

United action, at the very least among the workers of the civilised nations, is one of the prime conditions of the emancipation of the proletariat.[15]

As a result, the legacy of Marxism would be rather confused. National struggles were ultimately judged according to whether they furthered or hindered the development of the proletariat's 'true class consciousness', yet, at the same time, workers' attachment to nationalism was seen as undercutting the class struggle and was, therefore, viewed as a form of 'false consciousness', which had to be combated by Marxists.[16]

In the second half of the nineteenth century the divide between nationalist and socialist ideologies was seemingly underlined by the gulf between their respective social bases. The ideologies of nationalism and socialism were both fuelled by the substantial migration of peoples, in itself connected with the weight and pace of social transformation marking the onrush of modernity. This whirlwind of social change produced substantial groups of malcontents for whom either 'race' and 'nation' or 'class' became defensive mechanisms ensuring a sense of identity and continuity in a rapidly changing world. Whilst the social constituency of nationalism was increasingly lower middle-class or petty-bourgeois in character, socialism relied heavily on the support of the industrial working class. In future nationalism was to be regarded by many as the property of the right and socialism was its mirror opposite on the left. Furthermore, in the late nineteenth and early twentieth centuries, growing imperialist rivalries and the threat of war strengthened abstract socialist internationalism. The tone was set by the Brussels congress of the Second International in 1891, which approved a resolution explicitly stating that 'the Socialists and workers' parties of all lands have always maintained that there could not be any form of antagonism or struggle of race or nationality, but only class struggle between proletarians of all races and capitalists of all races'.[17] Over the next forty years many anarchists and anarcho-syndicalists, left socialists and, later, Communists continued to insist that international class solidarity and the national class struggle must take precedence over any idea of national collaboration.

One of the most uncompromising internationalist positions within the wide range of socialist thinking on the nation state was taken by Rosa

---

15 K. Marx and F. Engels, *Manifest der Kommunistischen Partei*, 44th edn (Berlin, Dietz, 1980), p. 66.
16 See in this respect Marx's and Engel's comments on antagonism between British and Irish workers in K. Marx and F. Engels, *Ireland and the Irish Question* (Moscow, Progress Publishers, 1971).
17 J. Joll, *The Second International, 1899–1914*, 2nd edn (London, Routledge, 1974), p. 71.

Luxemburg. Luxemburg, who refused to endorse the restoration of her native Poland in 1918, argued that class loyalty should be superior to national loyalty. In her view, the principle of national self-determination could all too easily sidetrack workers from their 'real interests'.[18] Whilst her party, the SDKPiL, rejected independence in favour of solidarity between the Russian and Polish working classes, the more nationalist PPS insisted that only after national independence would cooperation on an equal footing be possible.

The Polish example already indicates that there never existed a straightforward juxtaposition between bourgeois nationalism and socialist internationalism. As Eric Hobsbawm, among others, has pointed out, national and class appeals could work at one and the same time, forming a complex interlinking relationship: 'Men and women did not choose collective identification as they chose shoes, knowing that one could only put on one pair at a time.'[19] Middle-class intellectuals could be found in the forefront of socialist movements, whilst many workers were no doubt affected by the nationalist sentiments of their times.

However, the relationship between nationalism and socialism depended very much on the social, national and cultural context. In many large 'nation states', as we have noted, liberal nationalism had a considerable impact on left-wing circles. This found its way into Social Democratic parties through the Marxist stress on the historic role of the nation, with the result that a certain 'great state' nationalism lurked behind the internationalist rhetoric. This could, for example, be seen in the extreme virulence with which parties like the Guesdist POF in France and the PSOE in Spain greeted any whiff of anti-state regionalist or nationalist movements in their own countries. It was also present in the lack of sympathy within the SPD for the aspirations to autonomy voiced by minority groups in Germany (Poles, Danes, Alsatians).

In countries recognised as multinational empires, socialists were faced, at both a theoretical and a practical level, with a more difficult task. And arguably the two most famous and consequential attempts to come to terms with the national question from a socialist perspective, Leninism and Austro-Marxism, were elaborated in such a context. Lenin's attitude towards all questions of national identity was tactical. If nationalism furthered the cause of social revolution it was to be

18 However, as Jie-Hyun Lim has pointed out, it would be wrong to view Luxemburg as a 'national nihilist'. For the complex Luxemburgian thinking on the nation see Lim, 'Rosa Luxemburg on the Dialectics of Proletarian Internationalism and Social Patriotism', *Science and Society* 59:4 (1995–96), pp. 498–530.

19 Hobsbawm, *Nations*, p. 123.

endorsed; if it threatened to hold back progress towards Communism it had to be fought tooth and nail. Hence, before 1917, Lenin used the principle of national self-determination as an ally against Great Russian imperialism. Yet after the Bolsheviks had gained power in Russia he emphasised that the future lay with an international union of nation states. Whilst in the 1920s the Soviet republics enjoyed a good deal of autonomy, full independence was never an option. And when, at the end of the 1920s, Stalin emerged victorious from the internecine party strug-gles, the different nationalities of the CPSU were ruthlessly reined in. Henceforth Great Russian nationalism (complete with antisemitic undertones) would be the official creed of the Soviet Union, while the nationalist nation-building model was also exported to the East European satellites. Outside the Soviet Union Stalin continued to use national struggles as vehicles to further the internationalist proletarian revolution. From the 1930s to the 1970s Marxism-Leninism, as defined by the Communist International, was actively seeking to support national liberation movements across the developing world.

If Lenin perceived issues of national identity primarily with a view to the ultimate goal of world revolution (although the principle of national self-determination could also serve the purpose of integrating non-Russian workers into the Soviet Communist Party), Socialists in the Austro-Hungarian Empire developed their theories more exclusively in the context of forging a Social Democratic party within a multinational empire increasingly perceived as an anachronism by various nationalist movements within it. For Otto Bauer, one of the main protagonists of Austro-Marxist thinking on the national question, the nation was not an invention by capitalists to divert attention from the class struggle. Rather it emerged in the process of nation building across diverse social classes. Workers were not indifferent to the fate of their nation state. Bauer defined the nation as a 'community of fate' (largely based on a shared culture) which had a real existence and was shared by members of different classes.[20] Yet, whilst the bourgeois nation excluded workers from becoming full members of that community, it was the task of the Socialists to ensure that workers would be inte-grated. In order to prevent any one ethnic group from hegemonising the state apparatus and using it to enforce its own national identity on all citizens of the state, Bauer argued that, within one state, different nations could claim 'cultural autonomy'. Cultural affairs would be the sole responsibility of the different nationalities making up the large

---

20 O. Bauer, *Die Nationalitätenfrage und die Sozialdemokratie* (Vienna, Volksbuch-handlung, 1907).

central states. Bauer was thus paying tribute to the traditional Marxist predilection for large central states whilst at the same time hoping that smaller nations would not feel oppressed by those states. Yet the concept of the nation as 'cultural community' – whilst having the advantage of breaking through the economic reductionism of classical Marxist analyses – was too vague to allow a neat demarcation from the dominant right-wing cultural nationalism. Hence, in the case of the Austrian Socialists, a certain German cultural chauvinism was also to be observed.

Indeed, 'cultural autonomy' was propagated in order to head off calls from the non-German parts of the Austro-Hungarian Empire for independence. In such 'dominated nations' Socialists could be influenced by another basic element in the liberal nationalist creed: the right of the nation's people to rise up against foreign oppression. Anti-state nationalisms grew up in territories with an active middle class and intelligentsia, and a strong historical memory of separateness which was nourished by the state's repression of separate customs and identities. Poland is a case in point. Here it was very easy for Socialists to see national independence (in this case primarily from the Russian Empire) as a progressive democratic step, and, therefore, to link up demands for social and national liberation. This, as we have noted, was the position taken by the Polish PPS. Similarly, in Ireland Socialists like James Connolly consciously tried to fuse Marxism, Catholicism and Irish nationalism to form a popular mass basis for national and social emancipation.[21] However, lest it be felt there was always a clear ideological difference between 'great' and 'oppressed' nation nationalisms the case of Poland is again instructive. The PPS was quick to condemn Russian oppression, but once the country had achieved independence in 1918 it supported demands for a Great Polish federation based on the old Polish Republic ('from the Black Sea to the Baltic Sea'), which would integrate Ukrainian, Belorussian and Lithuanian-speaking borderlands, a move Socialists from these areas were quick to condemn as an example of Polish imperialism.

/In the large Western and Central European states and white settler colonies the relationship between nationalism and the labour movement was characterised by subtle change over time/As we have already noted, in the more reforming states the period between roughly the 1890s (the 1850s in Britain) and the 1920s was to see a certain 'integration' of sectors of labour into the state. The most spectacular example

---

21 D. Howell, *A Lost Left. Three Studies in Socialism and Nationalism* (Manchester, Manchester University Press, 1986).

was the fact that a minority of workers voted for ruling parties. Already in the second half of the nineteenth century the phenomenon of the working-class Tory had raised its head in Britain, and in France, it seems, not insubstantial numbers of workers flocked to the cause of Boulangism in the 1890s.

Elsewhere, workers may not have voted directly for liberal-conservative or right-wing parties but instead opted for reformist Social Democratic currents which were willing to reach at least a partial accommodation with the state. These Social Democrats took an evolutionary stance, arguing that social and political reform and/or socialism could be brought about gradually rather than through revolution. Concomitantly, acceptance of the parliamentary road inevitably led to more emphasis being placed on building wide coalitions for reform rather than appealing exclusively to the working class. And this in turn encouraged the use of the vocabulary of the 'people', 'nation' and 'national interests', alongside and eventually as a replacement for languages of class. In this respect the liberal nationalist heritage also helped provide a bridge, and it was, indeed, the case that even at the height of Second International orthodoxy at the end of the nineteenth century, languages of class and people overlapped. Such an emphasis led nationalist perspectives frequently to be translated into socialist phraseology – for example, in claims by the SPD that Germany was the fortress of European socialism and by the SFIO that France was the home of liberty. More ominously, it also made possible, claims by Socialists that, because of its special role, their country had to be defended at all costs from foreign threats. Such statements clearly demonstrate how easily such a theory could deteriorate into forms of negative ethnic stereotyping of those who were regarded as unworthy of acquiring national status.

These tendencies could be seen in a variety of national contexts. The most extreme example of a narrowing of the gap between 'official state nationalism' and labour was perhaps provided by the white settler-dominated countries. Thus in the United States the early twentieth century saw the rise of the AFL's 'business' trade unionism, which overwhelmingly endorsed the existing framework of state and economy, and in Australia the mainstream of the Labor Party remained on a steady accommodatory path. In the various Western and Central European labour and Socialist parties reformist currents were strengthened by the experience of collaboration in the war effort during the First World War, with labour representatives actually entering government in Britain, France and Germany. Reformist strands could even develop in southern Mediterranean countries such as Italy and Spain. Here

Socialists argued that, because of the country's 'backwardness' alliances had to be built with the 'progressive bourgeoisie' (i.e. the Republicans) in order to institute 'bourgeois democratic' reforms – a key stage, it was supposed, on the road to socialism.[22]

Reformism was to have several dangerous consequences. In the first place, it led to growing acceptance of or even support for colonialism. Whilst Karl Kautsky was one of the first Marxists to produce a coherent critique of colonialism in the 1880s, condemning it for its disregard of the human rights of the native peoples, key thinkers of reformist Social Democracy such as Eduard Bernstein and Ramsay MacDonald approved of imperialism on the condition that the European states had a 'civilising mission' in the world. The belief in the superiority of the 'white races', forged during the colonial waves of the sixteenth and seventeenth centuries, reinforced by the slave trade, and theorised in late nineteenth-century Social Darwinist thinking, was deeply ingrained in the European psyche and Socialists were affected.[23] Such thinking easily deteriorated into 'socialist racialism', as, for example, when the Webbs argued that socialism could be achieved only when the white race became the dominant one in world affairs.[24] Moreover, such thinking did not remain on the drawing board. It was, as we shall see, at the root of the virulent racism 'non-whites' faced in European and white settler societies.

However, most reformist Social Democrats attempted to strike a precarious balance between the evils of integral nationalisms and the, in their eyes, meaningless internationalism of many professed Marxists. Yet, not unlike the liberal nationalists, Social Democrats like Bernstein were quick in essentialising feelings of national identity. So, for example, Bernstein ascribed to all citizens in the nation state 'natural feelings of love for their own country and their people'. Like the Austro-Marxists, Bernstein perceived nations as 'organically developed social organisms' whose cultural distinctiveness and integrity needed to be preserved. Reformist Socialists like Bernstein tended to identify strongly with what they saw as the civic nationalism of Western Europe, irrespective of the fact that it could be every bit as violent and intolerant as the nationalisms farther to the east. For them civic nationalism was the basis on

22 For this process in Italy see, for example, J. A. Davis, 'Socialism and the Working Class in Italy before 1914', in D. Geary (ed.), *Labour and Socialist Movements in Europe before 1914* (Oxford, Berg, 1989), pp. 192–3.
23 The classic study is V. G. Kiernan, *The Lords of Human Kind. European Attitudes towards the Outside World in the Imperial Age* (London, Serif, 1995, first publ. 1969).
24 J. M. Winter, 'The Webbs and the Non-white World: a Case of Socialist Racialism', *Journal of Contemporary History* 9 (1974), pp. 181–92.

which true internationalism could be built and widespread ethnic nationalisms could be overcome.[25]

Yet, in reality, the delineation of good and bad nationalisms proved difficult and, as the chapters in this book demonstrate, left-wing nationalism tended to collapse time and again and merge with various state and integral nationalisms. This was particularly clear in the case of military and colonial policy. Support for colonial expansion could easily result in militarism. This could be fuelled by state propaganda, for while military discipline might be resented, the idea of military service could link into masculine values of physical strength and prowess and (at least until the true carnage of modern warfare became known) appeal to a spirit of adventure and escape from the worker's enclosed community. And, in time of war, propaganda urging the population to 'do its duty' would be all-pervasive. Again, as we have noted, nineteenth-century liberal nationalism could be a bridge here, with its notions of the West's civilising mission and the 'nation at arms'. And though Socialists could state they only favoured a humane colonialism and would only support a defensive war, because the nationalist myths and legends were often similar it was easy for the leftist alternative to blur into the dominant statist discourse.

The clearest example was the onset of war in 1914, which many German Social Democrats supported because of the supposed threat from reactionary Russia, while French Socialists and British Labour Party members could argue that they were fighting a defensive war against Prussian militarism. This stance has, moreover, to be put in the context of the penalties of not complying. Clearly any organisation which openly opposed the war would face repression. And for European Social Democracy, which had built large party and union federations of which it was immensely proud, the thought of this edifice's destruction was unbearable.

Yet, whilst there is no easy distinction between 'good patriotism' and 'bad nationalism', it should be recognised that by and large 'good patriotism' did – warts and all – provide a democratic alternative to the authoritarian right. This became clear in the 1920s and 1930s, when large sections of the left defended the continental European liberal democracies – Weimar in Germany, the Third Republic in France, the Second Republic in Spain – against the threat of fascism. These regimes should not be idealised. In both Weimar Germany and the Spanish

---

25 On Bernstein's 'noble patriotism' see M. B. Steger, *The Quest for Evolutionary Socialism. Eduard Bernstein and Social Democracy* (Cambridge, Cambridge University Press, 1997), pp. 197–204. For reformist nationalism within the German SPD see also S. Pierson, *Marxist Intellectuals and the Working-class Mentality in Germany 1887–1912* (Cambridge, Mass., Harvard University Press, 1993), pp. 205–28.

Second Republic, Socialists and republicans harshly treated workers not unionised in 'responsible' Social Democratic unions. And in France Socialist and even Communist unions showed themselves willing to ally with the right to stem immigration. But the alternative was anti-parliamentary authoritarian government. In these circumstances many on the left identified with the liberal regimes and their radical-democratic heritage. These were regimes which many on the left could identify with the radical-democratic heritage. Under them, national symbols were republicanised and the link between 'people' and 'nation' was emphasised. Indeed, a nationalist inversion could to a degree be seen to take place, with, for example in France and Spain, the far right accused of lack of patriotism because of its support for 'foreign' fascist ideals. Most remarkable was the transformation which the European Communist parties underwent. From the sectarian anti-Social Democratic strategy in the early 1930s, in 1934 they shifted 180° to support inter-class 'Popular Front' alliances against fascism. This was clearly undertaken on orders from Moscow (which, scared of an attack by Nazi Germany, was trying to build alliances with the Western democracies), but it did allow the Communist parties to play a more central role in European political life. It was also accompanied by an incredible reformulation of these parties' analysis of the national question; proletarian internationalism was overlaid if not replaced by a populist appeal to the heroic nation and its people to ward off the foreign fascist invaders.[26]

However, on the European continent the Achilles heel of state integrative policies and reformist labour politics was to be found in several interconnected issues: the consequences of imperial rivalry, the limits of reform and the sheer virulence social conflict was at times to acquire. In the pre-Second World War world it was these factors which truncated attempts by left-wing reformists to fashion 'catch all' parties which could attract a diverse social base.

In the first place, in order to ensure support or at least acquiescence, militarism and colonial expansion had to appear to achieve results, and, for obvious reasons, this was not possible everywhere at once. Thus defeat for Spain in the colonial war against Cuba and the 1898 war against the United States left a strong anti-militarist current in both the organised labour movement and wider working-class milieux. Military defeat at the end of the First World War was, at the same time, the pre-

---

26 For an overview see H. Graham and P. Preston (eds), *The Popular Front in Europe* (Basingstoke, Macmillan, 1987); on the reaction of Social Democracy to united and popular fronts see Gerd-Rainer Horn, *European Socialists Respond to Fascism. Ideology, Activism and Contingency* (Oxford, Oxford University Press, 1997).

condition for the Bolshevik revolution and the revolutionary crisis in central Europe.

Secondly, in both Europe and the white settler colonies, welfare reform and the institution of collective bargaining left sectors of the working class marginalised and unrepresented. And, as a result, the acceptance of piecemeal improvements and the attempt to build up inter-class coalitions of reform was almost everywhere challenged by the politics of class, championed by a mixture of left socialist, Communist and anarcho-syndicalist organisations. In Europe, it was within these bodies that the language of internationalism (in the Communist case, as we have seen, until the *volte-face* of 1934) remained at its strongest. It is not that these groups generally maintained an anti-national cosmopolitanism (though anarchists and syndicalists could come close), but stress was still laid on class conflict as against any attempt at national reconciliation, while ideas of international proletarian revolution were also extolled. In the white settler colonies, on the other hand, the importance of the republican-state heritage seems to have ensured that among more leftist groups radical democratic nationalism was more to the fore. Thus in the United States the CIO launched an assault on the narrow conservatism of the AFL on the basis of the return to the workers' republic, and in Australia the Communist Party's ideology was a mixture of internationalism and democratic, anti-imperialist-tinged, nationalism.

Beneath these political and ideological schisms could be seen a certain social differentiation among the working-class base. In general it was the case that the more reformist sectors of labour tended to recruit most strongly among the white collar and skilled workers. These men (and they were almost always men) had enjoyed improvements in wages and working conditions and were more likely to benefit from state welfare programmes and state-sponsored collective bargaining. On the other hand, there was to be found a 'poor working class', often in a desperate situation, given the high unemployment levels of the 1930s. In the United States, for example, the AFL was very much the preserve of the skilled white male, while the CIO recruited much more widely among the 'new' immigrants of the European south-east and east. And in Germany in the 1920s it was also the case that, while the SPD recruited most strongly among the skilled, the KPD had greater support among the unskilled and unemployed.[27] Indeed, as we shall see in the following

---

27 It should be noted, however, that this correlation has recently been called into question for Germany by Klaus-Michael Mallmann, *Kommunisten in der Weimarer Republik. Sozialgeschichte einer revolutionären Bewegung* (Darmstadt, Wissenschaftliche Buchgesellschaft, 1996).

section, such a divide could generate tensions among workers which can, in some cases, be considered at least partly ethnic in nature.

Labour culture within these organisations, as a result, varied greatly. In the more 'reformist' European organisations – the British Labour Party, the German SPD, the French Socialists, and part of the Spanish PSOE – national symbols, patriotic songs and plays made their appearance, whereas further to the left a more exclusionary labour culture still remained the norm. It is more difficult to measure the impact of nationalism in broader working-class milieux. The chapters in this book indicate that nationalist issues were for much of the time relatively peripheral to workers' thoughts and actions, and seemed often to occupy labour leaders much more than the broader community. Certainly, at times of national crisis broad sectors of labour could sometimes be mobilised behind the flag – as in the case of Poland during the Soviet–Polish war of 1920/21 – but this was quickly to subside to the back of people's minds. It was also generally the case that imperialist agitation galvanised students and the lower middle class more than workers. These could be mobilised, but at the end of a crisis jingoistic rhetoric and actions would quickly die away. This is important in order to put the relationship between labour and nationalism into perspective. A book of this type, centred on the phenomenon of nationalism, can give the impression that it was an all-pervasive concern in workers' lives. But the 'facts of class' were frequently more relevant because for much of the time they touched workers' lives more directly – the question of a wage increase, the threat of redundancy, the working-class friends one met off the job and in one's free time. Yet, as we have also seen, through the liberal republican inheritance, education, military training and state propaganda, nationalist assumptions and notions of cultural and racial superiority could insinuate themselves into workers' consciousness in complex and multiple ways, and help to ensure conformity and even enthusiasm at times of crisis. Moreover, though not unambiguous, there was no doubt a connection between organised labour culture and broader working-class culture, with, in Europe at least, notions of national pride more widely disseminated among white-collar workers, the 'respectable' and 'skilled' than among the more marginalised population of the unskilled, immigrants and the unemployed.

Labour and ethnicity

As previous sections have indicated, nationalist tensions within the working class and labour movement could easily lead to conflict. Such tensions were usually bound up with ethnic differentiation. While ethnic identities are no less constructed than national or class identities, they are much older – ranging back to the tribalism of small-scale communities before the onset of modernity. Yet modern nationalism has appropriated the inevitably diffuse ethnic boundaries – or even multiple and situative ethnic identities – to create fixed national-ethnic identities with the purpose of distinguishing between 'them' and 'us'.[28] Labour was by no means immune from such stereotyping.

Ethnic division took place within three fundamentally different social, cultural and institutional contexts. In the first place, in Europe one is dealing with the impact of immigration or of 'national minorities' on the broader host community. Outside Europe, in the white settler communities and colonies, the key social and cultural divisions could be between settlers and the state (if they remained colonies), between the various waves of settler immigrants, between settlers of different national origin, and, especially, between the aforementioned groups and – depending on the country – either the indigenous population or, where this had been decimated, ex-slave blacks. Finally, in non-settler colonies the major fault line would run between the colonial administration and the more politicised sectors of the indigenous population.

In Europe the experience of centuries of wars, and more directly, the growth of imperialist rivalries from the late nineteenth century, and especially the impact of the First World War, all served to extend and reinforce European national stereotypes, which, as we have noted, took in at least sectors of labour. At the same time, throughout the continent one could see a certain anti-Jewish prejudice, which extended both to established communities and to more recent immigrants from Eastern Europe. This prejudice was deeply ingrained in the culture of Christendom. In the nineteenth century Christian antisemitism was supplanted by racist antisemitism. Jews were rejected and persecuted not because of their religion but because of their race. Espousal of antisemitism and racism more generally found its main outlet in right-wing circles in pseudo-radical attacks on plutocratic Jewish financiers and capitalists, yet anti-Jewish outbursts were also to be found in the labour press.

Within the multinational European empires national division quickly acquired ethnic overtones in which labour became immersed. For example, in Austro-Hungary the Social Democrats had strongest support among German workers, and during the early twentieth century

---

28 E. Tonkin, M. McDonald and M. Chapman (eds), *History and Ethnicity* (London, Routledge, 1989); M. Díaz-Andreu, 'Constructing Identities through Culture: the Past in the Forging of Europe', in S. Jones, C. Gamble and P. Graves-Brown (eds), *Cultural Identity and Archaeology. The Construction of European Communities* (London, Routledge, 1996), pp. 48–61.

Czech workers broke away to form their own party and union. And, as Jie-Hyun Lim has pointed out, in Poland conflict between the PPS and SDKPiL had an ethnic dimension, for while the former had more success in recruiting among ethnically Polish workers the latter had a strong base among other groups (Ukrainians, Lithuanians, etc.).

Within the more industrialised European states ethnic-nationalist tensions were also fomented by foreign immigration. This quickened from the 1850s and, as almost all the chapters in this book emphasise, immigrants were regularly greeted with prejudice and, on occasion, xenophobia. The roots of this hostility are to be found in a complex mix of distrust of the 'other', whose customs and language varied so much from one's own, and fear of competition for jobs, housing and (not least) women, as well as the immigrants' possible depressive effect on wages. Of course, this did not apply only to workers from another land. It is clear that immigrants from rural hinterlands, when arriving in nineteenth-century cities, faced discrimination.[29] However, when such prejudices were racialised and nationalised they inevitably hardened and exclusionary practices became more difficult to break down.

Furthermore, in the late nineteenth century the distinction between the native and foreigner was being systematised by states themselves, through such measures as the institution of welfare programmes to which only natives were entitled, laws limiting immigration, and the pursual of assimilation programmes which, in some cases, left little space for the maintenance, at least in the public sphere, of non-national languages and customs. The various sources of prejudice were not, it should be stressed, independent. By participating in the stereotyping of immigrants as stupid and brutish and as capable of only the crudest tasks, native workers were, in fact, at the same time defending their position in the labour process. Indeed, as John Belchem has pointed out in this context, the local workers' stress on the value of possessing a craft was articulated in opposition to the unskilled and immigrants.[30]

Hostility could, moreover, be reinforced by religious differences. Especially in Protestant Northern Europe, the labour movement and its new religion of socialism found most of its converts among Protestant

29 And it is only by viewing these questions through a distorted nationalist mirror that one might suppose that, say, a late nineteenth-century Parisian worker would view a peasant immigrant from the south of France (who would speak Provençal, Langue d'Oc or Catalan) any differently from an Italian from, for example, Piedmont.

30 J. Belchem, 'Ethnicity, Labour History and Irish Migration', paper presented to the conference held in St Antony's College, University of Oxford, 'Racialising Class, Classifying Race. A Conference on Labour and Difference in Africa, the USA and Britain', 11–13 July 1997.

workers. One element of religious thought which had very effectively been disseminated by the Reformation and found its way into leftist culture was the belief in the reactionary nature of Catholicism and, especially, the Catholic Church (personified in the figure of the Pope). This no doubt was to exacerbate hostility towards Polish workers in Germany and Irish workers in Britain (and in the United States), especially as in both cases the religious divide also coincided with a political fault line.

In addition, the deep imprint of the colonial heritage and ingrained notions of white (in Britain, the United States and the British settler colonies, more specifically white Anglo-Saxon) superiority were revealed in the particular hostility faced by the 'non-white' non-European. This was very evident in France, where, during the First World War, imported Chinese, Indochinese and Turks faced crude racist abuse, and, finally, race riots. Indeed, the fact that Ireland was a British colony no doubt served further to accentuate the negative image: a comparison could be drawn with the subject non-European peoples; not for nothing were the Irish referred to in the United States in the nineteenth century as 'white negroes'.

In Europe, where the level of outside immigration had by the 1930s not reached great proportions, this was not yet a major issue. However, looked at on a world scale, the divide between 'whites' and 'others' was the central feature in the restructuring of social and cultural relations which accompanied colonisation. The fact is that within the dominant Western ideological framework non-white colonised peoples and ex-slaves were viewed as inferior races, with which contact on equal terms was virtually impossible.

This was to be seen in Australia, the United States and South Africa. In Australia the Labor Party supported a 'white Australia' policy, aimed at keeping Chinese, Pacific Islanders and Italians out. In the United States, in the second half of the nineteenth century, whereas 'old immigrants' from the British Isles (including Ireland) and the Northern and Western European continent were accepted as 'whites', who shared the white hosts' cultural assumptions and would uphold the 'American standard' of freedom, independence and working conditions, the next wave of 'new immigrants' from rural South-eastern and Eastern Europe faced wide-scale exclusion from organised labour. Chinese immigrants and southern blacks seeking a new life in the northern cities were faced with even greater hostility, which, on occasion, degenerated into race riots and lynchings. In South Africa, such exclusion was even more marked. On the one hand, British-born craft workers formed socialist unions and voted for the South African Labour Party with barely a thought for black workers. On the other, poorer Afrikaners were rapidly urbanised in the early twentieth century and when they started to feel the effects of black competition, attitudes hardened and they began to be drawn to the segregationist propaganda of Afrikaner nationalist groupings.

In order to gain a foothold, but later also as a response to exclusion, in both Europe and the United States immigrant workers (and in Europe 'national minorities') often pursued ethnic strategies to find a niche for themselves in the host society, using village, family and later 'national' networks to obtain work, security and social advancement. (This is also stressed for internal migrants by both Tim Moldram for South Africa and Rajnarayan Chandavarkar for India.) In this, of course, they were simply following the footsteps of their native immigrant forebears. But again national and racial stereotyping was significant in remoulding the political context. Often, it should be remembered, immigrants from rural areas were made aware of 'their' national identity only when they came into contact with the host society. The case of Italian immigrants in the late nineteenth and early twentieth-century United States, who often perceived themselves as 'being Italian' only when they were so labelled, is an oft cited example. This not only had social implications. It could also lead to a new ethnic-based politics in which politicians presented themselves as representatives of a sectional ethnic entity. This was, for example, widespread in major US cities, and could also be seen in Irish Catholic areas in Britain or in Polish Catholic areas in Imperial Germany. Of course, it is often forgotten that such 'ethnic' strategies were also being used by workers from the dominant community (but because they were the majority and it was seen as 'normal' and 'to be expected' it was usually regarded not as ethnic but as 'familial' or 'clientelistic'), who quite naturally used their own contacts to assure social advancement and, from the late nineteenth century, in the most industrialised areas could begin to use the educational system to try and get their offspring white-collar jobs or posts as primary school teachers or as minor civil servants. Indeed, it may usefully be asked whether an AFL or German Free Trade Union representative of native white skilled workers of Protestant stock was any less an 'ethnic broker' than his Afro-American or Polish counterpart.

However, to characterise the labour history of the period of study simply as determined by ethnic strife is insufficient. As the chapters in this book also point out, there were frequent attempts to structure broader inter-ethnic labour federations, which could meet with considerable success. Within republican thought there was a strong tradition of the free nation's duty to be a home to the poor and oppressed. And socialist ideology, with its emphasis on the emancipatory role of labour movements and on international class solidarity, did provide a language through which more all-encompassing movements might be structured.

In Europe, leftist labour leaders certainly showed more under-standing for the plight of the poor immigrant than most sections of the community. Many, as a result of their own prejudices and those of the rank and file, did rail against immigration, but there were attempts to integrate immigrants and ethnic minorities into wider unions. In the colonies, on the other hand, labour leaders had the difficult task of amalgamating workers from a wide variety of backgrounds into the same organisation, though in the United States and Australia at least they had some success. Yet as has been pointed out, racist attitudes made particu-larly precarious attempts to unionise the 'non-white' population, leading to claims that worker internationalism – particularly in the Anglo-Saxon world – was very much a 'white internationalism'.[31] This certainly serves to emphasise the chasm opened up by colonial racist and Social Darwinist thinking, but it should not hide the fact that there were attempts by white unionists to breach the gap.

At grass-roots level, relations between workers who belonged to the established, dominant group and outsiders were extremely complex. Within the labour process established groups of workers would defend their position if they could, but they might also have to reach compro-mises with newcomers or disadvantaged minorities. How this played out very much depended on power relations, which would themselves be related to such factors as the type of work involved, the number of immi-grants and the institutional context. The very different fate of immigrant Irish workers in different countries brings this issue out well. In Australia, perhaps because both Irish and other British workers arrived in large numbers during the same period, and because Irish nationalism could be channelled into an Australian anti-imperialist nationalism, Irish Catholic and Protestant workers were able to cooperate effectively within the Labor Party.[32] On the other hand, in the United States, while

31 P. van Duin, 'Proletarian Prejudices: the Impact of Ethnic and Racial Antagonism on Working-class Organisation', in W. R. Garscha and C. Schindler (eds), *Arbeiterbewegung und nationale Identität* (Vienna, Internationale Tagung der Historiker/-innen der Arbeiter/-innen und Arbeiterbewegung, 1994), p. 84.
32 Such co-operation did not, however, preclude high levels of ethnic tension between the Irish and non-Irish. On several occasions in the late nineteenth century, anti-Catholic riots and Catholic retaliation split Australian politics. Even worse forms of racism were targeted at the Chinese, the Pacific Islanders and the Italians, all of whom were targeted by legislation to exclude them as immigrants. We would like to thank Terry Irving for sharing these thoughts about the role of ethnic tensions in Australian politics with us.

Irish immigrants originally faced much prejudice, in the second half of the nineteenth century they were able to 'become white' and establish themselves in key positions in industry and the trade union bureaucracy. Finally, in England and Scotland they continued to suffer high levels of exclusion and discrimination. Yet, while the Irish in Britain did, at least, enter into competition with the locals (and indeed on occasion were able to dominate specific local industries), the Jews in Poland felt the safest approach was to restrain the level of anti-Jewish sentiment by remaining in low-paid employ in marginal workshops.

Despite this complexity, when assessing the response of workers from the dominant community a number of broad patterns can be discerned, which need to be related to our discussion in the previous section regarding ideological division and social differentiation within the labour movement and working class. First, as we have noted, during the first three decades of the century there was a tendency for skilled workers, who were able to carve out a niche for themselves within the system, to distance themselves from the poorer working class. These were usually either indigenous workers in Europe or workers of 'white' Western European ancestry in the settler colonies. Secondly, below this level there were attempts to form broader coalitions. In the United States the CIO was able to affiliate both 'old' and 'new' immigrants, and made some effort to organise Afro-Americans. In Europe, socialists, communists and anarcho-syndicalists were all also behind initiatives at united action. It was those unions which tried to articulate the 'poorer working class' that took most interest in organising immigrants.

In this respect it should not be forgotten that ethnic and class strategies were not necessarily mutually exclusive. A New York Italian who joined the CIO would not for that reason abandon his connections within the local community. These could, indeed, be very useful in order to extend the union at a local and factory level. Yet at the same time he could also be pursuing the strategy of integrating his offspring into the host society. And indeed it was the case that over some three generations the Irish, Italian and Jewish ghettoes did slowly become less ethnically self-enclosed (for Jews, this seems to have been the case in the United States and England but not in Eastern Europe, where 'official' antisemitism remained much stronger), more amorphous and interlinked with the dominant community. Yet as has already been indicated, the fault line most difficult to budge was that between 'whites' of European stock and workers of African or Asian origin. Where racism and segregation were strongest, as in South Africa, anti-black racism remained a central element of white labour movement ideology. In this particular case, moreover, integration was made even more difficult because blacks to a large extent were forced to remain migrant workers and because (in part through employer design) their chiefdom identities remained central to their conception of life. Indeed, for the reasons outlined above, general inter-working-class union and ideological divisions could sometimes acquire racial overtones, as when, for example, Communist organisers could be accused of being 'nigger lovers' in the United States, or the CNT of being a union of feckless *murcianos* (southern Spanish immigrants) in Catalonia.

Towards a new pluralism of identity politics?

As we have already seen, the more reformist sections of the labour movement in particular, in line with liberal thinking on the nation state, came to regard nations as quasi-natural entities based on a common culture, language and history. Hence Social Democrats, like liberals, were prone to essentialising the nation state and making it the 'normal' locus of identity politics. By contrast there is now emerging something like a scholarly consensus which perceives nations as invented and constructed. Whilst not being professed Marxists themselves, some time ago scholars like Ernest Gellner and Karl Deutsch stressed that the making of nations had material and structural determinants. For Gellner nationalism is essentially a 'common idiom', a 'shared culture' which allows the individual in modern industrial societies to negotiate his social position via a multitude of 'minor contracts' with others. He thereby pointed to the fact that for long periods in history other political units such as tribes, dynastic empires or city states dominated the scene. Only the emergence of capitalism or modernity meant that language communities were set up with the prime aim of sustaining complex educational systems producing in turn the social hierarchy characteristic of modern nation states.[33] That discursive elements also played a major role in the making and unmaking of nations was prominently discussed by Benedict Anderson and a collection of essays edited by Terence Ranger and Eric Hobsbawm.[34] For Anderson all national identities are necessarily constructed in a complex process through a variety of factors, among which the development of 'print capitalism' takes pride of place, yet it is

33 E. Gellner, *Nations and Nationalism* (Oxford, Blackwell, 1983); *id.*, *Encounters with Nationalism* (Oxford, Blackwell, 1994). See also K. Deutsch, *Nationalism and Social Communication. An Inquiry into the Foundations of Nationality* (Cambridge, Mass., MIT Press, 1966).

34 B. Anderson, *Imagined Communities. Reflections on the Origins and Spread of Nationalism*, 2nd edn (London, Verso, 1994); E. Hobsbawm and T. Ranger (eds), *The Invention of Tradition* (Cambridge, Cambridge University Press, 1983).

the 'style' in which nations are imagined which was contested and which differed substantially at different times and places.

Postmodernist approaches have taken the deconstruction of identity further by insisting that concepts such as class, nation and ethnicity belong to the 'grand narratives' which have structured the modern world.[35] The greatest insight of postmodernist approaches to the history of nation and class lies in its radical denial of attempts to fix their meaning once and for all, thereby ignoring the historical contingency in the shifting definitions of national and class identities. The meanings of both nation and class were and are continuously contested, challenged, destabilised and redefined. Both nationalism and socialism constantly constructed boundaries – mainly through a common 'memory of belonging', through symbolic spaces, representations, rituals and myths – which were in a process of continuous change. Nationalists as well as class warriors constructed their paradigms on the basis of an inclusion/exclusion mechanism. Certain stories had to be excluded to make the overall story a homogeneous one. Instead, a new historiography of class and nation (which could, in fact, build on the works of critical Marxist scholars such as E. P. Thompson and Eric Hobsbawm rather than trying to reinvent the wheel, as some postmodernists are suggesting) would concentrate on those groups written out of or marginalised by the super-paradigms of class and nation. It is because a nation is not a natural entity with a given soul or spirit and because class is not an objective description of one's social position in society that we have to turn to specific historical attempts of the left to define its own position *vis-à-vis* diverse forms of nationalisms. The construction of any kind of identity is usually dependent upon the existence of an elite with a high level of communicative and bargaining skills. The socialist labour movement and the national movements could provide those elites and construct powerful identities around the narratives of class and nation respectively.

Many chapters in this collection point towards the continuing appeal of liberal democratic versions of nationalism and their respective ability to strike at times impressive intra-class coalitions. It was this appeal of nationalism which made it paramount for both the political right and the left to come to terms with it and adopt, if possible, rival ideas of national identity and belonging which could challenge the dominance

35 On the impact of postmodernism on the national and class paradigms in historiography see Stefan Berger, 'The Rise and Fall of "Critical" Historiography? Some Reflections on the Historiographical Agenda of the Left in Britain, France and Germany at the end of the Twentieth Century', *Europa. European Review of History* 3 (1996), especially pp. 226–31.

of liberal nationalism in nineteenth-century Europe. On the right, official state nationalisms coexisted (albeit uneasily at times) with a variety of integral racist nationalisms, whilst sections of the left, in particular its Social Democratic variant, attempted to formulate left-wing nationalisms of their own. Whilst the latter had positive consequences as well as a wide appeal in specific historical circumstances (such as in the nineteenth-century struggle for democratisation in Europe or the struggle to create united and popular fronts against fascism in 1930s Europe or in the anti-colonial struggle of indigenous or white settler communities outside Europe) it never managed to come to terms with the Janus face of every type of nationalism. Left-wing nationalisms, just as their right-wing mirror images, have been capable of breeding intolerance and racial prejudice. Yet, as we have tried to emphasise, Labour's reaction to the challenge of nationalism has been a complex and multifaceted one. And, to end on a positive note, wider recognition of our contention that historical identity is contingent and forever shifting, could contribute to a more rational discussion of the benefits and pitfalls of nationalism as well as feelings of ethnic and class solidarity.

British and German Socialists between class and national solidarity

If Patriotism really meant true love of our native land, then I should claim that Socialists are patriots, and I should go further and claim Socialists are the only true patriots since they alone are striving for the real honour and the real welfare and the real advancement of their nation.[1]

I learnt what it means to be truely patriotic; it means being a Social Democrat! Patriotism means love for one's country. No one can love his Fatherland more than we Social Democrats.[2]

Thou shalt not be a patriot, for a patriot is an international blackleg. Your duty to yourself and your class demands that you be a citizen of the world.[3]

Today the only defence of all true national freedom is the revolutionary class struggle against imperialism. The fatherland of the proletarians is the Socialist International and its defence has to come before everything else.[4]

The basic ambiguity and tension between socialist and national identities in Britain and Germany, which can be gauged from the above quotes, had much to do with the integration of workers into and the positioning of the labour movement towards its respective nation state. In the first two sections of this chapter the degree of working-class integration and the character of the competing national discourses within the labour movement will be discussed at some length before turning – in the final section of this chapter – to examine key junctures in the relationship between class/Labour and nationalism/ethnicity. The increasing nationalisation and militarisation of British and German Labour before the First World War will be traced, and the reaction to the war efforts of Britain and Germany will be discussed. Furthermore, the post-

1 R. Blatchford, *Clarion*, 27 May 1899.
2 P. Scheidemann, *Memoirs of a Social Democrat*, I (London, Hutchinson, 1929), p. 12 f.
3 Second Commandment from the Ten Commandments issued by Glasgow's Red Sunday School in May 1917. Cited in R. Samuel, 'British Marxist Historians' I, *New Left Review* 120 (1980), p. 48.
4 K. Duncker in her speech at the conference of the left-wing opposition in the SPD in 1916 (*Reichskonferenz*), cited in D. Groh and P. Brandt, *'Vaterlandslose Gesellen'. Sozialdemokratie und Nation 1860–1990* (Munich, Beck, 1992), p. 169.

1918 period which saw a further turn of both Labour Party and SPD towards the national principle will be analysed. The many ambiguities, false dichotomies and dangerous pitfalls produced by various attempts to define alternative forms of 'good' left-wing patriotism (as opposed to 'bad' right-wing nationalism) will also be examined with reference to Labour's stance *vis-à-vis* the monarchy, imperialism, immigration and resident ethnic minorities in both countries.[5]

Levels of integration of Labour into nation state and society

When an independent labour movement appeared on the scene in both Britain and Germany, it met with hostility from state, employers, Churches and middle classes alike. By the late nineteenth century anti-socialism had become part and parcel of the countries' educational systems and played an important role in encouraging very different governments to experiment with social reform. Efforts to cripple and ultimately destroy the labour movement went hand in hand with attempts to wean the workers away from Labour's embraces. Consequently, both labour movements felt alienated from the nation state, and yet, at the same time, both increasingly felt that they had a stake in the nation, that they belonged to and even best represented the community of people making up the nation. Feelings of loyalty to the nation were carefully distinguished from the continuing hostility towards certain aspects of the way this nation state was organised. In the following paragraphs I would like to give a brief overview of the attitudes of Churches, state, army, judiciary, other political parties and employers towards organised Labour and reflect on the impact of social welfarism and parliamentarism on the attitudes of the labour movement towards the nation state.

In Imperial Germany, Social Democrats were widely denounced as 'fellows without a fatherland' (*vaterlandslose Gesellen*). They were excluded from 'respectable' bourgeois society. The Protestant Church in Prussia, the head of which was the king himself, preached continuously against the evils of Social Democracy. Whilst the Catholic Church railed against atheist socialism, it was more successful than Protestantism in retaining working-class allegiance – not the least because of its willing-

---

5 The focus of this chapter will be firmly on the organised labour movement and its relationship to national and ethnic identities in Britain and Germany. Whilst much could be said about the wider relationship between class, ethnic and national identities in the neighbourhoods and at the workplaces, such a perspective, valuable as it is, would go beyond the scope of the chapter.

ness to set up Catholic trade unions and workers' organisations.[6] In Britain, the official Churches also remained largely hostile to the labour movement whilst being more sensitive to the social problems of the working class. The high politicisation of Churches in the second half of the nineteenth century meant that the Labour Party had nowhere to turn for support. The Anglican state Church was widely known as the 'Tory party at prayer', and the Nonconformist Churches strongly supported the Liberal Party. In Scotland, the Free Kirk and United Presbyterians supported the Liberals whilst the Old Kirk supported the Conservatives.

The imperial German state could not only rely on the Churches to combat socialism, it also heavily recruited the educational system in this battle. Known Social Democrats such as Eduard David were dismissed as teachers, and the autobiographies of Labour leaders frequently recount the attempts to imbue schoolchildren with nationalism and anti-socialism. Victimisation of teachers who were active on behalf of the labour movement was not unknown in Britain. Dan Griffiths perceptively noted the similarities between Britain and Germany in this respect: 'The enemies of the workers in Germany . . . made a cult of inculcating subservience and "patriotism" in their schools . . . The same thing is being done . . . in this country. The celebration of Empire Day, for example, is a part of this process.'[7] As a result, the labour movements in both countries, which perceived themselves very much as educational movements, provided their own independent educational institutions for their members. The parties appointed educational officers and organised speakers' classes. Itinerant teachers travelled the country and workers' libraries were set up. The party school of the SPD in Berlin, the Socialist Workers' College in Hamburg, the Workers' Academy in Frankfurt, Ruskin College in Oxford, the Central Labour College in London and the many local branches of the Workers' Educational Association and the Plebs' League were testimony to the willingness of socialists in both countries to take education into their own hands. However, the more integrated Labour became locally and nationally, the more it sought to merge its independent institutions with those of the state. From providing their own for their own they sought to provide better facilities for all through local politics and national governments. Especially the exten-

6 However, as D. Blackbourn, *Class, Religion and Local Politics in Wilhelmine Germany* (London, Steiner, 1980), p. 52, has argued, the Centre Party's growing agrarian tendency before 1914 meant a steady decline of the party's urban working-class support.

7 D. Griffiths, *'The Real Enemy' and other Socialist Essays* (London, Richards, 1923), p. 65.

sion of municipal and recreational amenities became a prime task for socialist municipal policies after the First World War in Britain and Germany.

The Imperial German state feared socialist agitation in the army and hence sought to immunise that institution from the socialist virus. Conscription in Germany meant that almost all workers had to serve in the army for three years.[8] As is well known, Prussia was a society in which civilian life was militarised to a very high degree. The army was widely perceived as 'the school of the nation'. Yet the army functioned as an instrument of national cohesion only to a limited extent. The oppression and degradation which many workers experienced in the army often led them to identify with Social Democracy. As the agricultural worker Franz Rehbein remembers in his autobiography, it had been his experiences with the military which had converted him to Social Democracy.[9] Many working-class recruits perceived their military service as hell. The SPD's trenchant critique of militarism, which included frequent calls on party members to agitate for the party's aims whilst serving their stint, and the party's repeated attacks on the everyday maltreatment of soldiers by their superior officers increased the mutual feelings of hostility between German Socialists and those in charge of the army.

From the 1880s onwards Social Democrats were systematically excluded from veterans' associations in Imperial Germany. The army command, in conjunction with the Prussian government, explicitly aimed to make those associations an ally in the fight against socialism. The Kyffhäuserbund, with almost 3 million members in 1913, was the biggest organisation in Imperial Germany, and whilst many of its leading members came from the educated middle and upper classes, many of its ordinary members were workers. It reflected the fact that many workers, including many Social Democrats, had a rather ambivalent relationship to their military service. Despite the humiliation suffered, many were proud of the fact that they had managed successfully to complete their service. In several workers' autobiographies there are fond memories of a time which was perceived, at least with hindsight, as a kind of adventure playground releasing them, for a brief period, from their dull everyday routine and giving them the opportunity to live out their ideas of male virility and comradeship. Having been invalided out

---

8 This was the case until 1893, when compulsory military service was reduced to two years. However, class bias even penetrated the military service. Germans who had enjoyed some higher education, usually at the socially exclusive and elitist *Gymnasium*, had to serve for only one year.

9 F. Rehbein, *Das Leben eines Landarbeiters* (Jena, Diederichs, 1911), p. 7.

of the army was widely seen as dishonourable. Many official army reports in fact single out Social Democrats for special praise. They were perceived as good soldiers, and the connection was made between the strong party discipline in the SPD and their love of discipline on the parade ground. The Social Democrat August Winnig, for example, recalls: 'The part I liked best was the drilling . . . The more I mastered the movements and rifle positions, the more I loved to drill.'[10] 'Service' and 'discipline' became measuring rods for both the army and the party. Military ideals thus penetrated the labour movement and the working class at large.

Militarism pervaded British civilian life to a lesser extent, but it was far from insignificant. At the beginning of the twentieth century about 22 per cent of all British men aged between seventeen and forty had some experience of military life. Yet, in the absence of compulsory military service, many workers in peacetime encountered the army (as an adversary) only during periods of extensive industrial conflict. Workers on strike might well have perceived the army as ally of their oppressors, but this did not necessarily prevent them from enlisting in the army in times of national crisis and war. The labour movement – wary of the domestic consequence of British militarism – was contemptuous of the army at large. It was perceived as 'oppressive at home and inefficient abroad' and denounced as a 'refuge for misfits and mediocrities, dominated by a polo-playing, pig-sticking officer corps of mean intelligence and reactionary disposition from which respectable trade unionists recoiled in horror'.[11] As a military career in the ranks carried little status and esteem, those who enlisted came overwhelmingly from the least skilled and respectable end of the working-class spectrum. Perennial and endemic problems of drunkenness and venereal disease further contributed to the negative image that the army enjoyed among most Labour leaders.

Robert Blatchford, who had served in the army for six years and looked back fondly on the experience, remained rather the exception. Furthermore, veterans' organisations never played a similarly influential role in Britain as in Germany. The British Legion, set up after the First World War, never became a mass organisation comparable to the Kyffhäuserbund or the Stahlhelm. Although no doubt nationalist and conservative in outlook (despite its official 'unpolitical' stance), the

---

10 A. Winnig, *Der weite Weg* (Hamburg, Hanseatische Verlagsanstalt, 1932), p. 70 f.
11 D. Englander, 'The National Union of Ex-servicemen and the Labour Movement 1918–20', *History* 76 (1991), p. 25. See also D. Englander and J. Osborne, 'Jack, Tommy and Henry Dubb: the Armed Forces and the Working Class', *Historical Journal* 21:3 (1978) pp. 593–621.

British Legion, unlike the Stahlhelm, never became a quasi-front organisation for fascism. In fact, British veterans sympathetic to the labour
movement set up their own organisation after 1918 out of fear of the
radicalisation of the uprooted and traumatised soldiers returning from
the trenches. The National Union of Ex-servicemen campaigned against
war profiteering and for the democratisation of the army. Its pacifist
outlook as well as its critique of the ideologies of 'trench solidarity' and
the 'front generation' stood in marked contrast to the racist and illiberal
ideas propagated by veterans' organisations in Germany.

The anti-socialism of the judiciary in both Britain and Germany
alienated the labour movements in both countries. The whole of the
state bureaucracy, especially the police and the courts, came to be seen
as instruments of the ruling class by the SPD in Imperial Germany.
Unsurprisingly Richard Evans found the pub talk of Hamburg workers
full of complaints about police harassment, unfair imprisonment and
dubious legal proceedings.[12] However, the repression of Social Democrats always had its limits in the rule of law. And after 1918 state attention largely focused on the Communist Party. At the same time, the
sporadic authoritarianism of the British state is also not to be underestimated. The police were widely perceived as an instrument of class rule.
A series of court rulings against trade unions in the 1890s finally led to
the Taff Vale decision of 1901 and further to the Osborne judgement of
1909. These decisions demonstrated a firm belief among the British judiciary that the law should be used to enforce repressive controls upon
trade unions. The 1915 Munitions of War Act, which made strikes illegal
and introduced compulsory arbitration, and, more than anything else,
the 1920 Emergency Powers Act, demonstrated the will of the British
state to take all necessary measures to defeat any serious challenge from
the political left. Even as late as 1927 the Conservative government could
still pass the infamous Trade Disputes Act, which aimed at crippling the
political muscle of the union movement.

If the Churches, the schools, the army and the legal system were all
part of the stick with which to beat the organised working class, social
reform was the carrot to lure the workers away from Social Democratic
promises of emancipation. Both countries have been correctly described
as pioneers of the modern welfare state. In the second half of the nineteenth century questions of social reform surfaced in both societies and
were quickly to take the centre stage in public discussion, partly because
an impoverished underclass was more and more perceived as a revolu-

---

12 R. Evans, *Proletarians and Politics. Socialism, Protest and the Working Class in Germany
before the First World War* (New York, St Martin's Press, 1990), p. 151.

tionary threat. The aim of creating a kind of state control over the whole spectrum of working-class life was propagated as a remedy.

It was not only the state which did much to isolate and alienate the labour movement: employer and general middle-class hostility also played a large part. Employers, sometimes in conjunction with the state or, in Britain, with the Conservative and Unionist Parties, supported vociferous anti-socialist organisations such as the Imperial League against Social Democracy in Germany and the Anti-Socialist Union in Britain. No doubt the different features of German industry, with its higher levels of concentration and cartelisation, vertical and horizontal integration, and the interpenetration of financial and industrial capital, were important in shaping different industrial relations from those in Britain. British employers were more vulnerable to trade union pressure, not least because bargaining remained highly decentralised. Yet already in Imperial Germany trade unions were far from powerless. The rise in real wages after the 1880s was not least due to trade union pressure. In fact, by 1907, the British and the German union movements organised an almost identical number of workers – about 2.5 million in Britain and about 2.25 million in Germany. Well before 1914, two out of three industrial conflicts in Germany ended in compromise, another indication of a growing readiness on the part of employers to accept trade unions as representative organisations of the working class. The notion of the Weimar Republic as a trade union state did not only reflect employers' hostility, it also demonstrated the real power and political influence of unions in the 1920s. In Britain unions also continued to grow and certainly exercised important political influence, yet, at the same time, the 1920s saw a series of devastating defeats of the union movement, culminating in the failure of the General Strike of 1926. Ultimately, the domestication of industrial conflict was to become the rationale of employer strategies in both countries.

Both parties were committed to their respective parliamentary systems. Despite the existence of anti-parliamentary factions in both parties, parliament was regarded as the holy grail of people's sovereignty by the party leadership. As Scheidemann remembered in his memoirs, 'for Bebel the Reichstag was a truly great and significant thing . . . , the "High Court of Parliament", which he entered only in his Sunday best'.[13] Despite the limited influence of the German parliament on policy-making before 1918, the work of the SPD's parliamentary party was significant. In Weimar the parliamentary republic had no greater stalwart than Social Democracy. Unlike the German Social Democrats, the

13 Scheidemann, *Memoirs* I, p. 166.

British Labour Party did not have to help bring full parliamentary government about, nor did it ever have to fear for its existence. Partly as a result of the stability of parliamentarianism in Britain, there developed a very strong belief in parliamentary government within the British Labour Party, with anti-parliamentary sections, comprising Clarionettes, syndicalists, Guild Socialists and the SDF always rather marginal.

Within parliament both parties faced deep hostility from Conservative Parties. However, it is important to note that Conservatives rallied support from very different constituencies in Britain and Germany. In the latter case the backbone of support came from rural/agricultural areas and from a substantial number of artisans, dock-yard and postal workers as well as from various other sectors of state employment. The working-class Tory, who was at the heart of Conservative success in industrial Lancashire, found no real equivalent in Germany, unless one wants to draw a parallel with the Catholic workers in Germany opting for the Centre Party. The more substantial working-class support for the British Conservatives meant that they had to at least pay tribute to the interests of the working class. 'Tory democ-racy', a phrase coined by Randolph Churchill in his effort to mobilise popular support from all classes, consisted of a well organised and suc-cessful form of demagogic populism. In both countries Labour found it easier to cooperate with the Liberals. Many of the early Labour leaders in Britain and Germany came from a Liberal background and not infre-quently portrayed themselves and their parties as true successors to the Liberal traditions which the Liberals themselves had betrayed. The SPD's electoral agreements with left Liberals in 1912 led to cooperation between the bourgeois centre parties and the social democrats in the *Interfraktionelle Ausschuss* of parliament in 1917/18 and ultimately to the Weimar coalition after 1918. In Britain the Gladstone–MacDonald *entente* of 1903 led to the support of the Labour Party for the pre-war Liberal social reform governments and ultimately to Labour minority governments in the 1920s which were tolerated by the Liberals.

In many respects, therefore, the story of the labour movements in Britain and Germany between 1880 and 1930 can be read as one of increasing, if always contested, integration into the mainstream of the nation state. Initial hostility which found expression in the anti-socialism of the educational systems, the Churches and large sections of the middle classes, especially employers, as well as in legal attempts to cripple and destroy the labour movement, slowly but surely gave way to the realisation that a movement which represented millions of workers and citizens could not be kept at the gates of the nation state. Increasing cooperation with other parties within their respective parliamentary systems, a rising recognition that a regulated system of industrial relations was more beneficial than the continued repression of trade unions, the acceptance of workers as citizens and the setting up of welfare states all worked in the direction of giving workers and their organisations an increasing share in the nation state after 1918. Whilst the integration of the labour movement in Germany had made great strides and was certainly more comparable to Great Britain than to most other European countries, the victory of National Socialism in Germany in 1933, which saw the complete obliteration of the German labour movement, clearly demonstrated how much more volatile such integration was in the German context. However, in Britain the General Strike of 1926 and its aftermath were a powerful reminder that the process of the integration of the labour movement was rather uneven and incomplete.

The positioning of Labour within the national discourses

It was the alienation and exclusion from the nation state which predestined the labour movements in both countries to become sharp critics of nationalism and develop instead a distinguished tradition of internationalism. British trade unions formed the backbone of the First International, into which context the foundation of the German Social Democratic Party must be firmly set. In 1870/71 the leaders of German Social Democracy, August Bebel and Wilhelm Liebknecht, opposed the war against France and the annexation of Alsace-Lorraine and instead identified strongly with the Paris Commune. The SPD went on to become the dominant party of the Second International and was regarded as a model working-class party by many European Socialists. The Labour Party took a bold and vigorous stance for the reconstitution of the Second International after 1918. Without its attempts to mediate between German and French Socialists in particular, there would not have been such a speedy restoration of international Socialist links after the First World War.

Germany's belated unification meant that the process of nation building was under way at roughly the same time as the SPD raised the spectre of social revolution. For the German ruling classes it was tempting to make anti-socialism part of the cement which was supposed to hold the new nation state together. The anti-socialist law of 1878 and subsequent efforts to suppress the labour movement had highly ambiguous consequences: on the one hand Social Democrats began to internalise the external pressure and developed a slavish belief in legality. On the other hand, the SPD turned to revolutionary Marxism with the adoption of the Erfurt programme in 1891. Marx's ideas on the national question were, however, highly unsystematic and full of contradictions. Whilst the class war was necessarily an international one, it also had to be fought within specific nation states. Whilst workers ultimately were not supposed to have a fatherland, the different social and economic conditions of nation states at the same time conditioned the character of the class struggle. Whilst nationalism was exclusively interpreted as a mechanism of the ruling class by which to defeat movements for social emancipation, Marx also carefully distinguished between a justified nationalism in progressive 'historical' nations such as Britain and a counter-revolutionary nationalism in backward nations, which, in his view, for example, included the Czech and Croat national movements, which served only the interests of pan-Slavism, i.e. reactionary tsarism in Russia. The right of progressive nations to defend themselves against backward ones became a standard argument in the debates in the Second International on war prevention prior to 1914. Furthermore, the emotional ties that many, including many workers, felt for the nation state were hardly ever taken seriously before Otto Bauer's pathbreaking book on the national question.[14] Kautsky, for example, predicted that the nations would simply fade away the more the internationalisation of capital proceeded and the more the different languages became dialects.[15]

Yet the internationalism of the SPD did not only suffer from its own theoretical contradictions. Long before the Marxist turn of the SPD, there had been serious attempts by Social Democrats to merge the national and the social agendas. Ferdinand Lasalle, one of the founders of the German labour movement and a disciple of both Fichte and Hegel, firmly believed in the superiority of cultural nations and the special spiritual mission of the German nation in particular. Thus he could, for example, justify Prussia's annexation of Poland's western provinces as a victory of German culture over Slav barbarity. Nineteenth-century Social Democrats frequently claimed to be heirs to the nineteenth-century universalist Liberal nationalism. The national idea was perceived as the standard-bearer of democratic emancipation. The patriotism of Social Democrats thus became indivisible from a democratic concept of the nation state. Only truly democratic institutions and a greater degree of social equality, based on the abolition of the private ownership of the means of production and the substitution of a socialist for the existing capitalist economy, so the argument went, would integrate all citizens,

14 O. Bauer, *Die Nationalitätenfrage und die Sozialdemokratie*, 2nd edn (Vienna, Verlag der Wiener Volksbuchhandlung, 1924, first publ. in 1907).
15 K. Kautsky, 'Die moderne Nationalität', *Neue Zeit* 5 (1887), p. 541.

including the workers, and in turn all would feel loyal to the nation state. Socialists tended to stress that identification with the democratic, socially responsible nation state of the future would not necessarily exclude true friendship with other nation states of similar make-up.

In Imperial Germany, the reformist and revisionist wings of the SPD in particular argued that such patriotism formed the basis of all genuine internationalism, whilst anti-nationalist internationalism was perceived as counterproductive to national integration. A slow national-isation of Social Democracy was taking place in Imperial Germany which fed into the widespread interpretation of the First World War as a 'war of national survival' even among SPD members. However, the nation state that the SPD defended in 1914 was not the state of the Junkers and the Hohenzollern monarchy but the future democratic welfare state allegedly threatened by 'tsarist despotism'. In the German revolution of 1918/19 Social Democrats played a key role in establishing a democratic and social republic. This was achieved not only against right-wing oppo-sition but also against resistance from the left. Notably the left wing of the Independent Social Democratic Party (USPD) and the German Communist Party (KPD) represented a tradition of radical internation-alism which tended to perceive nationalism as part and parcel of bour-geois ideology. The fatherland of the workers, they argued, was the (Communist) International. Time and again the KPD in the 1920s stressed that only social revolution could solve the national question. At the same time, however, the party did not shy away from employing the language of nationalism for tactical reasons. So, for example, it rejected the Versailles Treaty and, at the height of the *Ruhrkampf* in 1923, Communists shared platforms with Nazis and other representatives of the extreme right in protest over the French occupation of the Ruhr. The Dawes plan, the Locarno treaties as well as the Young plan were all denounced as 'national treason' by Germany's ruling classes. Germany, Communists in the Weimar Republic argued, had become an oppressed nation and a victim of capitalist imperialism.

If the classed patriotism of the Communists post-1918 was increas-ingly linked with unconditional support for the Soviet Union as the fatherland of the international proletariat, the anarcho-syndicalist tradi-tion in Germany firmly rejected nationalism as the 'religion of the modern state'. Whilst they argued that national boundaries were largely arbitrary, anarcho-syndicalists did recognise cultural differences between peoples and argued strongly in favour of concepts of cultural autonomy. Rudolf Rocker's *Nationalism and Culture* (first published in English and Spanish in 1936) explicitly defined culture as 'non-domi-nation of man by his surroundings' and continued to argue that 'culture' formed the positive counter-concept to the modern nation state.[16] The anarcho-syndicalist tradition in Germany was certainly a minority one, both before and after the war, yet at times, as in the Ruhr between 1919 and 1923, it managed to win a mass following among workers. It could probably build on what Alf Lüdtke has described as the *Eigensinn* ('denoting wilfulness, spontaneous self-will, a kind of self-affirmation, an act of (re)appropriating alienated social relations on and off the shop floor by self-assertive prankishness, demarcating a space of one's own'[17]) of German workers. Such *Eigensinn* could be directed against the various efforts of employers to regiment workers, but it could equally be directed against a regimented Social Democratic labour movement and its claims to represent all workers. As far as non-organised workers were concerned, work, occupation, workers' origin, dialect, residential style, Church affiliation all were far more important than the nation for the make-up of working-class identities. Yet at times the language of the nation could mobilise workers. So, for example, the notion of German quality workmanship (*deutsche Qualitätsarbeit*) was something that many workers were proud of and which the Nazis made good use of in their attempts to win stronger working-class support.[18]

Unlike Germany, Britain was not a 'belated nation', yet it was a multinational state. 'Britishness' clearly served the purpose of papering over the deep cultural, linguistic and social differences between England, Scotland, Wales and Ireland. Such Britishness, however, could not be ethnically based, as any outright ethnic nationalism would necessarily destroy the state. At the same time, Britain's claim to a democratic nationalism was also in many respects seriously flawed, so that in the end, as Tom Nairn has argued, a mixture of royalism, imperialism and racialism became the substitute for a modern national identity.[19] From the late 1870s onwards the political right consciously used the language of the nation to counter class tensions and the perceived threat of socialism. As in the German case such anti-socialism was met by an extremely varied

16 H. van den Berg and D. Nelles, 'Nationalismus oder Kultur. Über die kulturpolitischen Vorstellungen in der anarchosyndikalistischen Exilpublizistik in den Niederlanden 1933–40', in H. Würzner and K. Kröhnke (eds), *Deutsche Literatur im Exil in den Niederlanden 1933–40* (Amsterdam, Rodopi, 1994), p. 130.

17 A. Lüdtke, 'Polymorphous Synchrony: German Industrial Workers and the Politics of Everyday Life', in M. van den Linden (ed.), *The End of Labour History?*, IRSH 38, Supplement 1 (Cambridge, Cambridge University Press, 1993), p. 49.

18 A. Lüdtke, 'The "Honor of Labor": Industrial Workers and the Power of Symbols under National Socialism', in D. Crew (ed.), *Nazism and German Society 1933–45* (London, Routledge, 1994), pp. 67–109.

19 T. Nairn, *The Enchanted Glass. Britain and its Monarchy*, 2nd edn (London, Verso, 1994).

response on the part of the labour movement. Especially on the so-called Celtic fringe, there emerged serious attempts to fuse socialism with Welsh and Scottish nationalism.[20] The Labour Party as a self-consciously British party could tag on to a tradition of 'radical patriotism' ranging back at least to the late eighteenth century. It had its own 'invented traditions', for example the idea of the 'ancient liberties of the freeborn Englishman', which amounted to an alternative vision of the nation state to the dominant right-wing nationalism. Labour's commitment to the nation state was nowhere more in evidence than in its 1928 programme *Labour and the Nation*. The author, R. H. Tawney, described the party's main aim in terms of creating 'a society in which the treasures of civilisation shall not be the monopoly of a class but the heritage of the nation'.[21] The workers, he argued, had yet to become full members of the nation state but they could do so through gradual social progress and reform within the existing nation state. That British socialism was inextricably bound up with national aspirations was very much in evidence in some of the most influential socialist writings of, for example, H. M. Hyndman and Robert Blatchford. The very titles of their books are revealing: *England for all, Merrie England,* and *Britain for the British.* Such positive identification with the nation state (inclusive of an even more problematic substitution of 'Englishness' for the whole of the British nation state) sat uneasily with a widespread distrust of Labour activists in the national discourse. The majority of Labour Party supporters, as Paul Addison has noted, 'behaved like outsiders in a country that belonged to someone else'.[22] In many ways it was only during the Second World War that the party faithful fully adapted the kind of 'social patriotism' which had long been part of Labour's discourse on the nation state.

The British left before 1939 widely rejected the dominant right-wing forms of nationalism and often underestimated the power of nationalist ideologies. Labour's thinking on nationalism owed much to the writings of J. A. Hobson and Norman Angell. Their aversion to nationalism was connected with the disorienting success of the 'new imperialism' after 1895. Worried by the illiberal and militarist side effects of imperialism, its success among the electorate was explicable

20 D. Howell, *A Lost Left. Three Studies in Socialism and Nationalism* (Manchester, Manchester University Press, 1986), pp. 8 and 247. Compare also J. Schmarzmantel, *Socialism and the Idea of the Nation* (London, Harvester and Wheatsheaf, 1991), p. 107.

21 *Labour and the Nation* (London, Labour Party, 1928), p. 45.

22 P. Addison, 'Britain and the Politics of Social Patriotism', in S. Aster (ed.), *The Second World War as National Experience* (Ottawa, Canadian Committee for the History of the Second World War, 1981), p. 48.

only with reference to the growing irrationalism of the British people, who were manipulated by vested interests, largely through the press. Like German Marxists, British Labourites were interpreting nationalism as a manipulative ideology of the ruling classes to defeat movements for social emancipation. Labour politicians feared that imperialism would lead to the rise to power of democratically unaccountable state bureau-cracies. After 1917 many on the left of the British labour movement – and most certainly the CPGB after 1921 – abandoned the earlier appeal to an indigenous alternative 'radical patriotism'. Instead, as in Germany, such concepts were sidelined by identification with the Soviet Union and the Communist International. However, it may be useful to distinguish between official party policy and the deeply ingrained beliefs of the rank and file. As Raphael Samuel pointed out, 'for my mother's generation, Communism, though not intended as such, was a way of being English, a bridge by which the children of the ghetto entered the national culture.'[23] Any such ambiguities did not prevent the CPGB from being, in the inter-war years, the party most visibly fighting racism and anti-semitism in British society.

Socialists in Britain and Germany were uncertain about their feel-ings towards the nation: emotions oscillated in a multi-layered patchwork between alienation from, critical reception of and commitment to the nation state. In both countries the language of an oppositional patriotism was spoken and developed by socialists who sought to demarcate a 'good patriotism' of the left, which could build on the national loyalties felt by the people, from the 'bad nationalism' of the political right. However, as we shall see in the next section, such attempts to establish democratic national credentials were to have highly problematic consequences.

The pitfalls of oppositional nationalisms in Britain and Germany

The nationalisation of Labour movement culture

Long before 1914 Bebel publicly demanded obligatory military training for German youth prior to military service. Social Democratic rhetoric also reflected the increasing militarisation of the SPD's milieu: party leaders were nicknamed 'the General' (Friedrich Engels), 'the Emperor' (August Bebel), 'the Red Czar of Prussia' (Otto Braun) and there were frequent references to the 'armies' and 'battalions' of the labour movement. Party conferences became 'army manoeuvres'

23 R. Samuel, 'The Lost World of British Communism', *New Left Review*, 154 (1985), p. 53.

(*Heerschauen*). The individual party member became a 'party soldier' (*Parteisoldat*). Working-class cyclists were described as 'red hussars of the class war'. Marching in step, militaristic rituals, mass demonstrations and the use of military vocabulary in the workers' sports movement were indicative of the prevalence of very traditional ideas of discipline and order within the Social Democratic milieu.[24] Labour movement culture thus often encouraged the nationalist, militaristic and authoritarian attitudes which its political movement sought to overcome. The SPD's educational programmes focused on national 'high culture'. Even if the works of, for example, Friedrich Schiller and Richard Wagner were interpreted not in the dominant middle-class nationalist vein but presented in the light of the struggle for social and political emancipation, labour movement culture still adopted values and norms implicit in bourgeois culture and society.

Similar tensions between the increasing nationalisation of labour movement culture and an attempted reappropriation of the national tradition existed in Britain. Of the two most popular hymns sung in the Labour Church movement of the 1890s, one was patriotic ('God bless our native land') and the other was class-conscious ('God save the working man').[25] One of the most popular songbooks in the British labour movement, the *Chants of Labour*, edited by Edward Carpenter in 1888, included songs such as 'England, arise', which was also sung regularly at Labour festivals. It celebrated national virtues and the English countryside and juxtaposed them with the 'wretched slum' and the 'dark cities where your babes are creeping', and it ended with a powerful call to arms to defend England against those who held it in misery:

> Forth, then, ye heroes, patriots, and lovers!
> Comrades of danger, poverty, and scorn!
> Mighty in faith of freedom your great mother!
> Giants refreshed in joy's new-rising morn!
> Come and swell the song,/ Silent now so long:
> England is arisen! – and the day is here.'[26]

Cartoons in the British socialist press often depicted the national saint,

24 G. Hauk, '"Armeekorps auf dem Weg zur Sonne". Einige Bemerkungen zur kulturellen Selbstdarstellung der Arbeiterbewegung', in D. Petzina (ed.), *Fahnen, Fäuste, Körper. Symbolik und Kultur der Arbeiterbewegung* (Essen, Klartext, 1986), pp. 69–89.

25 K. S. Inglis, *Churches and the Working Classes in Victorian England* (London, Routledge, 1964), p. 234.

26 E. Carpenter (ed.), *Chants of Labour. A Song Book of the People* (Manchester, Swann Sonnenschein, 1888), p. 18 f.

St George, as defender of the poor and the workers. Socialist visions of the future were frequently linked with the allegedly happier days of the Middle Ages, when rural England had not yet been marred by the ugly scars of industrial capitalism. Keir Hardie, for example, wrote: 'the golden age of the English workman was the fifteenth century . . . there were neither millionaires nor paupers in those days, but a rude abundance for all . . . ; a strong element of Communism . . . characterised town and village life.'[27] Many international May Day events in the interwar period celebrated the 'England of old' with *tableaux vivants*, theatre plays, 'Merrie England' model villages and parades in folk costume.

One of the overriding concerns of labour movement culture in both Britain and Germany was to counter what was perceived as the negative effects of popular culture, which was frequently regarded as amoral and degenerate. Instead the self-understanding of Labour as educational movements aimed primarily at introducing workers to the 'great national culture', at giving them a share in that national culture. Among the most popular metaphors of both the British and the German labour movements were those of the rise of Labour to the light. In the present workers were surrounded by 'darkness', but the socialist future was inevitably 'bright', 'clean', 'healthy' and 'light'. This story of the inevitable rise of the working class was in fact playing on the desire of many workers for a bourgeois life style, job security and material well-being. It was leading the workers out of the workers' existence and could thus accommodate the widespread longing for individual social mobility. As such Labour's most powerful metaphor could in effect work as a brake on class solidarity and enhance the further integration into an alleged 'national community'.

The impact of the First World War
The increasing nationalisation and militarisation of the British and German labour movements surfaced most dramatically with the remarkable outburst of national solidarity in 1914. Karl Bröger, one of the most popular worker poets, wrote a poem for the working-class soldiers: 'We have always loved you, but so far we have never declared our love. Now that we were called upon, we followed silently, the word "Germany" not on our lips but in our hearts.'[28] Whilst it is undeniable

---

27 K. Hardie, *From Serfdom to Socialism* (London, 1907), pp. 45–8.
28 'Immer schon haben wir eine Liebe zu Dir gekannt, bloß wir haben sie nie mit einem Namen genannt, als man uns rief, da zogen wir schweigend fort, auf den Lippen nicht, aber im Herzen das Wort: Deutschland.' Cited in P. von Rüden, *Beiträge zur Kulturgeschichte der deutschen Arbeiterbewegung 1848–1918* (Frankfurt, Büchergilde Gutenberg, 1981), p. 40.

that many ordinary workers in both countries enthusiastically joined their respective armies in August 1914, many expecting the adventure of a lifetime or at any rate a change from the monotonous work routine they were accustomed to, the reactions of workers were more ambiguous, multi-layered and less ecstatic than the war euphoria displayed by the middle classes. Cross-class alliances in pursuit of war-related national goals were at best intermittent and always remained volatile and contested. As the effects of food shortages and general misery were felt most rapidly among the working class, dissatisfaction with the war mounted throughout the war years. Malnourishment, a decline in real wages, longer working hours and clothing shortages quickly led to disillusionment and ultimately to widespread social protest, rent strikes, the growth of a revolutionary shop stewards' movement and – in Germany – to the revolution of 1918.

In both countries there was a marked hiatus between the disillusionment of many workers and the continued enthusiasm of many Labour leaders. Important leaders of both parties like Arthur Henderson or Eduard David perceived the war as an opportunity to integrate the labour movement more firmly into the nation state. In Britain Socialists sat in the War Cabinet and cooperated fully with the war effort. In August 1914 several Labour MPs joined in when the rest of the House gave a thundering rendition of 'Rule, Britannia'. Even opposition to the war often employed the language of patriotism. As Philip Snowden wrote, 'We . . . believed that the most patriotic duty we could render to our country was to seek peace; that the longer the war continued, the more the ideals for which the nation stood were in danger of being destroyed; . . .'[29] In Germany, Socialists like the trade union leader Carl Legien or the party historian Gustav Mayer worked with officials in a variety of ways, eager to help the war effort. Socialists like Paul Lensch and David argued that defeat would result in a catastrophic defeat of socialism, as Germany had the most advanced Socialist movement in the world and as such was the locomotive of historical change.[30] Victory for Germany, in that sense, was necessarily a victory for international socialism. Reformist Social Democrats such as David and Friedrich Stampfer sought to use the opportunity of wartime consensus to build an alliance with the liberal and centre parties in the Reichstag which could bring about a genuine parliamentarisation of the constitutional monarchy. In both parties, jingoist sentiments and racialist fan-

29 P. Snowden, *An Autobiography* (London, Nicholson and Watson, 1935) I, p. 415.
30 P. Lensch, *Die deutsche Sozialdemokratie und der Weltkrieg* (Berlin, Buchhandlung Vorwärts, 1915), p. 26 f.; E. David, *Die Sozialdemokratie in Deutschland* (Berlin, Buchhandlung Vorwärts, 1915).

tasies reached unprecedented heights during the war years. So, for example, Otto Braun, who became Minister President of Prussia in the Weimar Republic, wrote about 'the half Asian, drunken Russian hordes of Cossacks who trample down the German fields, torture German women and children and crush German culture.'[31] In Britain virulent anti-German feeling mingled with outspoken racism in many wartime statements by British socialists. Robert Blatchford ranted against the 'insatiable race of savages' and called for 'something very near to the extermination of the German people', and George Barnes fought 'a people with a "kink" in their mental and moral make-up'. Whilst such racist statements were indistinguishable from right-wing war propaganda, many German and British Social Democrats struggled hard to differentiate their own support for the war from the pan-Germans and John Bulls on the political right. MacDonald and Snowden, for example, carefully distinguished between the need to fight Prussian militarism and the allegedly peaceful attitudes of the majority of the German people.[32]

Continued nationalisation between the wars

After 1918 there was a further marked turn towards national sentiments in both parties. In the Weimar Republic no party was more committed to the democratic nation state than the SPD, despite the persistence of a social-revolutionary tradition which distinguished between 'formal bourgeois democracy' (i.e. Weimar) and 'true democracy' which had not yet been achieved. Social Democrats played a crucial role in holding the Reich together amidst defeat and revolutionary turmoil in 1918/19. The opposition to the Versailles Treaty which united all political parties in Germany further strengthened feelings of national solidarity on the left. The 1921 Görlitz programme of the Majority Social Democratic Party (MSPD), for the very first time, sought to overcome the language of the class struggle.[33] The Prussianism of the Weimar SPD has become almost legendary. 'Red Prussia' under Otto Braun was a bastion of Weimar democracy where the SPD made sustained efforts to overcome the old structures in Prussia and the Reich through reform of the admin-

---

31 Cited in Groh and Brandt, *'Vaterlandslose Gesellen'*, p. 160.
32 The quotes from Blatchford and Snowden are cited in Ward, *Englishness*, p. 152. For the most detailed analysis of the widely differing attitudes of British Labour towards Germany during the First World War see also F. Weckerlein, *Streitfall Deutschland. Die britische Linke und die 'Demokratisierung' des Deutschen Reiches 1900–18* (Göttingen, Vandenhoek und Ruprecht, 1994).
33 However, after reunification with the USPD in 1922, the Heidelberg programme of 1925 reinstated the language of the class struggle into official party policy.

istration and the judiciary. Its success, however, remained limited, and Erich Mühsam's neologism that the SPD had become 'Bismarxist' (*Bismarxistisch*) was probably nowhere more justified than in Weimar Prussia. Young Socialists, like Julius Leber, Carlo Mierendorff and Theodor Haubach, many of whom were organised in the so-called Hofgeismarkreis, explicitly endorsed the language of patriotism and sought to tie the rhetoric of the nation to the rhetoric of democratic socialism. They advocated a more positive attitude towards a democratised and republicanised army and favoured a more emotional endorsement and republican reinterpretation of national symbols. National democratic patriotism in the Weimar SPD found its most prominent expression in the republican paramilitary formation, the Reichsbanner Schwarz-Rot-Gold.

In 1933 the SPD stood firm against the Nazi Party, and it was the only party in parliament (the Communists had already been imprisoned or sent to concentration camps) courageously to vote against Hitler's Enabling Act which was to end parliamentary government in Germany. Yet the national orientation of some Socialists at times collapsed into sad attempts to collaborate with the new Nazi rulers. So, for example, the socialist unions decided to participate in the May Day celebrations organised by the Nazis and attempted to portray themselves as a national movement. Whilst some trade union and party leaders, such as Theodor Leipart, Lothar Erdmann, Otto Wels and Stampfer, were still speculating about a possible deal with the Nazis to preserve an independent labour movement of some sort, the SA and SS occcupied all union offices on 2 May 1933 and the General German Trade Union Confederation was forcibly dissolved. The SPD followed in June 1933. The ultimate failure of the SPD to reshape the nation in its republican image was rooted in its unwillingness to use the revolution of 1918 for a more thorough transformation of German society. However, after 1933 the Social Democratic Party in exile, in its attempt to come to terms with its defeat by National Socialism and analyse its past mistakes, chose to ignore the fatal impact of its own nationalism. Instead it placed special emphasis on the fact that it had overemphasised the economic class interest whilst simultaneously underrating the national loyalty of the working class. Social Democrats like Otto Friedländer and Julius Leber now came to argue that the nation was far more deeply rooted in the consciousness of workers than class. The nation – this was one of the main lessons that Social Democrats would draw from their defeat – had to be even more firmly integrated into the policital conception of Social Democracy.

Like the SPD, the Labour Party in the 1920s increasingly appealed to the nation. Labour leaders like Henderson and MacDonald self-consciously aimed at creating a national party. Whilst the party was seeking to destroy the impression that Labour was a class or, worse, a trade union party, it could not – again like the SPD – in any meaningful way leave its electoral working-class ghetto before 1945. If Labour's 'Appeal to the Nation' (the title of the Labour Party's 1923 election manifesto) was not reaching the bulk of the middle-class vote, there were also very few indications that it had a measurable impact on the working class. A Mass Observation report of 1938 emphasised how uninterested the majority of workers tended to be about national affairs and alleged 'national crises' – unless such crises were directly linked with the everyday lives of working-class families, e.g. regarding food prices, rents, employment conditions. If this observation is correct (and Mass Observation material has to be treated cautiously, for it has its own biases and agenda), then, as in the German case, the concept of the nation did not figure prominently in the *Eigensinn* of British workers. Thus the main impact of the nationalisation of the Labour Party in the 1920s may well have been on the party itself rather than on the working class. Party officials employed the language of the nation to demarcate their position clearly from the Communist one on their left, whilst, at the same time, they aimed to demonstrate to the electorate that Labour was indeed 'fit to govern' – contrary to Conservative Party scaremongering. In 1924, on the occasion of the first Labour government being sworn in, Snowden was haunted by the party's national responsibility: 'We must show the country that we were not under the domination of the wild men.'[34] In much of their rhetoric Labour Party leaders came to equate 'the pleasures of rural England' with Britain, thereby accepting the established cultural and political framework which was so successfully exploited by Stanley Baldwin's variant of Conservatism. The appeal of MacDonald's governments in the 1920s was, above all, to 'fair play', 'moderation' and 'national well-being'.

The belief that Labour was not a class but a national party also led to the debacle of 1931, when MacDonald and a handful of his ministers formed an alliance with the Conservative Party against the explicit wishes of the Labour Party. Following their expulsion from the Labour Party, they founded the National Labour Party. Their representatives such as J. H. Thomas had been responsible for (temporarily) crippling Labour Party representation in parliament, but they showed themselves 'convinced that what was done saved the country.'[35] However, the rapid

34 Snowden, *Autobiography* II, p. 596.
35 J. H. Thomas, *My Story* (London, Hutchinson, 1937), p. 198. Labour Party representation in parliament was slashed from 288 to forty-six at the 1931 general election.

decline of National Labour in the 1930s and the quick recovery of the Labour Party demonstrated the limited appeal of left-wing nationalism among the wider working-class electorate. As Viktor Kiernan has pointed out, 'It has been remarked that the average workman was not religious, but did not like to be dubbed an atheist; his patriotism may often have been of the same order.'[36] Whilst it seems valid to emphasise, with Gareth Stedman Jones, that workers 'were neither the instigators nor the chief participants on "patriotic" occasions'[37], one should not regard their class identities as incompatible with a strong national identity.

Immigrants and ethnic minorities

In both countries working-class nationalism and racialism were at their most visible and problematic in the relations of the indigenous working class with immigrants and ethnic minorities, i.e. those who did not belong to the 'national community'. Before 1914 Germany was not so much a country of immigration as a 'labour-importing country', where foreigners had no civil rights and were kept as a dependent and disposable labour force.[38] The labour movement's attitude to this state of affairs was ambiguous. On the one hand, it stuck by the 1907 Stuttgart resolution of the International, which had declared in favour of international freedom of movement, and they also campaigned hard to give foreigners the same rights as Germans. On the other hand, its frustrations in organising the immigrants (which had much to do with its failure to understand their needs) and its experience of foreign workers being used to break strikes and undercut wages, led Labour to demand the preferential employment of indigenous workers and restrictions on immigration. Furthermore, the millions of non-Germans who lived within the borders of Imperial Germany had no better champion of their rights than Social Democracy. The SPD's opposition to the ruthless Germanisation policies of Imperial German governments (which prevented national minorities from using their own language and finding outlets for their cultural identities) left little doubt that, as a party of government, the SPD would have initiated a more tolerant and liberal policy towards the national minorities. Yet the SPD found it excessively

---

36 V. Kiernan, 'Working Class and Nation in Nineteenth Century Britain', in M. Cornforth (ed.), *Rebels and their Causes. Essays in Honour of A. L. Morton* (London, Lawrence and Wishart, 1978), p. 129.

37 G. Stedman Jones, 'The Language of Patriotism', in R. Samuel (ed.), *Patriotism. The Making and Unmaking of British National Identity* (London, Routledge, 1989) I, p. 79.

38 Martin Forberg, 'Foreign Labour, the State and Trade Unions in Imperial Germany 1890–1918', in W. R. Lee and Eve Rosenhaft (eds), *State, Social Policy and Social Change in Germany 1880–1994*, 2nd edn (Oxford, Berg, 1997), p. 112.

difficult to recognise the national ambitions of Poles, Danes and Alsatians. Social Democrats tended to reduce the struggle for national independence to a constitutional problem of equal participation within the Reich, i.e. to a problem of citizenship. Hence they were unwilling to grant any degree of autonomy to the national minorities in the Reich. German Social Democrats constantly rejected the idea of setting up a separate Polish Socialist organisation for the millions of Polish-speaking workers living within the German borders until 1918, and there was constant tension with the Polish Socialist Party (PPS) in Prussia between 1893 and 1913. The socialist unions and the SPD were also reluctant to set up newspapers and journals in the Polish language. Influenced by the official nationalism, the trade unions in the Ruhr made only half-hearted attempts to organise the Polish or Masurian-speaking workers or cooperate with their organisations, despite the existence of a distinct Polish sub-culture in 'Polish cities' in the Ruhr. Yet it also has to be said that the SPD and Social Democratic unions were far less hostile to 'foreigners' than the avowedly nationalist Catholic labour movement, which used to brand both foreign workers and Social Democrats as anti-national. Polish miners found themselves routinely stereotyped as black-legs and rate busters who undercut wages. Overall, the nationalisation of German Labour often marred the potential for class solidarity.

In the Weimar Republic a strengthened labour movement could force employers in certain sectors of the economy to employ German workers rather than cheaper foreigners. As a result, the employment of foreign labour became a rather marginal phenomenon in the 1920s. Yet the shipping industry provides a compelling argument that, where they could, employers desired to return to the replacement of German by foreign workers, who were not only cheaper but also less militant. (The seamen, like other sections of the German working classes, had been radicalised by the events of the German revolution and its aftermath.)[39] The resulting xenophobia among German seamen should not be interpreted as an expression of working-class racism. It has to be put in its proper context of the conscious racialisation (and thereby segmentation) of the labour force by employers seeking to maximise their profits. The Social Democratic unions failed to point to this connection and instead contributed to the racialisation of labour relations by adopting the racial discourse and reappropriating it for its own purposes of fighting job insecurity, health risks, declining real wages and deteriorat-

39 H. Rübner, 'Lebens-, Arbeits- und gewerkschaftliche Organisationsbedingungen chinesischer Seeleute in der deutschen Handelsflotte. Der maritime Aspekt der Ausländerbeschäftigung vom Kaiserreich bis in den NS-Staat', *IWK* (forthcoming).

ing union membership. Recourse to the 'national interest' led unions to collude with employers in the racialisation of the labour force. As Laura Tabili's study of black seamen in Britain indicates, British employers, like their German counterparts, with the help of the state, employed a number of racist strategies and constructed racial differences to lower wages and divide opposition to capitalist exploitation.[40] Like the German Social Democratic union, the British National Union of Seamen failed, by and large, to expose those strategies. Instead, the union leadership under Havelock Wilson often colluded with employers and introduced racist practices and discourses as a means of achieving specific ends such as the establishment of wage hierarchies, the prevention of any rank-and-file radicalisation and the strengthening of their own position *vis-à-vis* the employers. The Yellow Peril campaign before 1914 and the NUS campaign against Arab seamen in 1929/30 were the clearest examples of such exclusionary practices. Hence, as the example of the British and German seamen shows, working-class racism was neither essentialist nor a necessary outcome of the introduction of an ethnically mixed labour force – rather it emerged out of the specific responses of diverse historical actors (employers, trade unionists, the state, the seamen) in the struggle over wages and working conditions in a capitalist and imperialist environment.

The SPD in Imperial Germany rejected antisemitism. Key social democratic thinkers like Kautsky, Bernstein or Luxemburg may have rejected Zionism and the Yiddish culture of Eastern European Jewry, but they were strictly in favour of assimilation and giving Jews full rights as citizens. The SPD rejected the idea of a separate Jewish national identity in favour of giving Jews full citizenship rights within the German nation state. The urban industrial working classes at large remained relatively free of antisemitic tendencies in Imperial Germany (certainly compared with middle-class or rural peasant sentiments).[41] Yet the potential for working-class xenophobia generally should not be underestimated. As Robert Michels observed in 1913, 'The proletariat tends to cut itself off in its national boundaries and favours protectionism, which sometimes displays itself in xenophobia.'[42] In the context of the Second World War, which saw the introduction of over 7 million slave labourers into the

---

40 L. Tabili, *'We Ask for British Justice'. Workers and Racial Difference in late Imperial Britain* (Ithaca, N.Y., Cornell University Press, 1994, especially chapter 5 on the NUS.

41 Rosemarie Leuschen-Seppel, *Sozialdemokratie und Antisemitismus im Kaiserreich. Die Auseinandersetzungen der Partei mit den konservativen und völkischen Strömungen des Antisemitismus 1871–1914* (Bonn, Dietz, 1978), especially pp. 87 ff.

42 R. Michels, 'Zur historischen Analyse des Patriotismus', *Archiv für Sozialwissenschaft und Sozialpolitik* 36 (1913), p. 428.

German labour market, German workers, as Ulrich Herbert put it, were
'by no means disinclined to maltreat foreign deployees, especially Soviet
workers'.[43] Experiencing rapid upward social mobility, German workers
quickly got used to the diverse forms of everyday racism and colluded with
the Nazi regime in a variety of oppressive and discriminatory practices.

The anti-tsarism of the German Socialists before 1914, which inci-
dentally was shared by all socialists everywhere in Europe, at times deteriorated into an openly racist anti-Slav bias. Take, for example, the
revered leader of the German SPD in Imperial Germany, August Bebel.
Already in 1891 he had argued that, in the event of war with Russia,
Germany had to mobilise all its forces. The war was desribed (rather ominously in the light of the German attack on the Soviet Union in the
Second World War) as a 'struggle for our existence' and a 'war of anni-
hilation'. In line with dominant nationalist tendencies, Bebel came to
see the Slav east generally as territory for the legitimate economic and
cultural expansion of Germany, and his enmity towards Russia in particular was motivated not just by opposition to the tsarist autocracy but also
by hostility towards pan-Slavism and 'Asian Tartarism'.[44]

Throughout the nineteenth and twentieth centuries Britain faced
several waves of immigration. The strongest contingents came from
Ireland, followed by Jewish immigrants from Eastern Europe in particular. Whilst there was a sizeable community of German immigrants settling in British cities before 1914, black immigration before 1945 was
important for only a handful of cities such as Cardiff, Bristol, Liverpool
and London. Anti-Irish feelings were stronger in Scotland than in
England but far from absent in places with substantial Irish immigration
like Manchester, Liverpool or London. The Irish communities in
Scotland and England were organised on ethnic lines, the influence of
the Catholic Church on the political behaviour of Irish immigrants
being paramount. Before 1918 the priests largely advised their flock to
vote for the Liberal Party as the best means of ensuring Home Rule for
Ireland. The relationship with the Labour Party was largely characterised by apathy, if not enmity. By putting class before nation, British (and
Irish) Socialists appeared to divide the Irish national cause, and the
tension between class and national identity formed the background of
John Wheatley's attempts to fuse Catholicism and Socialism. Judging by
the evidence from Manchester's Irish community, such attempts to fuse
the languages of religion, ethnicity and class correlated with 'the relative

43 U. Herbert, *Hitler's Foreign Workers. Enforced Foreign Labour in Germany under the Third
    Reich* (Cambridge, Cambridge University Press, 1997), p. 396.
44 Groh and Brandt, *'Vaterlandslose Gesellen'*, pp. 60, 94.

ease with which individual members of the Irish Catholic population combined class and ethnic sentiments'.[45] By and large, it was only after 1918 that the Irish entered tentative alliances with Labour in major cities such as Glasgow and Liverpool, where the Labour Party was willing to give power and influence to Irish representatives in exchange for Irish votes. Overall, and despite continuing, at times widespread and often savage, anti-Irish sentiments among English workers (for whom the Irish, it seems, never ceased to have the capacity of being identified as 'alien'), it usually took 'only' three generations for an Irish worker to become integrated into British society, which arguably made the Irish the least alien of all Britain's ethnic groups.

As in the German case, the attitude of the labour movement towards immigrants oscillated wildly. Labour attempted to defend them against discrimination, and, officially, the Labour Party always took a stance against restricting immigration. Britain, in its view, had to remain the 'home of freedom'. Yet many Labour leaders also believed that foreigners made effective unionisation of the work force more difficult, that the importation of foreign labour would lead to blacklegging, undercutting and deskilling. Therefore, in the 1890s and 1900s, the Trades Union Congress (TUC) passed several resolutions hostile to alien immigration. It was, after all, the internationalist Keir Hardie who, before a Select Committee of the House of Commons, argued in 1889: 'every foreigner throws one British workman out of employment.'[46] And it was the internationalist Bruce Glasier who declared in 1905 that 'neither the principle of the brotherhood of man nor the principle of social equality implies that brother nations or brother men may crowd upon us in such numbers as to abuse our hospitality, overturn our institutions or violate our customs.'[47] In London and Leeds Labour activists spoke the language of antisemitism in their vociferous campaigns against any further Jewish immigration. Ben Tillett could envisage no class solidarity between white and black workers. Although both suffered from capitalist exploitation, there could be 'no comradeship between these two sets of slaves; for ever the black is black – and the white is white'.[48]

45 S. Fielding, 'A separate culture? Irish Catholics in Working-Class Manchester and Salford *c.* 1890–1939', in A. Davies and S. Fielding (eds), *Workers' Worlds. Cultures and Communities in Manchester and Salford 1880–1939* (Manchester, Manchester University Press, 1992), p. 43.
46 Cited in A. Lee, 'Aspects of the Working Class Response to the Jews in Britain 1880–1914', in K. Lunn (ed.), *Hosts, Immigrants and Minorities. Historical Responses to Newcomers in British Society 1870–1914* (Folkestone, Dawson, 1980), p. 118.
47 Cited in J. Bourke, *Working Class Cultures in Britain 1890–1960* (London, Routledge, 1994), p. 196.
48 Cited in L. Barrow, 'White Solidarity in 1914', in Samuel (ed.), *Patriotism* I, p. 281.

Any comparison between the attitudes of the Lanarkshire Miners' Union and the Alte Verband in the Ruhr towards Polish and Lithuanian-speaking workers before 1914 reveals striking similarities. The latter were crudely stereotyped, and the most frequent complaints were about their alleged uncleanliness, drunkenness and taste for fighting. In Scotland and the Ruhr alike the prevalent identity of the indigenous miner as 'independent collier' who took pride in his skill often prevented solidarity with the unskilled immigrants. The language problem proved an important barrier and in both regions there were endless debates over the question of higher accident rates due to the foreigners. Yet in the pre-war strikes in both Lanarkshire and the Ruhr Polish and Lithuanian-speaking miners were among the most militant. In Scotland they joined the existing union and made a significant contribution to the stable and successful unionisation of Scottish miners.[49] By contrast, the Polish and Lithuanian-speaking miners in the Ruhr set up their own unions and organisations and formed their own sub-culture. If we ask why, the answer may well lie not so much in the different reaction of the unions as in the different reaction of the state. The British state certainly took decisive action to curb immigration before 1914, and the 1905 Aliens Act was in fact extended in 1914 and 1918. The 1908 Pensions Act even stipulated that all pensioners had to have been British subjects for at least twenty years. However, there were no Anglicisation policies comparable with the Germanisation policies of the Imperial German state, which attempted to strike at the heart of Polish and Lithuanian linguistic identity.

The more ethnically based nationalism of the German Empire was less capable of integrating foreign workers than the political nationalism espoused by the British state. Not being able to speak their own language at the workplace, and with the German authorities and the unions opposed to using the Polish and Lithuanian languages on signposts, notices, etc., the immigrant population withdrew into its own neighbourhoods and organisations. Yet, if there were Polish 'ghettoes' in the Ruhr, there were few difficulties in locating Irish or Jewish 'ghettoes' in major British cities.[50] Similar mechanisms of exclusion and self-isolation

---

49 This is by no means the only example of foreigners helping to build up unions in Britain. Whilst Spaniards brought socialism to the South Wales valleys, the Jewish immigrants in the London, Leeds and Manchester clothing trades belonged to the best organised in the country.

50 It should be noted, however, that ethnic minorities such as the Poles in Germany or the Irish in Britain were rarely uniform in their political and social behaviour. Non-Catholic Polish groups as well as Protestant Irish groups were obviously very different from non-Catholic Poles and Irishmen.

were at work to ensure the appearance of city quarters which looked like foreign enclaves and were overwhelmingly resented by the indigenous population. As a shopkeeper in Bradford put it before 1914, 'They should put every German on a Jew's back and make 'em swim to Ireland.'[51] Not unsurprisingly the British Union of Fascists won considerable support in working-class districts of London, Liverpool, Manchester and Leeds in the 1930s. Most certainly the working-class response to immigrants was no more liberal in Britain than it was in Germany. Yet, as the great strikes before 1914 demonstrated in both countries, there was space for solidarity and united class action between immigrant and indigenous workers. Also, in their daily relations on the shop floor and in the neighbourhoods, relations could be characterised by a considerable amount of cooperation and even integration. According to Richard Murphy, the story of the Polish coal miners of Bottrop can be seen as 'a success story of American dimensions. . . . they steadily adapted to the urban society and worked assiduously to secure a satisfactory place in it.'[52] Overall, however, both labour movements failed to unite ethnically diverse workers in their struggle for emancipation.

Rather than helping to overcome the xenophobia of the native workers, the labour movements at times played on such sentiment to win support among the natives or curry favour with employers. In both countries, expressions of racial hostility were closely tied to competition for employment and housing as well as to complaints about 'strange habits', i.e. an alien culture. Where a combination of technological change and immigrant labour threatened workers in a particular trade, their xenophobia was usually vociferous. Examples are provided by the British boot and shoe operatives, tailors and furniture makers as well as clerks, who in the 1880s and 1890s turned on German immigrant clerks perceived as serious competitors for jobs. In Germany the perfect example would be the building trade, where time and again German workers were dismissed and replaced by foreign workers. In the workplace, foreign workers often found themselves at the bottom of the pile. The Poles in Germany and the Irish in Britain just did not have the same chances of upward social mobility as the native workers. Instead they remained confined to low-skill employment. They often had a very alert sense of cultural isolation. Some workplaces in Britain were strictly segregated.

51 L. Slater, *Think on! Said Many. A Childhood in Bradford, Manchester 1911–19* (Swinton, 1984), p. 52.
52 R. C. Murphy, *Guestworkers in the German Reich: A Polish Community in Wilhelminian Germany* (Boulder, Colo., East European Monographs, 1983), p. 189.

In the Glasgow engineering trade and the shipyards of the Clyde, Catholics were deliberately kept out by strong Orange groups. Sometimes an inverse self-isolation could be found. So, for example, the National Union of Dockworkers in Britain was widely known as the Irish Union.

The working classes in both countries had been subjected to forms of 'class racism' which alienated them from the state and the dominant middle classes alike. The racialisation of manual workers which made them victims of racism at the same time led to a 'self-racialisation' of the working class which produced an 'inverted class racism' directed both against the bourgeoisie ('them *v.* us') and against foreigners.[53] Whilst social scientists and public administrators increasingly referred to the poor as 'backward people' or 'a race apart', the poor themselves felt the need to distinguish themselves from other groups in ethnic terms. So, for example, the uprising of Welsh miners and transport workers in 1910/11 was not only directed against employers but was accompanied by fierce attacks on Chinese laundries and Jewish shops. The unmitigated hostility of the SPD's main daily newspaper, *Vorwärts*, against the 'capitalist system' was accompanied by occasional outbursts against 'Russian garbage Cossacks' and uncleanly 'Pollacks'.[54]

Labour, monarchy and imperialism

The increasing nationalisation of Labour was also visible in the ambivalent attitudes towards monarchy in both countries. In Britain the republicanism of Keir Hardie sat side by side with a widespread acceptance of the monarchy by other Labour leaders. Republicanism was widely perceived as a vote loser. The monarchy, after all, was popular amongst the working people, and it had gone to considerable lengths to establish a monarchical cult. The only book-length study emerging from the British left before 1939 on the monarchy was by Kingsley Martin, the editor of the *New Statesman*.[55] He argued that the monarchy should be retained but that it had to be made more popular and less bound up with the establishment. He looked to Scandinavian constitutional monarchies as models for the royal family to emulate. British Labour leaders tended to accept invitations to court, always stressing their belief that such invitations honoured not so much their own persons as the class they represented. However, royalism remained a contested issue even in Labour

---

53 The extremely helpful categories of 'class racism' and 'self-racialisation' are taken from E. Balibar, '"Class Racism"', in *id.* and I. Wallerstein, *Race, Nation, Class. Ambiguous Identities* (London, Verso, 1988), pp. 204–16.

54 Cited in Lüdtke, 'Polymorphous Synchrony', p. 75.

55 K. Martin, *The Magic of Monarchy* (London, Nelson, 1936).

Party circles. The staunch royalist Jimmy Thomas admitted that many ordinary workers had little love for the monarchy and the establishment at large: 'I repeat that I sprang from the people and belong to the people; therefore I had always harboured notions about the austerity and aloofness of those of royal blood.' Whilst his memoirs tried hard to denounce such 'foolish fallacies'[56], others chose to take a different line. Hamilton Fyfe, the editor of the *Daily Herald*, for example, argued in 1924 that visits to court and socialising with the establishment would ultimately corrupt the values and ideals of the labour movement.[57]

In Imperial Germany, royalty, in particular the Hohenzollern emperor, was much less willing to receive representatives of the SPD at court. When, in 1889, the young Wilhelm II agreed to grant an audience to a deputation of striking miners from the Ruhr, he left them in no doubt that any involvement with Social Democracy would result in harsh punishment for the strikers. Hence it comes as no surprise to find much resentment against the monarchy in the Social Democratic milieu. When the Social Democrat Philip Scheidemann was elected to the presidency of the Reichstag in 1912, his party threw itself into a heated debate about whether Scheidemann should be allowed to go to court, as was usual for all members of the Reichstag presidency, whilst at the same time the emperor let it be known that he would be unlikely to receive a deputation that included a Social Democrat. Disillusionment among workers with the repressiveness and exclusionary practices of the Imperial state and its head meant that fervent royalism was much less widespread in working-class neighbourhoods than it was in middle-class ones. Striking workers and mutinous sailors and soldiers in 1918 rarely had second thoughts about their key demand – that the Kaiser should abdicate. Yet a critique of the Imperial German government and its anti-socialist policies could also go hand in hand with fundamental acceptance of the monarchy, and the institution of the emperor in particular.[58] Reformist Social Democrats, following the British model, argued well before 1914 in favour of retaining the monarchy in a properly parliamentarised political system. The economic determinism of the SPD's official and rather schematic Marxism in fact played into the hands of the reformists, as it substantially relativised the distinction between monarchy and republic. Furthermore, republicanism in the pre-war SPD was hampered by the threat of legal persecution and by the

56 Thomas, *My Story*, p. 159.
57 H. Fyfe, 'The House of Rimmon', *Socialist Review* 24 (1924), pp. 109–16.
58 M. Cattaruzza, 'Das Kaiserbild in der Arbeiterschaft am Beispiel der Werftarbeiter in Hamburg und Stettin', in J. C. G. Röhl (ed.), *Der Ort Kaiser Wilhelms II. in der deutschen Geschichte* (Munich, Beck, 1991), pp. 131–44.

SPD's own home-made Lasallean idealisation of a 'social monarchy'. Whilst the royalty cult enjoyed some sympathy among unorganised sections of the working class (notably miners and dock workers), Social Democrats developed their own festivals and celebrations. However, as Peter Domann has argued, such rejection of the official royal cult could go hand-in-hand with *de facto* acceptance of a constitutional monarchy even among broad sections of the left in the pre-war SPD.[59] The refusal of Friedrich Ebert in 1918 to endorse Scheidemann's proclamation of the republic hence seems to have followed a certain logic.

A fundamental ambiguity characterised not only Labour's stance on the monarchy but also its attitude towards imperialism and colonialism. The official imperialism of the German governments before 1914 and their desperate search for a place under the imperialist sun was widely criticised by German Socialists. Yet, especially on the reformist and revisionist wings of the SPD, such a critique was often combined with the notion of alternative 'good' forms of imperialism. Eduard Bernstein, for example, rejected the German variant of imperialism as illiberal and a threat to freedom, but he justified colonalism as such because he agreed with the general argument that Europe had a civilising mission in the world. British free-trade imperialism he accepted as progressive. In his justification of colonialism there was more than a hint of Social Darwinism, as, for example, when he talked about 'the struggle for survival between peoples and races' or 'superior cultures'.[60] On the party left, Karl Liebknecht's publication *Militarism and Anti-militarism* (1907) denounced German imperialism as a plot of very specific vested interests and perceptively characterised the special character of Prussian German militarism. Yet the SPD's parliamentary party more than once demonstrated its willingness to participate constructively in Germany's colonial policies. Gustav Noske, who spoke for the parliamentary party on questions of the military and colonialism, attempted to formulate a 'positive' Social Democratic colonial policy before 1914. Restricting his criticism to malpractices and 'reactionary colonialism', he supported an imperialist expansionism which was justified by reference to the alleged

---

59 P. Domann, *Sozialdemokratie und Kaisertum unter Wilhelm II. Die Auseinandersetzungen der Partei mit dem monarchischen System, seinen gesellschafts- und verfassungspolitischen Voraussetzungen* (Wiesbaden, Steiner, 1974). See also W. K. Blessing, 'The Cult of Monarchy: Political Loyalty and the Workers' Movement in Imperial Germany', *Journal of Contemporary History* 13 (1978), pp. 357–75; A. G. Bonnell, 'Socialism and Republicanism in Imperial Germany', *Australian Journal of Politics and History* 42 (1996), pp. 192–202.

60 H. Mommsen, 'Nationalismus und nationale Frage im Denken Eduard Bernsteins', in *id., Arbeiterbewegung und nationale Frage. Ausgewählte Aufsätze* (Göttingen, Vandenhoek und Ruprecht, 1979), p. 115 f.

superiority of European civilisation. In March 1919 most Socialists in the constitutional assembly voted in favour of a motion demanding that its former colonies should be returned to Germany.

Among the British labour movement there was widespread moral indignation and opposition to the aggressive imperialism and militarism which manifested themselves in the Boer War. Keir Hardie, Edward Carpenter and many other Labour leaders belonged to the pro-Boer section which faced public abuse for their anti-imperialist stance. The majority of the ILP and the SDF – where Rothstein's and Bax's anti-imperialism stood in blatant contrast to Hyndman's imperialist outbursts – opposed the war. The Fabian Society was badly split on the matter. Philip Snowden's stance against militarism and imperialism found expression in a well publicised speech in parliament, where he denounced both as a plot of the armaments industry to increase its profits. Hobson and Brailsford were the two writers who arguably had the greatest influence on Labour's understanding of imperialism. Hobson's theory of under-consumption in particular argued that imperialism benefited only the capitalist, not the worker, because of the obvious neglect of the home market. At its 1921 conference this view became official policy of the Labour Party. However, in the 1920s an influential Labour Common-wealth group argued that the empire should be reformed, not abandoned. The Colonial Minister in the first Labour government of 1924, Jimmy Thomas, in his autobiography defended the Commonwealth: 'we can with confidence say that the British Commonwealth of Nations stands out as a beacon light to the rest of the world.'[61] MacDonald strongly defended the idea of empire: it was England's mission to spread freedom to the rest of the world. Labour's attitude to India reflected how divided Labour was on the issue of imperialism. Whilst Hardie argued that India should be treated like the white colonies of settlement and be given a similar measure of self-government, MacDonald denied India the status of a nation. Left to its own devices, it would sink into chaos. The empire should not be wound up, MacDonald argued – quite the contrary, a democratised and humanised empire had to fulfil its civilis-ing mission in the world. British workers seemed to have had at best a blurred image of empire and, generally speaking, needed tangible material incentives to support imperialist ventures. Thus the empire made sense to the Lancashire textile worker, as India imported vast amounts of Britain's cloth production. The Admiralty, which refused to accept trade unions in the naval dockyards before 1914, instead attempted to win the loyalty of the workforce by offering secure employ-

61 Thomas, *My Story*, p. 307.

ment and an ideological diet of nationalism and identification with the empire which was to have a major impact on the political culture of dockyard towns.[62]

Conclusion

The relationship between Labour, nationalism and ethnicity in both Britain and Germany never was one of straightforward rejection or endorsement. Between the 1870s and the 1930s there were many indications that the moderate mainstream of Labour in both countries was becoming increasingly integrated into the nation state. Despite the strong hostility of the nineteenth-century state, Churches and employers towards organised labour, British and German Labour leaders time and again reaffirmed their Britishness and Germanness respectively. The earlier emergence of a welfare state in Germany did much to facilitate such feelings of belonging, as did the pride of Labour in Britain's long-established parliamentary tradition. Strong minorities in both labour movements continued to favour the transformation of the existing state, including its political and economic structures. Communists and anarcho-syndicalists wanted no part in the existing nation state and were excluded from it. However, the left wing of the SPD and of the Labour Party also continued to question the political, economic and social foundations of their respective nation states.

The anti-socialism of schools, the civil service, the army, employers, Church and judiciary had for too long discriminated against organised Labour to make for any smooth integration of labour into the nation state. In both countries Labour remained in a volatile position between integration and isolation, developing both a distinct national identity and at the same time reasserting the fundamental differences between the working classes it sought to represent and other classes in society. The tensions between national and class identities resembled walking a tightrope. The national discourses within both labour movements were for ever shifting between, first, anti-national internationalism, secondly an internationalism conscious of and endorsing national differences and identities, thirdly attempts to formulate an 'oppositional patriotism' which would allow national identification without giving up the internationalist creed, and, finally, at different times, the adoption of the dominant right-wing nationalism, racialism and imperialism. The key issue of organised labour in both countries remained the further democrat-

---

62 K. Lunn, 'Labour Culture in Dockyard Towns: A Study of Portsmouth, Plymouth and Chatham', *Tijdschrift voor sociale geschiedenis* 18:2/3 (1992), pp. 275–93.

isation of the nation state. To democratise the political, economic and cultural spheres of the nation state meant working towards the full acceptance of workers as equal citizens within that nation state.

Yet any demarcation between a left-wing national discourse and its right-wing equivalent, however well-meaning, never proved to be easy. There was no neat distinction between an authoritarian, anti-socialist, ethnic nationalism in Germany in which Labour had no part, and democratic nationalism in Britain, in which the Labour Party could easily participate and share. In both countries, as we have seen above, nationalism and racialism had made considerable advances among the working classes, and the labour movements had no clear idea of how to overcome the ethnic and national tensions preventing greater class unity, nor were they able to keep their 'oppositional patriotism' from collapsing time and again into more traditional nationalist and racist sentiments. The nationalisation of labour movement culture in Britain and Germany before 1914, the vociferous wartime nationalism in both parties between 1914 and 1918, their attitudes towards ethnic minorities and immigrants, as well as their unwillingness to find a coherent response to either monarchism or imperialism, all testify to the many pitfalls inherent in attempts to delineate a 'good' democratic nationalism from its 'ugly' brother. Whilst the national discourses within British and German Labour were never unopposed and always contested, the very elusiveness of the concept of 'national identity' furthered unholy alliances with traditional right-wing nationalism and demonstrated that there was no safe passage between the Scylla of a national cosmopolitanism which tended to underestimate the powerful hold of nationalism over people's imaginations and the Charybdis of adopting parts of the national discourse in the hope of linking it with the overriding concern for class emancipation.

Acknowledgments

I would like to thank Kenneth Lunn, Angel Smith and the anonymous reader for Manchester University Press for their helpful comments on draft versions of this chapter. Any remaining errors and inconsistencies are, of course, entirely my own.

Spaniards, Catalans and Basques: Labour and the Challenge of nationalism in Spain

I am not waging a war against Franco . . . so that its offspring is a provincial and stupid separatism in Barcelona . . . I am waging a war for Spain and its glory.
                    Juan Negrín, Spanish Socialist Prime Minister, 1937–39

'Let my verses be bombs which explode at the feet of the idols: be they called / Religion, Fatherland or Money.
                    Alberto Ghijaldo, Argentinian anarchist poet

In Spain, both the crystallisation of national identities and the imbrications between class-based organisations and, more broadly, working-class communities and the nation differed markedly from those of her European neighbours. In the nineteenth century, unlike the Ottoman and Austro-Hungarian Empires, the country had been considered without doubt a nation state, but from the early twentieth century the concept of the Spanish nation faced a powerful challenge from Catalan and Basque nationalisms. At the same time, while a strong Socialist Party and union grew up, uniquely in Europe, through to the 1930s a vigorous anarchist or anarcho-syndicalist movement, which combined revolutionary fervour with a seemingly equally intransigent internationalism, vied for hegemony over organised labour. Thus by the early twentieth century three separate national projects were trying to establish their legitimacy over the territory, and had, moreover, to deal with the threat of the working-class left. It is our contention that an understanding of the reasons behind the multiple threats to Spanish nationalism, and the complex connections between national and class-based identities in the various Spanish territories, offers key insights into the changing and contingent relationship between nationalism and labour in the modern world. It is on these themes that the chapter will focus.

The left, the Spanish nation and the crisis of 1898

As in much of continental Europe, modern nationalism entered Spain during the Napoleonic Wars of the early nineteenth century, when liberals began to disseminate the ideals of Spanish nationhood. The liberal tradition would, however, soon divide into two. On the one hand, from the years of the 'bourgeois revolution' in the 1830s, more conservative liberals were quick to reach a compromise with the old aristocracy, monarchy and arch-reactionary Church. Thus they came to represent the party of order, anxious to limit suffrage and the power of parliament, and quick to use military force to quell disturbances.

Conservative liberals were, at the same time, rather than fashion a bureaucratic state machine, to enter into a clientalistic alliance with local landowning elites, known as *caciques*. This was to have a number of interrelated consequences. First, state income, in any case ravaged by the cost of colonial revolt and civil wars, was by Western European standards to remain low. This was reflected in the country's appalling state education system and high illiteracy rates (some 64 per cent of the population in 1900). Second, political elites found it difficult to fashion policy to any extent independent of the oligarchy, with the result, for example, that taxes remained largely indirect and that military conscription was not introduced until 1912. Until then the middle and upper classes were able to buy their way out. The Catholic Church was seen as the new state's principal means of social control. Yet, by the early twentieth century, its convents and parishes centred on well-to-do urban areas, and it put far more effort into educating the sons and daughters of the elites and wealthy middle classes than attending to the needs of workers and peasants. Conservative Spanish nationalism was therefore accompanied by the whiff of incense and the military jackboot, and could not be attractive to wide sections of at least the urban population. Moreover, as has also recently been forcefully pointed out, the Spanish state did little to socialise the population in the new religion of nationalism. Its aim was to marginalise the people from the political process rather than to mobilise them behind government, flag and country; despite the adoption of the language of conservative-liberal nationalism, depoliticisation, not active enthusiasm, was what was required.[1] In nineteenth-century Spain, then, there could be no 'white revolutionary'

---

1 B. de Riquer i Permanyer, 'La débil nacionalización española del siglo XIX', *Historia Social* 20 (1994), pp. 97–114; J. Alvarez Junco, 'The Nation-building Process in Nineteenth Century Spain', in C. Mar-Molinero and A. Smith (eds), *Nationalism and the Nation in the Iberian Peninsula. Competing and Conflicting Identities* (Oxford, Berg, 1996), pp. 89–106; J. Pablo Fusi Aizpurúa, 'Centralismo y localismo: la formación del estado español', in G. Cortázar (ed.), *Nation y estado en la España liberal* (Madrid, Noesis, 1994), pp. 77–104; A. Smith, 'The People and the Nation: Nationalist Mobilization and the Crisis of 1895–98 in Spain', in A. Smith and E. Dávila-Cox (eds), *The Crisis of 1898: Colonial Redistribution and Nationalist Mobilisation* (Basingstoke, Macmillan, 1999), pp. 153–79.

like Bismarck in Germany or, significantly, any right-wing populist nationalist movements along the lines of French Boulangerism.

These 'statist' nationalists were opposed by more left-wing liberals who accused the new 'oligarchy' of having betrayed the 'people', who would achieve national plenitude only after throwing off the new shackles to which they were subject. By the 1860s the most radical and, in the larger urban areas, most popular wing of left liberalism was represented by the republicans. In urban Spain in particular, and also along the more prosperous Mediterranean littoral, republicanism was able deeply to penetrate middle and lower-class society, structuring a tradition which exalted 'freedom' and 'progress' in opposition to state repression and clerical 'reaction' and 'obscurantism'. It was, in particular, a tradition sustained in local party headquarters, which often functioned as centres for recreation, consumer cooperatives and mutual aid societies, and through the press. It also intersected with broader liberal milieux in freethinking and Masonic societies, while much of the republican world view could also be looked upon with some sympathy by anarchists and Socialists (and, of course, the further one gets away from political elites the more fluid ideologies become). In much of urban Spain, therefore, the liberal left, helped by the state's weak socialisation, was able to carve out a powerful position for itself in the evolving public sphere, and republicans could also gain the sympathy of labour.

The relation between republicanism and nationalism was a complex one. One tendency within the movement, known as Federalism, emphasised the locality over and above attachment to the nation. However, by the 1890s the dominant republican groups combined the call for democratisation of political life with an exultant Spanish nationalism.[2] This was to come to the fore during the lead-up to the crisis of 1898. As we shall see, the two decades before the crisis had witnessed the first stirrings of Catalan and Basque nationalism. Yet in the 1890s these movements were still weak, and at first it seemed that the colonial wars in Cuba and the Philippines, followed by the Spanish-American war of 1898, would serve to consolidate Spanish nationalist sentiment. In the major Spanish cities the approach of the war certainly led to a rise of patriotic and jingoistic rhetoric, with large crowds gathering to see the departing troops off and anti-American demonstrations and riots.[3]

2 The two most important sources for late nineteenth-century republicanism are A. Duarte, *El republicanisme català a la fi del segle XIX* (Vic, Eumo, 1987), and J. Alvarez Junco, *El emperador del paralelo. Lerroux y la demagogia populista* (Madrid, Alianza, 1990), chapters 1–3.
3 E. Hernández Sandoica and M. Fernanda Mancebo, 'Higiene y sociedad en la guerra de Cuba 1895–1898: notas sobre soldados y proletarios', *Estudios de Historia Social* 5–6 (1978), pp. 361–84.

This nationalist upsurge was promoted both by the dominant monarchist parties and by the republican opposition. Both used similar images of the bravura imperial Spanish lion, which would have little difficulty seeing off the money-grubbing *nouveau riche* American pig. Yet the war also became a battleground on which the republicans attempted to establish hegemony over nationalist discourse. The monarchists presented a conservative reading of the nationalist tradition as the unfolding of Spain's Catholic, Christian, destiny. In contrast the republicans accused the monarchists of having fatally weakened Spain through their corrupt and ineffective rule, claiming that only a republic could provide economic prosperity, political liberty and imperial expansion. Indeed, it was in the republican press that the most vociferous articles were published and it was republicans who organised anti-American demonstrations. This is important because, as we have noted, in urban Spain and in the poor south few outside the elite and well-to-do middle classes showed any sympathy for the monarchists, and it was left liberalism and then republicanism which had largely articulated discontent. Certainly it seems that workers were not unaffected. This, for example, could be seen in the nationalist agitation in Lavapiés, the popular quarter of central Madrid, and in the patriotic march held by the workers of Barcelona's largest textile factory, La España Industrial.[4]

Yet even in the run-up to war there were tensions which ruffled the smooth surface of Spanish nationalist rhetoric. The Cuban revolt had produced a collapse in the value of the Spanish peseta, and this, together with the rapid rise in government expenditure, led to accelerating inflation. Furthermore, the human cost of fighting the Cuban campaign was heavy and the existence of redemption payments rankled. And from 1896 the constant repatriation of ill and dying soldiers, who were given minimum support by the authorities, could not but produce sorrow, dismay and anger among lower-class families.

This disquiet was given some political focus by the working-class left. The anarchist and Socialist movements, it should be stressed, were extremely weak on the eve of the Spanish-American War. Nevertheless, through the press and through their presence in working-class cultural associations, the anarchists could still have some impact. And, as was to be expected, they came out in total opposition to the war, arguing that

---

4 C. Serrano, *Final del imperio. España 1895–98* (Madrid, Siglo XXI, 1984), pp. 72 and 80–9; Smith, 'The People and the Nation', p. 164 and n. 30, pp. 178–9. However, in the case of the Barcelona textile workers it is likely that the employers were influential in orchestrating the march.

patriotism was simply a cover for the interests of the ruling classes, while showing considerable sympathy for the Cuban rebels.[5]

The Spanish Socialist Party (PSOE) had never gained the same influence as the anarchists, but had, on the other hand, achieved a degree of organisational stability and, as a result, was to have a significant impact in the run-up to the war. The Socialists, like their counterparts in the Second International, adopted a schematic Marxist perspective, which proclaimed the class struggle the motor of history, and class solidarity the duty of workers of all nations. Yet at the same time, as noted in Chapter 1, Marxism had inherited from liberal nationalism the belief that the construction of the modern nation state was a key moment in human progress. And the Spanish Socialists had no doubt that Spain was (rather on the French model) a nation and, in the foreseeable future at least, the proper territorial unit on which to struggle for social transformation. It would, as a result, be difficult for Socialists to avoid being influenced by a certain left-wing nationalism despite official Second International anti-patriotism.

This could be seen in their extreme antagonism towards what they took to be 'reactionary' Basque and Catalan nationalist movements, who by endangering Spanish unity could only throw the country back into feudalism.[6] It was also reflected in the rather contradictory attitude adopted when they were confronted by the Cuban rebellion. At first the Socialists claimed that the war was simply a conflict between two rival bourgeoisies. Yet shades of nationalism could be perceived in comments that possession of the colonies could aid Spanish economic development, and in their failure to back the Cuban rebels. Nevertheless, as the war dragged on and the suffering of the Spanish workers and peasants intensified the party took an increasingly hostile line against Spanish intervention, centring its attacks on what it saw as the disastrous policies pursued by the Spanish authorities.

This ambiguity was also reflected in the grounds on which the Socialists attacked the war. Rather than developing a total critique of Spanish intervention *per se*, from September 1897 the PSOE launched a campaign against the practice of the well-to-do being able to buy their

5 J. Alvarez Junco, *La ideología política del anarquismo español 1870–1910* (Madrid, Siglo XXI, 1976), pp. 247–65; C. Serrano, 'Anarchisme fin de siècle', in *id.*, *Le Tour du peuple* (Madrid, Casa de Velázquez, 1987), pp. 123–72.

6 Here the position of the Spanish Socialists reflected Engels's views on 'ahistorical' nations, whose nationalist pretensions should be combated. Indeed, in an article written in 1849 Engels specifically identified the Basques, 'the supporters of Don Carlos', as one of the 'relics of a nation' who 'become fanatical standard bearers of counter-revolution'. Cited in I. Cummins, *Marx, Engels and National Movements* (London, Croom Helm, 1980), p. 38.

way out of military service. Implicitly, however, it anticipated the end of the war and Cuban independence, for it was argued that if the rich had to go the war would soon come to an end. In fact the campaign was to be a considerable success. The Socialists held about forty meetings across the country attended by an estimated 100,000 workers. For the first time, as a result, the Socialists were able significantly to raise their profile and get through to a wider audience than that of their small trade union base.[7]

Overall, then, it seems that sections of labour were drawn into the patriotic atmosphere of these years. Nevertheless, it tended to be the civil and military authorities, vociferous students, industrial interests and the middle-class republican leadership who were at the forefront of the patriotic campaigns. In working-class Spain any patriotic feelings had to be drawn against the heavy human price that was being paid. And the considerable success of the Socialist campaign does seem to indicate that by late 1897 the spectacle of the repatriation of troops and fear for the fate of loved ones was starting to override any interest in the maintenance of the colonies. Hostility grew after the disastrous end of the Spanish-American war. The summer once again saw bread riots, and, later in the year, the repatriation of large numbers of troops, many of whom were infirm and penniless, led to widespread disturbances around the ports. The government, military and Catholic elites were very much the focus of discontent. The reactionary Catholic Marqués de Comillas and his shipping line, La Transatlántica, became a particular target of the protesters' ire. It had been used to ship troops out from Spain and repatriate them, and was seen as the clearest example of the way cynical elites had used the war to their own advantage.[8]

Spanish labour and Spanish nationalism, 1900–39

The long-term impact of the war in working-class circles was equally telling. As we have noted, labour's attitude towards nation and empire was already ambiguous, but it is no doubt the case that, as Sebastian Balfour has pointed out, the defeat of 1898 and the terrible cost, served to stifle any 'incipient growth of popular imperialist sentiments'.[9] This

---

7 On the PSOE and the crisis of 1898 see, in particular, C. Serrano, 'El PSOE y la guerra de Cuba 1895–98', *Estudios de Historia Social* 8–9, (1979), pp. 287–310. For the Socialists' campaign I have also used *El Socialista* between September and December 1897.

8 Sandoica and Mancebo, 'Higiene y sociedad', p. 382.

9 S. Balfour, '"The lion and the pig": nationalism and national identity in *fin-de-siècle* Spain', in Mar-Molinero and Smith (eds), *Nationalism and the Nation*, p. 112.

became clear in the anti-military and anti-colonial protests and campaigns which were to pepper Spanish history between 1900 and 1923. These centred on opposition to Spanish imperialism in northern Morocco, which was almost unanimously seen in working-class circles as a scam by which the clerical, plutocratic, elite would make a killing at the expense of the lives of the working class. On occasion, protests were to reach levels of extreme virulence. This was the case in Barcelona during the so-called 'Tragic Week' of July 1909 when a general strike called against a flare-up in the war between the Rif tribesmen and the Spanish military degenerated into several days of church burning.

All the various leftist organisations supported the working-class protest. In the most awkward position were the Spanish republicans. As we have seen, most had adopted a vociferously patriotic stance during 1898. Nevertheless, their populist, anti-government mobilisation allowed them, in the aftermath of the defeat, rapidly to increase their support. In the 1890s the left of Spanish republicanism, represented by such figures as the Madrid-based journalist and adventurer Alejandro Lerroux, realising the need for republicanism to widen its working-class base, radicalised its discourse and seemingly committed itself to the cause of labour. This allowed it to dominate left-wing, anti-oligarchic politics during the first decade of the century. Lerroux himself moved to Barcelona in 1901, and was able to captain a powerful republican movement in the city. Similarly, in Valencia the novelist Blasco Ibañez was able to integrate important sectors of the lower middle and working classes into his organisation. And even in cities such as Madrid and Bilbao, where republicanism retained a more middle-class air, it still remained a significant repository of working-class votes.

As the run-up to the crisis of 1898 shows, republicans hoped to be able to integrate labour into a nationalist, colonial project, at least rhetorically along the lines of the major imperial powers. However, after the 'Disaster' the contradictory needs of simultaneously trying to appeal to a radical working-class base and stimulate nationalist and colonial sentiment proved impossible to manage. After 1900 left-wing Spanish republicans attempted, rather schizophrenically, to combine far-leftist rhetoric with an inflamed Spanish nationalist discourse, sympathy for the military (sections of which, they hoped, might bring them to power through a military *coup*), and support for colonial expansion. These contradictions were at their most extreme in the politics and language of Alejandro Lerroux. Lerroux, as shall be seen in the next section, was able to use Spanish nationalism as a club to beat Catalanism, which he portrayed as a archaic, ultra-clerical and reactionary movement. But at the same time, in order to attract working-class support, he had to adopt an extreme anarchistic, anticlerical and anti-government rhetoric. The contradiction came to the forefront during Tragic Week, when the Lerrouxists had to hold any colonial sympathies in check and, at least verbally, to sympathise with the strikers and rioters.[10]

Left-wing Spanish republicanism in fact proved a dead end. The attempt to forge a republican movement with a powerful working-class base was undercut by the rise of the Socialist and anarchist labour unions, the UGT and CNT, from 1910. This does not, however, mean that all left-wing Spanish nationalist projects were moribund. In the aftermath of 1898 it proved possible to maintain the belief that it was the monarchy that had sold out the nation and that the people could still be its salvation. Thus, though no one wished to hear of imperial aggrandisement, as the experience of the first decade of the twentieth century showed, sectors of the middle and working classes could still be integrated within a Spanish nationalist discourse. This was shown by the survival, alongside Lerrouxism, of a more moderate republican tradition, which was to have a greater long-term impact on the left. It was represented by such figures as Nicolás Salmerón at the turn of the century, and Manuel Azaña during the Second Republic. These republicans never tried to adopt a pseudo-anarchistic language in order to capture working-class support and were far more wary of promoting a military intervention in politics. Instead they maintained their nineteenth-century vision of a secular, socially reforming, democratic state. As a result, they retained considerable middle and lower middle-class (and some working-class) support, and were able to ally with more moderate sectors of the labour movement. Moreover, as we shall see, within the working-class left sections of the PSOE can also be seen to a degree to take up the baton of reformist Spanish nationalism.

Both anarchists and Socialists were to increase their weight in Spanish political life from 1900, and, especially, 1914, and both participated actively in anti-military and anti-colonial protest. At first they largely recruited workers into their trade unions. However, they also began to develop their own labour movement sub-cultures, based on workers' centres. It is important to emphasise in this respect that, because of the lack of state education, republican, anarchist and

10 Widespread working-class opposition to colonialism following the experience of the nineteenth-century colonial wars emerges very clearly from working-class autobiographical accounts. See, in particular, Emili Salut, *Vivers de revolucionaris. Apunts històrics del districte cinquè* (Barcelona, 1938), p. 105; Adolfo Bueso, *Recuerdos de un cenetista* (Barcelona, Ariel, 1976), p. 29. The southern Spanish peasantry's hatred of military service is brought out in Jerome R. Mintz, *The Anarchists of Casas Viejas* (Bloomington and Indianapolis, Ind., Indiana University Press, 1994).

Socialist centres were to offer for many the only route available into the world of literate culture. In urban Spain in general workers' children, if they were lucky, left school at the age of ten, but in rural areas peasants never went to school at all. As a result, the left hardly had to try and socialise workers in opposition to the state. This is, for example, clear in those parts of Andalusia in which from the late nineteenth century the anarchists gained a strong hold. In his splendid oral study of Casas Viejas Jerome B. Mintz shows how, with the exception of one worker who had learnt to read and write while undertaking military service, the only literate peasants in the village were the minority of so-called *obreros concientes*, who had become attached to the anarchist centre. They would start by being taught to read the anarchists' own elementary reading and writing books, before graduating onto the anarchist press and leading anarchist thinkers. Indeed, it even seems the case that, given the lack of Church attendance and the fact the mass was in Latin, some peasants received clear notions of the Christian faith only through their anarchist comrades, though, in this reading, Christ had been a liberator put to death by Roman capitalists.

It was the anarchists who tried to structure the most richly textured sub-culture. In the first place, they believed their total rejection of the state given it was only through their autonomous organisation that the workers could achieve liberation, and only in rejection of the state, bourgeois society and its values could the new world be forged. Furthermore, the anarchists' belief in the capacity of each individual, and fierce rejection of hierarchy, encouraged the brightest or most determined to go on and write articles in the anarchist press, poems, or even a novel, invariably depicting, in moralistic and romantic language, the exploitation and abuse to which the workers were subject, and their struggle for emancipation.

Both anarchists and Socialists provided an alternative to the nationalist historical narrative, in their emphasis on the global advance of science and technology laying the material foundations of the communist society of the future. The socialist narrative had its own heroic episodes. Thus, as against the nationalists' glorification of the resistance of the Spanish town of Numancia to Roman conquest, Socialists and anarchists celebrated the 'free' Syrian city of Palmyra, conquered and ransacked by the Romans after trying to forge an independent region. Nevertheless, whilst both anarchists and Socialists balked at the nationalist story, it was probably the case that from the first the anarchists' rejection of patriotism was more overt and vociferous. Anarchists saw the state and nation as inevitably twinned under capitalism, and though, therefore, the nation might, in a future libertarian communist society, form one link in the bottom-up federalist chain, under present conditions patriotism should be combated as the harbinger of war and conquest.[11]

However, it is important to note that only a small minority of workers were fully subsumed into these anarchist and Socialist cultural milieux. Moreover, particularly in the early twentieth century, socialist culture was inserted into, and influenced by, the wider 'democratic culture' patronised by left liberals and republicans. The overlap between these worlds can be seen in the artistic sphere. The liberal left's great literary patrons were the great liberal Romantic and realist figures of the nineteenth century, such as Victor Hugo and Emile Zola, and Spaniards such as Pérez Galdós, Clarín, Blasco Ibañez and the playwright Joaquín Dicenta. It was also clearly this genre of literature that was most enjoyed by the literate working-class elite, and it found its way into working-class libraries (and was widely read), along with the revolutionary classics and militant working-class novels. This could be justified by working-class radicals through the argument that they should inherit the greatest of human achievements. But it also needs to be understood in terms of the continuing impact of the liberal nationalist heritage. In literary terms this was made most blatantly clear through the popularity of Pérez Galdos's *Episodios nacionales*, which portrayed, in populist leftist terms, the great moments of the Spanish nation's past.[12]

Liberal nationalism was, therefore, able to insinuate itself into labour ideology and outlook in a variety of ways. Within the PSOE from the 1900s this was to feed into new political and ideological currents which put emphasis on the modernisation of the nation rather than social revolution. This departure needs to be seen in wider European terms. During the first decade of the twentieth century it quickly became plain that there was a considerable reformist potential within Second International Socialism.[13] Spanish Socialism very much followed the

---

11 Francisco Ferrer, the anarchist founder of the Modern School in Barcelona, rejected private Catholic but also state schools where 'God was replaced by the State, Christian virtue by cynical duty, religion by patriotism, submission and obedience to the king by obedience to the aristocrat and boss.' F. Ferrer y Guardia, *Postuma explicación y alcance de la enseñanza racional* (Barcelona, n.d. [1911?]).

12 For the analysis of labour culture I have used, in particular, J. Carlos Mainer, 'Notas sobre la lectura obrera en España 1890–1930', in A. Balcells (ed.), *Teoría y práctica del movimiento obrero en España 1900–36* (Valencia, Torres, 1977), pp. 173–240; Mintz, *Anarchists of Casas Viejas*; J. Maurice, B. Magnien and D. Bussy Genevois (eds), *Peuple, mouvement ouvrier, culture dans l'Espagne contemporaine* (Paris, Presses Universitaries de Vincennes, 1990); B. Hofmann, P. Joan i Tous and M. Tietz (eds), *El anarquismo español y sus tradiciones culturales* (Frankfurt, Veruert, 1995); F. de Luis Martín, *La cultura socialista en España 1923–30* (Salamanca, Ediciones Universidad de Salamanca, 1993).

13 See, in particular, Chapters 1 and 2 in this volume.

Guesdist–Kautkyist line dominant within the Second International.[14] Nevertheless, the PSOE could never compromise with existing state institutions. On the contrary, in consonance with the whole of the left, it believed that the 'oligarchy' had to be overthrown for 'progress' to be possible. In these circumstances no Bernstein-like revisionist tendencies could emerge in Spain. This, together with the negative experience of colonial war, explains why no Socialists could sympathise with imperial aggrandisement. Indeed, the PSOE was at its most radical when faced with the threat of war in Morocco.[15]

Yet it would, at the same time, be drawn into nationalist politics. As we have already seen, within the party certain liberal nationalist-derived assumptions could lurk behind internationalist rhetoric. Already in the late nineteenth century there was a certain ambiguity in Socialist language. On the one hand, of course, like anarcho-syndicalism it mobilised workers within its unions in the name of class. Yet in its campaigns and protest movements it also aimed to attract wider support, appealing to 'the people' and the 'sane element in the population'.[16] This aspect of Socialist discourse came further to the fore from the turn of the century when the PSOE dropped its belief in the short-term possibility of proletarian revolution and instead began to argue – in line with Socialist parties in other less developed countries – that in order for socialism to be possible Spain first had to go through a bourgeois democratic revolution. The most progressive and democratic elements within 'the bourgeoisie' were taken to be the republicans, but because of their weakness, it was maintained, the Socialists had to help them democratise the country, and hence, from 1910, the Socialists agreed to pact with them (the so-called *Conjunción*) in local and national elections.[17]

The PSOE was now embarked upon a strategy of achieving a liberal democratic (but capitalist) regime, and, indeed, launched a general strike in August 1917 for this objective. Thus its duty became to cooperate in the modernisation and 'regeneration' of Spain in order to bring the country up to the level of the most advanced capitalist states. And, in this context, the language of liberal Spanish nationalism could easily penetrate Socialist discourse, particularly because republicans and

14 For which see, for example, J. Joll, *The Second International*, 2nd edn (London, Routlege, 1974), pp. 77–107.
15 See X. Cuadrat, *Socialismo y anarquismo en Cataluña 1899–1911. Los orígines de la CNT* (Madrid, Revista del Trabajo, 1976), pp. 367–72.
16 See, for example, *El Socialista*, 29 October 1897, pp. 2–3.
17 In particular the PSOE wished to pact with more moderate republicans who stuck to their 'proper' task of attracting middle-class support. The PSOE was, on the contrary, highly antagonistic to the Lerrouxist republicans, whom they managed to have excluded from the *Conjunción* in 1910.

Socialists still, to a degree, moved in overlapping cultural milieux, and for many workers had at least some objectives in common. This could, for example, be seen in the writings of the president of both the UGT and PSOE until his death in 1925, Pablo Iglesias. Iglesias maintained that workers and republicans ('the productive people') should cooperate 'in the national interest' against the monarchist plutocrats, who were simply using patriotism as a shield behind which they hid their reactionary objectives.[18]

After 1914 this perspective became most closely associated with Indalecio Prieto, one of the two major figures within the party between 1918 and 1936. Prieto though born in Asturias was brought up in the liberal atmosphere of Bilbao (and worked as a journalist on the Bilbao republican daily *El Liberal*). He fervently believed in coalition with the republicans but did not arrive at this conclusion through Marxism. From the first, as Juan Pablo Fusi has pointed out, he adopted a language which had more in common with the regenerationist thought of Joaquín Costa than Marx, and which was firmly set within the liberal nationalist tradition.[19] Thus for Prieto, as for the nineteenth-century liberal nationalists, Spain had been reduced to a state of decadence by corrupt and inefficient administration, and only a revolution by the 'people' would make possible a resurrection. At times, indeed, his discourse was fervently nationalist. For example, he responded to Spain's disastrous military defeat in Annual in 1921 by lamenting that it had been a national humiliation, but he restated his faith in national regeneration, affirming:

We must adopt this optimistic conclusion because anything else, how black, depressing and horrible it would be! It would be tantamount to denying the attributes of the race, tantamount to believing that Spain already had one foot in the grave, tantamount to accepting that the racial drive which took us from one side of the world to the other, conquering and civilising peoples, had become perverted, had decayed and lay rotting among the carrion of Annual, Zeluá and Monte Armit.[20]

Indeed, Prieto had the opportunity to put his ideals into practice during the Second Republic's reforming biennium of 1931–33, when, as Minister of Public Works, he, significantly, looked to modernise Spain through a programme of irrigation works similar to that first championed by Joaquín Costa at the turn of the century.

This political and ideological shift was also accompanied by the

---

18 P. Iglesias, *Escritos* II. *El socialismo en España. Artículos en la prensa socialista y liberal 1875–1925*, 2nd edn (Madrid, Ayuso, 1976), pp. 235–7.
19 J. Pablo Fusi, *El País Vasco. Pluralismo y nacionalidad* (Madrid, Alianza, 1985), p. 111.
20 Cited in I. Prieto, *Discursos fundamentales*, intr. E. Malefakis (Madrid, Turner, 1975), p. 72.

opening of the Socialists' sub-culture to liberal influence. Already in the early years of the century the Socialists had shown themselves willing to cooperate with a group of liberal nationalist modernisers in the building of a popular education movement known as the University Extension. Later, in the 1920s, (unlike the anarchists) the party leadership dropped attempts to develop its own militant working-class art and music, and began to argue that great art should be cherished simply for its own sake.[21]

The reforming republican-Socialist project could carry considerable weight in working-class circles. At the trade union level it was bolstered, from the second decade of the century, by the building of bureaucratised unions integrated within collective bargaining machinery, and which used the language of negotiation and compromise. Further integration of labour into reforming state structures could then be promoted through state involvement in collective bargaining. Parity Committees in which labour and employers could negotiate under the presidency of a state representative were, in fact, at first promoted, with Socialist support, by the Primo de Rivera dictatorship, and were extended by the Socialist Minister of Labour, Francisco Largo Caballero, in 1931–32. On the other hand, it should be stressed, this process could only be further deepened if the prospect of reform was a real one. Moreover, in the trade union wing of the movement in particular, the belief that these were merely partial gains on the road to Socialism remained strong.

More broadly, in the imagination of many workers the republic was still perceived as a liberating force. Workers who voted Socialist, and even those integrated into the CNT, could still see the republic in almost mythical terms, as the regime in which all ills could be put right. It is in this context that one can understand the massive Socialist-republican victory in the first elections of the Second Republic in June 1931 and the popular celebrations which followed.[22] During the Second Republic so-called *Prietista* members of the PSOE, under pressure from the left, came to adopt a vocabulary in which class played a more prominent role, but Prieto still argued that the 'overwhelming impetus of Spanish genius' had to overthrow the oligarchs and 'reconstruct Spain'.[23] The Communist Party (PCE) would, indeed, tap into this language during the Spanish Civil War. The war itself, of course, made such a discourse

21 Mainer, 'lectura obrera', pp. 206–15; Luis Martín, *Cultura socialista*, pp. 66–67; Manuel Pérez Ledesma, 'La cultura socialista en los años veinte', in J. L. García Delgado (ed.), *Los orígenes culturales de la II República* (Madrid, Siglo XXI, 1993), p. 138.
22 S. Juliá, 'De revolución popular a revolución obrera', *Historia Social* 1 (1988), pp. 29–43.
23 Prieto, *Discursos fundamentales*, pp. 202–3 and 261.

particularly apt. The 'Republican nation' was literally in mortal danger, and the Communists were, under the impact of the Comintern's anti-fascist, popular frontist policy, to shed revolutionary objectives in favour of a republican-based language of the people. The tone was set by the famous 'No pasarán' (They shall not pass) speech of Dolores Ibárruri, 'La Pasionaria', immediately following the military uprising against the Republic: 'Workers, peasants, anti-fascists, Spanish patriots! Faced with the military fascist rebellion, everyone on their feet to defend the Republic, popular liberties and the people's democratic conquests!'[24] This perspective was vigorously pursued by the Socialist Prime Minister, Juan Negrín (who had been a close associate of Prieto's), between May 1937 and the end of the war in March in 1939. In this he was strongly supported by the PCE, which, by 1938, was comparing the war against Franco to the 1808–14 'War of Independence' against the Napoleonic armies.

Yet the attempt by the *Prietista* Socialists to integrate the working class into a national liberal democratic project of reform was always going to be a difficult one. In the first place, from the turn of the century all Spanish nationalist discourses came under challenge in Catalonia and the Basque Country, and, by the Second Republic, as will be seen in the following section, groups of workers came under the influence of rival Catalan and Basque national identities. In this case, nevertheless, it largely proved possible to accommodate the contradictory identities within an overarching republican reform programme (which accepted Catalan and Basque autonomy).

Second, and more seriously, such integrative discourses were at every turn challenged by social division and the politics of class. In part this needs to be seen in the context of continuing anti-unionism visible within wide sectors of the employer class, and exacerbated, moreover, by the 1930s economic depression. It was also stimulated by a distrust of liberalism, originally based on oligarchic manipulation practised by the Restoration regime, and rekindled by the Republic's failure to carry though rapid social reform (symbolised above all by the stagnation of its agrarian reform programme). It was, of course, the anarchists above all who represented a ferocious rejection of parliamentary politics, but the suspicion of politics as an arena of manipulation and deception was widely held in working-class circles. Finally, the pursuit by much of the Spanish right of an anti-democratic, corporatist agenda, and the rise of fascism and the authoritarian right in much of Europe, helped to undermine the credibility of parliamentary government. This also needs to be

---

24 Cited in M. Vázquez Montalbán, *Pasionaria y los siete enanitos* (Barcelona, Planeta, 1995), p. 398.

seen in the context of the vision of the Soviet Union as a beacon of hope among wide sectors of the working-class left.

The continued vigour of the anarchist tradition was the most prominent example of the extent to which labour remained alienated from the state and its institutions.[25] But the contradiction between integration within the reforming nation and class revolution would be at heart of schism within the PSOE and UGT between 1919 and 1923 and again between 1931 and 1936. Within the party and especially the union there was from the first disquiet at collaboration with republicanism. The first crisis was to explode between 1917 and 1923 when the failure of the 1917 general strike and then the impact of the Bolshevik revolution and the post-war economic recession provided ammunition for critics of the *Conjunción* to have it scrapped, and for left-wing 'bolshevisers' to call for a more militant union strategy and more overt class politics. Then, during the Second Republic, disappointment at the limited impact of social reform, together with the a growing sense of danger from the right, encouraged the Socialist youth and union militants to adopt an (at least verbally) revolutionary stance, with calls for proletarian revolution and the implantation of a 'social republic'. The rejection of state power and belief in the revolutionary potential of the unions was most forcefully brought home in the social revolution which engulfed much of Republican Spain after the right-wing military revolt of 18 July 1936. It was, finally, also to be seen in the anarchist and dissident Communist rejection of the attempt by republicans, Socialists and Stalinist Communists to rebuild state power during the war.

Indeed, it was in the highly politicised and conflictual 1930s that languages of class and revolution came to the fore. On the Marxist left it was in these years that the use of the term 'proletariat', the clenched fist salute and the singing of the 'Internationale' became widespread. In this context, there developed a new militant ascetic characterised by the uniforms of the youth movement, the parades, hymns and salutes. Relatedly, the Communist left (whether orthodox or non-orthodox) was to acquire a new intellectual and cultural vigour, in large measure predicated upon the portrayal and widespread acceptance of the Soviet Union as a symbol of modernity. It was on this basis that the Communists were to champion an invigorated revolutionary romantic realism, christened Socialist Realism at the congress of the Union of Soviet Artists in 1934, and which

25 I have dealt with these issues in more detail in my articles 'Spain', in S. Berger and D. Broughton (eds), *The Force of Labour. The Western European Labour Movement and Working Class in the Twentieth Century* (Oxford, Berg, 1995), pp. 171–209, and 'Anarchism, the General Strike and the Barcelona Labour Movement 1899–1914', *European History Quarterly* 27:1 (1997), pp. 5–40.

in Spain was able to take in such figures as the novelist Ramón J. Sender and the poet Rafael Alberti. This new Soviet ascetic and cultural militancy was to attract the Socialist left – and in particular the youth movement – between 1934 and 1936. And once the old evolutionist certainties were brought into question, other elements of the Socialist ideological paradigm could be jettisoned. Thus Luis Araquistáin, Largo Caballero's intellectual mentor, writing in the leading Left Socialist journal, *Leviatán*, attacked Second International Socialists for having saved 'national capitalisms' in 1914 and, given the 'feudal' nature of Spanish social elites, anticipated the Basque Country and Catalonia playing a key role in the forging of an Iberian federalist workers' republic.[26]

It was to a degree the case that political divisions could be traced to socio-economic differentiation within the working class itself. Thus it seems that rejection of the Republic became particularly pronounced among an amalgam of unskilled workers and workers particularly hard hit by technological change, escalating unemployment and deteriorating working conditions. It is noteworthy that the impetus to the radicalisation of the PSOE came, to an important degree, from the landless labourers of Andalusia, whose hopes of serious land reform had by 1933 been totally frustrated. Similarly, in 1933–34 the Asturian miners were, in part, also driven to question the Republic because of its inability to tackle the deep-seated structural crisis – worsened by the Great Depression – which faced their industry. It was, finally, also the case that the militant CNT-FAI, which from late 1931 declared war against the Republic, recruited heavily among the unskilled – with construction workers to the fore – who suffered heavy unemployment with no social security and who benefited little from established mechanisms of collective bargaining. On the other hand, it seems that it was more skilled sectors of labour, those who enjoyed greater job security, and white-collar workers (whom the Socialists began for the first time to recruit in large numbers) who tended to give greater support to organisations such as the UGT, and *Treintistas* in Catalonia, and were more willing to operate within the Republican framework.

However, this relationship between skill, political militancy and the language of proletarian revolution should not be seen in too mechanistic a fashion. Clearly, for example, growing unemployment and the

---

26 See, in particular, the articles by S. Juliá, M. Bizcarrondo and M. Aznar Soler, in Maurice *et al.* (eds), *Peuple, mouvement ouvrier*; H. Graham, 'Community, Nation and State in Republican Spain 1931–38', in Mar-Molinero and Smith (eds), *Nationalism and the Nation*, pp.133–48; John Langdon-Davies, *Behind Spanish Barricades* (London, Secker and Warburg, 1936); P. Preston (ed.), *Leviatán Antología* (Madrid, Turner, 1976), p. 23 and pp. 96–7.

increasingly fraught international climate during 1933 led the representatives of broad sections of labour to adopt a more radical tone. This was reflected in the October revolution of 1934, which, while called supposedly to defend the Republic against fascism, also contained – as events in Asturias were to make plain – elements of a working-class revolutionary uprising. Alternatively, after the failure of October 1934 most working-class radicals (including members of the CNT) voted for the Popular Front in February 1936 in order to remove the right from government. And during the Civil War the shift towards popular frontism was based – quite apart from Soviet aid – on the realisation that only through the reconstruction of the state would there be any hope of effectively combating the forces of General Franco.

Class, ethnicity and nationalism in Catalonia and the Basque Country

Given Spain's relative industrial backwardness, she was a net exporter of labour during the period under consideration. However, the growth of important industrial nuclei and urban centres in such areas as Catalonia, the Basque Country, Asturias and Madrid was to lead to large-scale internal migration. In Catalonia and the Basque Country, as has been indicated, autochthonous nationalist movements were to grow up from the late nineteenth century. As a result, at a cultural and political level, relations between immigrants and host workers would be mediated by competing nationalist discourses, especially as both Catalan and Basque nationalists tried to attract labour support, while, at the same time, alternative republican and class-revolutionary projects would be refracted through the different nationalist perspectives.

In their origins and evolution Catalan nationalism and Basque nationalism were, however, rather different. Catalanism was at the outset, in the 1880s, a middle-class, anti-monarchist movement. From the 1890s, however, much of the movement moved to the right. It integrated traditional Catholic, corporatist, ruralist thought and, after 1898, allied with the Catalan industrial elite. Yet at the same time it was to exist alongside other more liberal currents. It was, therefore, from its base in middle and upper-class Barcelona that Catalanism was largely to try and construct the Catalan 'imagined community'. This was reflected in the Catalan people's supposed *Volksgeist*. Catalan nationalist ideology, like all late nineteenth-century ethnic nationalisms, saw the nation's existence as based on a series of immutable characteristics. Race was one element (with the 'Celtic' Catalans favourably compared to the 'Semitic' Castilians), but more important in most renditions was the Catalan culture and spirit, which had supposedly forged a hard-working, thrifty, dynamic and entrepreneurial community (in contrast to the laziness and profligacy of Castilians and Andalusians). Within this mind set, moreover, the Catalan working class was portrayed as sober, sensible and conscientious at work. This set of attributes was rolled into the Catalan expression *seny*.

Yet it would not prove easy to integrate lower-class Barcelona into this 'cultural' community. During the first decade of the century, it should be stressed, most workers were of Catalan origin. Yet Catalanist discourse found difficulty penetrating all areas of Barcelona working-class life. In the first place, customs differed wildly from the Catalanist ideal. Thus the rather *risqué*, cosmopolitan and even 'Spanish' entertainments in working-class circles contrasted with the rather puritanical streak in Catalanist culture. Furthermore, at an ideological level Catalanism jarred somewhat with the dominant currents on the left. It is the case that decentralisation had been a demand of left liberals since the early nineteenth century, and this fed into Socialist and anarchist discourse. This led the more moderate wing of one of the republican parties of the 1880s, the Federal Republicans, to evolve towards Catalanism. But, as we have noted, majority currents saw 'progress' as coming within what was seen as the established nation state, and Socialists and anarchists viewed the future communist or collective world order in cosmopolitan terms as leading to the removal of all national boundaries. It is, therefore, not surprising that anti-state nationalisms were greeted with hostility, especially given the conservative, traditionalist characteristics of much of Catalan (and, as we shall see, to an even greater extent Basque) nationalism.[27]

This division between middle-class Catalanism and an anti-Catalanist left was to be the central fault line of Catalan politics during the first decade of the twentieth century. In Barcelona, once the monarchist parties had been ousted in 1901, the key political battle was fought out between the Lliga Regionalista, the dominant conservative Catalanist party, and the Lerrouxist republicans. From the first the Lerrouxists (and anarchists) were accused of being the dregs of society (*la púrria*): rootless interlopers (*forasterada*) sent to Catalonia by the

27 For more information see my article, 'Sardana, Zarzuela or Cake-walk? Nationalism and Internationalism in the Discourse, Practice and Culture of the Early Twentieth Century Barcelona Labour Movement', in Mar-Molinero and Smith (eds), *Nationalism and the Nation*, pp. 171–90. There was a minority, rather intellectual anarchist current which sympathised with Catalanist demands because, it argued, they could induce the collapse of the repressive centralised state. Such anarchists could, indeed, have turned to Bakunin's writings for support (see Chapter 1). However, given the cultural and political climate, they were to remain on the fringes, at least until the 1930s.

central authorities in order to undermine the natural harmony of the national community through their anarchistic doctrines. Hence Catalanists tried to ethnicise political divisions. In this way they were situating political debate on the nationalist plane, on which they felt most comfortable. At the same time, one may speculate, they sublimated class and cultural rifts within Catalan society. Much of the hatred directed towards Lerrouxism and anarchism, one suspects, reflected anxieties and fears at the kind of world which existed in lower-class Barcelona, and by portraying class fears in nationalist terms a ready solution could be found (ideological expulsion from the imaginary national home).

However, this rhetoric hid a number of contradicitions which the left was able to exploit. It is true that many immigrant workers felt attracted to the Lerrouxist fold. Yet this was only a minor part of Lerroux's power base. The party was also able to attract large numbers of Catalan workers, along with members of the lower middle class, who saw Lerrouxism as both taking up the city's republican heritage and adapting it to new times. And it was what these supporters experienced as an attempt by the Catalanists ideologically and culturally to expel them from the community to which they rightfully belonged which helps explain why their reaction was so virulent. Thus in the republican press the Catalanists were described as reactionary, backward-looking Vaticanists, whose ideals belonged to a bygone age.

There was much that separated Lerrouxist republicans, anarchists and Socialists, but in this analysis of Catalanism they could by and large agree. Yet Catalanism cannot be described solely as a self-enclosed middle-class movement. In the first place, from the first years of the century it also attracted considerable lower middle-class support, and this stretched to take in large numbers of white-collar and shop workers. Indeed, the Catalan nationalist white-collar union, the CADCI, founded in 1903, had considerable success.[28] Catalanism could also, from the turn of the century, interest some workers uncomfortable with the revolutionary traditions of Lerrouxism and anarchism. This could include the supervisory elite, workers in trades in which close relations were maintained with employers, and at a political level workers who gravitated around reformist cultural associations. These workers could be attracted by a common language of thrift and hard work which would make social advancement possible.

From 1905 to 1907 Catalanists were able to make further inroads during the so-called Solidaritat Catalana campaign; a broad movement

---

28 M. Lladonosa, *Catalanisme i moviment obrer. El CADCI entre 1903 i 1923* (Barcelona, Abadia de Montserrat, 1988).

under the *de facto* leadership of the Lliga Regionalista in protest at a military assault on its newspaper offices and a subsequent law making any criticism of the army subject to military jurisdiction. Lerroux opposed the alliance but many moderate republicans, who had followed Lerroux only reluctantly in the first place, broke away. As has been shown, these republicans tended to come from more established middle-class families, in close contact with the Catalanist milieu.[29] Two key consequences followed from this campaign. First, Catalanism could clearly appear as a reforming movement opposed to the reactionary Spanish state.[30] Second, from that date reformist politics would be refracted through the Catalanist mirror. This was particularly the case following the crisis of Lerrouxism between 1910 and 1918. That is to say, whereas in the rest of Spain projects aimed at democratising the state required, to be successful, alliance between Spanish republicanism and sectors of the working-class left, in Catalonia the alliance would be forged with Catalanist republican groupings.

More workers than ever before were attracted to Catalanism during the Solidaritat campaign. Lerroux, however, retained most of his working-class base, and, until 1914, Catalanism remained largely a middle-class movement which could only reach out and touch those workers closest to the middle-class cultural and ideological universe. The ideological range of Catalan nationalism was, however, to widen considerably during the war years. In the first place, a number of liberal Catalanists, impressed by the growth of labour politics in Western Europe, moved left and began to link the struggles of the 'oppressed peoples' of Europe with that of the working class for its emancipation. Broadly speaking, they maintained that both movements were complementary, for, while the first undermined the oppressive centralist state, the second destroyed capitalist tyranny.[31] Like the *Prietista* Socialists,

---

29 J. B. Culla i Clarà, *El republicanisme lerrouxista a Catalunya, 1901–23* (Barcelona, Curiel, 1986), pp. 153–5.
30 Junco, *El emperador*, p. 354.
31 See, for example, X. Cuadrat, 'El PSOE i la qüestió nacional catalana fins l'any 1923', *L'Avenç* 5 (1977), pp. 58–66, and 6 (1977), pp. 56–63; A. Nin, *Socialisme i nacionalisme 1912–34. Escrits republicans, socialistes i comunistes*, ed. Palai Pagès (Barcelona, Malgrana/Diputació de Barcelona, 1985); A. Balcells, *Rafael Camapalans, socialisme català. Bibliografia i textos* (Barcelona, Malgrana/Diputació de Barcelona, 1985). From this ideological perspective these socialists also used the dual class–people = nation discourse favoured by Prieto (though, of course, the national subject was a different one). Hence Rafael Campalans stated in 1923: 'We frankly and firmly proclaim the class struggle and all the principles of the International. But we desire even more that the whole people may be converted into a formidable army on the march, . . .'. Cited in A. Fabra Ribas and R. Campalans, *Catalanisme i socialisme. El debat de 1923*, ed. Jesús M. Rodés (Barcelona, Malgrana/Diputació de Barcelona, 1985), p. 27.

these nationalists also built on liberal traditions; in this case support for 'national' liberation struggles against oppressive rule. But while for the PSOE Spain was seen as a nation and thus the proper territorial unit in which to pursue 'progress', for the Catalanist leftists it was not a nation but merely a state machine – like Russia or the Austro-Hungarian Empire – which had to be totally reconstituted. They were given a considerable fillip as the national question rose to the top of the political agenda during the First World War, and were further encouraged by growing Catalanist agitation for an autonomy statute from 1916. Moreover, by 1918 Lenin's position on the national question, which stated that the proletariat should ally with national liberation movements in order to bring down authoritarian rule, was also being disseminated in left-wing circles.

The most dramatic developments took place within the Catalan Federation of the PSOE. A number of left Catalanists joined the party between 1914 and 1916. They were able to build on complaints within the federation that leadership was too centralised in Madrid, and managed to get resolutions approved in favour of the decentralisation of the PSOE and calling for a future reordering of state structures so that the 'peoples of Iberia' might link up to form a federation of autonomous governments. At first it seemed that the PSOE leadership would acquiesce (going so far as to support a Catalan autonomy campaign in 1918), but from 1919 it took an increasingly critical stance, leading a large group of Catalan Socialists to break away and form their own party, the Socialist Union of Catalonia (USC) in the 1920s.[32] Yet the party leaders quickly revealed that they still retained strong emotional links with the world of liberal Catalanism; they were resolutely social democratic and wished to establish no contacts with the CNT. Others, however, were willing to go further. A small Catalan Republican Party (PRC) established close contacts with the leader of Catalan syndicalism, Salvador Seguí, and tried to turn the party into a working-class organisation which would integrate the 'realist' wing of the CNT (see below). It was, however, Andreu Nin, who in the 1930s was to become Spain's leading Marxist theorist, who moved furthest to the left. After an odyssey which took him from Catalanism to social democracy and syndicalism, his final home became Leninist Bolshevism, and from 1923, with a group of colleagues within the CNT, he laid the basis of a movement which would

---

32 In the case of Prieto it was his experience regarding Basque nationalism (see following section) which particularly predisposed him to view all non-Spanish nationalisms in a negative light. Thus he was reported as stating in a meeting held in Reus in 1923, 'He did not sympathise with regionalism, because the one he knew - Basque regionalism – was reactionary to the core'. Cited in Cuadrat, 'El PSOE', p. 63.

combine Communism with support for the Catalan 'national liberation struggle' against the central state.

Nevertheless, it should be remembered that all these groups remained small, though they provided a series of options which in the more favourable climate of the Second Republic could begin to bear fruit. In Catalonia the CNT quickly rose to become the hegemonic force in these years, and, moreover, in general maintained the anti-Catalanist rhetoric dominant within the anarchist movement during the first decade of the century. This could be seen in the comments of the leader of the Catalan branch (CRT), Salvador Seguí, in 1919, when he accused Catalanism of being a movement of the 'organised bourgeoisie' and stated that the workers had no interest in nationalism.[33] Yet under Seguí's leadership the Catalan CRT began to evolve in a more 'realist' direction. Seguí was never a fanatical anarchist ideologue, his stance being more akin to that of the syndicalists on the moderate wing of the French CGT. He believed the CNT should be a broad movement which would take in all Catalan workers, whatever their ideology, and he was wary of calling general strikes which would put the organisation in jeopardy. Furthermore, though a convinced libertarian communist he never accepted the hard-line anarchist position that all 'bourgeois' governments were alike; rather, like many within the PSOE, he believed that a republic would give workers more freedom and allow them to organise more effectively. Thus under Seguí's auspices the CNT supported the Socialist-led strike of August 1917. He was also close to leftist Catalanists and in 1920–22 tried to work with them in order to halt the reactionary onslaught on the CNT in Barcelona. Seguí and his collaborators were, therefore, willing to enter into dialogue with the world of Catalanism in order to preserve or extend civil liberties.[34]

These contacts and projects were in the short term to come to nothing. Virulent social conflict on the streets of Barcelona was capped, in September 1923, by a military *coup* against the constitutional authorities. Similar issues were, however, again to raise their head in what would be for Catalanism the more favourable context of the Second Republic. The Primo de Rivera dictatorship was to see the radicalisation of Catalanism, with the result that during the Second Republic the dominant Catalanist party became the republican and socially reforming Catalan Republican Left (ERC). It was, fundamentally, a middle and

33 Cited in A. Elorza (ed.), *Artículos madrileños de Salvador Seguí* (Madrid, Cuadernos para el Diálogo/Edicusa, 1976), pp. 48–51.
34 Indeed, it has been argued – probably with some justification – that Seguí sympathised more with the left Catalanists than with his 'official' pronouncements as head of the CRT would indicate. For which see Salut, *Vivers de revolucionaris*, p. 173.

lower middle-class party, but its programme of autonomy, democratisation and social reform did, at the very least, attract some working-class electoral support. At the same time, there also emerged a whole range of Catalanist or para-Catalanist working-class parties, from the more reformist USC to the Communist Workers' and Peasants' Bloc (BOC).[35]

This was balanced by the rapid reorganisation of the CNT, which was to launch a series of violent strikes in the autumn and winter of 1931. Yet the CNT itself was soon faced with serious internal divisions. Between 1910 and 1923, below the surface, there was always tension between hard-liners who wished the CNT to operate as an anarchist-dominated overtly revolutionary force and syndicalists, like Salvador Seguí. During the Second Republic these divisions broke through to the surface, leading to a split between a minority of CNT members, who were willing to compromise with the Republic – the so-called *Treintistas* – and the anarchist militants. Among the defectors were, significantly, to be found most of Seguí's lieutenants, and as they developed contacts with the ERC and left Catalanists their own discourse began to incorporate Catalan nationalist categories.[36]

These divisions to a degree reflected the crystallisation of two worlds within the Barcelona labour movement. Politically, they were separated by their attitude towards the Republic. Within what might very loosely be called the 'pan-Catalanist camp' varying degrees of adherence to the Republican institutions were to be found. One can also up to a point see the forging of a specific mentality which owed much to Catalanist *seny*. This can, I would argue, be seen in the PSUC, an alliance of smaller parties and unions formed in July 1936 which was able to integrate much of the 'pan-Catalanist' labour movement. This followed the radicalisation of the working-class left following the rise to power of the right in the elections of November 1933. The fusion, as a result, would take place under the aegis of Marxism, and the PSUC declared itself a Communist party and affiliated to the Communist International. Yet, at the same time, the socialism of Joan Comorera, the PSUC's first general secretary, and the party more generally, would owe much to its Catalanist origins; thus the emphasis was on top-down planning and education, while revolutionary upheaval was not contemplated.[37]

It has also been pointed out that this milieu tended to articulate

35 See R. Alcaraz i González, *La Unió Socialista de Catalunya 1923–36* (Barcelona, La Malgrana/Institut Municipal d'Història, 1987); A. Durgan, *El Bloque Obrero y Campesino* (Barcelona, Laertes, 1996).
36 E. Vega, *El trentisme a Catalunya. Divergències ideològicas en la CNT 1930–33* (Barcelona, Curial, 1980).
37 M. Caminal i Badia, *Joan Comorera*, 3 vols (Barcelona, Empúries, 1984).

workers in smaller provincial cities, peasants' trade unions and, in Barcelona, white-collar workers and workers in the more highly skilled trades and/or in more stable employment. In this respect, therefore, some continuity can be seen with the early twentieth century, when Catalanism began to expand into the labour movement through these categories of worker. Nevertheless, during the Second Republic the expectations and opportunities for reform and improved working conditions to be had through dialogue with state institutions, and the consolidation of specifically working-class Catalanist options, served greatly to widen its base. Thus by 1936, on paper, non-CNT unions had at least as many affiliates as the CNT itself.[38]

Yet the CNT (or CNT-FAI as it was now often referred to) remained a powerful force. As previously, its firmest support was to be found among the industrial trade unions of Barcelona (textiles, transport, metallurgy and construction). Yet its working-class base had evolved significantly since the second decade of the century. The years from 1916 were to see massive immigration into the city, and, in the 1920s, immigrants came to an increasing extent from southern Spain – especially Murcia. The result was the growth of working-class shanty towns on the Barcelona periphery, and massive overcrowding in the working-class districts of Barcelona itself. During the Second Republic the 'poorer working class', including the unskilled immigrant workers, experienced heavy unemployment as the construction boom of the 1920s collapsed and the 1930s economic depression bit. These workers were also far less likely than the more skilled elite to benefit from collective bargaining and the decisions of the Republic's State-sponsored collective bargaining bodies, the *Jurados Mixtos*. It was within this world that the CNT-FAI was to recruit most successfully. Its militant strikes and 'direct action' tactics (including rent strikes and, indeed, the condoning of robberies and muggings) appealed to a labour force trying to eke out a living on the margins of 'official Barcelona'.[39]

Similar tensions to those in the Barcelona movement could, as we have noted in the previous section, be seen in other parts of urban Spain. Faced with anarchist agitation, the Spanish republican-Socialist and Catalan ERC governments also reacted similarly. Fearing the stability of the Republic might be called into question, and predisposed to see the CNT as a rabble of troublemakers, from the autumn of 1931 repres-

38 A. Durgan, 'Sindicalismo y marxismo en Cataluña 1931–36: hacia la fundación de la Federación Obrera de Unidad Sindical', *Historia Social* 8 (1990), pp. 29–45.
39 C. Ealham, 'Anarchism and illegality in Barcelona 1931–37', *Contemporary European History* 4:2 (1995), pp. 131–51; N. Rider, 'Anarchism, Urbanization and Social Conflict in Barcelona 1900–32', 2 vols (University of Lancaster Ph.D., 1988).

sion was severe. Yet in Catalonia the terms of the nationalist debate meant that fractures within society were again ethnicised. The ERC and, indeed, at least sections of the pan-Catalanist working-class left, drew on the traditions of anti-Lerrouxist invective of the early years of the century to anathematise the CNT. Attention focused in particular on the figure of the *Murciano*, who, in racist terms, was stereotyped as the prototypical anarchist; uneducated, unable to earn a proper living and of low intelligence, it was claimed, he was drawn into the twilight world of theft, vice and anarchism.[40] As in the early twentieth century this was a very partial and interested reading. Many Catalans, socialised in the insurrectionary and violent traditions of left-wing politics, stayed with the CNT. Yet the picture was not totally devoid of content. Inevitably larger numbers of workers in the 'pan-Catalanist' camp were of Catalan origin, whereas there was a higher percentage of immigrants in the world within which the CNT-FAI moved. This, when coupled with Catalanist discourse, no doubt strengthened the self-perception of contradictions being based on ethnic origin rather than class conflict and social stratification. These divisions came to the fore during the Civil War, when the Catalan Communist party, the PSUC, allied with the ERC against the CNT. And from the start the political in-fighting behind the lines very much became intertwined with the attempt not only to impose one's power but also one's identity markers on the city of Barcelona. This was, observers noted, most spectacularly embodied in the struggle over the use of the anarchist red and black emblem and Catalan 'four bars' flag between the CNT and ERC/PSUC.[41]

There were both similarities and differences in the development of class and nationalist politics in the Basque Country. The Basque Nationalist Party, the PNV, was at the outset, in the 1890s, an arch-traditionalist, Catholic party. Furthermore, to a greater extent than its Catalan counterpart, Basque nationalism was predicated on the concept of biological race. In its origins Basque nationalism represented a small-town ethnically Basque reaction against industrialisation and non-Basque immigration. Hence working-class immigrants were denigrated as knife-wielding degenerates who, through bringing crime, vice, blasphemous language and revolutionary agitation to the Basque Country, were undermining the traditional way of life.[42]

40 Rider, 'Anarchism, Urbanization and social conflict'.
41 G. Orwell, *Homage to Catalonia* (London, Secker and Warburg, 1938), pp. 146–54 and p. 190; J. Langdon-Davies, *La Setmana Tràgica de 1937. Els fets de maig* (Barcelona, Edicions 62, 1987), p. 116.
42 A. Elorza, 'Sobre ideologías y organización del primer nacionalismo vasco', in *id.*, *Ideologías del nacionalismo vasco 1876–1937* (San Sebastián, Haranburu, 1988), pp. 132–3.

This, not surprisingly, led to an extreme polarisation of Basque society. From the 1880s the PSOE began to organise Basque industrial workers. Many of the leading figures in the party were Basque but a majority of affiliates to the UGT – especially in the years before 1914 – were immigrants, and this, when added the ideological considerations already outlined, ensured that Basque Socialism would be passionately anti-Basque nationalist.[43]

Basque nationalism did not, however, remain as simply a backward-looking traditionalist force for long. From the first decade of the century, as Catalanism had done previously, it began to recruit among the urban middle and lower-middle classes, linked with the new indus-trial society but marginalised from centres of political and economic power. Yet, unlike Catalanism, Basque nationalism had only a very limited impact among the area's urban industrial elites. Most shipping and steel magnates, through state contracts and participation in Spain's financial system, were closely linked with Spain's ruling oligarchy. This very much conditioned the movement's evolution. On the one hand, it championed a model of economic development based on small-scale manufacturing in an ethnically Basque society rather than the world of large-scale industry promoted by the elite. On the other, the lack of elite participation meant that the PNV was able to promote a populist and vaguely anti-capitalist programme which could attract some ethnically Basque workers to its cause. This was formalised in 1911, when, faced with the failure of Catholic trade unionism, growing labour agitation and the strengthening of the PSOE, Basque nationalists created their own trade union, Solidarity of Basque Workers (SOV).

The union was social Catholic and spoke the language of class harmony within the Basque community. Thus it centred on mutual aid and social welfare activities and avoided conflict with employers if pos-sible. But, unlike Catholic unions set up in other parts of Spain during the first decade of the century, which were mixed worker–employer asso-ciations either under control of the Church hierarchy and/or with industrialists heavily involved, the SOV, to a degree at least, genuinely represented workers' interests. This helped it to succeed where Spanish Catholic unions had failed (and continued to fail). At first it was very small, but it grew rapidly in 1919/20 to reach a first peak of perhaps 10,000 members in the latter year. During the Second Republic it once again increased rapidly in strength, reaching the figure of 37,000 affili-ates in the Basque Country (against the UGT's 50,000) in 1936. It was not only distinguished from the UGT by its purely autochthonous

43 Fusi, *El País Vasco*, p. 45.

working-class base. As in the case of Catalonia, one can discern some structural differences between Basque nationalist and non-Basque nationalist workers. It tended to recruit most strongly among workers in small-scale industry and the more highly skilled trades, and particularly in smaller centres in which what may be referred to as more traditional, Catholic Basque values were dominant. This no doubt explains why, though the SOV (like the PNV) was born in Vizcaya, in the Second Republic it rapidly gained support in the less heavily industrialised province of Guipúzcoa. However, with the unionisation of the major Vizcayan shipbuilding and steel industries after 1914 it was also to make some headway. The particular circumstances in which this took place require additional comment. From these years the UGT was rapidly able to increase its strength in these industries, and, indeed, establish collective bargaining procedures with most employers. The one major figure who bucked the trend was Ramón de la Sota, a Basque nationalist who ran the great shipbuilding yard of Euskalduna. Rather than negotiate with the Socialists, he was to build a highly paternalist regime, employ native Basque workers and allow the SOV to organise in the factory.

   Given the SOV's nationalist and Catholic origins, and the links with Ramón de la Sota, it was, as may be expected, accused by the Socialists of being a yellow union under the control of Basque nationalist industrialists. And it does indeed seem the case that Sota and other industrialists made financial contributions to the union to keep the UGT at bay. Yet the SOV could not avoid the issue of social conflict altogether if it wished to retain a union base. Thus, in the years 1921–23, as the economic climate worsened and employers began to lay workers off, it increasingly began to criticise industrialists. Worst in its eyes was what it referred to as the '*españolista* plutocracy', but even Basque nationalist employers were warned that they would forfeit their right to form part of the Basque community if they did not treat their workers with respect. However, this did not necessarily lead it any closer to the Socialists. More moderate Basque nationalists had closer ties with the business community, and SOV identified more with the hard-line separatists who aimed to recapture the nationalist founder, Sabino Arana's, populism and seperatist racialism.[44]

44 On the SOV see, in particular, I. Gortazar Olábarri, *Relaciones laborales en Vizcaya 1880–1936* (Durango, Zuyaza, 1978), pp. 131–66; M. Ortaegui, 'Organización obrera y nacionalismo: Solidaridad de Obreros Vascos 1911–23', *Estudios de Historia Social* 18–19 (1981), pp. 7–83; L. Mees, *Nacionalismo vasco, movimiento obrero y cuestión social 1903–23* (Bilbao, Fundación Sabino Arana, 1992), pp. 139–84; Fusi, *El País Vasco*, pp. 45–51. An overview of the Basque labour movement is to be found in J. Javier Díaz Freire, F. Luengo, A. Rivera and L. Castells, 'El comportamiento de los trabajadores en la sociedad industrial vasca 1876–1936', in L. Castells (ed.), *Los trabajadores en el País Vasco 1876–1923* (Madrid, Siglo XXI, 1993), pp. 141–70.

As in the case of Catalonia, therefore, cleavages within society were ethnicised, and this ethnic divide cut through the working class. Yet the imbrications between national identity and social class were complex. As inter-class movements, both Basque nationalism and Catalan nationalism tended to reach out, in the first instance, to an important degree to sectors of labour in which social divisions were not perceived as particularly virulent. However, unlike the Catalan case, Basque nationalism remained Catholic and anti-liberal and ideologically based on biological race, and thus it could not but remain restricted to the autochthonous Basque population. Indeed, in the Basque case a radicalisation of the SOV after 1920 was to lead it, because more moderate regionalists were considered 'bourgeois', to re-emphasise the centrality of race. A similar process of radicalism and hardening of nationalism was to be seen in some sectors of Catalan nationalism. However, the fact that from the start there had been a liberal component in Catalan nationalism, and the emphasis on spirit rather than on race, meant that the connection with socialism was far easier, and also allowed Catalan nationalism to reach out further, and integrate at least second and third-generation immigrants. This juxtaposition of socialism and Catalan nationalism had interesting consequences. On the one hand, the situation in many ways represented a mirror image of the wider Spanish picture. In both cases, the more moderate sector of labour had either aligned with or entered into dialogue with the dominant left-wing nationalism, though the nationalist symbols of the respective *rapprochements* were, of course, antithetic. Nevertheless, a group of dissident Communists within the 'pan-Catalanist' camp (the BOC, later integrated into the POUM), because of their emphasis on proletarian revolution, during the Civil War actually ended up on the side of the CNT against ERC and the PSUC. Concomitantly, in both areas there remained an industrial working class, which, at an ideological level, had been schooled in a mixture of internationalism and (especially in the Basque case) liberal Spanish nationalism, and which was to a large degree impervious to the Basque and Catalan nationalist offensive. In both these sectors, it is important to note, class solidarity would be an important factor in blunting the new nationalist message. Thus the Catalan CNT continued to mobilise large numbers of native Catalans, and the Basque UGT had albeit a minority of ethnic Basques in its ranks.

Conclusion

The key to understanding the evolving relationship between nation and class would appear to be the weakness of the Spanish national project and the difficulties involved in building national-reforming coalitions. As we have seen, the Spanish liberal state's nation-building programme had from the start been marked by inefficiency and a lack of interest. This certainly stimulated the growth of peripheral Catalan and Basque nationalisms, which then went to try and structure their own national ethnic identities. From the left, republicans and the republicanised sector of the PSOE tried to construct their alternative, progressive liberal Spanish nationalist programme, and, during the Second Republic, put it into practice. They were able to build bridges with socially reforming Catalan nationalists through the concession of autonomy (and, during the Civil War, even reach out to more traditionalist Basque nationalism). Yet, as we have seen, they were subject to fierce challenge from the working-class left. The growth of an intransigent left wing needs, at an economic and social level, to be related to bitter social divisions in Spanish society and employer hostility to unionisation. But it also grew out of distrust of the Spanish state and of the political arena in general. This was most clearly manifested in the case of the anarchists, but, as we have seen, in parts of the Socialist movement the possibility of reform through a liberal state was also viewed with suspicion. The result was that the Spanish left was divided into a plethora of fractions. Divisions surfaced over what form of class or national project should be championed. And in these circumstances, of course, it was impossible to form a united front in the face of the authoritarian threat from the right.

Appropriating the symbols of the *patrie*? Jacobin nationalism and its rivals in the French Third Republic

Workers and the nation

There is no consensus about when France truly became a 'nation'. Some historians emphasise the importance of precocious Bourbon centralisation. Others see a secular religion of nationalism constructed after 1789 as a citizens' army was mobilised to defend the revolutionary *patrie*. Possibly many peasants became 'Frenchmen' only as railways, conscription and schools integrated peripheral regions into the national market and culture after 1870.[1] During the prolonged process of 'internal colonialism' provincial migrants were often treated as *horsains* (foreigners). Native workers in Paris or Saint-Etienne treated migrants from the Limousin or the Massif Central with quasi-xenophobic contempt – as dirty, ignorant, *patois*-speaking chestnut eaters.[2] Arab workers in inter-war car factories were dubbed 'brown Bretons'. Many workers developed a clear sense of their 'Frenchness' only when they used French – taught in primary school – as the lingua franca of conversation with migrants from other regions. The Socialist leader Jean Jaurès would begin his speeches in the Midi in French – to flatter his audiences that he knew that they now understood the 'national language' – before reverting to Occitan.

Recent attempts to define the 'distinctiveness' of French labour history – the paradoxical contrast between precocious and recurring militancy and endemic organisational fragmentation and weakness – have emphasised the survival of artisans with strong job-control priorities and the importance of informal direct action.[3] Two further 'peculiarities' are of relevance to our concern with the relationship between national and class identity. These are the unique importance of immi-

---

1 D. Bell, 'Recent Works on Early Modern French National Identity', *Journal of Modern History* 68 (1996), pp. 84–113.

2 J-P. Burdy, *Le Soleil noir. Formation social et mémoire ouvrière dans un quartier de St Etienne 1840–1940* (Lyons, Université de Lyon, 1989).

3 L. Berlanstein, 'The Distinctiveness of the Nineteenth Century French Labour Movement', *Journal of Modern History* 64 (1992), pp. 660–85; R. Magraw, 'The Peculiarities of the French', *Socialist History* 9 (1996), pp. 23–42.

grant labour to French industry during the 'second industrial revolution' and the crucial role in worker consciousness of workers' historic relationship with the republican Jacobin tradition.

In France 'democratic nationalism' had long been a key component of left-wing thinking. The Jacobins and the *sans-culottes* were 'patriots', the 'traitors' were the aristocratic *émigrés*. The Revolutionary and Napoleonic armies contained former *sans-culottes* who saw their mission as the export of anti-feudal revolution. In 1848 foreign exiles in Paris looked to the Second Republic to export revolution to their homelands. In 1871 Communard workers fought on for social revolution and national independence – and the right surrendered to Bismarck. Thereafter mainstream French Socialists saw no incompatibility between internationalist and national loyalties. They rejected *revanche*, supported the peace efforts of the Second International – but emphasised not 'cosmopolitan utopianism' but the equality of nations. In the existing condition of Europe, in the absence of a mature international proletariat, autonomous nations remained prerequisites of freedom and progress. Jaurès sought cooperation with the SPD to avoid war, urged the abandonment of France's Russian alliance and the replacement of its army with a defensive citizens' militia. Yet he was worried by the absence of genuine revolutionary traditions in the German working class and insistent that French workers should defend the Republican *patrie* if attacked.

Two decades later the PCF, after years of denunciation of French capitalist imperialism, reinvented themselves as the 'New Jacobins', defenders of the *patrie* against fascism – waving the tricolour, readopting the *Marseillaise*, praising Loire *châteaux* as part of the national heritage and urging young members of their Union des Jeunes Filles de France to become patriotic model mothers. Communist-led aircraft unions utilised a national productivist rhetoric which portrayed the production of military planes – even training as 'proletarian pilots' – as fulfilment of one's class duty in the anti-fascist battle. 'Our party,' Vaillant-Couturier insisted, 'did not fall from the sky. We have deep roots in French soil. The names of our militants have an . . . honest, native tang. Our party is a moment in the history of eternal France.'[4] Political class consciousness was higher in France than in Britain after 1945 because the outlook of many French workers was moulded by the PCF. Central to workers' self-awareness was the image of workers as the true patriots who defended

---

4 H. Chapman, *State Capitalism and Working Class Radicalism in the French Aircraft Industry* (Berkeley, Cal., University of California Press, 1991); S. Whitney, 'Embracing the *Status quo*: French Communism, Young Women and the Popular Front', *Journal of Social History* 30 (1996), pp. 29–51.

democratic France when, time and again, its elites – aristocratic *seigneurs* or industrial barons – colluded with the German enemy (1792, 1871, 1940–44).

Jacobin patriotism was not, of course, the only nationalist strand. Its rivals – 'official' Republican patriotism, traditional Catholicism, ethnic 'New Nationalism' – will be discussed below. The coexistence of these rival variants complicates any attempt to provide a clear, simple outline of the relationship of class, politics and *patrie*. Furthermore, the relationship changed over time. Firstly after 1880 some on the far left – notably anarcho-syndicalists – espoused an anti-militarist and anti-patri-otic discourse, and insisted that the tricolour, soiled by its association with the 'capitalist' Republic, should be tossed on to a dungheap. Subsequently, war-weariness and the appeal of the Bolshevik revolution sparked the unprecedented wave of labour militancy of 1917–20 and the formation of a mass Communist party.

Thus for several decades the right was given the opportunity to don the mantle of patriotism discarded by some – not all – of the left, and to appropriate the symbols of the *patrie* – tricolour, *Marseillaise*. During the 1920s it appeared resolutely anti-Bolshevik and anti-Boche – whilst branding Communists as Moscow's fifth column and the Socialist Party (SFIO) as naive dupes of League of Nations pacifism. Then, after 1930, the situation became increasingly convoluted. For as the left revived the rhetoric of Jacobin patriotism to mobilise resistance to fascism, so the right – whether through anti-Communism, or ideological sympathy with fascism, urged appeasement and branded those seeking rearmament as 'traitors' risking needless war on behalf of Stalin. In defence of internal bourgeois class interests the 'patriotic' right and elements of the Radical Party became openly defeatist. To make confusion worse confounded, some on the right put their anti-Boche patriotism before their class interests whilst some on the left remained so appalled by the carnage of 1914–18 that they believed anything, including Munich or Vichy, prefer-able to another war.

Labour and the Republican state

France achieved male suffrage by 1848 and by the 1870s was Europe's major 'democratic republic'. Workers had allied with 'progressive' bour-geois to revive radical republicanism in the 1860s, and to consolidate the Republic in the late 1870s.[5] Thereafter, reformist Socialists insisted that

5 R. Aminzade, *Ballots and Barricades: Class Formation and Republican Politics in France 1830–71* (Princeton, N.J., Princeton University Press, 1993).

workers had a stake in the republican system. Dissident minorities had long warned workers not to be 'duped' by siren songs flattering them as 'citizens' of a 'Republican *patrie*'. The *sans-culottes* favoured direct, not representative, democracy. Syndicalists emphasised the importance of an autonomous workerist culture and warned that Republican patriotism had betrayed its emancipatory promises and degenerated into a cynical manipulative tool designed to reconcile workers to the capitalist *status quo*. Patriotic prejudices persisted in the working class because of the brainwashing of children by the laic schools, established in the 1880s by Republican Education Minister Jules Ferry, in whose textbooks French history became less the celebration of popular democracy forged in the fires of revolution than an anodyne national consensus built around loyalty to an 'eternal France' whose internal conflicts were glossed over.[6]

Nevertheless, syndicalists scarcely dented working-class admiration for the laic school. Workers had been activists in the Ligue de l'Enseignement, which had campaigned since the 1860s for secular education.[7] Undoubtedly the school was central to subsequent attempts to boost popular identification with the *patrie*. Maps of 'the hexagon' on school walls, textbooks such as *Tour de France par deux enfants* and *bataillons scolaires* encouraged pride in a future role as 'citizen soldiers'.[8] Education in French eroded linguistic particularism. Whilst the elitism of secondary and higher education made the 'myth' of social promotion via education largely an illusion, it was possible for workers' sons to aspire to careers as primary teachers or minor *fonctionnaires*. And whereas German workers' autobiographies portrayed the Prussian schoolteacher as a reactionary bully, French workers give an affectionate portrait of the *instituteur* as keen to reason with pupils and to inculcate pride in France's democratic heritage – whilst *institutrices* provided a positive role model for girl pupils.[9] Of course the consequences of any pedagogic regime are not necessarily those intended. Future Communists could show gratitude to their *instituteur* and yet be highly critical of Republican patriotism – which was itself dented by the carnage of the

6 S. Citron, *Le Mythe national. L'Histoire de France en question* (Paris, Editions Ouvrières, 1987).

7 K. Auspitz, *The Radical Bourgeoisie* (Cambridge, Cambridge University Press, 1982).

8 J. Ozouf, 'Le thème du patriotisme dans les manuels primaires', *Mouvement Social* 49 (1964), pp. 37–51; G. Canini, 'The School Battalions in the East', in R. Tombs (ed.), *Nationhood and Nationalism in France 1889–1918* (Cambridge, Cambridge University Press, 1992).

9 M. J. Maines, *Taking the Hard Road. Life Course in French and German Workers' Autobiographies in the Era of Industrialisation* (Chapel Hill, N. C., University of North Carolina Press, 1995).

Great War, so that many inter-war teachers espoused an integral pacifism which, unwittingly, paved the way to Munich.

The appeal of secularist education to so many workers suggests that a shared anticlericalism united them with the Voltairean/positivist wing of the bourgeoisie. Conversely the religious beliefs of the *bien-pensant* bourgeoisie were shared by a sizeable minority of workers – particularly women, textile workers in the Flemish Nord and in Midi towns with a history of sectarian Protestant/Catholic hatreds. Since the post-revolution religious fault line divided both the elites and the proletariat it is difficult to provide any simple, schematic analysis of the relationship between religion, class identity and national integration. However, one may suggest that religion played a less central role than in Britain in integrating workers into the nation. For British identity was clearly constructed around the myth of a free, prosperous, industrious, Protestant people, for whom the 'other' was Catholic/despotic Europe or, later, godless revolutionary France. In Lancashire, Glasgow and Belfast Protestant workers were often Tory Unionists hostile to Irish Catholics. There remains some plausibility in Halévy's thesis that the religiosity of British workers played some role in preventing revolution. In industrial France the islands of working-class Catholicism were often resistant to the left and, after 1919, supported the Catholic union confederation (CFTC) which denounced its 'red' rivals as tools of Moscow. Yet, paradoxically, it may have been anticlericalism which played the key role in integrating workers into the bourgeois Republic. Both Marxists and syndicalists sometimes lamented that the atavistic detestation of the clergy which pervaded male working-class culture made it all too easy for secularist Republican bourgeois to pose as 'progressive'. However, it would be misleading simply to conclude that anticlericalism was the opiate of the French masses, a socialism of fools. For it was undoubtedly one of the bedrocks of French workers' precocious militancy. It made them suspicious of 'paternalist' Catholic employers and wary of attempts to use the clergy for industrial discipline. It made them wary, too, of the radical right which, it suspected of close ties with the old Catholic elites. And when Catholics accused the left of being 'unpatriotic', workers countered by arguing that Catholics' loyalties lay with Rome, and that countries under the yoke of clericalism were notable for their ignorance, poverty and oppression. Significantly the provocative secularist rituals of some working-class communities – secularist funerals, the 'de-baptising' of street names – were often accompanied by a rhetoric accusing God of being an ally of capitalism which was very different from that of 'official' Republican anticlericalism.

France was relatively precocious in family welfare provision, since the 'natalist' obsessions with falling birth rates, shared by Republicans and Catholics, led to support for 'maternalist' mainstream feminist demands for crèches, infant care clinics and maternity leave. Social care workers proliferated between the wars, though ironically many were Catholic 'professionals' who justified their apparent flouting of their own *femme au foyer* ideology by emphasising their mission to disseminate sound family practices to 'patriotic' working-class mothers.[10]

Wider claims have been advanced that the stabilisation of a capitalist-conservative Republic after 1880 was achieved by the coming together in 'para-political' groups of hitherto mutually antagonistic fractions of the elites – republicans, Radical 'solidarists', Catholic paternalists – to frame strategies capable of defusing rising working-class militancy. These embraced tariff protection and 'social imperialism' to safeguard 'French jobs', encouragement of profit sharing, palliative social legislation on mine safety (1890), child and female employment (1892), workers' housing (1894) and attempts to normalise industrial relations, culminating in Alexandre Millerand's attempts after 1900 to establish regular meetings between bureaucrats, employers and 'moderate' trade unionists. An increasing obsession with national 'degeneration' – as evidenced by high rates of venereal disease, alcoholism and tuberculosis – and the high proportion of doctors among Republican deputies, lent support to measures on medical provision and public hygiene.

Class cooperation and 'national solidarity' were emphasised. Industrialists and workers were NCOs and soldiers of an 'industrial army' engaged in 'battles' for national efficiency. Such rhetoric was derided by revolutionary syndicalists but in time pragmatists within the CGT and SFIO began to justify post-1914 collaboration with state and employers in the war effort as a prelude to a post-war neo-corporatist world in which such 'tripartite' collaboration in economic planning would allow France to escape from its economic backwardness into a high-productivity world of Taylorism and mass production which would guarantee decent pay and social provision. In this way former syndicalists such as Adolphe Merrheim or Léon Jouhaux adapted their emphasis on the worker-as-producer to fit a discourse about 'national efficiency'.[11]

However, whilst a plausible case can be made for the 'integrative'

10 P. Nord, 'The Welfare State in France', *French Historical Studies* 18 (1994), pp. 821–31.
11 S. Elwitt, *The Third Republic Defended. Bourgeois Social Reform in France* (Baton Rouge, La., Louisiana State University Press, 1986); K. M. Tucker, *French Revolutionary Syndicalism and the Public Sphere* (Cambridge, Cambridge University Press, 1996).

impact of Bismarckian welfare reforms, a similar case for France remains more questionable for several reasons.[12] First, deep rivalries persisted between different sections of French elites. These political fissures were exposed during the Dreyfus crisis. Catholic paternalists remained suspicious of 'statist' Radical-solidarist reforms. Secondly, the proportion of French workers covered by accident, sickness and pension provision varied between a quarter and half of comparable German levels. Thirdly, large employers, whose style and mind set remained essentially authoritarian, resisted 'intrusion' by factory inspectors, refused to negotiate with unions and were pushed into collective bargaining agreements only by quasi-revolutionary strikes (1919–20, 1936). Moreover they were adept at mobilising the anxieties of small employers reluctant to bear the tax burden of social reforms. Fourthly, Republican deputies were reluctant to break with *laissez-faire* dogma to fund worker housing – which remained among the worst in Western Europe – and the Senate regularly obstructed progressive income tax.[13] Finally even Radical governments – most notoriously that of Georges Clemenceau (1906–09) – regularly used troops against workers' strikes and demonstrations.[14]

Undoubtedly, therefore, many workers, faced with blatant contradictions between the 'fiction' of equal citizenship and continued social marginalisation, felt betrayed by the Republic. The failure of post-1918 governments to offer significant social reforms to reward workers for wartime sacrifices fuelled support for Communism. Wartime economic planning was abruptly dismantled, the aspirations of labour reformists to a role in post-war economic strategy ignored and many employers evaded the one major concession – the eight-hour day.

The Third Republic was dominated by centrist coalition governments reliant on middle-class, petty-bourgeois and peasant votes. Given France's gradual and uneven industrialisation, the working class remained, unlike in Britain, a minority class whose concerns were marginal to those of the Republican consensus. Whilst Republican politics, dominated by relatively modest doctors and lawyers, appeared 'democratic', the underlying power of the economic elite and of *grandes écoles-*

---

12 G. Steinmetz, *Regulating the Social. The Welfare State and Local Politics in Imperial Germany* (Princeton, N.J., Princeton University Press, 1993); J. Stone, *The Search for Social Peace. Reform Legislation in France 1890–1914* (Albany, N. Y., State University of New York, 1985).

13 A-L. Shapiro, *Housing the Poor of Paris* (Madison, Wis., University of Wisconsin Press, 1985).

14 A. Calhoun, 'The Politics of Internal Order. The French Government and Revolutionary Labour' *1898–1914* (University of Princeton Ph.D., 1973).

trained technocrats remained. In these circumstances the ability of labour to pressure governments into meaningful reform was always severely limited. But, in turn, this means that Republican attempts to woo the working class into a national consensus were only ever likely to achieve partial success.

Imperialism, popular culture and French labour

The 'peculiarities' of British labour history owe much to an imperial hegemony which created the super-profits to reward a 'labour aristocracy' and which nurtured popular assumptions of racial and cultural superiority which underlay much working-class Toryism. But in France, too, imperialism was an issue which left many labour activists and workers confused both in their ideological analysis and in their daily attitudes. For it was all too easy for the neo-Jacobin left to justify colonialism as part of France's emancipatory civilising mission, whilst the poverty of French Marxism precluded sophisticated analysis of capitalist imperialism. Consequently, even Jaurès, always ready to denounce the 'excesses' of colonial 'exploitation' (e.g. the Congo) praised French colonial schools as 'part of the difficult work of moral . . . assimilation' designed to turn Arabs into 'adoptive children of our country'. On the eve of 1914 M. Allard, in *L'Humanité*, described colonial peoples as 'grotesque primitives' requiring French tutorship.[15]

And yet 'social imperialism' was obviously a central strategy of Ferry's bourgeois Republicans, designed to woo metropolitan workers. Mass circulation newspapers and colonial expositions were used to emphasise the dependence of French industrial jobs on colonial markets and raw materials.[16] Socialist Paul Louis confessed that many workers were seduced by this propaganda, which began when schoolchildren were set class exercises composing admiring letters to conscripts in Indochina.

The left did criticise capital export to colonies as depriving domestic industry of investment, and deplored the blood shed by working-class conscripts to secure profits for colonial shareholders. But, too often, it felt obliged to pull its punches. For was not the economy of Marseilles – site of the 1906 Colonial Exposition – heavily dependent on colonial trade, and was not the Lyonnais silk industry reliant on raw silk from Indochina? Moreover, the reliance of the French economy on its colo-

15 F. Bédarida, 'Le mouvement ouvrier et l'impérialisme en France', *Mouvement Social* 88 (1974), pp. 25–42.
16 W. Schneider, *An Empire for the Masses* (New York, Greenwood Press, 1982).

nies increased in the inter-war period. The Colonial Exposition of 1931 helped sustain France's faltering image as a great power.[17]

The acute dilemmas posed by imperialism for the labour movement were apparent during the Rif War (1924–25), during which a combined force of half a million French and Spanish troops shelled Moroccan villages and burned crops in order to subdue Berber rebels. The far left, notably the Communist youth leader Jacques Doriot, made efforts to mobilise protest against these atrocities, culminating in a one-day General Strike in October 1925. Conscripts were urged to 'fraternise' with the rebels – and, indeed, some naval gunners were court-martialled for refusing to shell coastal villages. Yet the campaign exposed the multiple complicities of labour with the hegemonic imperialist culture of the bourgeois Republic. Aware of the anti-Arab racism permeating popular culture, the Communist leadership was lukewarm in its support for Doriot's anti-imperial rhetoric and merely reiterated the standard pre-1914 argument that colonial wars killed working-class conscripts to defend capitalist profits. SFIO spokesmen denounced Rif rebel leaders as 'feudal', justified France's 'civilising mission' to 'inferior races', warned that whites in North Africa faced the risk of massacre. They even championed the land settlement rights of small white *colons*. Socialist deputies failed to condemn the aerial bombing of Rif villages. Meanwhile Communist Party members in Algeria labelled the rebels reactionary fanatics, insisting that 'domination by cannibals is not desirable'. Whereas the Communists had had some success in 1923 in persuading conscripts to fraternise with German miners during the Ruhr occupation, anti-Arab racism proved a more formidable obstacle to internationalist solidarity than anti-Boche nationalism. Communist union organisers feared that they might push wavering members into rival reformist unions if they emphasised anti-imperialist rather than bread-and-butter economistic issues. Angry Comintern leaders denounced PCF leaders for being 'incorrigible social democrats' – and their party members in Algeria as 'possibly excellent Frenchmen but very indifferent Communists'.[18]

Most French workers appear to have given little thought to imperi-

17 J. Laffey, 'The Roots of French Imperialism: the Case of Lyon', *French Historical Studies* 6 (1969), pp. 78–92; A. Olivesi, 'Les Socialistes marseillais et le problème colonial', *Mouvement Social* 46 (1964), pp. 27–64; H. Lebovics, *True France. Wars over Cultural Identity* (Ithaca, N. Y., Cornell University Press, 1992); J. Marseille, *Empire colonial et capitalisme française* (Paris, Albin Michel, 1984).

18 All quotes in this paragraph are from D. Slavin, 'The French Left and the Rif War: Racism and the Limits of Internationalism', *Journal of Contemporary History* 26 (1991), pp. 5–32.

alism – an issue debated at only two of thirty-two labour congresses between 1886 and 1914. But in popular *roman feuilleton* novels and in the cinema the Legionnaire became a celebrated hero – and the 'Arab' a scheming, fanatical villain. The colonial army figured prominently in the popular cinema of the 1930s – for ever hunting down 'the bastards south of Sidi Bel Abbès' and 'making men' of its raw recruits. Then, as earlier, military service played a role in rites of passage into virile masculinity – 'bon pour l'armée, bon pour les filles'.[19]

Workers, army, nation and revolution

Conscription does appear to have been quite effective as an instrument of national integration in France, where the ethos of an equal civic duty to serve in the 'nation in arms' became a cornerstone of Republican ideology. The Achilles heel of protest strikes in 1916–18 was the vulnerability of strikers in the armament plants to accusations of being *embusqués* (shirkers), evading their Republican duty of paying the *impôt du sang*.[20] Moreover, many workers looked back with affection on their conscript days – perceived as a welcome break with the routine of family and factory, a chance to experience a wider world. Undoubtedly, too, army service helped to construct a sense of 'the foreigner'.[21]

However, it is misleading to present too unambiguously rosy a picture of army–worker relations. For the Dreyfus affair highlighted the reactionary political sympathies of many officers. Furthermore the image of the army in working-class communities was sullied by its regular role in strike breaking and by periodic shooting of demonstrators by troops, as at Fourmies in 1891 in the northern textile region or at Villeneuve-Saint-George in 1908, where cavalry charged a demonstration of construction workers protesting at an earlier police shooting of strike leaders.

Moreover there were traditions of resistance to conscription in 'peripheral' regions. In 'red' Lower Languedoc Prussian victories over the Bonapartist army in 1870–71 were widely celebrated. During the 'Révolte du Midi' (1905–07) local conscripts mutinied when ordered to control wine grower protests – an episode provoking rightist condemnation of southern 'mongrels' and fears that southern conscripts might

19 G. Vincendeau and K. Reader (eds), *La Vie est à nous. French Cinema of the Popular Front 1935–38* (London, British Film Institute, 1986)

20 J. Horne, 'L'impôt du sang: Republican Rhetoric and Industrial Warfare in France 1914–18', *Social History* 10 (1989), pp. 45–64.

21 V. Kiernan, 'Conscript and Society in Europe before the War of 1914–18' in M. R. D. Foot (ed.), *War and Society* (London, Elek, 1973).

refuse to defend France in the coming war. However, it is unwise to exaggerate the ideological or *occitan* regionalist implications of such 'anti-militarism'. Conscription evasion was as high in neighbouring Catholic conservative Lozère as in radical Hérault, the influence of Montpellier-based syndicalism waned after 1910 and in 1914 most Midi conscripts 'did their duty'.[22] Syndicalists, who sought to mobilise workers against a 'militarism' which denoted both internal social repression and the threat of war, attempted to develop links between trade unions and conscripts (the 'Sou du Soldat' campaign) and to convert European trade unions to the CGT strategy of an anti-war General Strike. Yet despite the strength of support for the 1913–14 campaign against the Three Year Conscription Act the overall impression remains that it was the military's internal role which was the source of most worker 'anti-militarism'.[23]

When war came, fears of widespread resistance to mobilisation proved groundless. The mood of August 1914 was one of resigned but dutiful Republican patriotism,[24] and the morale of France's 'citizens' army' was sustained more firmly than that of most belligerents. The attitudes of ordinary trench soldiers – among whom the working class was relatively underrepresented – suggest deep hostility to the gung-ho super-patriotism ('eyewash') of journalists like Barrès and to the army high command, combined with acceptance of discipline because it was consented to by 'citizen soldiers' rather than imposed by Junker *seigneurs*. There was a sense of alienation from civilian society, where armament workers enjoyed 'cushy' jobs and women excessive social and sexual freedom.

Such sentiments were complex, politically ambiguous. The left could hope to tap resentment against ultra-patriotic propaganda and against war profiteers. But there was comparable hostility to 'shirker' engineering workers whose complaints about excessive hours, 'deskilling' and industrial accidents cut little ice with troops hardened to trench horrors. For all their often expressed sense of alienation from civilian life, troops yearned for contact with and recognition by the 'hearth and home' for which they were fighting. The sense of defending the Republican *patrie* was made tangible by feeling that the only justification for the blood shed on Flanders soil would be the liberation of northern France. Hatred of 'the Boche' heightened the popular sense of national identity – even if there was a certain empathy with the

22 J. Maurin, *Armée–guerre–societé. Soldats Languedociens 1889–1919* (Paris, Sorbonne, 1982).

23 J. Howorth, 'French Workers and German Workers: the Impossibility of Internationalism', *European History Quarterly* 15 (1985), pp. 71–9.

24 J-J. Becker, *The Great War and the French People* (Leamington Spa, Berg, 1985).

sufferings of ordinary German soldiers. And, like soldiers on the eastern front in the Second World War expressing pride in 'quality German work', so the *poilus* ('tommies') referred to themselves as artisans determined to do a proper job.[25]

Trench experience proved 'the test of truth of national feeling . . . crowned with tragic success for the entire French nation'.[26] The trauma of personal and family loss was etched in the memory of millions. Over half (3 million) of surviving war veterans joined Ancien Combattants associations, which, although skewed towards villages and small towns, had many working-class members. The Catholic UNC was sometimes manipulated by the *patronat* (e.g. Lorraine) to mobilise loyal company workers. Conversely some 300,000 veterans joined a variety of Communist, trade union and laic associations. Undoubtedly the denunciation of futile carnage in Barbusse's *Le Feu* reflected the bitterness of those ex-soldiers who rallied to Communism in 1920.[27]

However, most working-class veterans joined mainstream associations. These were not bellicose or proto-fascist. They supported the League of Nations and disliked military parades – insisting that the *poilus* had fought against militarism. But their staunch Republican patriotism and pride in the virtues of the 'citizen soldier' show how profound the impact of the teaching in the laic school had been. France, home of the rights of man, could have fought the war only for democracy and freedom – not for sordid economic or imperial goals. The dominant rhetoric was of 'fraternity of the trenches', of inter-class and of Republican unity.

Yet this is not the whole story. The industrial unrest of 1917–18 revealed the strains on patriotic loyalties, whilst the unprecedented scale of the quasi-syndicalist militancy of 1919–20 reflected the appeal of the Soviet myth to workers disillusioned by the absence of post-war reforms. A war which drew labour leaders into collaboration with the state ended by deepening earlier fissures in the labour movement and driving large sectors of the working class into the Communist Party.

J-L. Robert's study of Paris suggests, however, a picture rather more

25 S. Audoin-Rouzeau, *Men at War 1914–18. National Sentiment and French Journalism during the First World War* (Oxford, Berg, 1992); A. Lüdtke, 'The Appeal of Exterminating Others: German Workers and the Limits of Resistance', *Journal of Modern History* 64 (supplement), 1992, pp. 46–67.

26 A. Prost, *In the Wake of War. Les Anciens Combattants and French Society 1914–39* (Oxford, Berg, 1992).

27 H. Barbusse, *Le Feu* (Paris, Flammarion, 1916); L. Barthas, *Carnets de guerre de Louis Barthas, tonnelier 1914–18* (Paris, Maspéro, 1978); D. Troyansky, 'Monumental Politics: National History and Local Memory in French *Monuments aux morts*', *French Historical Studies* 15 (1987), pp. 121–41.

nuanced than that of a reformist majority supporting the *Union Sacrée* whilst a growing 'pacifist' minority voice increasingly strident dissent.[28] Certainly key SFIO and CGT leaders (Henri Sellier, Jouhaux) were drawn into collaboration in the war effort – and dreamed of a post-war world where labour would, routinely, be consulted on national economic strategies. The proximity of German offensives made the 'German peril' feel real to working-class Parisians and served to tone down the 'pacifist' thrust of the 1918 strikes. And some reformist labour leaders lapsed into Barrèsian rhetoric about defending 'French soil' from 'Boche brutes'.

Yet among the most ardent supporters of national defence were neo-Blanquist workers whose bastions (e.g. Belleville) had been strongholds of the Commune. Belleville gave 60 per cent of its votes to the SFIO, 39 per cent of its funerals were secular and it staged annual clashes with the police during demonstrations to honour the martyred Communards. For Belleville militants France remained the world's emancipatory hope, Paris the revolutionary heart of France and Belleville the revolutionary *quartier*. To such Bellevillois workerist chauvinists the male skilled worker was the culture hero, everyone else – not merely capitalists but women, immigrants, provincial workers, peasants – an alien 'other'. Vaillant, the local deputy, evoked the assumptions behind Belleville's wartime stance:

The people of Paris, the working-class population, which suffers in its slums but which intends to stay free, master of its own destiny, and to transform the city. The people of Paris, incomparable in their beauty and moral grandeur, know that in [the city] beats the heart and thinks the mind of the Nation, which would be mortally wounded by its fall.[29]

The true bulwarks of the anti-war left included the building unions and the rapidly growing metal and rail unions, whose strongholds were in the industrial suburbs. Yet even left syndicalists remained aware of the German threat. 'Let us beware,' one warned, 'of our own *tempéramant exalté*, for it is futile to have made three revolutions only to fall under the jackboot of Junker *hobéraux*.' It was hazardous to build an anti-war coalition round the grievances of skilled *métallos* in the armament plants because *poilus* believed that 'while they are getting the shit kicked out of them in the trenches, we are "shirkers" earning forty francs a day . . .'[30]

Many workers were simultaneously committed to national defence,

28 J-L. Robert, *Les Ouvriers, la patrie et la révolution. Paris 1914–19* (Paris, Annales Littéraires, 1995).
29 Cited in Robert, *Les Ouvriers*, p. 45.
30 *Ibid.*, p. 216.

yearning for peace initiatives and filled with bitter social resentment. Armament manufacturers were denounced as authoritarian 'tsars' and as war profiteers. Peace was eagerly anticipated 'so that we can resume the [real] war – against capitalism'.[31] Sometimes women and immigrant workers were denounced, in misogynistic and xenophobic phraseology, by syndicalists – because their cheap labour helped prolong the war. And the response of many workers to Bolshevism reflected injured national pride. Was it not humiliating that France, *patrie* of the revolution, should allow 'backward' Russia to assume the leadership of world revolution?

Workers and the populist radical right

France developed a variety of radical right populisms which targeted the left's social constituency. Two of these, popular royalism and Bonapartist populism, began before our period but influenced the politics of the Third Republic. One response of opponents of 1789 was to claim that if the revolution's beneficiaries were bourgeois capitalists, then the ousted clerical-aristocratic elites could pose as 'paternalistic' defenders of 'little people' left exposed to the chill winds of the free market. The resultant *politique du pire* – flirtation with the left against hegemonic bourgeois liberalism – became central to Legitimist politics. During the Second Republic the royalist 'White Montagnards' welcomed mass suffrage and mobilised Catholic artisans in the Midi. In 1865 the Legitimist pretender Chambord claimed that the monarchy had always been the working class's protector. During the 1880s the royalist aristocrat de Mun advocated legislation to curb *laissez-faire* excesses – and two decades later the Action Française, which added a touch of 'modern' nationalism and positivism to the royalist tradition – was encouraging its jailed activists to fraternise with syndicalist prisoners and sing alternate choruses of the *Internationale* and *Vive Henri V!*[32]

Although royalists fantasised about alliances between 'sons of Chouans and sons of Jacobins', Bonapartism had more plausible claims to a share of the Jacobin legacy. In his final years Napoleon I posed as the 'people's emperor' – the champion of a revolution whose enemies were kings, aristocrats and priests and whose dream was emancipation of Europe's people. Much popular radicalism after 1815 was voiced in Bonapartist rather than republican phraseology – and much of Louis Napoleon's success derived from astute manipulation of his uncle's pop-

---

31 *Ibid.*, p. 192.
32 R. Gildea, *The Past in French History* (New Haven, Conn., Yale University Press, 1994), chapter 7.

ulist myth. Until the last years of the Second Empire Bonapartism retained mass support via populist gestures, the use of *dirigiste* economic policies to maintain full employment and an anti-Hapsburg foreign policy which won the applause of radical Lyons workers.[33]

By the 1880s Legitimism's blend of ultramontane Catholicism and social paternalism had little appeal in industrial France, whilst Bonapartism had retreated to a few rural bastions in the south-west. But as the Republic sought to consolidate itself it faced the challenge of a new radical right which exhibited a disconcerting capacity to appropriate elements of the left's ideology and to woo segments of its social base. Having alienated Catholics via the secular education laws, Republicans outraged 'Jacobin' patriots (e.g. Paul Déroulède) by apparent subservience to Bismarck and angered their urban 'little man' voters by failing to protect them against the Great Depression. 'Boulangism' was, thus, an ephemeral alliance of the discontented – ranging socially from Catholic landowners via threatened small businessmen to unemployed workers and politically from royalists and neo-Bonapartists via maverick radicals to neo-Blanquist socialists. Its ideological underpinnings included the rejection of 'corrupt' parliamentary government and an insistence that the Republican elites were failing to defend the national interest against Germany. A 'national anti-capitalism' directed against 'international' Jewish finance capital was combined with a 'national socialism' – hostile to internationalist, 'Jewish' Marxism – and the championing of 'national labour' against immigrant workers.

Much of this has affinities with elements of classic 'left-wing' ideology. From the *sans-culottes* onwards there had been populist suspicions of 'oligarchic' parliamentarianism. Concern over appeasement of Bismarck came naturally to heirs of the Commune. Proudhonists and Blanquists had long denounced the money power of the Rothschilds. Sternhell argues that whilst Boulangism's funding came from the royalist right, its cadres were recruited on the left.[34] When Barrès attracted anti-immigration working-class votes in Nancy his campaign manager was a Blanquist. One may, thus, define Boulangism as a movement of the 'left' – or, at least, of that sizeable element of the left which blamed the problems of the 'little man' on the machinations of the financial oligarchy. However, Sternhell pushes his case too far. Boulangism occurred

33 B. Ménager, *Les Napoléon du peuple* (Paris, Aubier, 1988); R. Magraw, 'The People's Emperor? Louis Napoleon and Popular Bonapartism', *Modern History Review* 8 (1997), pp. 28–30.
34 Z. Sternhell, *La Droite révolutionnaire en France 1885–1914* (Paris, Senil, 1978); P. Mazgaj, 'The Origins of the French Radical Right', *French Historical Studies* 15 (1988), pp. 287–315.

at a specific moment when a still inchoate labour movement was still recovering from post-Commune repression and when unions, legalised only in 1884, were weak. Populist anxieties could, thus, easily be channelled into a catch-all protest movement. However, during the 1890s the rise of socialism and of the CGT allowed Marxist and syndicalist ideologies to distance themselves from antisemitic populism. For Barrès antisemitism was designed to direct workers' anger against 'Jewish' capital, and hence away from productive French capital. He aimed not to recruit warriors for the class war but to build inter-class national solidarities against Jews and immigrants. In alarm most mainstream socialists stepped back, albeit belatedly, from the 'careless' rhetorical equation 'Jew' = Rothschild = capitalist of which even Jaurès was guilty. Those who refused to adapt, such as some neo-Blanquists, were marginalised. Simultaneously the growing militancy of CGT-affiliated Jewish artisans in the Marais led to the 'discovery' of a Jewish proletariat and the dispelling of tenacious stereotypes. In 1909 when electricians' union leader Emile Pataud called Jews the 'enemies of the proletariat' he faced both condemnation from the CGT and a mass protest by Jewish workers.[35]

Moreover, contacts between the populist radical right and traditional conservatism were closer than Sternhell allows. Eduard Drumont's ideology, for all his rhetorical sympathy with the Communards, had clear affinities with the traditional religious antisemitism of *La Croix*. Déroulède jettisoned his Jacobin past to espouse crude revanchism, whilst Barrès's blood-and-soil racism and cult of leadership were clearly proto-Fascist. By 1900 there was little in the New Nationalists' blend of irrationalism, Social Darwinism, Le Bon-ist crowd psychology, biological racism, or in their ties with army and Church which gave them affinities with the mainstream left.[36]

Efforts of the radical right to build bridges to 'patriotic' workers enjoyed only sporadic success. Syndicalism – despite its anti-militarist/anti-patriotic rhetoric – has, as the Italian example shows, certain affinities with fascism. Both glorify activist, heroic minorities and the cathartic role of violence in combating corrupt bourgeois liberalism. Both scorn parliaments and favour corporate representation of the workplace. But the notorious syndicalist/Action Française flirtation (1908–14) proved a marginal sideshow, involving maverick syndicalist

35 N. Green, 'Socialist Antisemitism, Defence of a Bourgeois Jew and the Discovery of a Jewish Proletariat', *International Review of Social History* 30 (1985), pp. 374–99.
36 J. Schwartzmantel, 'Nationalism and the French Working Class', in E. Cahm and V. Fisera (eds), *Socialism and Nationalism*, 2 vols (Nottingham, University of Nottingham Press, 1979–80).

intellectuals more than worker militants. The Cercle Proudhon, built around a selective reinvention of Proudhon as an anti-Marxist, antisemitic, patriotic socialist, remained tiny.[37]

Certainly working-class support for the radical right was never insignificant. Boulangism attracted anti-immigrant votes in frontier regions (Lorraine, Nord). 'Yellow' unions led by ex-syndicalist Biétry – and financed by employers and royalists – attracted Carmaux miners, Lille textile workers and Paris butchers in the 1900s by appealing to 'patriotic' workers, disgusted by the 'Jewish' Republic and the efforts of Marxist strikers to wreck the economy.[38] The social Catholic right, which dabbled in antisemitism, had support among the charity-dependent poor in company towns and among Nord textile workers. In the 1920s such workers voted for the centre-right Fédération Républicaine. But when the Depression heightened tensions with this party, some of its working-class electors drifted to the quasi-fascist Parti Social Français (PSF).[39]

Many who ostensibly sought a 'socialism of national unity' foundered for want of a sustained working-class base. George Valois's Faisceau sought to recreate 'the solidarity of the trenches' by uniting war veterans and producers against parliament and plutocracy – but most workers were made wary by his praise of Mussolini and his funding by the perfume magnate François Coty. Both Marcel Déat and Jacques Doriot – defectors respectively from the SFIO and the PCF – began by arguing that to defeat fascism one needed to woo the middle classes and cadres by promises of a productivist, managed economy but themselves drifted towards fascism when they found that the bulk of their working-class electors remained loyal to the emerging Popular Front. Undoubtedly both Jacques Doriot's Parti Populaire Français and the PSF did have blue-collar support in 1937–39 – but since neither ever fought a general election it is difficult to estimate its extent. For most of the 1930s the radical right lost the battle of the streets and made no really significant inroads into the left's core working-class constituency – although at a local level in Marseilles maverick ex-Communist Simon Sabiani developed an idiosyncratic blend of rightist populism, gangsterism and clientelist machine politics. What was disturbing, however, was

37 P. Mazgaj, *The Action Française and Revolutionary Syndicalism* (Chapel Hill, N. C., University of North Carolina Press, 1979); D. Roberts, *The Syndicalist Tradition in Italian Fascism* (Manchester, Manchester University Press, 1979).

38 G. Mosse, 'The French Right and the Working Class. Les Jaunes', *Journal of Contemporary History* 7 (1972), pp. 185–208.

39 J. Sweets, 'Hold that Pendulum: Redefining Fascism and Resistance in France', *French Historical Studies* 15 (1988), pp. 731–58.

the extent to which its xenophobia set the tone of debates about immigrants.[40]

Immigrant labour and the working class

France has long been Europe's melting pot, a fact largely obscured by historians' selective amnesia. From the 1850s onwards large-scale labour immigration influenced both the structures of the labour force and French workers' national consciousness. The need for immigrant labour was an indirect consequence of the survival of the peasantry. Anti-seigneurial revolution in 1789 had won it the right to stay on the land. To avoid subdivision of their farms peasants became precocious practitioners of birth control. After the advent of male suffrage (1848) no government could ignore the interests of peasant voters – hence the reintroduction of tariff protection in the 1880s to cushion agriculture against imports and the rhetoric of Third Republic politicians nurturing the aspirations of peasant parents for white-collar jobs for their newly literate offspring.[41]

The net outcome was that, when heavy industry began to expand, labour supply bottle necks developed. A pattern emerged of immigrant influxes in boom years (1850–65, 1896–1920s, 1950–60), interspersed with small net outflows during recessions (1880–96, 1930s). By 1850 Belgians were an established feature of Nord textiles. By the 1890s Lorraine's steelworkers and iron miners were overwhelmingly Italian, and by the 1920s Polish miners were ubiquitous throughout the Pas-de-Calais coalfield. Immigrants were prominent in the engineering and chemical plants of the Parisian and Lyonnais banlieues, in Midi vineyards and in the Bouches-du-Rhône, where, by 1930, they comprised 20 per cent of the labour force. Chinese, Indochinese and Turks were among those imported to work in war industries in 1914–18, whilst colonial immigration expanded in the 1920s.[42]

It is not inevitable that an ethnically diverse labour force must succumb to nativist racism. The dominant ideologies of French labour – neo-Jacobin, Marxist, syndicalist – were all, in theory, sympathetic to

40 P. Jankowski, *Communism and Collaboration. Simon Sabiani and Politics in Marseille* (New Haven, Conn., Yale University Press, 1992).

41 G. Noiriel, *Le Creuset français. Histoire de l'immigration* (Paris, Editions du Seuil, 1988); G. Noiriel, 'Amnesia and Memory', *French Historical Studies* 19 (1995), pp. 367–80.

42 Immigrant Workers in France: 1830, 380,000; 1871, 700,000; 1891, 1,130,000; 1911, 1,160,000; 1929, 3,000,000; 1935, 2,500,000. See G. Cross, *Immigrant Workers in Industrial France* (Philadelphia, Temple University Press, 1983).

oppressed workers of all races. And there were encouraging examples of the successful integration of immigrants into local labour movements. In Nord textile towns second-generation Belgians played an active role in the 1880s in building the Marxist POF – although its leader, Guesde, revived his earlier complaints about an 'alien invasion' when, after 1900, employees used *frontaliers* (cross-border commuters) as strike breakers. Similarly, years of anti-Italian violence around Marseilles were halted when exiled cadres of the Italian Socialist Party began to unionise their compatriots and persuade them not to act as blacklegs. By 1899–1901 Italians were participating in major dock and construction strikes and Jaurès addressed mass rallies to celebrate new-found internationalist solidarities. In 1906 the Voiron (Isère) textile strike was led by an Italian.[43]

In time many second-generation immigrants came to identify with the labour movement as a vehicle of their aspirations. Many adapted to French working-class culture, became dechristianised and took advantage of the 1889 law to become naturalised. From the inter-war years to the present – to Le Pen's disgust! – many of France's international football players have been working-class immigrants. The vibrant combative labour movement of the 1900s or of the Popular Front offered a positive pole of attraction. And certainly the Communist union confederation (the CGTU) made real efforts to mobilise immigrants and to champion their cause.

Xenophobia was contained, at least during economic booms, because immigrants accepted jobs – in steel mills, chemical plants, sewers, coal pits – with little appeal to French peasants and artisans. 'What French worker,' asked *L'Humanité* (1920), 'would choose the "Calvary" of inhaling lung-wrecking dust "sanding" down Citroën car panels?'[44] French craft industry and peasant pluri-activity were, indeed, offered an extended lease of life only because immigrants filled gaps in the labour market by doing heavy, unskilled jobs. This also allowed French employees to move 'upward' into supervisory and white-collar jobs. In short, the classic trajectory which saw sons and grandsons of peasants and artisans ascend into the professions by way of jobs as primary school teachers or minor civil servants built on the sweat of

43 P. Milza, *Français et Italiens à la fin due XIX siècle*, 2 vols (Rome, Ecole Français de Rome, 1981); J. Reardon, 'Belgian and French Workers in Nineteenth Century Roubaix', in C. and L. Tilly (eds), *Class Conflict and Collective Action* (Beverly Hills, Cal., Sage, 1981); D. Bigorgne, 'Main d'oeuvre étrangère et mouvement ouvrier: l'example des Belges dans les Ardennes frontalières', *Mouvement Social* 178 (1997), pp. 10–25.
44 Cited in S. Sirot, 'La condition du travail des ouvriers coloniaux à Paris 1918–36', *Revue Française d'Histoire d'Outre-mer* 83 (1996), pp. 65–92; quote on p. 77.

blue-collar immigrants. Hence it is misleading to assume undifferen-
tiated, unrelenting hostility towards immigrants. Colonial workers in
1920s Paris faced underlying currents of racism, yet they did such poorly
paid, unhealthy jobs that few French envied them and the labour market
was so segmented that there was little direct job competition. However,
when, during economic slumps, unemployed French skilled workers
were pushed into seeking labouring jobs they found them already occupied by immigrants. This was the context of the xenophobic violence
which erupted in Midi vineyards in the 1880s or on big-city building sites
in the 1930s.

The role played by immigrants in the strategies of the *patronat* was
bound to anger French workers. Many immigrants came from low-wage
countries with weak trade union traditions. Lacking the vote in France,
they feared deportation if they offended police or employers. Employers
thus viewed them as a cheap, flexible, docile reserve army of labour –
which could be used to depress wage levels, break strikes or, as in the
Rive-de-Giers glass industry in 1894, to 'dilute' skilled jobs. Hence when
French militants reacted in such circumstances they exhibited an incon-
gruous blend of class consciousness and xenophobia. In La Mure
(Isère), in 1901, armed miners forced 800 Italians to flee – and
demanded that management should employ sacked strikers from
Montceau-les-Mines in their place. Racist terms (*Kaffir*) came to rival
renard as slang for a blackleg. Strikers questioned the 'patriotism' of
employers who denounced 'Marxist internationalism' yet gave 'French'
jobs to immigrants. In extreme cases workers' demonstrations could
alternate singing the *Internationale* with chanting anti-immigrant
slogans!

There was a 'workerist' logic in critiques of 'docile' immigrants.
Poles and Italians were accused of being *cléricos*, whose docility stemmed
from lack of sound Gallic anticlerical instincts – even if immigrants from
the Romagna inherited an anticlericalism whose ferocity put that of
most French workers to shame! But undoubtedly French workers'
responses could degenerate into open and murderous racism – most
notoriously in the lynching of at least fifty Italians at Aigues-Mortes
(Gard) in 1893. Levels of violence were lower in the 1930s, but racist kill-
ings were still not uncommon.[45] Most victims of such collective violence
were newer, less assimilated, immigrants. In Marseilles in the 1880s
established Piedmontese participated in attacks on recent arrivals from

45 M. Perrot, *Workers on Strike. France 1871–90* (Leamington Spa, Berg, 1987); P. Milza,
    Les Français devant l'immigration (Brussels, Editions Complexes, 1988); R. Schor,
    L'Opinion français et les étrangères 1919–39 (Paris, Sorbonne, 1985).

central Italy. Colonial workers were a particular target. Many of the 150,000 non-Europeans employed during the Great War were, in effect, forced labour. Lodged in segregated barracks, they suffered several race riots in 1917–18. Bureaucrats and workers alike appeared obsessed with the danger of sexual relations between them and French women – and trade unionists warned of a future France populated by the offspring of these promiscuous racial inferiors. Even CGTU militants who in the 1920s made genuine efforts to mobilise colonial immigrants sometimes evoked their 'natural savagery' to explain recruitment difficulties.[46]

Two-thirds of major xenophobic incidents in the period 1867–83 occurred between 1883 and 1889 – at the height of the depression. The departure of some immigrants during economic slumps failed to prevent simplistic correlations between immigration and unemployment levels. Cyclical and structural capitalist crises were all too easily blamed on immigrants, who became more 'visible' as unemployed French workers found unskilled jobs occupied by 'foreigners' whose children were perceived as imposing an extra burden on the education and welfare services. The mass press of the 1880s and the 1930s, local and national, gave the 'problem' publicity by publishing letters from 'outraged' patriotic workers denouncing immigrant job stealers, scroungers and criminals.

International rivalries heightened such economic tensions. During the 1880s anxieties about Bismarckian Germany were compounded when Italy, Germany's new ally, challenged French hegemony in North Africa and erected tariffs against French exports. Anti-Italian riots in Marseilles (1881) were triggered by Italian workers jeering at French troops disembarking from Tunisia. Striking Italian dock workers (1900) were accused by the right of being a fifth column whose aim was to wreck the Marseilles economy for the benefit of Genoa. However, the Franco-Italian *rapprochement* after 1898 reduced these ethnic tensions in Provence. The Italian government, fearing German financial and technological hegemony, was seeking access to French financial markets to service Italy's debts. Ironically, Italian government officials actually encouraged exiled Italian socialists to persuade Italian immigrants to join trade unions in order to reduce tensions with French workers.

The radical right always saw immigration as the left's Achilles heel. Marginalised intellectuals of the populist right could carve out a distinct political niche by denouncing Republican politicians who sat idly by whilst 'childless', 'Malthusian' France was 'swamped' by 'niggers' (Drieu

---

46 T. Stovall, 'Colour-blind France? Colonial Workers during World War I', *Race and Class* 35 (1993), pp. 41–56.

la Rochelle) whilst themselves gloating over the discomfiture of an 'internationalist' left unable to protect its proletarian base against immigrant job stealers without jettisoning its principles. There was, crowed the *Action Française*, 'a healthy revival of national sentiment' even in the 'gangrened heart' of the labour movement. For 'the most ardent revolutionary worker, . . . internationalist in theory, reacts like the most ardent patriot' as soon as his livelihood was affected.[47] The right-wing press warned workers that it was not only was the nation that was under threat but also the more homely, local *chez nous* of the popular *quartier*. Doctors were cited warning that 'unhygienic' immigrants spread disease. Immigrants, the royalist writer Pierre Gaxotte reminded his readers, were those with funny names who polluted the *quartier* with foul cooking smells and held up post office queues because they could not read the forms.

Faced with such crude populist appeals to the 'common sense' of 'ordinary' workers, the left felt obliged to 'bend' its principles. In the 1880s Guesde fulminated against the 'immigrant invasion'. In 1899 the CGT pressured for quotas on immigrants in public works contracts and in the 1920s secured union representation on job placement agencies in order to channel the flow of immigrants away from its members' skilled, big-city jobs. By 1932, when the SFIO voted for tighter immigration restrictions, voices on the left were insisting that France could no longer afford its historic humanitarian principles, that immigrants lacked French labour's heritage of struggling for social justice and that the Great War had not been fought simply to hand jobs to immigrants. Sadly, even the Communists, who had hitherto fought hard for immigrants' rights, began for electoral purposes during the Popular Front to adapt to the prevailing mood as in their new 'patriotic' guise they 'held out their hand' to 'all good Frenchmen' – among whom were not only Catholics but members of the quasi-fascist Croix de Feu.

The late 1930s witnessed a rare moment of national consensus – based on the protection of French culture against aliens. Despite the Popular Front's anti-fascist rhetoric, the left appeared mesmerised by an agenda set by the xenophobic right. The building union leader Emile Caporali was criticised by his own union for urging the CGT to defend immigrant workers. Henri Dubreuil was saddened by the shift in the language of labour leaders. 'How is it possible,' he asked, 'that to a worker and a socialist a man can be a "foreigner"? It all shows the futility of fifty years of internationalist propaganda.' The Communist Henri Constant clearly diagnosed the danger faced by the left:

47 Cited in Schor, *L'Opinion français*, p. 483.

The goal of chauvinist propaganda is to weed out from workers' consciousness the concept of class struggle and to replace it by the belief that the national community, the solidarity of all Frenchmen, will save the proletariat from the disaster into which capitalism has plunged it.[48]

But an ageing France, alarmed at the spectre of war, insecure, made anxious by the challenge of industrial change to its 'stalemate society', found immigrants the ideal scapegoats. By 1939 much of the left remained silent whilst the right denounced Spanish Republican refugees as atheistic nun killers. These refugees were the living embodiment of the bad tidings which an insular, ostrich-like French public did not wish to hear: that Europe was a continent on the brink of disaster. Insults to immigrant workers in cafés, on buses, in the workplace, became the daily norm. The rhetoric of 'invaders', 'Attila's hordes', 'leprosy' was voiced even by some trade unionists. Arthur Koestler's account of his experiences as a foreign refugee in the France of 1939–40 – aptly entitled 'Scum of the Earth' – provides graphic evidence of how France's plight was blamed, by countless 'ordinary' Frenchmen, on immigrants.[49]

Immigrant labour proved extraordinarily useful to the *grand patronat*. Because immigrants supplied the cheap labour which underpinned the 'second industrial revolution' it was, unsurprisingly, right-centre pro-business parties (e.g. the Fédération Républicaine) that were the staunchest advocates of free entry for foreign workers. And yet, whenever the labour movement sought to recruit such workers, businessmen politicians adeptly played the patriotic card. The textile magnate Eugène Motte defeated Guesde in Roubaix (1898) by claiming that socialists were 'soft' on immigrant labour! Lorraine steel barons like François Wendel cultivated the loyalty of their French company workers by playing on the 'patriotism' of this frontier region – presiding over war veterans' ceremonies at war memorials. During the 1900 CGT-led strike they appealed to 'loyal' French workers against 'knife-wielding' Italian strikers. They funded Pierre Biétry's xenophobic 'yellow' unions. And yet when labour leaders sought to woo French workers by advocating quotas to prevent 'excessive' immigration these same employers claimed to be the 'true internationalists', since they alone believed in a free international labour market.[50]

In the 1840s attacks on Belgian workers were shrugged off as regrettable expressions of local job rivalries in the midst of economic

---

48 *Ibid.*, p. 503.
49 A. Koestler, *The Scum of the Earth* (London, Hutchinson, 1968).
50 D. Gordon, *Liberalism and Social Reform. Industrial Growth and 'Progressive' Politics in France 1880–1914* (Westport, Conn., Greenwood Press, 1996); G. Noiriel, *Longwy. Immigrés et prolétaires. 1880–1980* (Paris, Presses Universitaires de France, 1984).

depression. But the 'dangerous classes' of the big cities were French rural migrants, whilst to many settled workers 'foreign' immigrants were no stranger than Limousin or Auvergnat provincial migrants. Two developments of the 1880s and 1890s signalled a major watershed. Firstly the emerging welfare state began to construct clear distinctions between 'French' and 'foreign'. 'Foreigners' were those denied the benefits of social legislation – eligible neither to be mine safety delegates (1890) nor for free medical treatment (1893). The Belgian parliament protested at the 'chauvinistic' exclusion of Belgian immigrants from the 1898 Accident Compensation Law. Simultaneously, immigrants faced specific exclusion from posts in the civil service, municipal government and the public services and were subjected to new styles of surveillance and policing. By 1922 they were obliged to carry identity cards containing data on the size of their fingers and ears. Complaints that immigrants were treated 'like criminals' were correct – since the dominant contemporary school of criminology, influenced by Cesare Lombroso, explicitly correlated propensity to criminality with race. The press highlighted 'scientific' criminal statistics purporting to show an immigrant crime propensity four times higher than that of the native population.

Conclusion: 'good' and 'bad' nationalisms?

In contrast to the racist, xenophobic cultural authoritarian-populist nationalism, of which Le Pen is the heir, Jacobin republican patriotism appears the decent child of the 'good' Enlightenment – civic, political, voluntarist, democratic, cosmopolitan. Its defenders emphasise that in sharp contrast to the German laws of 1913, which define 'nationality' in terms of ethnicity and culture, Republican citizenship has been open to anyone born or resident in France – of whatever 'race'- who chooses to become 'French'.[51] Moreover, Jacobin republican patriotism was universalist and emancipatory. 'Patriots and Internationalists,' claimed the Socialist Saint-Mandé programme (1896), 'these are two titles that our French Revolution ancestors knew . . . how to reconcile.' Why, Jaurès asked, did self-proclaimed 'nationalists' lay special claim to that word? 'We, too, seek to defend the Nation's independence . . . from foreign aggression . . . a precondition of . . . human progress.' A 'free . . . and powerful France,' he added, 'remains a force . . . for human progress and the emancipation of workers.'

Such rhetoric was more than mere self-delusion. For two centuries

---

51 C. Mondinoco-Torri, 'Aux origines dès la code de nationalité en France', *Mouvement Social* 171 (1995), pp. 31–46.

many foreign progressives have felt Paris to be their second spiritual home. Yet there remain certain problems with this optimistic interpretation of the Jacobin legacy. For the radical right was not just a pale imitation of unsavoury 'German' ethnic nationalism. It had authentic French roots, and some of these derived from the culture of the left – from Jacobin obsession with national unity to anti-capitalist antisemitism – and it did recruit a steady trickle of defectors from the left. Furthermore there is surely a real danger of arrogance in a tradition which views France not as *a* but as *the* nation and as the emancipatory hope of the world. It assumes that foreigners lack the commitment to struggle for equality and freedom. Such assumptions surfaced when 'anti-patriotic' syndicalists (Georges Yvetot, Victor Griffuelles) failed to persuade German labour leaders to adopt the anti-war General Strike. Their instinctive response was that, however large and well funded, German unions lacked fighting spirit – because sheep-like German workers had never made a revolution. In 'heart and gut', therefore, such syndicalists remained Jacobin nationalists – for all their rhetoric about the republican-revolutionary heritage being a bourgeois con trick.[52] Absent from neo-Jacobin analysis was any appreciation that Germany's *Sonderweg*, in particular its anti-Enlightenment culture, might itself be a backlash against the French occupation of Germany in the Napoleonic period. And often missing, too, was a willingness to criticise French imperialism.

It is dangerous, too, to tie 'progressive' aspirations to any one national tradition – because it is bound to be exclusive. The radical artisans who 'made' E. P. Thompson's working class drew on the heritage of the 'free-born Englishman'. Yet their culture built around the white, male English Protestant skilled worker, implicitly excluded blacks, women, Irish, Catholics and the unskilled.[53] French 'new nationalism' excluded Jews, Protestants, Freemasons and *métèques*. But Jacobinism, too, had its exclusions – and not merely aristocrats and clergy. After all, women were not 'citizens' until 1945 – because Republicans viewed them as 'clerical', 'reactionary', 'irrational', and many labour militants saw them as 'docile' cheap labour. The urban left had an underlying suspicion of rustics, particularly those from peripheral regions whose culture was perceived as clerical and backward ('Fanaticism speaks Basque'). Until recently the left appeared to assume the necessity of

---

52 J. Jennings, 'Syndicalism and the French Revolution', *Journal of Contemporary History* 27 (1992), pp. 43–65.
53 L. Colley, *Britons. Forging the Nation* (New Haven, Conn., Yale University Press, 1992).

Jacobin centralisation, with most regionalist critiques of an over-cen-
tralised state coming, with a few neo-Proudhonist exceptions, from the
Catholic right.

Similar assumptions informed attitudes to immigrant workers.
Neo-Jacobinism left little scope for cultural pluralism. Poles, Algerians
and others were paid the 'compliment' of the assumption that they
could, and naturally would, wish to assimilate to French (laic) cultural
values. Also immigrant workers were assumed – often incorrectly – to be
'docile', unwilling to fight for rights. Thus, as Antoine Prost insists,
Jacobin republican 'humanitarian' and 'cosmopolitan' nationalism
often 'conceals a subtle national pride . . . , disguises an immense affir-
mation of French superiority'. Since all nationalisms share the same
underlying exclusionist logic, all, Steven Vincent argues, are a form of
measles. Jacobin nationalism may be 'more benign than most', yet 'it
remains measles nonetheless'. If one has lost faith in the Trinity
God–Christ–King it is possibly better to be an atheist than to reinvest
one's faith in Nation–Republic–People.[54]

And yet it may be churlish to finish on this negative note. Maurice
Agulhon still feels justified in offering us a progressive meta-narrative of
republican Jacobin patriotism. It was, he admits, challenged by xenophobic New Nationalism before 1914 and then by a Moscow-orientated
PCF and a quasi-fascist right flirting with foreign totalitarianism. Yet by
1945 the latter were discredited – whilst the twin victors of the
Resistance, both incarnating Republican patriotism, were Gaullism and
the Communist Party.[55] Can one still justify such a meta-narrative? To do
so for our period one might begin by accepting the sheer strength of
those forces which, after 1870, were drawing hitherto local popular
classes and peripheral regions into the nation state. These included railways, which meant that no longer was travel within France a minority
phenomenon, involving tramping artisans, seasonal migrants and soldiers – it became a mass phenomenon. Universal conscription allowed
the barracks to function as the 'school of the nation'. And many ex-con-
scripts did not return to their villages, but secured jobs on the railways
or in the Post Office. Schools taught in French, not *patois*, and made
national cultural unity a key goal. Moreover, an emerging mass culture
of cheap newspapers, *romans feuilletons*, embryonic consumerism and,
later, the cinema rendered the syndicalist dream of using the *Bourses du*

54 Prost, *In the Wake*; K. S. Vincent, 'National Consciousness, Nationalism and
   Exclusion: Reflections on the French Case', *Historical Reflections/Réflexions
   Historiques* 9 (1993), pp. 433–49; S. Englund, 'The Ghost of Nation Past', *Journal of
   Modern History* 64 (1992), pp. 55–70.
55 M. Agulhon, *The French Republic 1879–1992* (Oxford, Blackwell, 1992).

Travail as the bastions of an 'autonomous' workerist culture utopian. At the apogee of the new culture of commercialised sport the Tour de France cycle race, echoing in its title the most famous textbook of the Republican school, became a symbol of the unity of the hexagon. Imperialism served both to guarantee French jobs and as a source of national pride, whether in the 'civilising mission' or in racial supremacy, whilst the embryonic welfare state drew not only reformist socialists (e.g. Albert Thomas) but also ex-syndicalists like Léon Jouhaux into the processes of a *socialisation étatique*. Finally mass suffrage, which made workers citizens with votes, gave them the chance to elect socialist deputies to a national parliament. The goal of socialist parties was, precisely, the *nationalisation* of railways and coal mines. It was, thus, by 1914 almost inevitable that adherence to the interests of one's class was articulated within the realities of the nation.

It was, of course, possible for labour militants to seek to fly in the face of these realities. One could defiantly assert internationalist ideals, 'anti-militarist' and 'anti-patriotic' values. One could reject the broad 'natalist' consensus and champion 'neo-Malthusianism' (i.e. birth control and abortion), insisting that too many working-class babies would simply provide the army with cannon fodder and the capitalists with a reserve army of labour. One could reject the symbols of the Republican *patrie* as 'bourgeois', urge that the *tricolour* be buried in a dung heap, allow the Catholic right to appropriate Joan of Arc and conservative Republicans – even fascists – to claim the *Marseillaise*.

The alternative approach – that of most of the SFIO, a growing number of ex-syndicalists in the CGT and, finally of the PCF, after 1935 – was, however, to accept the reality of national identity and to recognise that it was suicidal to abandon the *patrie* to one's enemies. For had not workers played an active, central role in the struggles to establish a Republic? Was not the Republic, for all its inadequacies, the least bad major regime in Europe? Was not the Place de la République a worthier national *lieu de mémoire* than the Sacré Coeur? Was not Marianne, even deprived of her red Phrygian bonnet, preferable as a national symbol to the Virgin Mary? And was it not tactically sensible to seek to rescue, as Marianne's sister, Joan of Arc from the clutches of the far right by emphasising that she was a girl of the people betrayed and killed by the clergy and the royalist élites?[56]

It may, indeed, be possible to argue that Republicanism, including the left Jacobinism espoused by the labour movement, had already

---

56 M. Agulhon, *Marianne au pouvoir* (Paris, Flammarion, 1989); G. Krumeich, 'Joan of Arc between Left and Right' in Tombs (ed.), *Nationhood*, pp. 63–73.

occupied the symbolic ground of the nation by 1880. Clinging to that terrain in the Dreyfus and Popular Front crises, the left thwarted the New Nationalist proto-fascist right by preventing it from laying claim to the imagery and symbolism of the *patrie*. If this is so, then those of us condemned to live under Europe's last *ancien régime*, whose national flag has been – until the arrival of 'New Labour' – the shared property of the Tory Party and of the BNP, will continue to look across the Channel with a degree of envy and to admire the achievements of the Jacobin-nationalist heritage.

Labour and the national question in Poland

The Polish national movement could play the tune of every nationalist ideology: from right-wing nationalism to left-wing patriotism, from gentry nationalism to socialist irredentism and from integral national-ism to Risorgimento nationalism. The 'gentry nation', the 'propertied nation', the 'people's nation', the 'statist nation' and the 'racist nation' can be used as conceptual shorthand to describe a wide variety of com-peting and coexisting ideas about what the Polish nation state should look like.[1] The 'gentry nation' was the ideological concept of the feudal gentry who had led the successive national insurrections up to the January Uprising of 1863. It excluded not only the peasant and plebeian mass but also the bourgeoisie from the Polish nation. With the failure of the January Uprising, the gentry's elitist and romantic nationalism suc-cumbed. The bourgeoisie could now enter national politics through the concept of the 'propertied nation'. Warsaw positivists articulated the Polish bourgeoisie's new ideology. They proposed the slogan of 'organic work' as a means of furthering economic and cultural modernisation. It fitted the social demands of the emerging bourgeoisie well. In this bour-geois concept of the 'propertied nation', however, there was still no room for the peasant and plebeian mass. Polish nationalism remained a nationalism without people.

Only when an organised labour movement began to assert itself in the late nineteenth century did Polish nationalism shift towards the 'people'. At that moment the national movement drew on a popular coalition and an ideological alliance with labour. This in turn gave rise to a new dialectical tension between the class solidarity of labour and the supra-class solidarity of nation, between socialism and nationalism, between social emancipation and national liberation. For the Polish workers who had suffered from both social and national oppression it was not a question of choosing one or the other. The real question was what should be the relationship between class and nation. A failure to

---

1 T. Łepkowski, 'Historyczne kryteria polskości', in A. Kłoskowska (ed.), *Oblicza polskości* (Warsaw, Wydawnictwo Uniwersytetu Warszawskiego, 1990), p. 90.

understand either the class aspect of the national struggle or the national aspect of the class struggle would hold back the advance of social emancipation and national liberation.

This tension was the engine of the Polish socialist movement in both theory and practice, but it was not always creative. It is undeniable that the Polish Socialist Party's (PPS) strategy of pursuing a united front policy gave parts of the Polish nationalist movement a more democratic outlook. The social patriotic wing of the labour movement emphasised its Polishness in populist terms. This was particularly true of the PPS-Right after the split with the PPS in 1906. In their theory and practice class emancipation was subordinated to national emancipation. The revolutionary internationalist wing represented by the Social Democracy of the Kingdom of Poland and Lithuania (SDKPiL) reversed this order of preference. Though this internationalist stance acted as a safeguard against the complete degeneration of Polish socialism into populist nationalism, its proletarian solipsism made it vulnerable to criticism by Polish nationalists. Any historical analysis of this irreconcilable controversy between the PPS and the SDKPiL will have to start by asking how ordinary Polish workers responded to the claims of socialism and nationalism.

The independence of Poland in 1918 was a watershed in the history of Polish nationalism. Suddenly Poles found that they were no more an oppressed nation but a hegemonic nation in a multinational independent Poland. A 'crucified' nation changed into a 'crucifying' nation, leaving its own memory of captivity and hardship behind. The working class, which had suffered from national oppression, now experienced the impact of Polish 'little imperialism'. The independent Poland was still vulnerable to its powerful neighbours – Germany and Russia – but the White Eagle was strong enough to harass weak neighbouring nations such as Lithuania, Belorus and the Ukraine. This paradoxical experience conditioned the Polish labour movement in the inter-war years. Along with the concept of a 'people's nation', concepts of a 'statist nation' and a 'racist nation' infiltrated working-class discourse. This explains how and why some workers moved from 'good' left-wing patriotism to 'bad' right-wing nationalism. 'Ethnocentrism or racial prejudice could well go together with class militancy and class consciousness.'[2] If we ask the question whether class consciousness outweighs national consciousness among workers or vice versa, we will inevitably get the wrong answer. The right questions are: where was the dividing line

2 P. van Duin, 'Proletarian Prejudices: the Impact of Ethnic and Racial Antagonism on Working Class Organization 1830–1930', in W. R. Garscha and C. Schindler (eds), *ITH-Tagungsberichte. Labour Movement and National Identity* 30 (1994), p. 95.

between class consciousness and national consciousness among Polish workers? Was the division solid or fluid? What factors channelled the energy of workers into the class struggle and what factors made them abandon class in favour of nation? Should nationalist mobilisation among workers be interpreted as simply reflecting the ideological hegemony of the ruling class? Or does it involve deep psycho-ontological roots of labour in the national tradition? Although difficult, to pose these questions serves to shed some light on the complex socialist perspectives on the national question which otherwise remain rooted in the banality of the 'the working class should have been like that' thesis.

Socialist irredentism: the 'people's nation' or the 'nation's people'?

Successive Polish national insurrections in the first half of the nineteenth century had been based on the concept of a 'gentry nation'. The alienated plebeian mass, mainly peasants, remained indifferent to nationalism. In so far as the national movement aimed at the resurrection of the glorious gentry republic, the independence of Poland simply meant the restoration of serfdom to the peasantry. After all, it had not been the Polish nobility but the emperors of partitioning powers who had emancipated the peasants. The Polish peasants could see no reason to support a national movement based on the gentry's feudal illusions of 'Golden Freedom'. They preferred 'benevolent foreign emperors' to compatriot landlords.[3] In fact the Tsar's peasant emancipation decree of 2 March 1864 proved to be a counter-blow to the January Uprising. It left insurgents without a popular base of support. Aimed at sharpening the class conflict between the gentry and the peasants, it succeeded in hampering the national solidarity between them.

The abolition of serfdom also triggered the rapid industrial development of the Polish Kingdom and gave rise to an industrial working class who, in time, turned out to be the gravediggers of tsarism. Peasant emancipation greatly increased the number of landless peasants as well as the number of small peasant holdings. The landless grew from 220,000 in 1870 to 849,000 in 1891. As industrialisation accelerated, peasants freed from the land were to be incorporated into the army of wage labourers. The number of industrial workers and artisans grew from 164,184 in 1864 to 440,000 in 1897. The growth rate of industrial

---

3 J. Molenda, 'The Formation of National Consciousness of the Polish Peasants and the Part they played in Regaining of Independence by Poland', *Acta Poloniae Historica* 63/4 (1991), pp. 130 f.

workers far outstripped that of the artisans. The former increased by roughly four times in the same period. This labour force, including 600,000 agrarian labourers, rose to 47·7 per cent of the whole working population by 1897.[4] Moreover Polish workers were concentrated into a few industrial centres such as Warsaw, Łódź and the Dąbrowa basin. The declassed gentry joined the working class and often acted as opinion leaders among workers.

In contrast to the working class, the bourgeoisie never really developed. The 'Prussian road' of Polish capitalism undermined the bourgeoisie. The ideology of 'triple loyalism' and 'organic work' led the bourgeoisie to make compromises, to live in harmony with the aristocracy at home and the absolutist powers abroad. Its mosaic multinational composition of Germans, Jews and Poles made it more difficult for the bourgeoisie to manoeuvre on its own. In fact the Polish bourgeoisie had never attempted a bourgeois democratic revolution. Hence the proletariat, aided by peasants and the intelligentsia, was faced with the task of carrying through both the democratic revolution and the building of a modern nation. Polish Socialists had to perform the double act of social emancipation and national liberation.

The first generation of Socialists was influenced by Ludwik Waryński, the leader of the first Polish Marxist party, Proletaryat. He stated that 'Poland suffers, but there is a nation which suffers much more than Poland – the proletarians all over the world.'[5] Contrary to Marx's and Engels's advocacy of Polish independence, uncompromising internationalism prevailed in Polish socialism in its initial stage. The Socialists favoured autonomy over independence. It was Bolesław Limanowski who stood up against the dominant current of revolutionary internationalism. He believed firmly that 'socialism and patriotism do not contradict but reinforce each other', and drew a sharp distinction between 'good' patriotism and 'bad' nationalism. While nationalism was an ideology of the immoral modern state, which pursues its own interests at the cost of others', patriotism stood for social equality at home and the brotherhood of nations abroad.[6] Along with his social

---

4 E. Kaczyńska, *Dzieje robotników przemysłowych w Polasce pod Zaborami* (Warsaw, PWN, 1970), p. 105; A. Żarnowska, *Klasa robotnicza Królestwa Polskiego 1870–1914* (Warsaw, PWN, 1974), p. 16.

5 L. Blit, *The Origins of Polish Socialism. The History and Ideas of the First Socialist Party 1878–86* (Cambridge, Cambridge University Press, 1971), p. 44.

6 This dichotomy between good patriotism and bad nationalism is still alive in contemporary Polish usage. This makes it difficult to take on board that good patriotism and bad nationalism are the head and tail of the same coin – Janus-faced modern nationalism. It precludes the possibility that the good social patriotism can degenerate into bad nationalism.

organicism, this stress on patriotism as a basic social bond made him reject the Marxist concept of class struggle. Limanowski preferred class collaboration to class struggle, socialist evolution to socialist revolution. According to him, socialism was destined to consolidate national unity.[7]

It presupposed an independent democratic nation state where socialist evolution was possible on the basis of national consensus. That is why he suggested independence as the primary goal of Polish Socialism. His theory of socialist patriotism was the gospel of the patriotic radical intelligentsia, who saw the main material force for the irredentist movement in the rising working class. The bourgeoisie owed allegiance to 'throne and altar' because of the integration of Polish capitalism into the Russian market, and the peasantry had not yet been awakened politically. This class structure forced the patriotic intelligentsia to seek support from workers. They gathered around the Union of Polish Youth, the Polish League and the National Socialist Community and tried to bridge the rift between intelligentsia and workers, nationalism and socialism. In general their nationalism outweighed their socialism. They never hesitated to attack Marxism and revolutionary socialism and their emphasis was on regaining independence. Socialism would be achieved in the future independent democratic republic of Poland by way of parliamentary reform. They were in favour of Fabian socialism and distrusted the revolutionary labour movement.

At the Paris Conference from 17 to 23 November 1892 they established a unified socialist leadership. It was the social patriotic wing of the *émigré* socialists, represented by the journals *Przedświt* and *Pobudka*, which attained ideological hegemony at the conference, which passed a resolution in favour of 'the separate democratic republic' as the primary goal of the Polish socialist movement and subordinated all other issues to that aim. Alongside this proposition the so-called Paris Programme offered a number of reformist demands largely borrowed from the Erfurt Programme of the German Social Democratic Party. It saw the state boundaries of a future independent Poland, or 'People's Poland', as coinciding with the territory of the historic 'Polish Republic' before the partition. It emphasised the necessity of broadening the party's activities into the frontier borders of the republic, roughly covering the present-day states of Lithuania, Belorus and the Ukraine. It guaranteed the full equality of the rights of nationalities on the principle of voluntary federation.[8] This territorial conception was reaffirmed by the

7 K. J. Cottam, *Bolesław Limanowski 1835–1935. A Study in Socialism and Nationalism* (New York, Columbia University Press, 1978), pp. 79–86.
8 'Szkic programu PPSej', in F. Tych (ed.), *Polskie programy socjalistyczne 1878–1918* (Warsaw, KiW, 1975), pp. 253, 259.

famous slogan 'From [Baltic] Sea to [Black] Sea'. This argument was in line with Marx's and Engels's call for the restoration of historical Poland as a strong buffer state against tsarist reaction. Engels's dichotomy of 'historic nations' and 'non-historic nations' categorised Poland as an 'historic nation'. By that standard Lithuanians and Ruthenians would be classified as 'non-historic nations'. In fact the main argument of PPS theoreticians was that non-historic and backward nationalities on the borderlands (*kresy*) would develop a civilisation under the guidance of Poland.[9]

Such arguments provoked sharp criticism from Ukrainian Socialists. Mykhailo Drahomanov condemned the Polish radical democrats as well as contemporary social patriots for wishing to resurrect the old Poland, including Galicia. He denounced, among other things, Limanowski's reference to Galicia as a 'Polish land'. Polish landlords and Ukrainian peasants both lived there. Contrary to Limanowski's proposal of federation based on the Polish–Lithuanian Union of Lublin (1569), Drahomanov preferred the concept of a Slav Federation gathered around Russia. Ivan Franko, a co-author of the 'Programme of Polish and Eastern Galician Ruthenian Socialists' (1880), stressing the class solidarity between the Polish and Ukrainian workers, reproached the Poles for their stubborn aim of restoring historical Poland, including Ukrainian territory. In the eyes of Ukrainian Socialists the Poles represented feudal landlordism, whilst Ukrainians embodied the democratic and radical peasant aspirations.[10] By contrast, Polish socialists argued that the Cossack Ukrainians needed to be civilised under the guidance of Polish high culture.

Lithuanian Socialists were also critical of such Polnocentrism. The historical experience that class antagonism between feudal lords and peasants coincided with the national division between Poles and Lithuanians made it difficult for them to accept the PPS's proposal for the restoration of the old Polish republic. After the foundation of Lithuanian Social Democracy (LSD) in 1896, it immediately clashed with the PPS. The orthodox wing of the LSD preferred to cooperate with Russian Social Democracy. The PPS largely ignored any criticism, arguing that political and economic conditions in Lithuania were not mature enough for the emergence of a genuine social democratic movement. The Jewish Social Democrats in Vilnius were also opposed to the PPS's plan for an independent Poland. They regarded the emancipation

9 J. Kancewicz, *PPS w Latach 1892–96* (Warsaw, PWN, 1984), pp. 349–50.
10 J. Radziejowski, 'Ukrainians and Poles: the Shaping of Reciprocal Images and Stereotypes', *Acta Poloniae Historica* 50 (1984), pp. 117–27.

of Jewish workers as depending on the victory of the united revolutionary and socialist forces of all Russia, including Poland. They could see no reason why the Jewish proletariat should favour the demand for an independent Poland to demands for social emancipation and national equality for all inhabitants of the Russian Empire. Polish independence would be a wedge dividing the Jewish community between Poland and Russia. They considered the PPS's Polonocentric attitude divisive and nationalistic.[11]

The Paris Programme also met with fierce criticism among many of the rank and file at home. According to the recollections of Leon Falski, who supported the programme, the majority of organised workers were against the Paris Programme. In particular, militants of the Union of Polish Workers (ZRP), just released from tsarist prison, contemptuously labelled the advocates of the Paris Programme 'nationalists'. Other reminiscences equally show that many organised workers stuck to Waryński's position that international social revolution would liberate all peoples, including Poland, and, therefore, Polish Socialists should not treat the Polish question separately. They favoured common action with the Russian Socialists in the struggle for political freedom in the Russian Empire.[12] A prison letter of an organised worker attributed social patriotism to the 'white-collar workers' aspiring to fill the positions of the Russian occupants. According to him, national independence was not the business of 'blue-collar workers'.[13]

The PPS's difficulty in winning workers to its social patriotic cause is verified once again by the fact that party leaders hesitated for a while to campaign openly on the slogan of independence. This does not necessarily mean that ordinary workers shared the anti-nationalist views of the ZRP. In the General Strike of 1892 workers in Łódź sang songs about 'the basic truths of the substance of class exploitation' like *Czerwony Sztandar* (Red Flag)[14]. Yet highly patriotic songs like *Boże coś Polskę* (God save Poland) and *Jeszcze Polska nie zginęła* (Poland has not perished yet) were equally popular, though the primary aim of the struggle lay in improving their workers' living conditions. Whilst this does not necessarily indicate that the workers were preoccupied with social patriotism,

11 H. J. Tobias, *The Jewish Bund in Russia* (Stanford, Cal., Stanford University Press, 1972), pp. 51–3.
12 B. Radlak, *SDKPiL w Latach 1893–1904* (Warsaw, PWN, 1979), pp. 54, 111–12; E. Kaczyńska, 'Robotnicy w Królestwie Polskim wobec idei narodowych', in *Narody. Jak powstały i jak wybijały się na niepodległość?* (Warsaw, PWN, 1989), pp. 287–8.
13 'Robotnicy z SDKP i PPS o kwestii narodowej (1986 r.). List Nr 1', *Archiwum Ruchu Robotniczego* 10 (1986), p. 18.
14 W. L. Karwacki, 'Piosenka w środowisku robotniczym cz 1', *Polska Klasa Robotnicza. Studia Historyczne* 5 (1973), pp. 131, 143.

it demonstrates that tódź workers were partially attached to the vestiges of 'traditional' culture.

Working-class culture and vestiges of traditional culture coexisted among workers. All that we can say with certainty is that ordinary workers who suffered from a long working day, low wages, chronic unemployment, lack of social security and labour legislation were much more sensitive to the slogans of economic struggle than to those of political struggle, including national liberation. The demands of striking workers in the years 1893–96 centred on wages and the working day.[15] The foundation of Social Democracy of the Kingdom of Poland (SDKP) in 1893, reorganised as SDKPiL in 1899, was a reaction of international socialists to the social patriotism of the Union of Polish Socialists Abroad (ZZSP), which renamed itself PPS in *Przedświt* of July 1893.

Broadly speaking, the SDKPiL, led by Rosa Luxemburg, was attached to Marxist internationalism, whereas the PPS (later the PPS-Right, led by Józef Piłsudski) inclined towards social patriotism. This does not mean that the SDKPiL was anti-national and the PPS was anti-class. Rather there was a difference of emphasis. If the SDKPiL's concept of a 'people's nation' meant that the nation was subordinated to the people, the PPS's concept of the 'nation's people' was putting it exactly the other way round. How did Polish workers react to the choice put before them by these two socialist parties?

The revolution of 1905–07 provides us with a good litmus test for this analysis. In the revolutionary ferment the fierce competition for popular support between nationalists and socialists, on the one hand, and among socialists, on the other, came to the fore. Polish workers were politicised by the experience of revolution and displayed both national feeling and class conciousness. The national flag and the red flag were displayed in strike action, mass meetings and on the barricades. They shouted 'Long live Poland' along with socialist slogans and sang the traditional patriotic songs of national insurgents along with the class songs. These scenes were a sign of the workers' patriotism, inspired by the need for self-protection and protest against the Russian gendarmes and Cossacks.

It was an eruption of patriotic feeling based on the widespread resentment of the suppression of objective national ties (language, religion, culture, customs and so on) by the forced Russification policies of the tsarist state. Socialist propaganda was careful not to offend key elements of the workers' national consciousness, including their Catholicism, which penetrated deep into the everyday life of Socialist

---

15 Kancewicz, *PPS*, p. 17.

activists as well as ordinary workers. Hence it was rather clericalism, Catholicism as an institution, that was the main target of socialist criticism. The strength of these objective national ties among the mass is verified by the fact that the peasants in *gmina* (village community) action wanted to replace Russian with Polish as the official language in the communal administration, judicial courts and schools. Parents removed their children from schools and tore up the official textbooks and the Tsar's portrait.[16] If disputes over servitude were likely to promote class antagonism, the *gmina* action strengthened the commitment to the national struggle. Class and nation were thus interwoven in the peasant struggle.

It is, however, another question whether this primitive patriotic feeling evolved into a politicised national consciousness. The collective autobiographies of the peasants and agrarian proletarians in inter-war Poland show that their consciousness was tied to the local community. Even after independence they did not immediately overcome their traditional local patriotism. Most workers recruited from the countryside had no politically matured national consciousness in the first decade of this century. The workers of the Warsaw metal industry were exceptional in their attachment to the national cause. Polish national emblems such as the White Eagle or the flag of the January insurgents were frequently on display in the workers' demonstrations in Warsaw. This was mainly due to the fact that the demonstrators were largely recruited from the city's artisans, who had retained the historical memory of fighting in the national uprising of 1863.

Class consciousness and solidarity were not unproblematic, either. In 1905 the working class demonstrated determined class solidarity which overcame ethnic cleavages, for example in Łódź, where the industrial working class consisted of Poles (57 per cent), Germans (23 per cent), Jews (12 per cent) and others (6 per cent). Although there were occasional signs of animosity towards Jewish shopkeepers and small merchants, attempts by the authorities to stir up anti-Jewish feeling met with decisive opposition from the Polish workers. The PPS joined the funeral demonstration for the Jewish workers organised by the Bund and SDKPiL. A mass meeting at the Warsaw Philharmonia on 2 November, attended by members of the PPS, SDKPiL and Bund, passed a joint resolution. Of course there were also conflicts among these three socialist groups. The PPS and Bund criticised each other as Polish and Jewish nationalists. If the SDKPiL attacked the PPS for its nationalist deviation, the PPS counter-attacked the SDKPiL for its indifference to the Polish

---

16 S. Kalabiński and F. Tych, *Czwarte powstanie czy pierwsza rewolucja* (Warsaw, Wiedza Powszechna, 1976), pp. 155–61.

national cause. The SDKPiL and the Bund fought each other for hegemony among Jewish workers in spite of a similar revolutionary line.

Despite such potential for inter-ethnic cooperation, Socialist party
politics were, broadly speaking, organised along ethnic lines. The
SDKPiL appealed to non-Polish workers because of its internationalism,
and it was centred on multi-ethnic cities such as Łódź. By contrast, the
PPS was strongest among ethnic Poles. Judged by party membership
figures, the social patriotism of the PPS proved more attractive to
workers. At the turn of 1906–07 the workers affiliated to all socialist
parties and trade unions reached about 100,000. Some 15 per cent of
the labour force in the Kingdom had been recruited to left-wing organisations. Among them the PPS-affiliated members numbered 55,000, the
SDKPiL and Bund claiming 35,000 and 6,500 respectively. However, ultimately party membership figures are an inadequate index for measuring the nationalism of Polish workers, as the motives for joining a
particular party were extremely diverse and cannot be reduced to an
assumed agreement with key programmatic statements. In many cases a
worker's decision to join the party depended on private connections
with colleagues, the local leadership's ability, the dominant mood of the
factory or workplace and so on.

A lack of nationalist fervour among Socialist workers is suggested
by the fate of the PPS-Right after the party's 1906 split. Approximately
26,000 workers, including the whole Jewish section, joined the class-oriented PPS-Left (Lewica), and 19,000 affiliated to the patriotic PPS-Right
(Frakcja Rewolucyjna). The latter was obsessed with the irredentist
struggle, disregarding the bread and butter issues of the workers' everyday life. Consequently it quickly lost influence among workers. Within a
year of the split, the PPS-Right had to dissolve its organisation in Łódź,
which had declined into banditry organised around the party's paramilitary formations.[17] Later, when Piłsudski organised the First Brigade with
the remnants of PPS-Right veterans, they were shocked once again by
the lack of interest of their working-class compatriots in the nationalist
cause. This clearly shows that patriotic propaganda isolated from the
reality of worker's lives was ineffective, though class propaganda could
to a certain extent stand on its own. Needless to say, a blend of class and
national propaganda was most effective. Maybe we need to amend
slightly Feliks Kon's famous estimation that the workers were 'as much
socialists as patriots'.[18] Workers were not so much patriots as socialists.

17 R. E. Blobaum, *Rewolucja. Russian Poland 1904–07* (Ithaca, N. Y., Cornell University
    Press, 1995), p. 209.
18 F. Kon, *Narodziny Wieku. Wspomnienia* (Warsaw, KiW, 1969), p. 23.

Nevertheless we should not take it for granted that class solidarity was stronger than national solidarity in principle.

From the outbreak of the 1905 revolution the right-wing National Democrats (Endecja) tried to win the support of the Polish working class for its blend of nationalism and racism. In the course of 1906 the National Workers' Union (NZR), organised by the Endecja, experienced remarkable growth. By June of 1906 it numbered 16,000 members. The number had risen to 23,000 by October.[19] If we include the 22,000 members of the Christian Workers' Association, the workers in non-socialist organisations numbered 55,000. As the Endecja's antisemitic stance grew, the influence of socialist Zionism among the Jewish workers also increased. When the Endecja won the second Duma election in 1907 with the support of PPS-affiliated workers, the nationalist tide seemed to extend to the working class as well.[20]

Yet workers did not necessarily join the NZR because of its nationalism but because it campaigned hard to improve workers' conditions. Though firmly against the political General Strike, the NZR proclaimed itself in favour of the economic strike to better the material conditions of workers. This was in sharp contrast to the PPS-Right's indifference to the bread-and-butter issues of workers. Hence workers moved from one union to another, according to which one best defended their immediate economic interests at a given time. Despite its facade of extreme nationalism and antisemitism, Endecja took back its original proposal for the independence of Poland and confined its immediate aim to the broadest possible autonomy for Poland. It was only in 1916 that Endecja called for full independence again. Such a modest stance stood in stark contrast to the PPS-Right's plan for a national uprising for independence. If the Endecja's rapid growth resulted only from working-class nationalism, the ardent irredentism of the PPS-Right should have been even more welcome to workers. However, such was not the case. When they could not see any possibility of overthrowing tsarism, especially after 1906, the Polish workers, exhausted by the revolution, found an alternative in the Endecja's legal line that seemed economically to satisfy their material concerns and emotionally to please their awakening national sentiments. But membership of the NZR also dropped rapidly to 13,600 by January 1908. By the end of the decade, most workers had withdrawn from the organised labour movement altogether. Many

19 T. Monasterska, *Narodowy Związek Robotniczy 1905–20* (Warsaw, PWN, 1973), p. 40.
20 P. Samuś, 'The Jewish Community in the Political Life of Łódź in the Years 1865–1914', in A. Polonski (ed.), *From Shtetl to Socialism* (London, Littman Library of Jewish Civilisation, 1993), pp. 114–16.

workers remained politically passive. The task of realising the 'people's nation' had to be left to the Second Republic.

Little imperialism: the 'statist nation' or the 'racist nation'?

Piłsudski, once the leader of the PPS-Right, emerged as the national saviour in the social and political turmoil accompanying independence. His political philosophy was that 'the state is superior to all other political organisations'.[21] The legendary saying of Piłsudski that he stepped off a 'red tram' (socialism) at the station of independence depicts well his self-image as a national figurehead. Already when he emphasised national aspirations rather than social emancipation in the era of partitioned Poland, Piłsudski transformed the 'people's nation' into the 'nation's people'. When, after independence, he started promoting the 'statist nation' he deprived the 'nation's people' of the people. If the classical Marxists had seen the national liberation movement as an instrument of the socialist revolution, the Piłsudskites turned this socialist-centred instrumentalism upside down in favour of the nation. Ironically it was Roman Dmowski, a lifelong nationalist rival, who caught the essence of Piłsudski. He estimated that 'socialist principles have been purely secondary to Piłsudski's commitment to the continuation of the traditions of 1830 and 1863 [the gentry national uprisings, *Lim*] and the eastern, Jagiellonian conception of the Polish state'.[22]

Even after independence, the Communist Workers' Party of Poland (KPRP), founded as the result of a merger between the SDKPiL and the PPS-Left, rejected Polish independence. This limited the party's influence in spite of some success in factory council movements encouraged by the Bolshevik revolution. The Provisional Revolutionary Committee of Poland, established during the Soviet–Polish War by leaders of the KPRP who supported the Soviet Union, became an easy target for nationalist propaganda, which quickly dubbed the KPRP activists 'national traitors', 'Russian agents' and 'Jewish Commies'. The success of such nationalist propaganda, exploiting the national sentiments of the masses aroused during the Soviet–Polish war, left the KPRP, later the Polish Communist Party (KPP), on the margins of the political arena during the Second Republic, although it appealed to the Ukrainian and Belorussian ethnic minorities in the borderlands.

21 A. Garlicki, *Józef Piłsudski 1867–1935* ed. and trans. J. Coutouvidis (Aldershot, Scholar Press, 1995), p. 137.
22 A. M. Fountain II, *Roman Dmowski. Party, Tactics, Ideology 1895–1907* (New York, Columbia University Press, 1980), p. 84.

Lacking political muscle, it withdrew into ideological sectarianism, denouncing the parliamentary left as 'people's fascism' and criticising the PPS in particular for its 'social imperialism'.[23]

The PPS had kept its distance from the Russian revolution. During the First World War it had supported the central powers in the belief that their victory would bring independence to Poland. When the delegates of the Petersburg Soviet visited Poland in search of moral support by Polish Socialists they received only a lukewarm welcome from the PPS. The Polish comrades were critical of the Bolsheviks' revolutionary dictatorship and, in line with the right wing of the Second International, they criticised its lack of democratic legitimacy. Their prime concern, however, was an independent Poland. Any interest in the Bolshevik revolution within the PPS focused on its meaning for the future Polish state.[24] The geopolitical location of the infant Polish state between the two great powers Germany and Russia made the PPS stick to the idea of the great federation of Poland along the lines of the historic Polish Republic.

The PPS suggested an alliance with the 'little Entente' states, Finland, Estonia and Latvia, in a so-called 'bloc of the peoples' which fitted well into the party's traditional vision of a Poland stretching 'from [Baltic] Sea to [Black] Sea'. Such an alliance was designed to prevent any possible connection between Moscow and Berlin. It was very similar to the Piłsudskites' conception of the Baltic States' Union as an anti-Soviet bloc.[25] In the eyes of the PPS leaders Soviet Russia was still a Russia which had occupied Poland for over 120 years. The Bolshevik revolution could not eradicate the anti-Russian prejudice rooted deep in the tradition of the PPS-Right. The Molotov–Ribbentrop pact of 1939 confirmed Polish socialists' anxiety about Soviet imperialism. When the parliamentary members of the PPS stressed the importance of a strong state and order, they shared Piłsudski's dictum that 'Poland will be a great power or she will perish'. In this way they replaced class and people with state power and order in their national identity discourse, thereby moving close to Piłsudski's definition of the nation.

The PPS differed from the Piłsudskites only in that it was firmly against the use of military means to realise the Polish federation. The

---

23 P. Samuś, 'Syndrom Oblężonej Twierdzy w KPP', in A. F. Grabski and P. Samuś (eds), *Między Wschodem a Zachodem* (Łódź, Wydawnictwo Uniwersytetu Łódzkiego, 1995), pp. 195–201.

24 J. Holzer, 'Attitude of the PPS and PPSD to the Russian Revolution of 1917', *Acta Poloniae Historica* 16 (1967), pp.78, 84.

25 M. Śliwa, 'Kwestia narodowościowa w publicystyce i programach socjalistów polskich w okresie Drugiej Rzeczypospolitej', *Dzieje Najnowsze* 15:1–2 (1983), p. 111.

PPS socialists never doubted the superiority of Polish culture and its assimilating power. Such megalomania was accompanied by ignorance of the national aspirations of the Lithuanians and Ukrainians. This position did meet with criticism from within the party. The PPS-Opposition reproached the PPS's idea of federation as 'masked imperialism' and resolutely opposed the Soviet–Polish War. Soon this group joined the KPRP. There was criticism from the inner circle of the PPS leadership as well. If Feliks Perl criticised the rehabilitation of the old Republic as a 'historical anachronism', Adam Próchnik stood for the independence of the Lithuanians, Ukrainians and Belorussians. But these opinions were in the minority. In 1920, during the Soviet–Polish War, the central executive committee of the PPS passed a resolution in favour of peace talks between Russia and Poland. It suggested specifically that the free will of the nationalities living in the eastern borderland, mainly Ukrainians, Belorussians and Lithuanians, was to be subordinated to the will of Poland and Russia.[26]

However, when the Polish military squad of General Lucjan Żeligowski occupied Vilnius on 9 October 1920, thereby undermining attempts by a group of Lithuanian Poles (*krajowcy* who rejected Piłsudski's idea of federation as thinly veiled Polish hegemony[27]) to build an independent Polish–Lithuanian federal state, the PPS betrayed its own principle of opposing any military aggression and kept silent. Indeed, we find satisfaction in the party press, which was preoccupied with the idea of the Great Polish federation. The nineteenth party congress of 1924 approved the nationality programme. Its most distinctive point was the idea of 'territorial autonomy' for the national minorities in the borderlands of Poland. An autonomous body would be set up with powers in every field of public life. It would have its own judicial court, local Ministry and local Diet. The 'Diet of country', endowed with legislative power, would control education, culture, religion, administration, the law courts, security, the police, industry, public works, communications and so on. This idea of the broadest possible autonomy seemed so impressive that Otto Bauer publicly approved it at the Marseilles congress of the Socialist Workers' International in 1925.[28]

It should be pointed out, however, that the programme was very similar to the SDKPiL's concept of 'autonomy for Poland'. It had first been put forward by the SDKPiL in its programme *What do we want?*

26 E. Koko, *W nadziej na zgodę* (Gdańsk, Wydawnictwo Uniwersytetu Gdańskiego, 1995), pp. 31, 36, 39.

27 J. Tomaszewski, *Mniejszości narodowe w Polsce w XX wieku* (Warsaw, Spotkania, 1991), p. 17.

28 Śliwa, 'Kwestia', pp. 120–1.

(1904), whose author was Rosa Luxemburg. Indeed 'territorial autonomy' was exactly the same term that Rosa Luxemburg had used.[29] It is
interesting that most Socialists of the PPS tried to apply the concept of
territorial autonomy to the Ukrainians, having rejected its application to
Poland. The Ukrainians refused it just as the Polish Socialists had repu-
diated it twenty years earlier. The Polish Socialists would have recognised
the national aspirations of the Ukrainians if they had examined their
own past. The obsession with making Poland strong so as to maintain its
independence blinded them to the reality of the Ukrainians' yearning
for independence. Above all, the unity of the state was important to the
PPS. Confronted with the authoritarian statism of the Sanacja (which literally means 'cleansing') government in the 1930s, the PPS was largely
disarmed ideologically. The state-centrism of the PPS circumscribed by
socialist irredentism could not compete with the forthright statism of the
nationalist right. It was no coincidence that 'many a representative of the
Sanacja elite was an old activist or fighter of the PPS before 1914 and
even before 1905'.[30]

Considering the unfavourable conditions for nation building, the
PPS's desperate effort at state unity can be understood. Before 1918
the socio-economic structure of the country had been developed
according to the divergent interests of the partitioning powers, with
the result that the creation of a single economic system was almost
impossible after independence had been achieved. Until 1920 six cur-
rencies circulated in the country. There was no unified transport
system and the railways were of different guages. Forms of taxation also
varied. Four legal systems coexisted and by 1939 there was still no
unified law code. The problem of national minorities, who made up
over 30 per cent of the whole population, was a great barrier to
national integration. Poles formed only about 66 per cent of the whole
population and the rest were Ukrainians (15·3 per cent), Jews (8·6 per
cent), Belorussians (4·3 per cent), Germans (2·6 per cent) and others.
That is why Poland was fertile soil for cultivating the statism of both the
right and the left.

The process of national integration was not easy, even among the
ethnic Poles. Most peasants sought their identity in religion. Till the
early twentieth century they had used often the word 'Polak' as a term
of contempt for Poles, even if they shared a language, religion and

---

29 J. H. Lim, 'Rosa Luxemburg on the Dialectics of Proletarian Internationalism and
Social Patriotism', *Science and Society* 59:4 (1995), pp. 510–11.
30 J. Żarnowski, 'Rozwój narodu polskiego w okresie międzywojennym', in R. Heck
(ed.), *Studia nad rozwojem narodowym polaków, czechów i słowaków* (Wrocław,
Ossolineum, 1976), p. 98.

culture . When some of their colleagues joined the January Uprising of 1863, the Galician peasants depicted them as joining the 'Polak' camp.[31] In the economic crisis of the mid-1920s they even felt nostalgia for the Golden Age of Partition. A survey in the years 1926–27 showed that peasants had little conception of their own state. The prevalence of local patriotism is a good indicator of the dominance of 'pre-national' loyalties among the peasants who represented over 70 per cent of the population. Their allegiance was confined to the estate, the local neighbourhood and the parish church.[32] The commitment to broader social systems such as the nation and state was still weak. Some 706,000 peasants, mainly of Belorussian and Ukrainian origin from the remote Podlasie region, when asked in a survey in 1931 about their national identity, answered that they were *tutejszy* ('from here').

The statistical indices that indirectly indicate the extent of national integration were also unfavourable. The railway system, as the main tool of interregional connections and thus of further national integration, was underdeveloped. Poland had about 660 km of railway per million inhabitants in 1931, which left it trailing far behind contemporary Germany, France and Britain. While, in 1910, nearly 100 per cent of all Prussian, French and British brides and bridegrooms were able to write, the illiteracy rate among Poles over fifteen years old reached 34·1 per cent in 1921. This large portion of illiterates was exempt from the patriotic indoctrination which compulsory education provided. Nevertheless, the army played an important role in the process of national integration. In 1918 50–60 per cent of the Polish Armed Organisation were peasants. Many workers and peasants were proud of being recruited to the army. They thought it was evidence of their physical prowess, which was one of the most important values in the world of labour. The officers and commandants, many of whom were ex-soldiers of Piłsudski's Brigade, not only taught the recruits military skills but also bolstered their nationalism.

In the course of the First World War, especially after the Russian revolution, Polish workers became more and more class-conscious. A study of the censored letters exchanged between soldiers and their families shortly after the February revolution is very suggestive. It shows that in the spring of 1917 the dominant mood among the peasants and workers conscripted by the Habsburg Empire was the desire for peace and social transformation, whereas the main concern of opinion leader

---

31 J. Tomaszewski, *Rzeczpospolita wielu narodów* (Warsaw, Czytelnik, 1985), p. 35.
32 J. Chałasiński, *Drogi awansu społecznego robotnika* (Poznań, Księgarnia św. Wojciecha, 1931), pp. 94–5.

groups and intellectuals was independence.[33] If war had led to sharp-ened class antagonism and class consciousness among the poor, it made intellectuals more sensitive to the nationalist cause. Likewise the workers in the Polish Kingdom also revealed their appetite for revolution through the factory occupation movement. It was the Soviet–Polish War that changed workers' socio-revolutionary mood into one of patriotic exultation. The Polish working class felt a certain 'hegemonic impulse'[34] from the triumphal parade of Piłsudski's army in Kiev, just as British or German workers were proud of popular imperialism. And the Red Army's threat to Warsaw induced a mood of national unity as well.

The war experience of nascent Poland helped to establish the statism of the Piłsudski faction as the ruling ideology. The PPS leader-ship consented to it, though not without reservations. Workers agreed to it by affiliating to the National Solidarity trade union. Between 1919 and 1923 membership of the class-oriented trade unions fell from 544,200 to 377,900 whilst the membership of nationalist trade unions rose from 442,600 in 1919 to 651,800 in 1923. In the same period the Christian trade unions increased their membership from 91,600 to 154,100. The socialist trade union had already lost its quantitative super-iority by 1921. The votes for the socialist list decreased further in the general election of 1923.[35] It is striking that the National Workers' Party (NPR) had a higher percentage of workers among its members than the PPS or KPP.[36] This indicates that the Polish nationalist camp succeeded to some extent in integrating the working class into the 'statist nation'. This interpretation is supported indirectly by the fact that the socialist trade union was most successful among Ukrainian and Belorussian workers, who did not share the hegemonic impulse or nationalist ideas with Polish workers. The KPP's internationalism appealed to them most.

With the concept of a 'statist nation' as state ideology, political energies concentrated on the task of creating 'a maximum of internal cohesion'. The democratic impulses of the 'people's nation' that social-ist irredentism had kept alive were pushed to the sidelines. Now social-ist irredentism was transformed into the social imperialism of the state

---

33 P. Hanak, 'Die Volksmeinung des letzten Kriegsjahres in Österreich-Ungarn', in R. G. Plaschka and K. Mach (eds), *Die Auflösung des Habsburgerreichs. Zusammenhang und Neuorientierung im Donauraum* (Vienna, Verlag für Geschichte und Politik, 1970), pp. 61, 65.

34 M. van der Linden, 'The National Integration of the European Working Class', *International Review of Social History* 33 (1988), p. 292.

35 L. Haas, 'Aktywność polityczna i organizacyjna klasy robotniczej drugiej rzeczy-pospolitej', *Dzieje Najnowsze* 15:1–2 (1983), p. 36, table 5.

36 K. Rzepa, 'Nieklasowy ruch robotniczy w Polsce do 1939 r.', *Dzieje Najnowsze* 15:1–2 (1983), p. 286.

apparatus. But the success of the ruling elite's integration policy towards the working class was variable. Out of 500,000 workers who withdrew from the trade unions in 1924–26, 311,400 had been members of the National Solidarity trade union. In other words it lost about 48 per cent of its members. The socialist trade union lost fewer members by comparison, only about 100,000. The implication is that class consciousness had remained more or less solid among workers, whilst national consciousness fluctuated according to the changing socio-political situation. As the patriotic tide stimulated by the Soviet–Polish War began to ebb, the integration process of the working class again found itself stranded on the shore of economic difficulties and competing identities.

National integration had to be achieved through a steady nation-building process. Given retarded economic integration, the state machinery had to fulfil this task. Whereas in Western Europe the creation of a national market aided nation-building, it was the state that had to create the national market in Poland. The Piłsudski *coup d'état* of May 1926 was a desperate attempt to fulfil the task of national integration by strengthening state power. The PPS, which shared Piłsudski's concern with national integration as a means of national survival, welcomed it. The KPP consented to it in the hope of recovering the party's legal existence. When Piłsudski expressed his contempt for parliamentary government in an interview in 1928, the PPS split into the pro-Piłsudski politicians who formed the PPS-Former Revolutionary Faction and his critics, who remained the main current of the PPS.

Roman Dmowski and the Endecja remained unconvinced by Pilsudski's 'statist' path towards nation building. Endecja's antisemitic propaganda aimed at national integration by adhering to the concept of the 'racist nation'. It was based on the conscious attempt of creating a feeling of superiority among the ethnic Poles. If Western European popular imperialism sought the hegemonic impulse in the colonies, Endecja targeted the national minorities, especially the Jews. Thus its ideology may be defined as an 'internal' popular imperialism. In fact Endecja treated Jews not as a national minority but as an internal enemy. During the Soviet–Polish War the stereotype of the 'Jewish Commie' or 'Soviet agent' was so widespread that Jewish volunteers wanting to serve with the Polish army were temporarily put into an internment camp. The 'murderous Red Army' portrayed in the government's propaganda posters depicted a stereotypical Semitic figure.[37] The Litvaks, the Russian Jews who emigrated to the Polish Kingdom/Russian Poland in the late

---

37 S. Bronsztejn, 'Polish–Jewish Relations as Reflected in Memoirs of the Inter-war Poland', *Polin* 8 (1994), p. 81.

nineteenth century, were particular reviled among ordinary Poles, as they clung to Russian culture and language, rejecting assimilation to Polish traditions. Poles anxious for national identity regarded the Litvaks as agents of Russification – the fourth partitioning power of Poland.[38]

The Endecja shifted the emphasis of its antisemitic propaganda to job competition between Poles and Jews in the 1920s. It argued that Jews were putting native Poles out of jobs. Such propaganda, voiced most vociferously in the years of economic crises, was specifically aimed at the ethnic Polish workers who were supposed to be in competition with the Jews over jobs and housing. Though there were far fewer Jews than Ukrainians living in Poland, most Jews lived in towns, and 78·8 per cent of them were engaged in trade and industry. It was a remarkable figure in comparison with the 66·7 per cent of the Christian population making a living from agriculture. Yet Polish workers seemed reluctant to respond positively to antisemitism, owing to the fact that job competition between Polish and Jewish workers was not as fierce as that between English and Irish workers in Britain, or between black and white workers in America. Jews occupied complementary rather than competitive positions in the labour market. Hence antisemitism could not halt the decline of the National Solidarity and Christian-social trade unions during the years of the economic slump. Between 1930 and 1932 the membership of these unions dropped by 39·4 per cent and 43·3 per cent respectively. As a result the class trade union became the most influential, incorporating about one-third of all organised workers.[39]

In inter-war Poland there existed a segmented or ethnically stratified labour market. Among the workers of the large factories that employed over 200 workers the proportion of ethnic Poles reached 92 per cent. The labour force of medium-size industry was composed of about 80 per cent Polish workers. Enterprises in the public service sector employed almost exclusively Poles. The skilled factory workers and the public service employees enjoyed the highest wages and benefited most from labour legislation. They belonged to the highest stratum of the working class.[40] By contrast, Jewish workers employed in small workshops with less than five paid employees amounted to 83·4 per cent of the total number of Jewish workers. These small workshops provided the artisan-like workers with none of the benefits of labour legislation or

---

38 P. Wróbel, 'Jewish Warsaw before the First World War', *Polin* 2 (1987), pp. 163, 181.
39 L. Haas, 'Układ sił i zasięg oddziaływania ruchu zawodowego wśród klasy robotniczej w Latach Drugiej Rzeczypospolitej', *Polska Klasa Robotnicza. Studia Historyczne* 4 (1974), pp. 164–7.
40 J. Żarnowski, 'Klasa robotnicza 1918–39', in A. Czubiński (ed.), *Historia polskiego ruchu robotniczego 1918–39* (Warsaw, KiW, 1988) III, pp. 61–2.

social security. Most of them suffered from long working hours and starvation wages. The miserable condition of this Jewish artisan proletariat
was confirmed by an opinion poll showing that only five artisans in 200
wanted to manage their own workshop. Jewish workers were thus in a
state of near isolation in *de facto* work ghettoes.[41] This polarised labour
market was only partly due to the Jewish custom of observing the
Sabbath and to the language problems of many working-class Jews who
spoke only Yiddish. Such polarisation was also the result of a systematic
boycott of Jewish labour. Jewish employees were constantly dismissed
from state-owned enterprises in the 1920s. From 1921 to 1931 the
number of Jewish workers employed by the railway and public transport
companies decreased by 75 per cent. When the tobacco industry was
subjected to a state monopoly, almost all Jewish workers were fired. Jews
were also often dismissed from the municipal enterprises in districts
where the nationalists won the local elections. Whilst Polish white-collar
workers developed a different ethos from that of blue-collar workers, the
Jewish working-class milieu remained unified. Jews could not find
employment in the civil service or the military. This ethnically stratified
labour market favourable to Poles strengthened ethnic identities among
workers. This is verified by the fact that Poles and Jews addressed each
other in a non-symmetrical way. Even though a Jew addressed a Pole as
'Sir', a Pole never addressed a Jew as 'Sir', but only as 'You Jew'.[42]

There is little evidence that such structural discrimination in the
labour market led workers of both nationalities into direct antagonism
in their personal lives. The memoirs of Łódź workers reveal Polish
workers' positive attitude to poor Jews, their everyday next-door neighbours. It is interesting that the positive views are much more concrete
whilst the negative views are more general.[43] This suggests that the latter
owed more to the propaganda of the Endecja than to real-life experience. In fact the relationship between the Jewish and Polish workers was
more intimate than has been thought. Polish workers often regarded
Jewish workers as equal partners and expressed sympathy for the misery
of their Jewish colleagues. The Yiddish literature of the inter-war period
depicted the Polish–Jewish workers' relationship as not antagonistic at
all.[44] It could even be argued that Polish and Jewish workers at times

41 B. Garncarska-Kadary, 'Some Aspects of the Life of the Jewish Proletariat in Poland
    during the Inter-war Period', *Polin* 8 (1994), pp. 239–42.
42 M. Kamińska, 'References to Polish–Jewish Coexistence in the Memoirs of Łódź
    Workers: a Linguistic Analysis', *Polin* 6 (1991), p. 209.
43 *Ibid.*, pp. 211–19.
44 C. Shmeruk, 'Jews and Poles in Yiddish Literature in Poland between the Two
    World Wars', *Polin* 1 (1986), pp. 176–95.

joined hands in a symbiotic relationship circumscribed by the structural discrimination of the labour market.

It was in the Prussian partition areas such as Poznań and Upper Silesia that the Endecja was most successful despite the fact that the Jewish population in these regions was negligible in comparison with the whole of Poland. The *Kulturkampf* (i.e. Bismarck's fierce struggle against Catholicism in the 1860s) and the Germanisation laws of the 1870s stirred up nationalist feelings among the Poles. Attacks on the Catholic Church provoked Polish peasants and the agrarian proletariat who attached themselves to the parish church. The Prussian officers reported that 'even among the lower classes of the Polish population, among peasants and workers, a lively and excited national feeling and even a mood of exasperation'[45] prevailed in 1886–87. This tradition was alive among workers who migrated from the countryside to the towns at the turn of the century. An ethnically loaded class conflict between German foremen and Polish workers provided the Endecja with a good climate for its nationalist propaganda. It should also be noted that the Polish petty-bourgeoisie was particularly strong in this region. They predominantly worked in the retail trade and in small workshops and faced intense rivalry from Jewish shopkeepers and artisans. The fiercest job competition between Poles and Jews took place here.

As for the industrial heart of central Poland, Łódź was an exceptional case in that the Endecja was very active. This reflected the fact that the investment of German and Jewish capital was concentrated around Łódź. Some workers would have seen the foreign capitalists not only as exploiters but also as an alien people with a different culture and nationality. Furthermore, many textile workers in Łódź were recruited from the peasant emigrants who attached themselves more to the national culture than to the class culture. The antisemitic campaign, however, was much more severe in intellectual circles. Jews were overrepresented in the legal profession (41·5 per cent of all lawyers came from a Jewish background). 34·5 per cent of all artists and 31·8 per cent of all medical doctors were Jewish. The most fanatical antisemitism was to be found among the young student nationalists who campaigned for *numerus clausus, numerus nullus, ghetto bench* and so on.[46] Quite apart from the small trade and workshop sector, educated Poles had to compete very hard for academic or professional jobs.

Though a few theoreticians of the PPS-Left recognised the excep-

---

45 W. W. Hagen, *Germans, Poles and Jews. The Nationality Conflict in the Prussian East 1772–1914* (Chicago, University of Chicago Press, 1980), p. 148.

46 S. Rudnicki, 'From *Numerus Clausus* to *Numerus Nullus*', *Polin* 2 (1987), pp. 246–68.

tional significance of culture in Jewish national identity, the main current of Polish socialist thought viewed the Jews as 'a scattered nationality' which did not have a material basis for national autonomy. The SDKPiL-KPP denied national cultural autonomy to the Jews on the basis of its Marxist theories, and the PPS did likewise for reasons of the national security of an independent Poland. Many PPS activists thought that the extraterritorial autonomy of Jews would hinder the unity of the Polish state and accelerate the tendency to secession. They believed that the equality of all nationalities stipulated in the constitution would guarantee the freedom of socio-cultural development of the Jews.[47] Though the PPS resolutely struggled against antisemitism, it closed its eyes to the ethnically stratified labour market. By refusing to make the Sabbath a public holiday it revealed its lack of interest in correcting the unequal working conditions of the split labour market.

The PPS's statist nationalism made it rather insensitive to the basic social inequality suffered by workers from ethnic minorities in the job market, which legal equality could do nothing to redress. Yet Mishkinsky went too far when he argued that, regarding their attitude towards Jews, the dividing line between the Socialists and the Endecja was not always as clear as it should be.[48] Equally, the condemnation of the PPS as nationalist by the Bund and the left wing of Poalej-Syjon was rather onesided. But the accusations were not absolutely without foundation. Although PPS workers attacked the pickets hired by the nationalist and Polish shopkeepers for the boycott of Jewish shops, the right wing of the PPS was against the affiliation of Jews to the party's ancillary organisations.[49] Peasant members in many local organisations of the KPP complained about their Jewish comrades.

As the Sanacja government and the Endecja converged around ultra-nationalist ideology and practice in the 1930s, the PPS and Jewish Socialist organisations tried to form a united front. A good example is provided by the electoral bloc of Łódź workers in the election of 1934 which was called Socialist Workers' Unity and Class Trade Unions.[50] Jewish Socialists, disenchanted with the reality of Soviet Communism, sought an ally among Polish Socialists in an attempt to erect barriers against the growing antisemitic mood both at home and abroad. Polish

---

47 M. Śliwa, 'Kwestia żydowska w polskiej myśli socjalistycznej', in F. Kiryk (ed.), *Żydzi w Małopolsce* (Przemyśl, P-WIN, 1991), pp. 280–5.
48 M. Mishikinsky, 'A Turning Point in the Theory of Polish Socialism and its Attitude towards the Jewish Question', *Polin* 1 (1986), p. 117.
49 J. Żarnowski, *PPS w Latach 1935–39* (Warsaw, KiW, 1965), pp. 133–4.
50 B. Wachowska, 'The Jewish Electorate of Inter-war Łódź in the Light of the Local Government Election', *Polin* 6 (1991), pp. 162–8.

Socialists awoke from their delusions of the powerful nation state in the face of Sanacja's oppressive statism. At long last the thirty-fourth congress of the PPS, held in Radom in 1937, passed a resolution in favour of the national cultural autonomy of the Jews. It conceded the extraterritorial autonomy that the Jewish Socialists had for so long demanded.

Unfortunately it was too late. Ideologically, the frontal attack by both Endecja and Zionists had put the Socialists on the defensive. The concept of the 'people's nation' was defeated by both the 'statist nation' and the 'racist nation'. However, integral nationalism also failed to fulfil the task of nation building. As a result the Second Republic of Poland remained 'not a nation state but a nationalities state'.[51] The task of realising the 'people's nation' had once again to be tossed to the next generation.

Conclusion

The People's Republic of Poland, or 'People's Poland', to use the colloquial term of the post-1945 Communist regime, should have been based on the concept of the 'people's nation'. What was actually achieved was, however, the consolidation of right-wing concepts of a 'statist nation' decorated with socialist phraseology. Lenin's definition of the Communist state as 'national in form, social in content' was, in fact, turned upside down. What had been realised was a state which was 'national in content, social in form'. As preoccupation with the national survival of Poland led the Piłsudkites and the right-wing Socialists to endorse notions of a 'statist nation', the syndrome of the besieged fortress reinforced Communist notions of a 'statist nation'. What made things worse was that the Polish United Workers' Party (PZPR) did not hesitate to use the concept of the 'racist nation' in the anti-Zionist campaign of the late 1960s. The PZPR differed from the Endecja only in that it suffered from the chronic schizophrenia between proletarian internationalism (in theory) and statist nationalism (in practice) so characteristic of Polish Socialism in the period under consideration.[52]

Whilst its statist nationalism helped to legitimise the PZPR's monopoly of power there was no room for the people in this operational nationalism. Solidarity rejected the statist nationalism by drawing on the concept of the 'people's nation' and leaving the concept of the 'statist nation' exclusively to the Communist *nomenklatura*. By identifying the

51 J. Pajewski, *Budowa Drugiej Rzeczypospolitej 1918–26* (Kraków, PAU, 1995), p. 164.
52 M. Zaremba, 'PRL: internacjonalizm w cudzysłowie: Partia i Naród', *Polityka*, 2 December 1995, pp. 72–73.

nation with the people it made explicit its will to put the people at the centre of the nation. It succeeded in ending Communist rule in Poland, but the road to the 'people's nation' is still a long one. Many political currents such as Social Democracy, populist Liberalism and ultra-nationalism are now locked in fierce competition to induce the people, i.e. largely workers and peasants, into their camps. They are conjuring up the concepts of the 'people's nation', the 'statist nation', the 'propertied nation' and the 'racist nation' from the tomb of history. The result of the present competition will depend largely on Polish workers' attitude to nation and class.

Acknowledgements

I should like to express my special thanks to Professor Anna Żarnowska, who organised a colloquium on this article, and to Polish collegues who made useful suggestion. All translations from Polish are my own.

Stalin's victory over Lenin: Russian Social Democrats and the nationality problem

Uniquely to the countries studied in this collection, for much of the period under consideration the territory of the Russian Empire was ruled by politicians who thought they had solved the national question. And, if Russia moved from being in 1870 an autocratic empire governed by the trinity 'orthodoxy, autocracy and nationality' to being in 1939 a dictatorship which in the terms of Stalin's chauvinistic post-war national anthem 'had been united for centuries by Great Russia', then in the long revolutionary decade 1917–30 new forms of government and inter-state relations, inspired by Lenin, were adopted by politicians from the labour movement which genuinely sought to address the national question and prove that in Russia labour did have the measure of nationalism and its leading theoretician was able to understand properly the power of nationalism over people's minds.

Pre-revolutionary populist nationalism of the right

Although Russian nationalism was the official policy of the multinational tsarist empire until its overthrow, there was only one serious attempt by ruling circles to develop a populist nationalism to support that policy and to integrate labour into a broader 'national community': the campaign launched by the Union of the Russian People, founded in November 1905 at the height of the revolutionary disturbances of that year. Earlier attempts to integrate labour never had the full support of the regime: thus the Moscow chief of the political police, S. Zubatov, had some success in organising a loyal workers' movement, based on legally recognised mutual aid societies, which operated between 1901 and 1903 in Moscow, Odessa, Minsk and Vilnius; however, Zubatov was dismissed in disgrace in 1903. The idea of confessional trade unions, like the Assembly of Petersburg Factory Workers established by the Russian Orthodox priest Father Gapon during 1904, was similarly doomed to failure: launched with the cautious approval of the authorities, the Assembly was soon in the hands of revolutionaries and it was Gapon's action which sparked off the 1905 revolution. The Union of Russian People (URP), however, had the public support of the Tsar.

The URP was founded during the October General Strike of 1905 which forced the Tsar to grant an elected assembly, the Duma. What distinguished this organisation from the start, and has prompted suggestions that the URP was a fascist movement before fascism, was the attempt to rally the masses to the cause of the nation with a populist call to defend the Russian tradition from the attacks of alien, largely Jewish, forces. Formally founded on 8 November 1905 'to firmly unify the Russian people of all estates and statuses in order to work together on behalf of our beloved fatherland – Russia, one and indivisible', its programme was essentially one of slavophile nostalgia for a mythical past before Peter the Great when Tsar and people allegedly had been at one. At its peak, in 1907, the organisation claimed 4,000 branches and millions of members, and even verifiable records suggest 1,000 branches and 300,000 members; between May and November 1906 it issued 13 million copies of its various brochures. The great mass of its supporters came from a broad range of small shopkeepers, clerks, artisans, industrial workers and peasants; its leaders, however, tended to be members of the commercial middle class or the professions. Many of its key figures were clerics, and, while the most senior clergy, the Metropolitans of Petersburg, Moscow and Kiev, kept their distance, many abbots and bishops were very actively involved. This gave the organisation much respectability, and an impressive distribution network for its pamphlets. The URP benefited extensively from government donations.

Like all populist organisations, the URP was a firm believer in direct action. Its first 'fighting organisation' (*druzhina*) was founded in December 1905 at the time of the workers' uprising in Moscow, which the authorities feared might spread to Petersburg. The Petersburg city governor issued the URP fighting organisations with revolvers and in January 1906 there were armed clashes with radical workers; the five district fighting organisations in the capital, all several hundred strong, were the preserve of industrial workers. In its propaganda the URP made repeated reference to the plight of industrial workers and, alarmingly to the authorities, suggested that relations between employers and employees needed to be regulated by law. But the URP found it easy to twist its attack on Jews into a vague anti-capitalism, with the whole world of business and finance being portrayed as somehow un-Russian.

All the organisations on the right blamed the Jews for the state of the country: what distinguished the URP from its elite-oriented fellow organisations was the way the Jews were linked with the key question of the land. Like other parties on the right, the URP argued that behind

the entire constitutional movement lurked Jews, who, with no attachment to their place of residence, were bent on subverting traditional
institutions and getting control of the state. For them the Duma proposals on land reform were simply a trick to enable the Jews to acquire land.
The fact that the URP won a substantial following in Duma elections
among the peasant electors of provinces like Tula, Orel and Kursk shows
that, where the URP was well organised, its programme was not without
appeal. Election returns showed that the URP also did well in the
western borderlands of the Russian Empire, in places like Volynia,
Bessarabia and Minsk, where the Russian population saw itself as threatened by an amalgam of Polish landlords, Jewish tradesmen and
Belorussian or Ukrainian peasants. On this topic the attitude of the URP
was clear and unashamedly Great Russian chauvinist: Russia was for the
Russians; the national minorities had to recognise that it was the Russian
people who had created the present state and therefore deserved a
superior role in its governance.

On the day of the Tsar's *coup d'état* against his own Basic Law, 3 June
1907, when the electoral franchise was changed to secure a less radical
Duma prepared to work with Prime Minister Peter Stolypin, the Tsar
sent a telegram to the URP leader fulsome in its thanks. However,
Stolypin quickly abandoned the project of rallying mass support for the
regime and in 1911 his government refused to support a rightist campaign in which URP politicians declared from their seats in the Duma,
'oppressing the minorities does not contradict the ideals of good healthy
government: the state is not a charitable organisation . . . [and] the place
for the backward peoples is behind the Russians'.[1]

Russian Social Democrats and the national question

The 1905 revolution not only gave birth to the populist nationalism of
the right, it also ignited the nascent nationalisms of the subject peoples
of the Russian Empire. For much of 1905 the Tsar's government lost
control of the borderlands, with nationalist unrest affecting such diverse
areas as the Caucasus, Ukraine and the Baltic seaboard. What was so
striking about these events, however, was the role played by the Social
Democrats in giving coherence to these popular movements. Thus, even
before the revolution of 1905, Social Democrats in the Guria region of

1 This summary history of the URP is taken from D. C. Rawson, *Russian Rightists and
the Revolution of 1905* (Cambridge, Cambridge University Press, 1995), to whom I
owe a great debt; the quoted passage is on p. 199. For the debate about the URP
as Russia's fascists see H. Rogger, 'Was there a Russian Fascism? The Union of the
Russian People', *Journal of Modern History* 36 (1964), pp. 398–415.

the Caucasus had encouraged peasants to cease paying taxes to the government and, in practice, to secede from the empire by recognising only their own elected authorities. After the events of Bloody Sunday on 9 January 1905 the Guria revolt overtook the whole of Georgia, with government officials being lynched and newly elected popular committees distributing land to the landless. The Tsar's authority was restored in 1906 only by means of bloody repression.

And that set the tone for Social Democratic activity elsewhere. On 13 January 1905 workers in Riga staged a 10,000 strong demonstration to protest at the Bloody Sunday massacre. When some of the demonstrators cornered a group of policemen and disarmed them, troops opened fire and seventy workers were killed and a further 200 injured. This unleashed a wave of protest which soon spread far beyond the confines of the urban working class. Peasants joined in workers' protest strikes, and soon they too were refusing to pay taxes and burning estates. Because of the shortage of reliable police and troops, the predominantly German aristocracy of Latvia had soon assembled a military force of its own and over the summer a vicious undeclared civil war developed, involving thousands of casualties. At the end of the year regular Russian troops were used to crush the peasants' and workers' movement, but, before the authorities restored order, popular committees had been established in large parts of the country in rural as well as industrial areas, taxes were no longer being paid, freedom of the press had been established and the Latvian language restored to the schools; in short, Latvia had become self-governing. And this was the work of the Social Democrats.

Events were less dramatic in Ukraine, although dramatic enough. Just as in Russia, towns were shaken by strikes in sympathy with the victims of Bloody Sunday and subsequent developments. The peasant movement, while not as widespread as in Georgia or as violent as in Latvia, witnessed significant insurrections in Chernigov and Poltava, and, once again, it was Social Democrats who proved most effective in mobilising the peasantry. However, the Social Democrats could claim only indirectly to have influenced the most important decision affecting Ukraine in 1905. The ruling by the Russian Academy of Sciences that Ukrainian was a language in its own right, and not a dialect of Russian, helped remove the ban on the use of the language in public and spawned in 1905 and 1906 a plethora of, albeit short-lived, Ukrainian cultural institutions. Social Democrats played a larger role in the other cultural phenomenon of 1905, the establishment of co-operatives, which soon became widespread throughout the country and, because of their ostensibly economic focus, were less likely to be closed by the authorities when, after 1907, all the concessions made to Ukrainian culture began to be undone.[2]

From the earliest days, then, the Social Democrats succeeded in mobilising the aspirations of both workers and peasants from a variety of national backgrounds. As the experience of the URP made clear, labour never experienced much competition from the populist right, despite the presence of workers in the URP fighting organisations. Put succinctly, the great bulk of the working class in the Russian Empire supported the Social Democrats, as the Duma elections of 1907 and 1912 made crystal-clear.

Of course, Labour in Russia was not a homogenous entity. It was divided according to levels of skill, and the divisions were frequently complicated by questions of ethnicity. As Ukraine industrialised in the second half of the nineteenth century it was largely migrant Russians who formed the labour force in the new factories. When the future Bolshevik leader S. I. Kanatchikov arrived in Petersburg at the turn of the century to seek employment in a metalworking plant he was struck by the predominance in the skilled trades of 'Finns, Estonians and Latvians – stern and taciturn people whom it was hard to get to know'. But, with no political party bent on making political capital out of such divisions, there was little ethnic tension; in the third Duma the Latvian for Riga, A. I. Predkaln, and the Petersburg deputy N. G. Poletaev formed a close working relationship. Later, between the two revolutions of 1917, skilled metalworkers did call for the expulsion from Petrograd of unskilled 'Chinese' migrant labour, but it was in the context of a debate over who should, and who should not, be the first to be evacuated from the city; no group wished to accentuate such divisions, and the workers' resolutions were keen to stress how the immigrant labourers 'had been duped into leaving Asia'.[3]

This absence of inter-ethnic tension, on top of the Social Democrats' success in mobilising the popular movement of 1905, was largely due to the success of the nationality policy adopted by the Russian Social Democratic Labour Party (RSDLP). Like so much else in the history of the RSDLP, the question of nationality policy became inter-

---

2 A clear account of the role played by the national minorities in the 1905 revolution can be found in A. Ascher, *The Revolution of 1905. Russia in Disarray* (Stanford, Cal., Stanford University Press, 1988), chapter 6. For additional information see A. Bilmanis, *A History of Latvia* (Princeton, N.J., Princeton University Press, 1951), p. 266, and O. Subtelny, *Ukraine. A History* (Toronto, University of Toronto Press, 1988), p. 297.

3 R. E. Zelnik (ed.), *A Radical Worker in Tsarist Russia* (Stanford, Cal., Stanford University Press, 1986), p. 86; S. A. Smith, *Red Petrograd* (Cambridge, Cambridge University Press, 1983), p. 172.

woven with the factional struggle between Bolsheviks and Mensheviks. The Bolsheviks wanted the highest degree of organisational centralism, the Mensheviks the reverse. When the issue of nationality first surfaced, at the Second Party Conference in 1903, the issue was that of the organisational structure best suited to Jewish workers. The Bolsheviks feared that if the Bund, the organisation of Jewish workers, was allowed to affiliate to the RSDLP, its policy of 'national cultural autonomy' – the idea that national autonomy depended on the existence of a common culture, not the inhabitance of a common territory – would lead to Jewish workers and Russian workers organising separately within the same factory, thus dividing the working class. The Bund was not allowed to affiliate in 1903, but when in 1906 the Mensheviks won control of the RSDLP the decision on the Bund was reversed and the Bund, the Polish–Lithuanian Social Democratic Party and the Latvian Social Democratic Party were admitted to the RSDLP as autonomous organisations with representation on the Central Committee. However, this reversal of policy on the question of affiliation did not change the party's stance on 'national cultural autonomy'; it favoured 'local self-rule' and 'self-determination', both of which implied territorial, not cultural, autonomy.[4]

Lenin showed little interest in the nationality question at this stage, and the 1906 decision suited him, since after the Fifth Party Congress in 1907 his majority on the Central Committee was wafer-thin and depended on the support of the two Poles and one Latvian member (the two Bund representatives always supported the Mensheviks). By 1911 arrests had changed the power balance on the Central Committee, depriving Lenin of his majority. His solution was to relaunch the Bolshevik faction and summon his own party conference at Prague; his Menshevik opponents summoned a conference in Vienna – and the Bund, Poles and Latvians either attended the rival Vienna conference or refused to attend either. It was in this angry frame of mind, deserted by the so-called 'national parties', that Lenin began to reconsider the national question, and denounce the Austrian concept of 'national cultural autonomy' which the Mensheviks had adopted in Vienna. Lenin welcomed the appearance of the 'wonderful Georgian', Stalin, who

---

4 This is the first of a number of occasions when I am indebted to Dr Jeremy Smith of Edge Hill University College for allowing me to read his 1996 University of London Ph.D. thesis 'The Bolsheviks and the National Question 1917–23', in this case his chapter 2. In a number of important ways the new archival material now available enables Dr Smith to challenge the standard interpretation of R. Pipes, *The Formation of the Soviet Union* (Cambridge, Mass., Harvard University Press, 1954). I have not always interpreted things in the same way as Dr Smith, but his scholarship has vastly improved this chapter.

offered to write on the national question, denouncing the Mensheviks and all their works.[5]

Stalin had first rejected 'cultural autonomy' in 1904, and took essentially the same line in the articles he wrote at Lenin's request in *Sotsial Demokrat* in November 1912 and January 1913, and in *Prosveshchenie* in March, April and May 1913. These stressed clearly that, while culture was an essential element of nationality, it meant nothing without territory; the policy of national cultural autonomy was wrong, and needed to be replaced by national regional autonomy. Stalin's writings were in tune with Lenin's immediate needs, and he chose to overlook Stalin's rather lukewarm comments on the party's commitment to self-determination. Stalin's theme was the future relationship between those nationalities who were prepared to continue in some sort of common state structure with Russia; he said little about those who might chose not to do so. He made clear that 'the right of self-determination is an essential element in the solution of the national question', which 'one or another nationality' might take up: but he added that, when it came to the question of self-determination, support for the principle 'did not mean that Social Democracy would not combat and agitate against the harmful institutions of nations and against inexpedient demands of nations'. It was, 'on the contrary, the duty of Social Democracy to conduct such agitation and to endeavour to influence the will of nations so that the nations may arrange their affairs in the way that best corresponds to the interests of the proletariat'.[6]

To Lenin, however, the policy of self-determination was essential. During the First World War his support for self-determination led him to clash with Bukharin. In November 1915 Bukharin tried to get the Central Committee to abandon self-determination, and throughout 1916 he and Lenin engaged in a heated exchange of letters and statements. During this bitter controversy, in which Lenin came down clearly on the side of self-determination, Stalin took a very different line. In the draft of an unpublished article planned for 1916 Stalin seemed implicitly to deny that the right to self-determination implied the right to secede.[7] The disagreement between Lenin and Stalin over the right to self-determination had little importance before the Russian revolution, since the detail of precisely what self-determination meant could not be explored.

5 For factional in-fighting see G. Swain, *Russian Social Democracy and the Legal Labour Movement 1906–14* (London, Macmillan, 1983). For Stalin on the national question see E. Van Ree, 'Stalin and the National Question', *Revolutionary Russia* 7 (1994), pp. 214–20.
6 J. Stalin, *Works* II (London, Red Star Press, 1973), p. 369.
7 Ree, 'Stalin', p. 224.

Yet it would have disastrous consequences for nationality policy when Stalin emerged as the dominant figure in the Bolshevik Party by the end of the 1920s. During the years of revolution, civil war and post-war reconstruction however, Lenin's views predominated and the nationality policy of the Bolshevik Party was successful in persuading a majority of the national groups within the former Russian Empire to collaborate with Soviet Russia on the formation of various new federal states.

Soviet federations under Lenin

During the first months after the seizure of power by the Bolsheviks in October 1917, their hold on power was often tenuous and they were forced frequently to respond to events rather than shape them; but to the extent that they could influence events they tried to reshape the Russian Empire into a federation of soviet republics. The first model for such a federation of nationalities was seen in the relationship which evolved between the Russian and Latvian soviets in the autumn and winter of 1917–18. As the November 1917 Constituent Assembly results showed, the victor in that contest in Latvia was the Latvian Social Democratic Party (LSD), which polled on average over 70 per cent of the vote.[8] The LSD was both nationalist and socialist. Founded back in the 1890s, it owed its early origins to the German Social Democratic Party and, while a constituent part of the RSDLP from 1906 onwards, did not split into Bolshevik and Menshevik factions until May 1918. Its relations with Lenin had always been ambiguous, and in the decade before 1917 the LSD was peripheral to the great party schism of Bolshevik *v.* Menshevik, never committing itself fully to Lenin but always siding with those calling for revolution rather than reform. The party leader, P. Stuchka, true to that tradition, was quick to support Lenin's 1917 April theses when it came to opposing the Provisional Government and was among the first to rally to the slogan 'All power to the Soviets'. When the First Latvian Congress of Soviets met on 29–30 July 1917 it was firmly under the control of the LSD, which established the Soviet Executive, Iskolat, as the *de facto* government of Latvia. In effect, the Latvian soviet state already existed when the Bolsheviks seized power.[9] The attitude of

---

8 A. Ezergailis, *The Latvian Impact on the Bolshevik Revolution. The First Phase, September 1917 to April 1918* (Boulder, Colo., Westview Press, 1983), p. 89.

9 A. Ezergailis, *The 1917 Revolution in Latvia* (Boulder, Colo., Westview Press, 1974), pp. 11–31, 67–73 and 93–127. For the early history of the Latvian Social Democrats see B. Kalnins, 'The Social Democratic Movement in Latvia', in A. and J. Rabinowitch, *Revolution and Politics in Russia. Essays in Memory of B. I. Nicolaevsky* (Indiana, Indiana University Press, 1972).

the LSD to the national question was in many ways contradictory. Despite the fact that the LSD had always campaigned for a federal structure for the RSDLP which would allow the LSD to pursue its own policies on the territory of Latvia, when it came to the future of Latvia as a nation LSD policy verged on the anti-national. Enigmatically Stuchka told the Fifth LSD Congress in July 1917: 'Latvia will be an autonomous part, perhaps the most democratic one, in a democratic republic of Russia. It will be united with Russia as a much as possible and yet independent as much as possible.'[10]

The other nationality to enter into some sort of federative arrangement with Russia in the first months of Bolshevik rule was Ukraine. Here the situation was very different. Unlike Latvia, with its large working class constituency and numerous landless peasants, Ukraine was predominantly rural and in the Constituent Assembly elections voted for the Ukrainian Socialist Revolutionary Party (SRs) and its allies, polling 80 per cent of the vote in their strongest areas and never receiving less than 45 per cent. While only formally constituted in April 1917, the SRs drew on long traditions and its programme was simple: the nationalisation of all land, the formation of a Ukrainian Land Fund, and democratic control of the Land Fund through elections to an autonomous and separate Constituent Assembly for Ukraine. This call for a Ukrainian Constituent Assembly made it the most radical party in Ukraine in 1917 on the national question, and the party's purpose and logic were clear: in this way there would be a separate Land Fund democratically controlled by Ukrainians and land would go to Ukrainian peasants on the principle of individual farming, long practised in Ukraine, rather than the tradition of communal farming common in Russia. In 1917 the SRs was an important participant in the Rada (Council) through which Ukrainians hoped to pressurise Kerensky to acknowledge some degree of autonomy for Ukraine.[11]

The attitude of the SRs to the Bolsheviks was far from straightforward. Since Kerensky was opposed to any meaningful concessions on Ukrainian autonomy the SRs was willing to help the Bolsheviks overthrow the Provisional Government; but it was unwilling to see Lenin dissolve the Constituent Assembly simply because the elections to it had been won by the SRs' allies, the Russian SRs. Soon Russia and Ukraine were facing in opposite directions: in Ukraine the SRs ignored the Bolshevik-dominated Congress of Soviets; and in Russia the Bolsheviks

10 Ezergailis, *1917*, pp. 84–5.
11 S. L. Guthier, 'The Popular Base of Ukrainian Nationalism in 1917', *Slavic Review* 38 (1979), pp. 36–46.

dissolved the SRs-dominated Constituent Assembly. To make an already complicated situation yet more complex, the Ukrainian SRs sought international recognition by opening separate talks with the Germans at Brest Litovsk. To prevent this, the Russian army entered Ukraine in early January 1918. Stalin greeted the decision to interfere in the affairs of another state with the comment 'It is necessary to limit the principle of free self-determination of nations, by granting it to the toilers and refusing it to the bourgeoisie.' Lenin remained silent.[12] But although Lenin may have been embarrassed by the use of Russian troops on Ukrainian soil, there was a large element of truth in the Bolshevik claim that what was happening in Ukraine was in essence a civil war in which the Russian army had intervened, not a war of conquest. By January 1918 the Ukrainian SRs was deeply split: many felt it had been wrong to turn to imperial Germany for support, arguing that it would not have been necessary if they, like the Bolsheviks in Russia, had implemented radical land reform. As the Russian army advanced, it brought with it the Ukrainian People's Secretariat, formed by the Ukrainian Congress of Soviets, and several leading Ukrainian army units quickly rallied to its side. Prominent members of the Ukrainian SRs had to be detained during the war for fear they were planning a *coup* against their own government.[13]

Although most of Ukraine was soon abandoned to German occupation, the Second All-Ukrainian Congress of Soviets met in Ekaterinoslav on 17–19 March 1918 and declared Ukraine an independent soviet federated republic. In April 1918, meeting in Taganrog on 19–20 April 1918, Ukrainian Communists established their own independent Communist Party of Ukraine (KPU) with powers to hold its own congresses, linked with the Bolsheviks only by the yet to be formed Third International.[14]

The decision provoked a typical response from Lenin. The Third Congress of Soviets resolved in January 1918 to establish 'a free union of free nations, a federation of Soviet national republics'. From the evidence of both Latvia and Ukraine in early 1918, this was to have been a fairly loose federation. However, self-determination for the nation did not equal autonomy for the party. When the KPU retreated to Moscow

12 Pipes, *Formation*, p. 109. See also G. Swain, *Origins of the Russian Civil War* (Harlow, Longman, 1996), pp. 92–6.
13 Y. Bilinsky, 'The Communist Take-over of Ukraine', in T. Hunczak (ed.), *The Ukraine 1917–21. A Study in Revolution* (Cambridge, Mass., Harvard University Press, 1977), p. 112; J. Mace, *Communism and the Dilemmas of National Liberation: National Communism in Soviet Ukraine 1918–33* (Cambridge, Mass., Harvard University Press, 1983), p. 53.
14 J. Reshetar, 'KPU and its Role in the Ukrainian Revolution' in Hunczak, *Ukraine*, p. 175.

in summer 1918 Lenin was determined to overrule the Taganrog deci-
sion that the supreme ruling body of the KPU was the Communist
International; this would have put the KPU on an equal footing with the
Bolshevik Party, or, as it was now known, the Russian Communist Party
(RKP). The KPU was forced to backtrack and when the First Congress
was formally held in Moscow in June 1918 it conceded that it was, like
the LSD, a constituent part of the RKP, ultimately responsible to the
Politburo and Lenin.[15]

The end of the First World War and the prospect of German with-
drawal from the territories it occupied opened the way for the restoration of soviet governments in Ukraine and Latvia. In 1919 soviet regimes
were re-established in both countries, but remained short-lived. Their
rapid collapse, however, had nothing to do with the failure of Lenin's
nationality policy. What destroyed the soviet republics in 1919 was the
question of land.

Ignoring the decision of 'bourgeois' nationalists to declare Latvia
independent on 18 November 1918 while German troops still occupied
the country, on 4 December the LSD established a provisional government of the reformed Latvian Soviet Republic. Its party leader, Stuchka,
still favoured close links with revolutionary Russia. Yet, once installed in
Riga, Stuchka found himself acting as a nationalist. The first clash came
with Estonia. As part of the same move to establish soviet regimes in
Latvia and Ukraine in 1919, rather shaky soviet governments were established in Estonia and Lithuania. At once a dispute arose as to whether
the town of Valk was Latvian or Estonian: Stuchka and his government
insisted it was Latvian, and as a result found themselves being attacked
in the Moscow press as 'chauvinists'. The town of Polangen was similarly
disputed with Lithuania.[16]

More alarming were the problems which developed over the future
of Latgale. Latgale, economically the most backward part of Latvia, had
a large Russian population in Dvinsk and Rezhitsa (Daugavpils and
Rezekne). Soon the Russians started to cause trouble, playing on the fact
that for some time after January 1919 Russian wage rates continued to
be paid in Latgale, and asserting Latvian control in Latgale meant reducing wages to the Latvian level, some 20 per cent lower. The Latgale issue
took on even greater significance when it came to the question of the
army. During the Sixth LSD Congress news came through that Moscow
had countermanded the order of the Latvian Soviet Government to

---

15 Reshetar, 'KPU', p. 176.
16 P. Stuchka, *Pyat' mesyatsev Sotsialisticheskoi Sovetskoi Latvii* (Moscow, Gospolizdat,
   1919), pp. 7–16, 21–6.

introduce conscription in Latgale, and had organised conscription in
the area through the Russian soviet authorities, thus recruiting to the
Russian Army of the Western Front, not the Latvian army. In closed
session the congress unanimously appealed to Lenin, pointing out that,
while the LSD remained a constituent part of the Russian party, Latvia
was an independent state and Latgale, according to the agreement of
the previous year, part of Latvia. Cancelling mobilisation to the Latvian
army when the whole of Latvia had not been freed from German occupation and anti-soviet forces were staging a comeback was a 'crime'. 'The
act of independence is still in force and we will not put up with any dis-
organisational work within our territory.'[17]

Clearly, whatever Stuchka's personal views, he pursued policies in
line with the nationalist aspirations of his supporters. What made his
rule so unpopular was his agrarian policy. The LSD programme looked
forward to immediate collective ownership: the first task was to nation-
alise all manorial, Church and state land, then transfer it to the landless,
who would arrange their collective management; small landowners,
forced at once to implement such reforms as the eight-hour day for their
workers, would gradually see the benefits of communal farming and vol-
unteer to join collectives. So, having expropriated the land, the Latvian
Soviet Government established 239 state farms of equal size, which peasants had no choice but to join. By April 1919 even Stuchka was aware of
the excesses involved in this process. He could fool himself into believing that, given peace and time, the state farms would bed down, but even
he had to admit that the so-called 'kulak' rebellions which the state farm
policy inspired throughout Latvia in spring 1919 were not led by kulaks
at all but by poor peasants. The peasants expected land, and the politician to give it to them was the 'bourgeois' politician who had declared
Latvia's independence on 18 November 1918, Karlis Ulmanis. On 23
May 1919 Riga fell to his forces and the experiment with soviet government was over.[18]

The history of the Ukrainian Soviet Republic in 1919 was in many
ways similar, although the leader of the Ukrainian Soviet government,
Khristian Rakovskii, was not himself Ukrainian and was less sympathetic
than Stuchka to national sensitivities. He embarrassed many when, in
March 1919, he doubted the validity of the Ukrainian language.[19] After
some hesitation, Lenin committed himself at the end of November 1918

17 Stuchka, *Pyat'*, pp. 27, 45.
18 Stuchka, *Pyat'*, pp. 75, 84–90. The LSD land programme is summarised in
   Ezergailis, *1917*, p. 67.
19 A. E. Adams, *Bolsheviks in the Ukraine. The Second Campaign, 1918–19* (New Haven,
   Conn., Yale University Press, 1963), p. 232.

to the re-establishment of a Soviet Ukraine and, in a repeat of events during spring 1918, pro-Soviet forces very quickly took control in January and February 1919. Their 'bourgeois' opponents, whose co-called 'Directory' had overthrown the German puppet dictator Skoropadsky on 14 December 1918, had only the most confused of programmes when it came to the question of land and was completely isolated from the peasant masses. In January 1919 the left-wing within the Ukrainian SRs, now the Borotbist Party, called for the re-establishment of the Soviet regime. When the Third All-Ukrainian Congress of Soviets met on 6–10 March 1919 it established the Ukrainian Soviet Republic as an 'independent and sovereign state' with such powers as proclaiming war and peace, forming an army, and financial independence. As it origins make clear, the Ukrainian Soviet Republic was not a Bolshevik creation but a creation of other Socialist parties as well, most notably the Borotbists.

Yet, even though the revived Ukrainian Soviet Republic was a multi-party creation, the KPU insisted on ruling alone. It did so because of its policy on land. As the Red Army advanced through Ukraine it established in its wake not soviets, as promised, but revolutionary committees. In theory these were to prepare for the election of soviets, but in practice they continued as all-powerful, if interim, organs appointed by the Commissar of Internal Affairs and open only to members or supporters of the KPU. Below the revolutionary committees came the 'committees of the poor', an institution imported from Soviet Russia and founded on the Bolshevik notion of class struggle in the countryside. The 'committees of the poor' were to identify and confiscate any grain surpluses, playing out the fiction that the poor peasants in the village saw the better-off peasants not as neighbours but as grain hoarders, who revelled in the prospect of urban proletarians and Red Army soldiers starving to death. The Borotbists did not believe in class struggle in the countryside, arguing that all but the richest of peasants had common interests. To make matters worse, the 'committees of the poor' also took on the task of implementing the government decree on communal farming. By February and March 1919 the forceful implementation of collective farming was well under way.[20]

The agrarian policies of the Latvian and Ukrainian Soviet Republics of 1919 highlighted the mechanism through which their relations with Soviet Russia were to be co-ordinated: Lenin insisted that, while Latvia and Ukraine could be independent states, the LSD and KPU could not be independent parties. In December 1918 Lenin made

20 Adams, *Bolsheviks*, pp. 100–14, 125–30, 217.

a series of speeches in which he called explicitly for the development of collective and state farms as the only way to secure the growth of a socialist economy, and this policy was loyally echoed in Latvia and Ukraine.[21] As Lenin began to comprehend the scale of the impending catastrophe, he instructed the KPU to drop all talk of collectives and state farms and appeal instead to the 'middle peasants'. 'Overzealous' officials, however, continued with the campaign, even though in April 1919 it led to ninety-three anti-government peasant uprisings.[22] So, using the ultimate authority of the RKP Politburo, to which the KPU was subservient, on 18 April 1919 Lenin insisted that, to ensure a change of agrarian policy, the Borotbists must be brought into the Ukrainian government. As the Russian Soviet government struggled to survive in summer 1919, Lenin intervened more than once through party channels in the affairs of the Latvian and Ukrainian Soviet Republics. With the two republics facing military disaster in May 1919, first the armies and then the key defence industries were brought under the overall command of Russia.[23] With the resuscitation of the Soviet Ukraine at the end of 1919 control over the defence industries was at once restored to the Ukrainian government. The situation regarding the army was more of a problem. For the RKP, and therefore the KPU, the issue was clear-cut: the Russian Civil War had proved that, if the non-Russian soviet republics were to survive in the era of capitalist encirclement, they needed a common army; the Borotbists insisted that a separate army for Ukraine was essential. After debates at the highest level, the Politburo in November and the Eighth Party Conference on 3–5 December 1919, the issue was eventually resolved in favour of the KPU. In March 1920 those Borotbists prepared to compromise on the question of an army merged with the KPU to form a united party, winning in return significant concessions for Soviet Ukraine in terms of agrarian policy.[24]

Lenin *v.* Stalin

Lenin's nationality policy was endorsed at the Eighth Party Congress (18–23 March 1919). His policy was clear: the RKP was supreme, and the

21 V. I. Lenin, *Collected Works*, English ed., XXVIII (Moscow, Gospolitizdat, 1963), p. 339.
22 Adams, *Bolsheviks*, pp. 224–9.
23 Adams, *Bolsheviks*, p. 218; Pipes, *Formation*, p. 147. Lenin's letter to Rakovskii in mid-May 1919 in *Works* XLIV, p. 233, shows clearly how the authority of the RKP Central Committee was invoked.
24 Adams, *Bolsheviks*, p. 396; Mace, *Communism*, pp. 60–6; Smith, 'The Bolsheviks', pp. 107–9. Note: page references from Smith's thesis are from a disk copy kindly made available by the author and do not always correspond exactly to the printed version.

KPU and other national parties were subject to the RKP Central
Committee and Politburo, but the peoples themselves had the right to
self-determination to the point of secession. He insisted that self-determination should remain in the newly adopted party programme, despite
the fact that Bukharin's original draft had dropped the phrase and many
delegates had argued that the previous two years' experience had shown
how the slogan had become a rallying point for counter-revolutionar-
ies.[25]

Once the Civil War was over five independent soviet republics came
into existence: Ukraine, Byelorussia, Azerbaijan, Armenia and
Georgia.[26] Relations between these republics were governed by treaties
and came under the jurisdiction of the Commissariat of Foreign Affairs.
However, a series of disputes concerning Ukraine and Georgia
prompted the Bolsheviks to establish a commission chaired by Stalin to
review the situation, and the result was the so-called 'autonomisation'
proposal of autumn 1922. Since 1920 Stalin had been busy resolving the
national problem within Russia itself, the Russian Socialist Federative
Soviet Republic (RSFSR), and had done so by establishing autonomous
national regions for such non-Russian peoples as the Bashkirs, in line
with his writings of 1913. In 1922 he concluded that the simplest solution to the relations between the independent soviet republics was to
extend this principle: Ukraine and the other republics would enter into
the RSFSR as autonomous regional units.[27]

Stalin had clashed with Lenin as early as June 1920 on whether
there was any difference between the status of a nationality like the
Bashkirs, who were granted regional autonomy within the RSFSR, and
the Ukrainians, who formed a separate republic. Stalin's writings of 1913
had made clear that he wanted, in future, to grant 'regional autonomy'
to Lithuania, Ukraine and the Caucusus.[28] His increasing disdain for
national self-determination was not shared by Lenin. At the end of
December 1922, in some of his last writings, Lenin opposed Stalin's idea
of 'autonomisation' as 'basically wrong and inopportune'. Stalin's justification for it had been pragmatic, the 'need for unity of the apparatus';
but that Lenin dismissed as the demand of the apparatus itself, the old
apparatus inherited from tsarist days which had no interest or commit-

25 Smith, 'The Bolsheviks', p. 23.
26 Georgia was forcibly sovietised by an invading Russian army early in 1921, a further
   example of Lenin's ambivalence on the national question when the fate of the
   revolution was at stake.
27 Smith, 'The Bolsheviks', p. 165.
28 Smith interprets the 1920 incident rather differently; see 'The Bolsheviks', p. 161.
   For regional autonomy see Stalin, *Works* II, p. 375.

ment to the Bolshevik project. He made it clear: 'I think that a fatal role was played here by haste and the administrative impetuousity of Stalin.' Lenin mused about the failings of members of great nations, how they were often unaware of how others interpreted their actions. The solution was to concede that the next Congress of Soviets could 'decide to return to the former situation, i.e. that we retain the Union of Socialist Republics only in the sphere of military affairs and diplomacy, while in other matters each of the People's Commissariats will be fully independent'. Any lack of co-ordination of work with Moscow could be overcome by using 'the authority of the Party'.[29]

When the Twelfth Party Congress met in April 1923 to debate Stalin's proposals, Lenin's views were known and the representatives of the national republics, particularly Rakovskii for Ukraine, subjected them to sustained criticism. Rakovskii came closest to Lenin's position by repeatedly insisting that the proposed Union Commissariats should be deprived of nine-tenths of their powers, and those powers handed back to the national republics. When a special meeting of delegates was held on 25 April to debate the national question, Rakovskii made it clear that what he envisaged was that only defence, internal economic policy and trade needed to be controlled by Union commissariats. In the end, compared with Stalin's original proposals, the constitutional status and powers of the national republics were greatly enhanced. These concessions were included in the new USSR constitution approved on 31 January 1924. Stalin held firm on just one issue. The constitution established a second Chamber, the Council of Nationalities. Rakovskii wanted to reserve that chamber for representatives of the federating republics. Stalin insisted that the nationalities within the RSFSR should also have a voice. This apparently reasonable request was granted, but its consequence was to give the RSFSR a dominant position in the Council of Nationalities, a Trojan horse that Stalin would be able to exploit by the end of the decade.[30]

National Communism?

Until Stalin's collectivisation campaign, as the example of the Ukraine shows, the constitution offered genuine opportunities for the separate republics of the Soviet Union. The Borotbist tradition was not lost, and one of its former leaders, O. Shumskii, became Commissar of Education in 1925, helping to attract back to the country many of those who had

29 Lenin, *Works* XLV, Russian 5th edn (Moscow, Gospolitizdat, 1970), pp. 356–60.
30 Smith, 'Bolsheviks', pp. 192–206.

emigrated during the course of the Civil War. Shumskii fell foul of Stalin for suggesting that the time had come for a former Borotbist to head the KPU, but his replacement in 1927, Mykola Skrypnik, was if anything more committed to the flowering of Ukrainian culture within the confines of the Soviet Union and seemed 'sincerely to have believed that the Soviet Union could be a socialist world in embryo, and the relations between Soviet Ukraine and Soviet Russia the model for the future relations between a socialist Germany and France'.[31]

Skrypnik had been a firm supporter of an independent Ukraine. Back in February 1918, when the first Ukrainian Soviet Republic had been established, he headed an 'extraordinary plenipotentiary embassy' to Moscow to proclaim the new state's independence. Then, in the work of the 1922 commissions which established the Soviet Union, he had argued for the republics retaining a say in foreign affairs and foreign trade and had joined in the criticism of Stalin at the Twelfth Party Congress. Finally, within the Council of Nationalities he became the leading defender of the rights of the republics. In particular he tried to prevent the adoption in 1927 of an all-Union agricultural plan and in 1928 of central restrictions on the budgets of the national republics.

Skrypnik's vision of Russia and Ukraine building socialism together as equal partners did not fit into Stalin's world of collectivisation and five-year industrial plans. Skrypnik's fate was sealed when he demanded a reduction in Ukraine's grain delivery quotas at the Third All-Ukrainian KPU Conference (6–9 July 1932). Famine in the republic, brought about by the collectivisation campaign, prompted Skrypnik to challenge Stalin in this way. Stalin's response was to conclude that the Borotbist pro-peasant wing of the KPU was back in the ascendancy and had succumbed to its tradition of opposition to collective and state farming. Subject to repeated denunciations for 'sheltering national deviationists' and defending the 'bourgeois nationalism' of the Ukrainian kulak, Skrypnik committed suicide on 6 July 1933.[32] With him died any notion that the USSR could be anything more than Stalin's 1922 'autonomisation' proposal, a Russian-led state offering limited regional autonomy to its member nationalities. Stalin had triumphed over Lenin.

Skrypnik's death was just the start of a purge of alleged nationalists; between January 1933 and 1934 100,000 were expelled from the KPU, while nearly the entire staff of the Commissariat of Education were sacked. In January 1934 there were 453,526 KPU members, by May 1938

31 Mace, *Communism*, p. 192.
32 Mace, *Communism*, pp. 297–9.

there were only 285,818; the entire KPU Politburo and Central
Committee Secretariat, with one exception, died, as did the entire
Ukrainian government.[33] While Ukraine suffered more than most, all
nationalities were under attack. When the purges were at last over the
nationality policy of the Soviet Union was a far cry from Lenin's vision
and well on the way to the Russian-dominated state celebrated in the
words of the Soviet anthem, a state which assigned the Russian people a
leading role, and which in the 1940s would develop an undercurrent of
antisemitism which brought it even closer to the ideology embraced in
1905 by 'Russia's fascists', the URP.

In pursuing his anti-national policy, Stalin was well aware that he
could exploit the latent great-nation chauvinism of Russian workers,
which had never been allowed formal expression. Most industrial
workers, in Ukraine were ethnic Russians; urban culture was, broadly
speaking, Russian; yet the policy of Ukrainianisation pursued in the
1920s involved developing Ukrainian as a state language. The problem
always came with industrial workers, who were unwilling to learn
Ukrainian and preferred to stick with Russian or the near Russian dialect
of eastern Ukraine. In 1926 Stalin warned the Ukrainian leaders that
'any attempt to force Ukrainian ways on Russian proletarians would only
serve to alienate the Party and would constitute a violation of their right
to their own national culture'.

Although ethnic Russians in Ukraine had the right to education in
their native tongue, some resentment at the Ukrainianisation policy was
natural, and provided fertile ground for Stalin to pose as the defender
of the Russian proletarian who would restrict 'nationalist excesses'.
Despite all the efforts of the Ukrainian government, as peasants flocked
to the new factories thrown up during the first five-year plan, most abandoned Ukrainian and took up the industrial dialect.[34] During the years
of industrialisation, Russian was the language of skill, the language of
Stakhanovism. Beneath the surface a sense of cultural superiority
lurked, and every now and then burst out in the form of antisemitism:
in 1930 the press recounted occasions on which managers lost control
of factory meetings addressed by officials with Jewish names and populist resolutions were passed calling for a 'USSR without Communists or
Jews'. The first part of this slogan Stalin deplored. The second he did
not mind, turning it to his advantage, and references to the leading role
of Russian proletarians ensured Stalin could harness such prejudice

---

33 B. Krawchenko, *Social Change and National Consciousness in Twentieth Century Ukraine*
    (London, Macmillan, 1985), pp. 145–50.
34 Mace, *Communism*, pp. 100, 214.

without it ever emerging as an independent political force.[35] Lenin, of course, was no democrat and was prepared to take undemocratic measures both to export revolution and to save the course of revolutions in other countries he saw as linked with his own. But he did understand the power of nationalism over people's minds, and did, by proposing the dialectic of self-determination for the state but centralisation for the party, offer a vision of how the interests of the nation and of revolution could be reconciled.

35 V. Anderle, *Workers in Stalin's Russia* (Hemel Hempstead, Harvester–Wheatsheaf, 1988), p. 144. In his *Stakhonovism and the Politics of Productivity in the USSR 1935–41* (Cambridge, Cambridge University Press, 1988) p. 127, L. Siegelbaum notes how Russian language courses were organised for prospective Stakhanovites.

The working class in the United States: between radical republicanism and the 'American standard'

While organised labour's attitudes and practices in the United States towards the discrete areas of nationalism and ethnicity have received considerable historiographical attention, fully integrated studies of labour, nationalism and ethnicity have been conspicuous mainly by their absence. This chapter constitutes such an integrated study and aims, in the process, to make a contribution to filling gaps in historical knowledge and to breaking new substantive and methodological ground. A related and subsidiary purpose is, where appropriate, to incorporate the issues of social class, gender and cross-national comparisons and contrasts into our framework of reference.

Before proceeding to our main task, it is important to outline the key methodological assumptions and procedures which underpin this chapter. These assumptions and procedures will then be incorporated into a substantive discussion with respect to three distinct, if linked, chronological periods. The first, marked by the hegemony of 'radical republican' ideas, dates from the post-Civil War years to the 1890s. The second, embracing the decades from the 1890s to the late 1920s Depression – with the First World War and its aftermath constituting something of a watershed in relation to all three of our subject areas – experienced fierce ideological conflicts and the eventual ascendancy of the conservative ideas and practices of the American Federation of Labour (AFL). The final period – the 1930s decade – saw the revival of radical notions of 'Americanism' and organised labour significantly extending its ethnic and class appeal. In moving, finally, to assess the relative weight of radical and conservative influences upon organised labour and questions of nationalism and ethnicity, the chapter will address the issue of American 'exceptionalism'.

In terms of methodological assumptions and procedures, central importance is attached to the *historical construction and reconstruction* of labour, ethnicity and nationalism – as opposed to a notion of their unchanging and 'naturally given' characteristics – and their complex – indeed often contested – articulations and interpretations.

As we shall see in more detail below, organised labour and the working class in the United States have been 'made' and 'remade' more often and more profoundly than in many other societies, not only as a result of the transforming actions of capital and the state to maximise capital accumulation, but also as a consequence of repeatedly massive and changing waves of immigration and migration, and patterns of occupational change and mobility. Within the labour movement conflicting forces have vied for control. And working-class experience and consciousness have been complex sites for the interplay of forces conducive either to unity or to fragmentation, or to a mixture of both.

The terms 'ethnicity' and 'nationalism' must likewise be divested of fixed and one-dimensional associations and meanings. Along with the late Herbert Gutman, David Roediger and James Hinton, we wish to emphasise the frequently synchronised and related, as opposed to the sequential and discrete, nature of the processes or constructions of ethnicity and nationalism, and, we might usefully add, social class.[1] Furthermore, as Cecelia Bucki has perceptively argued, 'We need to historicize the social construction of ethnicity in the early twentieth-century United States in order to comprehend how immigrant workers saw themselves in American society and how they "fit" into an emerging American citizenship.' This necessity is anchored in the historical facts that 'The patterns of ethnic identity-building and their relation to American society have quite different elements before and after World War I' and that, far from being monolithic in character, immigrant communities contained their own differences and divisions with respect to class structure, the use of American political ideals and definitions of ethnicity.[2] Similarly, the often interdependent identities of ethnicity, class, race and gender interacted in multiple and by no means necessarily antagonistic ways.

Nationalistic, or patriotic, feelings and principles also manifested themselves in a number of ways and could assume different and conflicting meanings with respect to time and place, class, race and gender.

---

1 H.G. Gutman, *Work, Culture and Society in Industrializing America. Essays in American Working Class and Social History* (New York, Vintage Books, 1977); D. Roediger, 'Race and the Working Class Past in the United States: Multiple Identities and the Future of Labour History', *International Review of Social History* 38, Supplement 1 (1993), especially pp. 130–1; J. Hinton, 'Voluntarism versus Jacobinism: Labor, Nation and Citizenship in Britain 1850–1950', *International Labor and Working Class History* 48 (1995), pp. 68–90.
2 C. F. Bucki, 'Workers and Politics in the Immigrant City in the early Twentieth Century United States', *International Labor and Working Class History*, 48 (1995), pp. 32–4.

For example, radical, revolutionary and conservative notions of 'Americanism' were present among workers, at various points of time and to varying degrees, during the period from 1870 to 1939. And nationalistic and class-based considerations were often interlaced.[3]

To highlight the importance of historical change, complexity and contestation to the study of the subjects of labour, nationalism and ethnicity is to offer a competing perspective to those viewpoints which treat these subjects as possessing either largely unchanging and 'natural' and/or uniform characteristics. For example, many 'old' (i.e. predominantly pre-1960s) labour historians, working within the 'exceptionalist' or 'market-embedded' paradigm of the 'Wisconsin school', maintained that the conservative, sectional and 'business-unionist' American Federation of Labour attained, more or less inevitability, its leading position within the early twentieth-century labour movement on the grounds that it derived its characteristics from the enduring hegemonic values and norms of the wider society. The latter were seen to reside in fundamental 'liberal' commitments to a market-based economy and society, to individualism, competition and acquisitiveness, and to pluralism and democracy. Furthermore, the very ethnic heterogeneity of the work force, allied to the supposedly unique and high material rewards, 'openness' and responsiveness to individual talent and character offered by the American social and political systems, underpinned American 'exceptionalism'. American workers were held, by a long line of distinguished 'old' labour historians and political commentators, to have lacked the 'true' class consciousness of their European and Brtish counterparts.[4]

Since the 1960s the 'natural common sense' of the 'old' labour history has quite properly been subjected to searching criticism by the 'new' labour history. However, one can still encounter the misleading viewpoint that late nineteenth and early twentieth-century US labour was more or less uniformly reactionary, anti-black, anti-immigrant and sexist.[5] By way of contrast, we suggest that detailed attention to the historical record reveals a far more nuanced and complex picture. We will begin with the post-Civil War period.

3 Hinton, 'Voluntarism', p. 68.
4 For a guide to, and trenchant critique of, the position of 'exceptionalism' see S. Wilentz, 'Against Exceptionalism: Class Consciousness and the American Labor Movement 1790–1920', *International Labor and Working Class History*, 26 (1984), pp. 1–25. See, also, the replies to Wilentz by Salvatore and Hanagan in the same issue of *International Labor and Working Class History*.
5 For the expression of such a viewpoint see G. Mink, *Old Labor and New Immigrants in American Political Development. Union, Party and State 1875–1920* (London, Cornell University Press, 1986).

Radical republicanism 1870–90s

As Leon Fink has suggested, 'labor republicanism, or some variation on that term, has served to define the characteristic ideology of the orga-nized labor movement in the nineteenth century'.[6] Labour's republican-ism was synonymous with radical patriotism, with, to borrow David Montgomery's phrase, 'a deep and abiding faith in the republican insti-tutions created in the eighteenth century, which guided the movement through its many forms until the depression of the 1890s'.[7] At the heart of organised labour's republican faith and vision were commitments to active citizenship and democracy – significantly, by the 1830s most white adult males possessed the suffrage – weak central government and the achievement of human happiness mainly through voluntary endeavours in the sphere of civil society. Labour also believed in a suitably moral-ised, regulated and civilised market place which would promote eco-nomic progress and meet human needs; and an 'open' social order based upon 'equal rights' – in which merit and character would receive their due reward, as opposed to the 'accident' of birth and the 'foul privileges' of heredity. Great store was set by the values and norms of per-sonal and collective independence, 'respectability', hard, honest endea-vour, and mutuality and brotherhood. Labour's ideal type was the staunchly independent-minded, virtuous and honest 'producer citizen', prepared to fight to the death in defence of his (*sic*) home and family and the modern world's first republican nation. Support was given to westward expansion in order to 'extend the "empire" for liberty', and to democratic and republican movements and ideas abroad.[8] Chattel slavery, 'European-style' 'closed', centralised, undemocratic and author-itarian forms of government, and 'aristocratic' and other forms of 'monopoly' and/or class privilege, were regarded as incompatible with the republican virtues of liberty, democracy and independence.

Between the immediate post-Civil War years and the 1890s organ-ised labour's republicanism was, as observed by Montgomery, 'decisively shaped' by three developments: 'the political triumph of the northern bourgeoisie, chronic deflation, and the nation-wide ascendancy of cap-italist relationships'.[9] Increasingly, the 'facts of class' – in terms of both

---

6 L. Fink, 'The New Labor History and the Powers of Historical Pessimism: Consensus, Hegemony and the Case of the Knights of Labor', *Journal of American History* 75:1 (1988), p. 116.

7 D. Montgomery, 'Labor and the Republic in Industrial America 1860–1920', *Mouvement Social* 111 (1980), p. 201.

8 M. H. Hunt, *Ideology and US Foreign Policy* (New Haven, Conn., Yale University Press, 1987), p. 23.

9 Montgomery, 'Labor and the Republic', p. 202.

structured exploitation and the expression of common worker interests, values and ideas in opposition to other social groups – informed workers' ideologies alongside and in engagement with cross-class 'liberal' commitments to 'economic markets and representative democracy' and to individual choice and freedom.[10] As Sean Wilentz has demonstrated, the growth of industrial capitalism and proletarianisation, combined with the perceived concentration of wealth and power in in fewer and fewer 'monopoly' hands, had served, albeit intermittently and unevenly in the face of ethnic and other divisions, to promote class-based sentiments and actions among workers in the ante-bellum decades.[11] During the Civil War nationalist and secessionist sentiments had prevailed over those of class. But, as Montgomery informs us, the triumph of capitalist power and social relationships throughout the post-bellum nation greatly extended proletarianisation, and increased the insecurity of many small urban and rural producers straddling the fine line between property ownership and 'wage slavery'. Furthermore, mounting instances of 'tyrannical' government, judicial and employer actions towards workers and their collective organisations – in order to offset declining prices and profit margins and firmly to assert their 'mastery' of the nation's life – did provide labour's republicanism with a sharper, more militant and in many ways more class-based, if largely non-socialist, cutting edge.

For example, and notwithstanding continued diversity and even conflicts among post-bellum workers, the main organisations of the labour movement – the National Labor Union (1866–72), the Knights of Labor (formed in 1869), the various currency, land reform and socialist movements and members of the infant American Federation of Labor (established in 1886) – found a common faith in the ideology of the 'universal brotherhood of labor'.[12] This ideology took as its starting point the 'inevitable and irresistible conflict between the wage-system of labor and the republican system of government', and, in class-conscious fashion, attributed the 'demise of the American republic and the growing concentration of wealth and power' to 'the inequalities and unnatural dependencies of the wages system'. Labour's aims

---

10 I. Katznelson, 'The "Bourgeois" Dimension: a Provocation about Institutions, Politics and the Future of Labor History', *International Labor and Working Class History*, 46 (1994), pp. 21 and 23–6.

11 Wilentz, 'Against Exceptionalism'; S. Wilentz, *Chants Democratic. New York City and the Rise of the American Working Class 1788–1850* (New York, Oxford University Press, 1986).

12 Montgomery, 'Labor and the Republic', p. 202; S. J. Ross, *Workers on the Edge. Work Leisure and Politics in Industrializing Cincinnati 1788–1890* (New York, Columbia University Press, 1985), chapter 8.

were to oppose the workings of the unregulated market and its attendant 'acquisitive individualism', and to promote equity and justice for
the 'producers' by means of economic regulation (in relation to the
conditions of work and the banking and currency systems), the restoration of independence (via trade unionism, co-operative production
and land reform) and the wider and more effective dissemination of
the principles of mutuality and democracy. In such ways was the late
nineteenth-century republic to be redeemed from 'the corrupting
power and "class legislation" of "the monopolists"'. Finally, primary reliance was to be placed upon the voluntary self-activity of working
people, the labour movement and their allies rather than upon the *dirigiste* state.[13]

Familiarity with the main features of labour republicanism places
us in a good position fully to understand workers' and their movements'
stances towards the issue of ethnicity. As astutely observed by A. T. Lane
in his study of American labour and European immigrants to the United
States, the primary social division drawn by the post-bellum labour
movement between 'producers' and 'parasites' meant that 'there should
be no distinctions between workers on the grounds of race or nationality'. As the 'Address to Workingmen', issued before the National Labor
Union's convention in 1867, stated, it was 'a grand ennobling idea that
the interests of labor are one; that there should be no distinction of race
or nationality . . . that there is one dividing line, that which separates
mankind into two great classes, the class that labors and the class that
lives by others' labor'.[14] Solidaristic and internationalist sentiments,
strongly generated by the traditional standing of the republic as a haven
of liberty for the poor and oppressed of other countries and the valuable
contributions made by immigrants to the economic, social and political
life of the nation, were further expressed and developed from the 1870s
to the 1890s by idealistic and class-conscious members of the Knights
and the early AFL and the socialists. As noted by Lane:

Admittedly, all these organizations made compromises over the immigration
question, but the essential point is that in tracing the roots of working-class
impoverishment to the financial manipulators and the capitalists, they averted
the search for scapegoats for social problems and concentrated attention on the
real rather than the symbolic causes of labor's dissatisfaction – for example, the
diminution of opportunity, the loss of worker autonomy, and the impersonality
of the work process.

13 Montgomery, 'Labor and the Republic', pp. 204–8; Wilentz, 'Against
   Exceptionalism', pp. 14–15; Fink, 'New Labor History', pp. 118–19.
14 Quoted in A. T. Lane, *Solidarity or Survival? American Labor and European Immigration
   1830–1924* (London, Greenwood Press, 1987), pp. 40–1.

And, more problematically,

immigration was a peripheral matter or an irrelevance; what was necessary was fundamental social and economic reform, which could best be attained by a united movement of all workers, of whatever ethnicity, religion or culture.[15]

It is instructive in this context to note the 'occupational inclusiveness' of the Knights, who, notes Fink, 'barred only lawyers, stockbrokers, bankers, and saloonkeepers from membership'. The 'classed producerism' of the Knights also permitted the organisation to 'extend itself beyond a constituency of old immigrants and old-stock Americans toward new immigrant, Afro-American, and female recruits'. Similarly, in the early years of the AFL, Gompers, himself an immigrant from London and the Federation's first president, strongly opposed racism, promoted inclusive rather than exclusive trade unionism and demanded equal pay for equal work on behalf of men and women.[16]

The ante- and post-bellum involvement of immigrants in workers' movements, combined with their growing numerical and strategic importance within both the population as a whole and the working class, were also conducive, within limits, to the development of positive and inclusive attitudes on the part of organised labour towards the question of ethnicity. The researches of Clifton K. Yearley, Ray Boston, Maldwyn Jones, Herbert Gutman, Montgomery and other scholars have clearly demonstrated the important contributions made by British and North and West European immigrants to the formation and development of nineteenth-century labour movements in the United States. Particularly striking was the prominence of these 'old' immigrants in positions of labour leadership.[17]

In the early decades of the nineteenth century largely native-born artisans and others had *formed* the emerging US working class. However, as shown by the pioneering research of Gutman and Ira Berlin, relatively few of these native-born artisans were to play a central part in the subsequent *development* of the working class up to 1880. Rather, while upward occupational mobility and economic indepen-

---

15 Lane, *Solidarity*, p. 211.
16 Fink, 'The New Labor History', pp. 118–19; N. Kirk, *Labour and Society in Britain and the USA 1780–1939* II, *Challenge and Accommodation* (Aldershot, Scolar Press, 1994), p. 141.
17 M. A. Jones, *American Immigration* (Chicago, University of Chicago Press, 1969), pp. 221–2; Gutman, *Work*; D. Montgomery, *Beyond Equality. Labor and the Radical Republicans 1862–72* (Urbana, University of Illinois Press, 1981); R. Boston, *British Chartists in America 1839–1900* (Manchester, Manchester University Press, 1971); C. K. Yearley, *Britons in American Labour. A History of the Influence of United Kingdom Immigrants on American Labour 1820–1914* (Baltimore, Md., Johns Hopkins University Press, 1957).

dence maintained, with some important exceptions, their real promise for many of the white native-born population, immigrants and their children increasingly provided – 'from New England's mill towns to Rocky Mountain mining camps' – 'the overwhelming majority of industrial wage earners'. During the middle and later decades of the century white manual workers of native-born parents did admittedly form a conspicuous presence in parts of New England, in Pennsylvania and in the Hudson and Mohawk valleys. But increasingly, while the shops, offices and farms of the country were staffed mainly by the native-born, the working class of the urban areas of the Middle West, west and south-west was composed of foreign-born immigrants and their native-born children; and by 1880 immigrants and their children 'dominated the wage-earning population in most Middle Atlantic cities of any size'.[18]

Three conclusions may be drawn from this evidence. First, as argued by Gutman, 'over the entire nation, native white workers of native white parents composed a small percentage of the developing working class'. Second, as highlighted by Montgomery, by the end of the century 'immigrants and their children were not intruders on the working class and the labour movement. They were the working class, and they made the labour movement.'[19] Third, as a corollary, a one-dimensional identification of the late nineteenth-century and early twentieth-century US labour movements with the native born and with more or less uniform opposition to immigrant participation is clearly false.

Simultaneously, however, we must include the necessary caveat that labour's acceptance of – indeed, support for – immigration was by no means unconditional. The validity of this proposition will be amply demonstrated in the next chronological section of this chapter dealing with the years from the 1890s to the late 1920s. However, it is also immediately apparent that labour's overall support for an open-door policy towards immigration in the pre-1890 period contained within it significant limitations and boundaries and notions of the unwelcome 'other'. Furthermore, labour's attitudes and practices towards Afro-American workers in both the north and the south were frequently, if not invariably, contradictory and hostile.

18 H. G. Gutman and I. Berlin, *Power and Culture. Essays on the American Working Class* (New York, Pantheon, 1987), pp. 380–94; D. Montgomery, *The Fall of the House of Labor. The Workplace the State and American Labor Activism 1865–1925* (Cambridge, Cambridge University Press, 1987), p. 48.
19 D. Montgomery, 'Gutman's Agenda for Future Historical Research', *Labor History* 29 (1988), p. 307.

In turning to address the issue of organised labour's ethnic limits, it is first of all advisable to outline the immigrant demographic context in which the issue of ethnicity must be placed. As Jones has informed us, there were three great waves of immigration into the United States between 1815 and 1914. The first and second of these waves – those of the 'old' immigration – were drawn predominantly from the British Isles, Germany, Scandinavia, Switzerland and Holland, and embraced approximately 5 million immigrants in the ante-bellum period and 10 million between 1860 and 1890. As late as 1882, 87 per cent of immigrants came from the countries of Northern and Western Europe. However, towards the end of the nineteenth century the 'old' immigration was increasingly overshadowed by 'new' immigration from capitalism's 'rural periphery' (to use Montgomery's term) in the countries of Southern and Eastern Europe. Thus, of a total of 15 million immigrants entering the United States between 1890 and 1914 the vast majority were drawn from the rural villages and towns of Austria-Hungary, Italy, Greece, Rumania, Turkey and Russia. Indeed, by 1896 the volume of the 'new' immigration had outstripped that of the 'old', and 'the disparity between the two groups became really marked . . . after the turn of the century'. Finally, the proletarian character of much late nineteenth-century immigrant life became even more pronounced with the arrival and settlement of the 'new' immigrants.[20]

As we will see in due course, the development of 'new' immigration saw a significant change of attitude, in favour of overall restriction, among influential sections of the twentieth-century labour movement. But we should first substantiate our thesis that organised labour's stance towards immigrants in the pre-1890s period was conditional and was characterised by important exceptions to the inclusive norm. Broadly speaking, immigrants were accepted – indeed, often welcomed – by nineteenth-century US workers and their movements on the condition that three requirements were met: that the immigrants were not perceived to pose a serious threat to the living standards, workplace controls, independence, skill or general economic standing and security – the 'American standard' – of their 'hosts'; that abidance by this standard, in its economic form, was accompanied by a commitment to adopt, uphold and protect the norms, values and patterns of behaviour associated with labour's 'radical republicanism', 'true citizenship' and 'honest and manly independence'; and that the immigrants should display solidarity with their worker-producer-citizen 'Americans'.[21]

20 Jones, *American Immigration*, pp. 178–9.
21 Lane, *Solidarity*, pp. 213–14.

Failure to meet one or more of these assimilative requirements could, and often did, result in hostility and conflict. For example, during the 1840s and beyond Irish Catholics had been the object of violent nativist outpourings, involving strongly 'producerist' native-born artisans and workers, on the alleged grounds that they were acting as the agents of a despotic Papacy intent upon undermining republican political, religious and civil liberties, honesty in public affairs and politics, and the 'sober and industrious' habits and living standards of the native born. Ante-bellum German immigrants' 'fondness for drink and their tendency to violate the sanctity of the Sabbath', combined with their strong attachment to their native tongue and customs and the socialism of those who had fled in the wake of the revolution of 1848 (the Forty-eighters) had also, and notwithstanding the considerable diversity of German immigrant life, met with nativist disapproval and, at times, physical violence during the 1850s. And during the latter decade nativist groups, involving craft and artisan workers, sought to 'restrict the holding of public office to the native born and to extend the period of residence for naturalization from five to twenty-one years'.[22]

During the period from 1865 to the 1890s labour movements repeatedly voiced their opposition to the importation of immigrant labour under contract, on the grounds that the latter had a marked tendency to 'cheapen and degrade' the resident work force. Significantly, contract workers themselves were thought to be lacking the independence of mind and action required by the 'republican standard'. They were widely viewed as the pliable instruments of capital, as strikebreakers, and as interested less in permanent settlement and the attainment of the 'American standard' and labour solidarity than in the achievement of a temporary 'stake' under bad working conditions and thereafter a return to their native lands. 'Coolie' labour, associated especially with Chinese, and later Japanese, immigrants in California, also met with profound and sustained opposition. In the case of the Chinese the negative stereotypes of servile, cheap and dependent labour (with the Chinese 'acting as the unthinking agents of monopolistic corporations like the Central Pacific Railway') and competition in the labour market merged with widespread racist beliefs in white superiority and the 'alien' nature of Chinese customs to produce 'a virulently anti-Chinese movement' in California and elsewhere. Indeed, as noted by Montgomery:

22 Ross, *Workers on the Edge*, chapter 7; Lane, *Solidarity*, chapter 2.

The unions and the Knights of Labor in the Far West not only lobbied for legal prohibition of Chinese immigration but also, after passage of the Exclusion Act of 1882, unleashed an 'abatement' campaign to drive Chinese by force away from mines, shops and lumber camps and formed a League of Deliverance, which attempted to compel all San Francisco employers to replace Chinese workers with white union members.[23]

Many Afro-Americans also felt the negative effects of labour's limited definitions of republican citizenship, producerism and class. As Nell Painter has claimed, racism 'has affected the whole of American society (and) the whole of the American working class'. As a consequence, 'White supremacy made it extremely difficult for workers who thought of themselves as white to combine with those they thought of as non-white. In the short term, lack of solidarity undermined numberless strike actions, making "Negro" and "Scab" virtually synonymous terms early in the twentieth century.'[24] Notwithstanding the widespread support for the cause of abolition in the ante-bellum period, anti-black attitudes and actions exerted a powerful influence among white workers. During the 1840s and 1850s increased labour market competition provided a spur to a sharp escalation in racist violence. During the Anti-draft Riots of 1863, which witnessed the 'bloodiest urban violence in the country's history', New York City experienced three horrendous days of lynchings of black people and 'devastation of their dwellings'. In the post-bellum years the newly enfranchised Afro-American adult males encountered formidable barriers against their active involvement in the labour movement. As in the ante-bellum decades, most unions continued to bar blacks from membership, and white working-class and trade union opposition to the employment of black workers meant that the latter were repeatedly forced, often as strikebreakers and a source of cheap labour, into the embrace of sympathetic employers. In turn, the latter frequently promoted ethnic and racial divisions within the working class in order to maintain the supremacy of capital over labour. Finally, much of the labour movement during the Reconstruction era and beyond 'displayed little understanding or sympathy with the desires of the freed people of the South for ownership of land, control over their own labour and for equal rights'. And the close identification between Afro-Americans and the Republicans (as the party of Lincoln and black emancipation) curried little favour with those workers who identified the Democrats as the party of 'the common man' and the

---

23 Montgomery, *The Fall*, p. 85; A. Saxton, *The Indispensable Enemy. Labor and the Anti-Chinese Movement in California* (Berkeley, University of California Press, 1971); Lane, *Solidarity*, pp. 41–4 and 69.
24 N. Painter, Symposium, *Labor History*, 30 (1989), pp. 119 and 131.

'true home of the working classes'.[25] Finally, American Indians were effectively excluded from membership of labour's producers.

Yet we must be careful to strike a proper balance in relation to the question of labour and ethnicity. Of overriding significance is the fact that the limits and exclusions characterising workers' attitudes towards immigrants, native Americans and Afro-Americans up to the 1890s can be properly set within the dominant frameworks of inclusive, 'producerist nationalism' and support for mainly unrestricted immigration into the United States. As Lane reminds us, even the powerful nativist movements of the 1850s, concerned to reduce 'the pernicious political influence of the foreign-born population', nevertheless upheld the 'traditional right of asylum' and excluded from their political programmes 'any reference to legislative resrictions on immigrants'.[26] We should also take care not to view class and ethnicity as necessarily and fixedly standing in mutual opposition. Rather we can identify a changing historical relationship in which, at least in terms of the nineteenth-century United States, was based upon a complex, and often contradictory and simultaneous, interplay of elements of harmony and discord.

Furthermore, as indicated earlier, in a number of contexts harmony and cooperation outweighed disagreement and conflict. For example, during the 1830s immigrant and non-immigrant workers, Protestants and Catholics, drinkers and abstainers, and 'traditionalist', 'revivalist' and 'radical' men, and, to a certain extent, women, had joined together in impressive and increasingly class-conscious radical movements. In the immediate post-Civil War years, and again at various key moments in the following three decades – 1873–77, 1884–86, 1890–94 – the bonds of unity overshadowed fragmentary forces. As Eric Foner has observed, 'drawing upon the traditional ideals of artisan independence and republican equality, the postwar labour movement mobilised the skilled and unskilled, the native and foreign-born'.[27] This mobilisation also included women, albeit in relatively small numbers. There were several instances, between 1866 and 1872, of Irish and German immigrants, Afro-Americans and native-born white workers putting aside their past differences and marching together in support of

---

25 D. Montgomery, *Citizen Worker. The Experience of Workers in the United States with Democracy and the Free Market during the Nineteenth Century* (Cambridge, Cambridge University Press, 1995), pp. 139–41; Kirk, *Challenge and Accommodation*, pp. 86–7 and 214–15.

26 Lane, *Solidarity*, pp. 28–9.

27 E. Foner, *Reconstruction. America's Unfinished Revolution 1863–77* (New York, Harper and Row, 1988), p. 477.

demands for improved working conditions and, albeit more infre-
quently, engaging in joint strike action. Notwithstanding its lack of
support for interracial trade unionism, the National Labor Union's convention in 1869 marked 'the first occasion in American history when a
national gathering of white workingmen advocated the formation of
labor unions by Negroes and authorized the admission of blacks to the
annual sessions'. And a number of historians have pointed to the existence of 'an incipient labor movement among black workers during
Reconstruction'. The massive strike waves of 1877, 1884–86 and the early
1890s saw the breakdown of ethnic and economic divisions within the
labour force and the ascendancy of class-based constituencies. Finally,
many of labour's late nineteenth-century institutions sought to build
their strength by promoting inclusive policies towards the issues of ethnicity and gender. For example, the Knights of Labor counted about
60,000 Afro-Americans and 65,000 women among their total membership of 750,000 in 1886. The extremely impressive and massive Alliance
and Populist movements of the 1880s and early 1890s – the former
attracting a membership of 3 million in the south alone in 1890 – also
embraced white and black families. And a minority of unions within the
young AFL, and especially the United Mineworkers of America, with
20,000 back members in 1900, attempted seriously to translate fine anti-
racist words into practical deeds.[28]

In sum, by the early 1890s the inclusive perspective of radical
republicanism enjoyed great and seemingly enduring strength within
the American labour movement. But by the end of that decade there was
mounting evidence of a marked swing towards growing exclusivity and
racism. The failure of the Populist movement saw increasing fragmentation and disunity between white and black and many urban and rural
workers and petty producers. Populism's attempt to unite black and
white poor farmers and workers was also met by a strong conservative
and racist backlash which resulted in the widespread adoption of Jim
Crow segregation policies and the disfranchisement of large numbers of
poor whites and blacks. In addition, growing fears on the part of many
of organised labour's 'old' immigrant and native-born constituents concerning the allegedly deleterious effects of 'new' immigration underlay
organised labour's support for the literacy test for immigrants in 1897.
More generally, as argued by Montgomery, from the 1890s onwards
labour's 'moral universality' began to fragment. Three competing ideological voices could be heard within the labour movement: that of the
Socialist Party; that of the Industrial Workers of the World; and that of

28 Kirk, *Challenge and Accommodation*, pp. 118–28.

the Gompers-inspired ruling group within the AFL. Between the 1890s and the 1920s it was the increasingly accommodating and conservative voice of the latter which became dominant. By the mid-1920s the AFL was actively opposed to the transforming goals of radicals and revolutionaries at home and abroad, was purging itself of radical and 'un-American' voices within its ranks, and was anchored in the increasingly beleaguered and narrow trade union base of white 'skilled' males in traditional industries such as construction and printing. Furthermore, AFL support was extended to a conservative and repressive state machinery committed to immigration restriction, anti-radicalism, 'free-trade' or 'open-door' imperialism, and the active and mass propagation and enforcement of a uniformly conservative and socially integrating version of Americanism. We can now usefully turn to a more detailed examination of these processes of fragmentation, competition and conservative ascendancy.

Conflict and conservatism 1890s–1920s

Three broad structural changes underlay labour's increasingly fragmented responses to the issues of nationalism and ethnicity. Of fundamental importance was the very rapid development, between the 1880s and the 1920s, of corporate or 'monopoly' capitalism. Out of the deflationary crisis of competitive capitalism during the late nineteenth century there emerged large, bureaucratic and increasingly hegemonic corporate enterprises, closely linked with investment banks and concerned to control, regulate and stabilise markets by means of vertical and horizontal combination and to increase managerial controls and reduce the costs of production by mechanisation, extended division of labour, deskilling, Taylorism and, increasingly, the pursuit of 'open shop' (i.e. non-union) policies combined with welfarism in the workplace.

Second, there was the marked growth of a centralised state machinery designed to promote the more efficient and smooth operation of corporate capitalism and an increasingly complex urban society, and to resolve the escalating social tensions, contradictions and pressures which accompanied corporate capitalism's phenomenal growth. The 'managerialist' intentions of many prominent figures in business, professional and government circles were reflected, albeit tentatively and unevenly, in the modification of their earlier 'acquisitive individualism' into 'capitalist collectivism'. 'Their new watchwords,' notes Montgomery, 'were "organization", "efficiency", "responsibility", and "management".' The collective task of making American society 'more orderly, efficient and united' demanded that 'both private associations and the state deliberately seek to reshape human relations' in order to 'overcome controversies at home and to face international conflict with greater military might and patriotic ardor'. The schools, the press, the Churches (especially the Protestant bodies), professional associations and citizens' leagues, the corporations (very much in the vanguard), the leaders of immigrant communities (as brokers between 'their' communities and the 'host' society), the political parties (and particularly the newly ascendant Republican Party) and the Progressives promoting urban and social reform – all these agencies were involved, albeit to varying degrees, in the tasks of promoting (state-assisted) individualism, self-help and consensus, loyalty to the nation, the 'Americanisation' of immigrants, the 'orderly' (i.e. segregated) 'arrangement of race relations', temperance or teetotalism, and opposition to 'negative' class consciousnes and 'extreme' and 'irresponsible' forms of labour collectivism.[29]

In terms of external matters, Presidents McKinley and Roosevelt and leading figures in the armed forces actively encouraged, in combination with the agencies outlined above, the American people to support a shift in foreign policy from a predominant isolationism towards a jingoistic 'nationalistic eagerness to assert American power'.[30] It was thus claimed that, 'in a world of growing imperialistic rivalries', the United States 'could find security and protection for its interests only in expansion'. The 'new imperialism', manifest in the war with Spain in 1898 and in wider US activities in the Caribbean, the Pacific and Latin America, provided both external outlets for internal tensions and overseas markets 'capable of absorbing the burgeoning surplus of farm and factory and supplying the raw materials that American industry depended upon'.[31] This phase of imperialism was also predicated upon the Darwinian belief in the 'survival of the fittest'. And 'the fittest' were assumed by those in the leading echelons of the state, business and the professions to be American, white, Anglo-Saxon and Protestant (WASP). For such people the 'natural superiority' of the WASP justified opposition to unrestricted 'new', non-WASP immigration, the necessary assimilation to 'American ways' on the part of those 'new' immigrants who stayed in their adopted land, and overseas 'action' against 'lesser races'. In such ways, and notwithstanding the presence of prominent restrain-

29 Montgomery, *The Fall,* pp. 176–8.
30 M. A. Jones, *The Limits of Liberty. American History 1607–1980* (Oxford, Oxford University Press, 1983), p. 397.
31 Hunt, *Ideology,* p. 9.

ing and dissenting voices on issues such as the annexation of the Philippines, did the state and various agencies within civil society seek to instruct workers and organised labour in the ways of 'official' nationalism and imperialism.[32]

The state's cultivation of a conformist and conservative form of nationalism was simultaneously combined with high and chronic levels of hostility and repression visited upon striking workers. Thus, while it is true that neither the state in general nor the military in particular pervaded American life to anything like the extent that they did in many European countries – peacetime conscription, for example, did not exist in the United States – nevertheless the state, in the form of the National Guard, the regular army and the courts adopted a prominent and increasingly coercive stance towards labour during this period.[33] 'Between 1880 and 1931,' records Fink, 'more than eighteen hundred injunctions were issued against strikes.' By 1910 the strike was 'severely handicapped by judicial censure', and the boycott effectively curtailed. Matters got worse in the post-war years, and on the eve of the Great Depression it was extremely difficult to ascertain what constituted legal action on behalf of a trade union. Certainly, the legal immunities enjoyed by their British counterparts and the British state's predominantly mediatory and conciliatory role in industrial disputes – a situation long envied by the AFL leadership – remained largely unfulfilled dreams for American trade unionists. And state hostility and coercion towards organised labour were accompanied by the political hegemony enjoyed by the 'party of big business', the Republicans, between the late 1890s and the early 1930s. It did, indeed, appear to many in the labour movement that their nineteenth-century republican state had been hi-jacked and geared up to meet highly repressive sectional needs by the 'monopolistic' corporations and their powerful allies and creatures in the state and the political parties.[34]

Third, a predominantly 'new' immigrant and Afro-American migrant working class, mainly semi-skilled and unskilled in character, was recruited to meet the labour needs of the corporate giant. By 1920 some 13 per cent of the entire population of the United States were foreign-born, a figure which rises to almost 35 per cent once the children born in the United States of foreign parentage are included. And while not all these people were working-class, it is, notes Montgomery,

32 Jones, *The Limits*, pp. 397–411.
33 Montgomery, *Citizen Worker*, pp. 95–104 and 114.
34 L. Fink, 'Labor, Liberty and the Law: Trade Unionism and the Problem of the American Constitutional Order', *Journal of American History* 74:3 (1987), pp. 911 and 918–19.

'safe to say that the immigrant milieu dominated urban working-class life at the time'. Furthermore, whereas the 'new' immigrants had constituted only 1·2 per cent of the foreign-born population in 1860, by 1910 they made up 37·5 per cent. Heavily concentrated in the burgeoning mass-production and predominantly 'open shop' industries of steel, automobiles, mining, meat packing and electrical goods, the 'new' immigrants were increasingly joined by a massive exodus of Afro-Americans from the south, seeking work and a better life in the urban areas of the north. Between 1916 and 1918 some 450,000 Afro-Americans were so attracted by the economic 'pull' of the northern cities and the opportunity to escape the 'racial bondage' of the south. In the wake of immigration restriction in 1924, which banned Asian immigration and virtually ended 'new' immigration, new labour market opportunities arose for migrants from the American countryside, immigrants from Europe, women and growing numbers of Mexicans and Canadians. In such ways was the US working class subjected to further massive demographic changes and ruptures.[35]

While 'new' immigrants played a conspicuous part in the strike waves which convulsed these years (Afro-Americans being generally far less prominent), nevertheless they also became, in the eyes of many people, the demoniacal 'other'.[36] As we will observe in more detail below, both the 'new' immigrants and black migrants often became the scapegoats for many of the insecurities, threats and ills which the rise of corporate capitalism inflicted upon skilled and other native-born and 'old' immigrant workers. Simultaneously, alarmed during the period of the First World War both by the scale of, and the large numbers of 'new' immigrants involved in, labour radicalism and militancy, by strong immigrant ties with central Europe, and by Socialist-led opposition to American involvement in the war, 'panicked government officials and private citizens . . . launched Americanization campaigns, unprecedented in scope and intensity, to strip the masses of their foreign ways and allegedly radical beliefs'. The Committee on Public Information, set up to whip up support for the war, achieved voluntary censorship on the part of the press, churned out literature on patriotic themes, enlisted the support of public speakers and 'energized loyalty committees within each of fourteen immigrant nationalities to argue the links between their national causes and America's victory in the war'. In addition, there

---

35 Jones, *American Immigration*, p. 208; D. Montgomery, 'Immigrants, Industrial Unions and Social Reconstruction in the United States 1916–23', *Labour/Le Travail*, 13 (1984), p. 108.

36 J. Higham, *Strangers in the Land. Patterns of American Nativism 1860–1925* (New York, Atheneum, 1963).

took place 'a vast expansion of the Secret Service and enrollment of 250,000 citizen volunteers into the American Protective League to ferret out disloyal activties in every factory and neighborhood of the land, as well as by compulsory registration of all aliens, six thousand of whom were detained under presidential warrants'. The overriding aim of the government was to 'generate a mass citizenry, essentially homogeneous in its cultural and political attitudes'.[37]

The corporations played a leading role in the process of Americanisation. For example, as James Barrett has observed,[38] Henry Ford's Sociology Department sought, from 1914 onwards, to 'remake the lives of their immigrant workers and win them over to thrift, efficiency, and company loyalty'. And, in order to achieve this goal,

case workers fanned out into Detroit's working-class neighborhoods, ready to fight for the hearts and minds of the immigrant auto workers. They investigated each worker's home life as well as his work record, and one could qualify for the Five Dollar Day incentive pay only after demonstrating the proper home environment and related middle-class values. Thus the company sought to show workers not only the 'right way to work' but also the 'right way to live'.

Ford, himself, argued that 'these men of many nations must be taught American ways, the English language . . .'. And when some 900 workers of Greek or Russian origin missed work to celebrate Orthodox Christmas he 'summarily fired them', declaring that 'If these men are to make their home in America, they should observe American holidays.' The Ford English School likewise put on a language and civics programme for the company's immigrant workers. And Ford's Director of Americanization declared, without the slightest trace of irony or embarrassment, that 'Into the pot fifty-two nationalities with their foreign clothes and baggage go and out of the pot after vigorous stirring by the teachers comes one nationality, viz American.'

Other major corporations, such as International Harvester and the Colorado Fuel and Iron Company, likewise set up their own sociology departments and established uniform 'American' standards and patterns for their immigrant employees' eating, cooking, drinking, cleaning and working habits. 'By the spring of 1919,' observes Barrett, 'there were at least eight hundred industrial plants sponsoring their own

---

37 Montgomery, *The Fall*, pp. 375–6; G. Gerstle, *Working Class Americanism. The Politics of Labor in a Textile City 1914–60* (Cambridge, Cambridge University Press, 1989), p. 3.
38 J. R. Barrett, 'Americanization from the Bottom up: Immigration and the Remaking of the Working Class in the United States 1880–1930', *Journal of American History* 79:3 (1992), pp. 996–1020. The following account of corporate Americanisation schemes is heavily indebted to Barrett's excellent article.

classes or working in conjunction with the YMCA and other agencies to put on evening or plant classes.'[39] And efficiency and Americanisation drives went hand in hand. Thus

efficiency justifications and corporate muscle began to be put behind older welfare causes, such as the closing of bars between the worker's job and his home, preventing immigrants' fraternal lodges from serving liquor, bringing college students to the factories to deliver noon-hour talks on 'clean living, character-building and vital religion', and surveying the home living conditions of employees.[40]

As we will observe below, vigorous attempts further to promote 'the Americanisation of aliens' would continue into the 1920s.

Labour responded to the broad developments outlined above in three main ways. First of all, and notwithstanding continuing and important ideological, tactical and strategic divisions within its ranks, the AFL came to terms with the demise of the traditional republic and the ascendancy, however unwelcome, of the new corporate reality in increasingly accommodating, conservative and exclusive ways. Above all, there occurred a narrowing of focus and vision – as reflected in a shift away from the concern to refashion the republic in the image of the independent 'producer citizen' towards the realisation, as unionised wage earners, of 'home ownership, a steady job, decent wages and, increasingly, of the consumerist pleasures of modern corporate America'. In sum, corporate capitalism and wage earning became accepted by Gompers and many others within the AFL as inescapable 'facts of life'. Accordingly, working-class 'emancipation' was to be achieved not by the 'pie in the sky' revolutionary schemes of the socialists and syndicalists – the employing class and the state being too strong, united and generally anti-labour to be suddenly transformed – but by a hard-headed and 'realistic', long-haul programme of 'incremental gradualism'.[41]

Situated in a predominantly hostile and repressive world, the AFL nevertheless sought to gain official approval by advertising its non-radical and thoroughly 'American' commitment to 'pure and simple' and 'prudential' trade unionism, voluntarism, to 'civilised' collective bargaining with 'responsible' employers, to American 'adventures' overseas, to President Wilson's war effort (the AFL would refrain from seeking to 'change existing standards' at the workplace for the duration of the war), and to immigration restriction. As a corollary, strong opposition was registered to 'un-American' and 'unpatriotic' syndicalists,

39 *Ibid.*, p. 1003.
40 Montgomery, *The Fall*, p. 244.
41 Kirk, *Challenge and Accommodation*, pp. 136–7.

socialists and 'alien Bolsheviks' engaged in attempts to 'excite' mass militancy. Indeed, during the period of the First World War and its aftermath the AFL actively opposed the Industrial Workers of the World, expelled from its ranks all those deemed to be opposed to America's interests, and supported the state's coercive measures agsinst revolutionaries and radicals. In such ways did the AFL come to commit itself to the 'official' nationalism, imperialism and anti-radicalism of the state and big business.

The AFL did undoubtedly derive important returns from its commitment to 'pragmatic realism', moderation and patriotism.[42] In 1914 the Clayton Act, promising the reduced use of federal injunctions in labour disputes, was introduced. During the war years President Wilson's administration 'was keen to consult with Gompers, to provide mediation and conciliation services in industrial conflicts, to encourage employers to negotiate with the responsible AFL', and 'to shun the IWW and other groups deemed "outlaw" by the AFL'. AFL leaders were invited into the councils of state during 1917 and 1918 (America having officially declared in favour of war in April 1917); and the National War Labor Board, an important body on which the AFL was represented, promised in 1918 and 1919 'federal protection for the right to organize as well as standards of wages, hours and pay'. Finally, and perhaps most significantly in view of the traditionally evanescent and, in general terms, weak character of trade unionism in the Unites States, the AFL had not only survived depression and official hostility but had increased its affiliated membership from 500,000 in 1898 to 4·75 million in 1920.

Simultaneously, these returns had been won at considerable cost.[43] First, as indicated earlier, a high level of official hostility towards organised labour by no means disappeared. Second, most of the AFL's membership was concentrated in the traditional and predominantly skilled sectors of the economy such as construction, printing and mining. The new and dynamic mass-production industries and their workers, including many black, immigrant and female workers, remained non-union and largely neglected by the AFL. It is true that the Federation did mount large-scale organising drives in steel and meat packing in the late 1910s, and that these campaigns saw 'new' immigrants and others traditionally on the margins of trade unionism join the cause in impressive

---

42 See Fink, 'Labor, Liberty', p. 921; Montgomery, *The Fall*, p. 374; Kirk, *Challenge and Accommodation*, pp. 136–9.

43 D. Montgomery, *Workers' Control in America. Studies in the History of Work Technology and Labor Struggles* (Cambridge, Cambridge University Press, 1986), pp. 65–6; P. S. Bagwell and G. E. Mingay, *Britain and America. A Study of Economic Change 1850–1939* (London, Routledge, 1970), p. 203; Montgomery, *The Fall*, chapter 8.

numbers and with great enthusiasm. But these drives foundered upon the rocks of internal working-class division and fierce official disapproval and successful repression. The severe race riots in 1917 in East St Louis and in Chicago in 1919 – the latter following an impressive attempt at mass organisation of the stockyards – provided massive setbacks to hopes of black and white working-class unity and interracial unionism.[44] Third, defeated working-class radicals and immigrants paid very dear for their post-war militancy, being systematically purged from the labour movement by AFL leaders and thrown into jail and or deported in their thousands by the forces of law and order.[45] Indeed, by the mid-1920s, and following the crippling defeats suffered by the mass strikes of 1922, strongly conservative and exclusionary voices were in the ascendancy in the Federation. However, the affiliated unions' favoured 1920s policies of restricting union membership largely to 'skilled' white males, forfeiting any claim over 'control issues' at the workplace, and supporting immigration restriction and an obsessively 'anti-Red' state, did not bring the anticipated rewards in terms of union recognition. Rather, the years between 1923 and 1933 constituted a very depressing decade for American trade unionism. Anti-labour sentiment prevailed in business and government circles. And the AF of L's membership had declined to 2,805,000, or a mere 7·3 per cent of the eligible labour force, by 1933.

There were, of course, responses to the structural changes identified above which constituted radical alternatives to those of AFL accommodation, exclusion and conservatism. Most prominent in this respect were the voices of members of the Socialist Party – many of whom remained within the AFL from the party's foundation in 1901 – and of the Industrial Workers of the World, founded in 1905. Notwithstanding their increasingly conflicting views – upon, respectively, the ballot box and direct industrial action – as the optimum path to the achievement of socialism, both party and IWW members did share key emphases upon capitalism as a system of class-based exploitation and the need actively to cultivate proletarian solidarity and internationalism in order to transform the system. Accordingly, both the IWW and the Socialist Party did make far more determined efforts than most AFL unions to pursue inclusive policies towards the 'new' immigrants, Afro-Americans, women and the non-skilled in general. For example, the

44 R. Halpern and R. Horowitz, *Meatpackers. An Oral History of Black Packinghouse Workers and the Struggle for Racial and Economic Equality* (London, Twayne, 1996), chapter 1; Montgomery, *The Fall*, pp. 382–4.
45 Montgomery, *The Fall*, pp. 407–10; D. Frank, *Purchasing Power. Consumer Organizing, Gender and the Seattle Labor Movement 1919–29* (Cambridge, Cambridge University Press, 1994), part III.

IWW, with its revolutionary syndicalist goal of 'one great industrial union . . . founded on the class struggle', played an important part in the struggles and organising endeavours of migrant, seasonal and casual workers on the docks and railroads and in lumber and agriculture, in the successful city-wide strikes of 1912 in Lawrence and Lowell and in the strikes of a wide range of workers between 1916 and 1922.[46] The Socialist Party enjoyed a significant presence among immigrant men and women, especially Germans, Jews, Finns, Slavs and Italians; and in the wake of the Russian revolution of 1917 immigrants drawn largely from South-eastern and Eastern Europe flocked into the party. Indeed, the party's foreign-born membership increased from 20 per cent in the pre-war years to 53 per cent in 1918. Many socialists were also active in the fight against racial discrimination and developed 'powerful allies in some black communities'. Furthermore, alone among major Western socialist parties, the American party remained resolute in its opposition to the 'imperialist war'. Similarly, the party never endorsed the literacy test.[47]

Socialist attitudes towards race, ethnicity and gender were, however, limited and conditional. The central importance attached by the party to class, and especially the achievement of class solidarity and power, meant that special concerns with questions of racial, ethnic and gender-based exclusion and discrimination, were often seen as incidental to, and indeed diversions from, the all-important class struggle (a viewpoint carried into the 1920s and 1930s by the Communist Party). Furthermore, as Erik Olssen has remarked, the Socialist Party was by no means 'immune to racism and nativism'. For example, as the volume of 'new' immigration increased, so many socialists began heavily to qualify their unconditional internationalism of the 1890s. Both within the AFL and outside, socialists could be heard voicing the fear that some of the new immigrants and black migrants *were* posing a threat to the economic position of 'American' workers -that they were being used by employers to break strikes, to replace skilled men, to depress wage levels and to staff the most dynamic, increasingly 'Taylorised' and non-union sectors of the economy – that they did not display sufficient levels of solidarity with organised labour, and that they did show signs of failing to appreciate and assimiliate to 'American' ways and values. While such fears were often expressed within an enduring general framework of commitment

46 Montgomery, *The Fall*, pp. 310–14; Montgomery, *Workers' Control*, chapter 4.
47 Kirk, *Challenge and Accommodation*, pp. 233–4; Lane, *Solidarity*, p. 183; E. Olssen, 'The Case of the Socialist Party that failed, or, Further Reflections on an American Dream', *Labor History* 29:4 (1988), p. 434.

to internationalism and solidarity, they did nevertheless illustrate 'the erosion of socialist solidarity over immigration'. For example, in 1917 a majority of socialists within the AFL voted for the literacy test.[48]

The Socialist Party and the IWW did nevertheless provide important sites of radical competition to AFL orthodoxy. Furthermore, in criticising 'un-republican' corporate greed and power, and in characterising their movement as the inheritor of American revolutionary and democratic ideals, the socialists gained a significant following in America up to the First World War and beyond. As Paul Buhle has declared: 'They brought under their banner native-born small-town workers, miners, lumberjacks, tenant farmers, railroad men, and petty merchants who saw capitalism destroying the old American ideals and who accepted the Socialists as proper successors to Tom Paine and Abe Lincoln.'[49] As late as November 1917 widespread anti-war feeling resulted in the Socialist Party winning 'very impressive numbers of votes' in the local elections. Furthermore, and notwithstanding the attempt of immigrant leaders during 1917 and 1918 to link their support for nationalist causes in their homelands with 'the tide of American patriotism' by supporting Liberty Bond drives, recruiting efforts and flag-raising ceremonies, some immigrants preferred to identify 'Americanisation' with organised labour's struggle for the 'American standard', for economic democracy as against 'czardom', with mutuality as opposed to acquisitive individualism, with internationalism and, as seen in their considerable influx into the Socialist Party, with socialism.[50]

Such radical political, ethnic and (American) nationalist manifestations did not, however, long withstand the conformist advance of 'official' patriotism and repression. Both the Socialist Party and the IWW suffered badly as a result of growing support for the war effort, the 'Red Scare', and mounting opposition to and repression of strikers. By early 1918 the tide was fast turning against Socialist-led opposition to the war. Montgomery observes that 'mass dissent had been effectively silenced':

48 Lane, *Solidarity*, p. 183; Olssen, 'The Case', pp. 432–4; Mink, *Old Labor*, pp. 228–5.
49 P. Buhle and A. Dawley, *Working for Democracy. American Workers from the Revolution to the Present* (Urbana, Ill., University of Illinois Press, 1985), p. 53; J. Weinstein, *The Decline of Socialism in America 1912–25* (New Brunswick, N.J., Rutgers University Press, 1984); E. Foner, 'Why is there no Socialism in the United States?', *History Workshop Journal* 17 (1984), pp. 57–80
50 Barrett, 'Americanization'; D. Montgomery, 'Nationalism, American Patriotism and Class Consciousness among Immigrant Workers in the United States in the Epoch of World War I', in D. Hoerder (ed.), *Struggle a Hard Battle. Essays on Working Class Immigrants* (De Kalb, Ill., Northern Illinois University Press, 1986), pp. 327–51.

'factories were saturated with agents of military and naval intelligence, and War Industry Committees, made up of workers and foremen, staged patriotic rallies and combatted "slackers" on the job'. Four years later, 'Soldiers swarmed over American industrial towns' effectively to combat the huge strikes launched by over a million workers.[51] Furthermore, immigration restriction, combined with renewed official campaigns for '100 per-cent Americanism', and the massive expansion of the Ku Klux Klan (which by 1920 'had millions of members, supported the open-shop drive and denounced all immigrants as "un-American" and "agents of Lenin"') severely curtailed immigrant radicalism, with beleaguered immigrant communities retreating increasingly into predominantly conservative forms of ethnic nationalism.[52]

As Gary Gerstle has suggested, led by the corporations, with their mass, standardised markets and national media chains, 'centralizing tendencies in economics, communications and culture' were well under way in mid-1920s America. The world of 'cultural and political diversity had narrowed significantly' in the face of the increasing 'nationalization and homogenization of the American experience'. And the state's policies towards immigration, its prohibition of the man-ufacture and sale of alcohol (in opposition to the 'excesses' of the largely immigrant 'masses') and its citizenship training courses (initially set up 'to enforce political loyalty on the foreign-born'), which became 'a permanent part of the public school curricula in every state', consti-tuted an integral part of the widespread drive for political and cultural conformity'.[53]

In sum, by the late 1920s labour's experience in the United States did take on the appearance of being very different from the situation prevailing in Britain and much of Europe. A conservative body, the AFL, the dominant 'House of Labour' since the early 1900s, now ruled the roost. Radical and revolutionary forces were either of minority standing, in serious retreat, or both. And racism and ethnic divisions were marked features of a working class seemingly given over to a celebration of the pleasures of consumerism and privatisation and support for a conserva-tive, indeed chauvinistic, form of American nationalism. Conspicuous by their absence or extreme weakness were European- and British-style Labour, Socialist and Communist parties and their mass influence. Mainstream American labour remained wedded to its non-partisan political strategy. Finally, the mass organisation of the non-skilled, such

---

51 Montgomery, 'Nationalism', pp. 334–5; Montgomery, *The Fall*, pp. 407–8.
52 Kirk, *Challenge and Accommodation*, pp. 303–4.
53 Gerstle, *Working Class Americanism*, pp. 3–4.

a strong feature of British trade unionism, was, for the most part, lacking in the United States. Open-shop big business and its political allies in the political parties, the judiciary and the state machinery as a whole were hegemonic. Did not American labour thus appear in the 1920s to be entering upon the path of 'exceptionalism'?[54]

The revival of radicalism in the 1930s

The dramatic chronology of labour's development during the 1930s and its changing attitudes to ethnicity and nationalism would suggest a largely negative response to the question of exceptionalism. Indeed, a number of events and processes converged to challenge the continued legitimacy and hegemony of 'open shop' corporate America and the dominance of the AFL within the labour movement, and to promote a 'culture of unity' and a radical form of American nationalism within the working class. In this final section we can provide a skeletal overview of these developments.[55]

The sudden, unexpected, precipitous and sustained nature of the Great Depression in the United States constitutes our starting point. Between 1929 and 1933 unemployment rose from 1·6 million (3·2 per cent of the labour force) to a staggering 12·8 million (25·2 per cent). The boom of the 1920s came to a shuddering halt and the bottom fell out of the economy. In the early '1930s 'wages plummeted . . . the banking system fell apart, millions of small businessmen and farmers were ruined, and 1920s welfare capitalism was no longer a viable proposition'. Matters improved somewhat from 1934 onwards, but in 1936 17 per cent of the labour force, or 9 million, were out of work. The recession of 1937–38 saw unemployment rise to almost 10·5 million, or 19 per cent, in the latter year. And as late as 1939 9·4 million Americans, some 17 per cent, lacked work. In sum the 1930s constituted the most profound economic crisis in the history of the United States.

The effects of this crisis were far-reaching. For example, increasingly unable to maintain the welfarism of the 1920s, and largely wedded to their sectional, anti-union and *laissez-faire* attitudes and policies, the nation's major corporate employers were perceived to be acting from

54 S. Sapolsky,'Response to Sean Wilentz's "Against Exceptionalism"', *International Labor and Working Class History*, 27 (1985), pp. 35–8.
55 The following section is heavily indebted to: Gerstle, *Working Class Americanism*; L. Cohen, *Making a New Deal. Industrial Workers in Chicago 1919–39* (Cambridge, Cambridge University Press, 1990); R. H. Zieger, *American Workers, American Unions 1920–85* (Baltimore, Md., Johns Hopkins University Press, 1986); Kirk, *Challenge and Accommodation*, chapter 5.

narrowly selfish goals rather than in the national interest. As a result they forfeited much of the trust and respect of their employees and the public at large, and an effective space was created for the development of pro-labour policies and attitudes.

Within this context there occurred major shifts in government and state policy which did favour strongly organised labour. Having defeated Hoover in the 1932 presidential election, Franklin D. Roosevelt committed his National Recovery Administration to the restoration of capitalism's health by the attempted resurrection of consumer demand, regulation and stabilisation of the market and the banking system, and the achievement of a more economically productive balance between capital and labour. Roosevelt, himself, was not particularly favourable towards the claims of organised labour, but influential figures within the New Deal administration did recognise the importance of increasing workers' bargaining power, via trade unionism, as a means of boosting demand in the economy. Some within the administration saw the recognition of the CIO as a means of incorporating the revitalised labour movement within the confines of a reformed capitalist system, and, as such, as effectively preventing any adoption by organised labour of independent labour or socialist politics. And one of the main results of the rise of the CIO and the development of an institutionalised, bureaucratic and legally enmeshed system of industrial relations was indeed the accommodation of the 'new' trade unions to the dominant social order. But we must be careful not to confuse results with causes. For, in truth, a great deal of frustration and challenging anger had underpinned the widespread popular radicalism which preceded, gave rise to and informed the early CIO. Finally, the close links which had developed by the mid-1930s between trade unionists who were to play a leading role in the CIO and a number of New Deal administrators meant that sections of the labour movement were already enmeshed in the machinery of state to an extent which a post-1935 picture of 'incorporation', complete with labour as earlier 'outsider', does not suggest. What was at work during the 1930s was, in fact, a complex and continuing interplay between the forces of assimilation and opposition, rather than the straightforward incorporation of labour or a simple 'sell-out' on the part of trade union 'bureaucrats' in opposition to the wishes of a predominantly 'radical rank and file'.[56]

Two pieces of New Deal legislation, section 7a of the National

---

56 Kirk, *Challenge and Accommodation*, pp. 342–9; D. Montgomery, 'Labor and the Political Leadership of New Deal America', *International Review of Social History* 39 (1994), especially pp. 353–60.

Industrial Recovery Act (1933) and the Wagner Act (1935), were of crucial importance in, respectively, recognising the right of workers to 'bargain collectively with their employers through representatives of their own choosing' and in the legal enforcement of workers' wishes. As a result of the Wagner Act, employers could no longer ignore, as so often in the past, the demands of a majority of workers for trade union recognition and collective bargaining. Henceforward the state would intervene to guarantee workers' rights. This constituted a remarkable change of policy from past practice. The overall health of capitalism was to be restored not by *laissez-faire* and hostile and repressive actions on the part of the state towards organised labour but, in the face of considerable employer opposition, by union recognition and collective bargaining. Assured of their safety, workers flocked into the unions, defied the considerable opposition of capital in the 'sit-down' and other strikes of 1936–37 and emerged victorious. By 1939 the American trade union movement had more members than its traditionally superior British counterpart.

This brings us logically to our final key ingredient: the actions and thoughts of workers themselves. As revealed in their hunger marches and other forms of protest in the late 1920s and early 1930s, in the mass strikes of 1933–34, and in their support for John L. Lewis's Committee for Industrial Organization (1935–38) and its successor, the Congress of Industrial Organizations (1938–55), workers rediscovered the capacity for the kinds of radicalism and mass, collective action which had all but disappeared in the barren post-1922 years. The CIO, with its commitment to organise the mass-production industries, soon developed into a major rival of the AFL. But during the later years of the 1930s both the CIO and the AFL enjoyed spectacular increases in appeal and membership. By the outbreak of the Second World War the cause of 'new' unionism, for so long limited and frustrated in the United States, was in fine shape.

Two features of the workers' movements of the 1930s merit special comment. First, in relation to the issue of labour and ethnicity, the upsurges of the 1930s signified a return to – indeed an extension of – earlier inclusive strategies. Notwithstanding certain limits, the CIO and preceding radical movements, complete with their emphases upon what Lizabeth Cohen has aptly termed a 'culture of unity', did make serious efforts, in many cases successful and certainly far more extensive than those of the AFL, to appeal to the sons and daughters of the 'new' immigrants, Afro-Americans and women. Indeed, second-generation 'new' immigrants, who had witnessed and endured the awful effects of employer 'tyranny' and poor wages and conditions during the 1920s, were 'at the forefront of the 1930s mass struggle for citizenship rights at the workplace'.[57]

Second, as implied in the previous sentence, central to the struggles of the 1930s was the language of radical nationalism – of an Americanism which, as highlighted by Gerstle, spoke the language of 'citizenship rights', the 'American standard' and 'democracy at the workplace' and which was quick to invoke the 'official voice of authority' in its cause. Lewis, in 1933, and the CIO, in 1936, thus announced to their potential constituents that 'The President wants you to organize'. Whether labour's resort to the language of radical patriotism constituted a continuing link with the nineteenth-century language of radical republicanism is open to question.[58] But of its renewed and central importance during the 1930s there can be little doubt.

Both these features point to the conclusion that US labour during the 1930s was not 'exceptional'. After all, the British labour movement was in the doldrums for a good part of the 1930s and the Conservatives, in the form of the National Goverment, dominated the decade. And in Europe the rise of fascism cast serious doubt upon the notion of a linear and uniform 'forward march of labour'.

Conclusion

Having completed our survey of labour, nationalism and ethnicity in the United States between 1870 and 1939, we can usefully bring together the methodological and substantive concerns which have occupied us throughout this chapter.

We have observed, above all, the complex, contested and changing ways in which workers and their movements defined their ethnicity, their ethnic boundaries and their attitudes towards the question of what it meant to be an American. Furthermore, the complex interplay between radical, conservative and indeed revolutionary definitions make it impossible to label workers' attitudes in static and one-dimensional ways. We have seen that exclusionary and conservative attitudes towards ethnicity, nationalism and gender did play a prominent role within the AFL, which was, for a considerable length of time during the period under review, the dominant force in American labour. However, during the late nineteenth and early twentieth centuries, and again in the 1930s, strong inclusionary and radical forces were at work and were, at times, in the acendancy.

---

57 Kirk, *Challenge and Accommodation*, p. 340.
58 Gerstle, *Working Class Americanism*, introduction and conclusion.

The importance of change, complexity and contestation also renders the rather flat notion of American 'exceptionalism' wide of the mark, not only in relation to the 1930s but also as a general judgement upon the entire period under review. The United States did, of course, possess many distinctive, rather than 'exceptional', features which bear heavily upon the concerns of this chapter. As we have seen, the republican heritage, the official cultivation of 'Americanism', the legacy of slavery and chronic and widespread racism, the heterogeneous character of its increasingly immigrant and frequently reconstituted working class, and the hostility and repression for so long practised by those in power and authority upon workers and their movements were important factors in the unfolding story of labour, ethnicity and nationalism. And, as Bucki has concluded, 'the malleability of the concept of "American", shaped as it was by the social and political activities of immigrant workers, gave the notion of citizenship in the United States a flexibility that it has in few other nations'.[59] But such distinctive features did not constitute exceptions from some supposed 'norm' of working-class formation, development and consciousness. And they were by no means entirely absent from labour's diverse experience in Europe and elsewhere.

59 Bucki, 'Workers and Politics', p. 44.

Terry Irving

Labour, state and nation building in Australia

Between 1891 and 1901 an eruption of national consciousness in Australia coincided with the emergence of Labor parties and with a process of constitutional debate that culminated in the federation of six colonies as the Commonwealth of Australia. Since that time, historians and would-be history makers have revisited that moment often for clues to the links between labour and nationalism. Thus, to European Social Democrats in the early twentieth century, contemplating the problem of reconciling class and nation, it seemed that Labor in Australia had opted from the start for a nationalist solution. It was, after all, Lenin who denied in 1913 that the Australian Labor Party (ALP) was socialist, characterising it instead as a liberal bourgeois party dedicated to developing Australia as an independent capitalist state.[1] To scholars this conjuncture has often explained the relative success of the Australian labour movement. Thus, in 1997, a Spanish historian, writing about Labour parties in the 'new world', explained Labor's success in Australia as 'due to the fact that the party's creation and development coincided with the growth of a national consciousness that would lead to independence and to the creation of the Australian Commonwealth in 1901'. With workers' organisations supporting the federation of the colonies, 'the new Labor Party became *the* party of national construction'.[2]

In some circumstances a nationalist approach has also suited the purposes of Australian Labor leaders. Looking back in 1991 on a century of the ALP, a Labor intellectual wrote: 'Who Australians are, where they have been in their story and what they might be yet, are questions asked by Labor. First defining Australia and then advancing that definition

---

1 V. I. Lenin, 'In Australia' (1913), in N. Ebbels (ed.), *The Australian Labor Movement 1850–1907. Extracts from Contemporary Documents* (Sydney, Australasian Book Society, 1960), pp. 243–5.
2 A. Bosch, 'Why is there no Labor Party in the United States? A Comparative New World Case Study: Australia and the United States 1783–1914' *Radical History Review* 67 (1997), pp.61 f. The discussion of Australia in this article is defective because it relies on scholarship, much of it over thirty years old, that assumed that theories of class, nation, state, and so on, could be transferred unproblematically from Europe to Australia.

into practice is a function of Labor, which presents a dynamic picture of pro-Australianism.'[3] Claims for Labor's hegemony over nationalism in Australia were to be expected as the party's centenary celebrations approached, at a time too when Labor governed and the conservative parties were in disarray. No wonder that the party's logo was then fashioned out of a version of the Australian flag. Yet Labor's capacity to mediate between class and nation has a longer history, and has proved attractive to voters. Labor governments were elected in moments of national emergency or strain: in the First and Second World Wars, at the onset of the Great Depression of the 1930s, at the end of the post-war boom and, most recently, as Australian capital adjusted to economic globalisation in the 1980s.

However, privileging nationalism in the Australian case is misleading. In the first place, Australia did not become fully independent in 1901. Not only did the Crown retain important powers, but Australians assumed that the British government would make our foreign policy and protect us with its navy. Secondly, in the analysis of social forces and movements, it is always a mistake to place too much emphasis on voting and electoral rhetoric. Labor governments, supposedly riding the nationalist wave, soon lost office, by party splits in the First World War and in 1931, by failing to face a massive ruling-class mobilisation in 1949, and by vice-regal *coup* in 1975. Nor are Labor's nationalist credentials without blemish if we look at policy. In the 1980s 'nationalist' Labor sold off the family silver and opened the doors to transnational companies. Even in Lenin's time, as this chapter will show, Labor's various successes cannot be attributed to its nationalism. Labor was not the *sole* party of national construction, and workers' organisations did *not* support federation along the lines allowed by the new Commonwealth constitution. It is wrong, too, to see the working class as instinctively or essentially nationalist. This chapter will contest the simple identification of Labor and nation, and offer a richer political understanding of Labor, ethnicity and nationalism.

Of course, compared with Europe and North America, Labor and nationalism in Australia are differently articulated. The difference lies in the opportunity that Australian Labor had to influence and participate in state building. In the settler capitalist colonies in the second half of the nineteenth century, state formation was not coextensive with nation building.[4] It is because scholars and commentators neglect this

---

3 R. Macdonald, *Reflecting Labor. Images of Myth and Origin over 100 Years* (National Library of Australia, Canberra, 1991), p. 10.
4 Nation building is the process of creating a nation state, that is, a process driven by a ruling bloc using state power to impose 'national' unity on subordinate forces.

distinction that Labor is mistakenly pigeonholed with the bourgeois nationalists, and the existence of a special kind of Labor nationalism in Australia is overlooked. The argument of this chapter is that while the labour movement exhibited a wide range of the kinds of 'nationalisms' found in other countries, its distinctive radical or democratic national-ism was the result of a specific state-building experience propelled from below, and that at crucial moments this protected Labor from the patri-otic excesses of anti-democratic nation building.

The argument requires a focus on state building, as does the fact that nationalism defines itself in relation to the state. The chapter is organised around a narrative of Labour, state building and nation build-ing from the 1850s to the 1930s. We will examine four moments in the story: the transfer of state power in the 1850s, the federal redistribution of state power that produced the Commonwealth of Australia in 1901, the brief moment of progressive state building after 1901, and the anti-Labor nation state that emerged during the First World War. This narra-tive will address the question of Labor's integration into the state and community. To unpack 'Labor', the chapter concludes with a discussion of three sets of actors: the working class, the organised labour movement (unions and parties), and the Labor intellectuals. In this discussion we will sum up the overall impact of nationalism on Labor, in terms of Labor definitions of nationalism, the imperial context, and the relation-ship between class and national identities.

National awakening and the transfer of state power

It is necessary to start this story in the middle of the nineteenth century, during the era known as 'the coming of self-government', when the liberal aspects of the colonial state were put in place. This was also an early moment of national awakening. Despite the continuing colonial status of the Australian governments, the intertwined processes of state building and nation building were under way. The first crucial point for the analysis of Labour and nationalism is that at this time male workers gained access to the state through enfranchisement, the secret ballot

---

State building is the process of enlarging state power and creating the institutions to do that. State building may be undertaken for various purposes, and in some situations may be open to subordinate forces. Thus, in the Age of Nationalism, state building may recognise and embrace a democratic or civic nationalism. Scholars of European nationalism emphasise top-down nation building and the 'official' status of nationalism. Scholars of the Third World, and the colonies of European settlement, separate nation building from state building to account for the insertion of popular interests into the state's organisations.

and equal electoral districts. As a result of this democratic extension of political rights, by 1860 wage earners in the cities and larger towns were active citizens. Henceforth, although the Australian colonies were now using the same map of nationhood as the emerging states of Europe, the *democratic* current in the process of nation building would flow too strongly to be blocked or diverted.

The second crucial point concerns the relationship with the mother country, and this is a more complicated story. In 1852 the British government conceded the right to frame their own constitutions to the colonies of New South Wales, Victoria, Tasmania and South Australia.[5] By so doing Britain was acknowledging both a decade of agitation for self-government and its own imperial interest. When the British state in the 1840s adopted free-trade policies to entrench its economic hegemony over much of the world, it was no longer rational for Whitehall bureaucrats to exercise direct political control over distant colonies settled by Britons. If the white settler colonies continued to attract Britain's surplus capital and population, and placed no obstructions in the way of the export/import trade with the mother country, then why should the British government resist self-government? Of course, the self-governing colonies would still be subordinate to Britain, but any contradictions in the colonial situation were confidently expected to be contained by the ties of 'race' and sentiment.

In terms of nation building, the critical aspects of the transfer of state power to the new colonial governments were that it happened without bloodshed, and that it was delayed until the new societies could support a diversifying economy and a liberal polity. The absence of bloodshed meant that no tradition of national political or cultural resistance to the mother country was established. The paradoxical promise of this moment was that Australia would become a nation without a national movement, an independent country without a pre-existing independent culture. This indicates how inappropriate it is to assimilate nation building in Australia to the models of cultural assertiveness and political mobilisation used in European studies.[6] Similarly, the delay in the transfer of power should also undermine a simple identification of

5 Queensland was separated from New South Wales in 1859, with the same right to self-government; Western Australia, which continued to accept convicts until 1868, did not receive self-government until 1890.
6 The contributors to J. Coakley (ed.), *The Social Origins of Nationalist Movements. The Contemporary West European Experience* (London, Sage Publications, 1992), offer a good sample of European ways of theorising nationalism. An example of the tendency to assimilate Australian history to 'universal' processes of nationalism in the nineteenth and twentieth centuries can be found in S. Alomes and C. Jones (eds), *Australian Nationalism. A Documentary History* (Sydney, Angus and Robertson, 1991).

political nationalism with bourgeois interests. Britain resisted self-government until the early 1850s because it was waiting for a balance in the colony of social forces that would support the new imperial system. In the new empire of free trade Britain could no longer rely on the sheep-raising 'squatters' who had dominated politics in the previous decade. As the operators of a plantation-style economy in the pastoral industry, they favoured continuing the convict system and supplementing it with coloured labor from Asia. Their economic vision was narrow and their politics conservative. If self-governing parliaments fell into their hands the attraction of the colonies to British investors and free immigrants would be limited. Thus Britain had to wait until the urban anti-squatter alliance of merchants, small shopkeepers and working men was consolidated.

By 1852, as a result of a series of popular political campaigns to end convict transportation, extend democracy and make ministers responsible to the parliament under the new constitutions, there was a working alliance between the liberal business community and the radical working men. Now it was possible to build a liberal state, with strong democratic participation. Within a few years of self-government the new colonial parliaments had enacted adult male suffrage, equal electoral districts and the secret ballot.[7] The transfer of power, thus, left a contradictory legacy for nationalism, on the one hand producing a kind of 'sub-British nationalism' among those who responded to the continuing imperial relationship and, on the other, strengthening the trend to the civic or democratic nationalism that would eventually find its expression in parts of the labour movement.

An awareness of separate interests within the empire, and sometimes outside of it, began to take shape in the middle of the nineteenth century. The movement against transportation was called the Australasian League, and coastal shipping at that time flew the first attempt at a distinctive flag for the colonies. It was a Presbyterian cleric who called for 'freedom and independence for the golden lands of Australia'.[8] Thus the emergence of a national consciousness was associated with the economic and political activities of the liberal strata: professionals, traders and small-scale producers. The few trade unions were small, and their dream for working men was economic independence, not labourist meliorism. For a decade after the Gold Rushes began in 1851, this independence was pursued mainly through small-scale alluvial mining.

---

7 R. W. Connell and T. H. Irving, *Class Structure in Australian History. Poverty and Progress*, 2nd edn (Melbourne, Longman Cheshire, 1992), chapter 3.
8 J. D. Lang, *Freedom and Independence for the Golden Lands of Australia* (London, 1852).

When miners at Eureka, near Ballarat, took up arms in 1854 against the Victorian government, raising for the first time the Eureka flag, their demands were characteristic of working men's movements in other 'new countries': freedom from government regulation and the right to representation in parliament. The Eureka rebellion, although easily suppressed, was to become a history-making moment for the democratic national tradition in Australia.[9]

Small-scale, independent economic activity was not viable in the long term for most colonists. Raising sheep required too much capital, and despite land Acts in the 1860s small farmers ('selectors') faced many difficulties, not least the relative absence of fertile land and reliable rainfall. Panning for alluvial gold, as a mass economic activity, was over by the early 1860s. Consequently the economic frontier shifted to the cities in the 1870s and 1880s, and a labour market for workers in building, transport and manufacturing was consolidated. This acceleration of the spread of wage labour occurred within an imperial economy. Colonial businessmen were not a native bourgeoisie, formed by an anti-imperialist logic, but a regional sub-set of the imperial ruling class. There was a parallel tendency among the colonial working men. Workers formed unions that were often branches of British craft unions, and their members were often British immigrants defending work practices that had been fashioned in Britain.

However, in this regional variation of British imperialism, as relations of production became fully commodified, a stage reached by the late 1880s, the mobilising focus of workers and employers had to be national.[10] In fact the trade unions were among the first civic organisations to envisage 'national' activity. The first Inter-colonial Trade Union Congress was held in 1879, three years before professionals and businessmen formed the Australian Natives' Association, a moderate nationalist organisation. At the third Inter-colonial Trade Union Congress in 1884 a broad national federation of labour was proposed and eventually, in 1889, the Australian Labour Federation (ALF) was brought into existence by the socialist Queensland Trades and Labour Council. New South Wales and Western Australia joined later, but as colonial loyalties were still stronger than national, the ALF existed only in name until it

---

9 See G. Gold (ed.), *Eureka. Rebellion beneath the Southern Cross* (Melbourne, Rigby, 1977). The Eureka flag designed by one of the Eureka rebels, five white stars arranged in a cross on a blue background, has been adopted throughout Australia's history by a range of protest movements, as well as left and right nationalist groups.

10 A. Wells, *Constructing Capitalism. An Economic History of Eastern Australia 1788–1901* (Sydney, Allen and Unwin, 1989), especially chapters 1 and 8.

faded away a decade later. After the failure of the ALF, inter-state trade union congresses periodically considered a more modest model of co-operation. At least one commentator at the time was surprised by Labor's national modesty. Writing in 1921, J. T. Sutcliffe felt it necessary to add as an appendix to his *A History of Trade Unionism in Australia* a survey of the repeated failures to establish an effective inter-state federation of unions. It was not until 1927 that a continuing organisation of unions at the national level, the Australian Council of Trade Unions, was formed along the lines discussed in 1902. Whenever claims of national significance for Labor are made, it should not be forgotten that the initial locus of trade union consciousness, and much of the strength of trade union action at any time, is a stubborn localism that is not easily overcome.

Labor and the federal redistribution of state power

It was not nationalism that propelled the trade unions beyond parochialism in the 1890s but class consciousness. To understand this we have to consider the second and third key moments of state building, when the weaknesses of the political and economic settlement of the 1850s were revealed. These were the moments when the colonies federated, the party system structured by the competition between Labor and the non-labour parties emerged, and the first majority Labor government was elected.

The depression of the 1890s starkly revealed three aspects of a crisis in the existing arrangement of state power.[11] First, as the colonial economies became more integrated and investment moved more freely it was difficult to confine economic downturns to one area of the economy or country. A national economy demanded a national approach, particularly to restore the confidence of overseas lenders and to attract immigrant workers. But each colony had its separate government. Second, the public policy programme of the mid-century settlement (land sales and low taxation to encourage immigration, and reliance on British investment for infrastructure) no longer functioned. The limit on disposable land had been reached and British funds had dried up by the end of the 1880s. Revenue tariffs, first introduced by Victoria in the 1860s, were the obvious solution, but by the 1890s, in an emerging national economy, it was clear that they created an impediment to inter-colonial trade. Third, there was a political crisis, caused by the entry of a class-conscious working class into the parliamentary arena where hitherto liberal interest-group

11 I rely here on Wells, *Constructing Capitalism*, chapter 9.

politics had prevailed. A series of 'great strikes' in the early 1890s were fought on the issue of trade unionism *v.* 'freedom of contract', following a rapid expansion of union membership in the 1880s. The defeat of the strikers, the intervention of colonial governments on the side of the employers, and the debates that led unionists and radical intellectuals to form Labour parties, all consolidated a sense of class identity among wage earners. Nowhere was this clearer than in the new Labour parties, which were organised, via the 'pledge', the caucus and the annual conference, to allow the extra-parliamentary membership to control their politicians. The ethos of party solidarity so created, with its potential for introducing class interests into politics, was regarded, correctly, by the conservative press 'as opposed to the principles of sound parliamentary government'.[12]

The matter of timing is crucial to the explanation at this point. The Labor Party, in its New South Wales and Queensland heartland, was set on this path from the early 1890s, before the movement for the federation of the colonies reached its climax in 1900. Federation, in one sense, was a ruling-class response to a working-class mobilisation. Indeed, Cardinal Moran, the head of the Roman Catholics, was supposed to have said that federation was a way of preventing one or more of the colonies becoming socialist. Whatever the likelihood of this happening, a redistribution of state power, such as federation would entail, was enthusiastically embraced by conservatives at this time. A new level of the state would restrain unionism and regulate wages, work and the labour supply. A national political framework signified that the national economy would be taken seriously by political leaders, thus reassuring overseas investors. A new federal government might even revive the economy by eliminating customs wars. Given this context, it is not surprising that the colonial bourgeoisie dominated the federation movement.

Federation never became a popular cause, despite the boosterism of the liberal and conservative press. While some Labor leaders supported the federal movement, the Labor press revealed widespread indifference or suspicion. The outcome was that Labor was largely absent from the debates in the constitutional conventions, which took place 'in an ocean of public apathy'. Although the constitution was passed at a referendum, only 43 per cent of electors voted in favour,

---

12 Labor politicians signed a pledge to abide by party policy as laid down by the caucus and conference. The quote is from the *Sydney Morning Herald*, 13 November 1893. On Labor's class theory of democracy see T. H. Irving and A. Seager, 'Labour and Politics in Canada and Australia', *Labour/Le Travail* 38 (1996), pp. 258–61.

and where Labor was strongest so was the 'no' vote.[13] While Labor intellectuals worried about the anti-democratic tendencies of the constitution, among the rank and file the concern was more basic. An article entitled 'Federation and food' told Labor supporters in Hobart in 1896 that

> The great and ever-present problem to most Australians is the tucker question, and we can't get away from that fact no matter how loudly and vehemently the upper crust may howl for Federation. Food is of more importance than federation in these times when the world is being forced to think of its stomach first in order to think at all.[14]

This was hardly a sentiment likely to encourage nationalism, but it was typical of the Labor press in the years leading up to federation. In the *Worker*, published in Sydney by the Australian Workers' Union, the regular articles on the constitutional debates and the federation referendum revealed not the slightest nationalistic rhetoric – except in rueful recognition of the real rules of the game:

> We feel a boundless yearning
> Our nationhood to claim
> To call Australians brothers
> To bear the same grand name
> And then we pause and ponder,
> These glories have their price –
> For present satisfaction
> A lasting sacrifice.
> We gain a piece of bunting,
> A continent, and since
> We're going to be a nation,
> Perhaps a royal prince.[15]

So, at the end of the second moment of nation building, Labor's integration into the state and community was uncertain. The party's policies envisaged enlarged state capacity in the areas of welfare and worker protection, and changes in state organisations as a result of democratic pressures. The Commonwealth of Australia, the new level of state power that emerged in 1901, had neither an enhanced capacity for action nor a fully democratic basis. There was no Bill of Rights, the powers of the

---

13 The quotation is from N. McLachlan, *Waiting for the Revolution. A History of Australian Nationalism* (Ringwood, Penguin Books, 1989), p. 167, and the voting figure *ibid.*, p. 179; R. Gollan, *Radical and Working Class Politics. A Study of Eastern Australia 1850–1910* (Melbourne, Melbourne University Press, 1960), pp. 180–3, is still the best source on federation and the New South Wales Labor Party.
14 W. A. Woods in *The Clipper* (Hobart), 1 July 1897.
15 W. H. D., 'For our Country's Sake', *Worker*, 17 June 1899.

federal government were limited, and the Crown, with its reserve powers preserved, was the paramount authority. The *Worker* was worried that socialist policies of state and municipal governments could now be impeded at the federal level. Moreover, campaigning in the new national political arena would be expensive and tend to throw Labor into the arms of the popular, and generally anti-Labor, press.[16] However, a different process of integration, class-based rather than national, was proceeding in the community. The arguments about federation had strengthened Labor's identification as the party of democracy, and the formation and immediate electoral successes of the party had confirmed that the labour movement was a serious player in the state, with the potential to influence later developments. When its policies were crossed with national consciousness, the product was a nationalism inflected with democratic, working-class sentiments.

Labor and the 'national' settlement

The third and fourth moments of state and nation building lasted from 1901 to 1939. This was a long period, unified by a balance of class forces: on one side an uneasy alliance between the colonial pastoral–financial bloc and the emerging industrial bourgeoisie, facing on the other side a working class mobilised in the trade unions and the Labor Party but weakened from within by fierce ideological conflicts. It was also a period, especially in the fourth moment, defined by the closing down of democratic state building by the forces of conservative nation building. This was just one expression of the more damaging discovery by Labor, that governing was not equivalent to ruling. Moreover, the experience of governing was mainly in the states, for at the federal level Labor was out of office for about thirty-one of the thirty-nine years after 1901. In this situation it was not surprising that Labor began to listen more attentively to the voice of the nation, or that differences over how to align the labour movement with nationalism would become an issue in the ideological conflicts in the movement. This was not the period, therefore, to which later commentators should look for evidence of Labor as the leading party in the construction of the national state.

The third moment of state building in the decade after federation was a passing moment, one whose significance is distorted by placing it solely in a nationalist trajectory. It may seem implausible that the creation of a new country should not have inaugurated a prolonged period

16 *Worker*, 18 February and 15 April 1899.

of state building, but, as Frank Castles has shown, modernity was well advanced in Australia in 1901. The country had a 'startlingly modern' economic structure (only 25 per cent of workers employed in agriculture), the highest GDP *per capita* in the world, it was among the most urbanised countries in the world, and its democratic labour movement was on the verge of winning majority popular support and legitimacy. Moreover, as 'a colonial settlement, the state had been the creator of civil society'.[17] Compared with European and North American countries, Australia did not lack a modern state in 1901. In these circumstances, if there were to be any post-federation building of the nation state, the emphasis would fall on developing national consciousness, not on enlarging the democratic capacities or scope of the state. It would be, in McLachlan's words, a nationalism without a nationalist revolution.[18]

Elections to the new federal parliament of Australia between 1901 and 1909 produced three parties of roughly equal strength, Labor and two conservative parties. The dynamics of capitalist competition meant that the protectionist party, with its support in the manufacturing and urban sectors of capital, was more liberal and more sympathetic to Labor. Because both were committed to a programme of state building, a series of policies were initiated in these years that gained for the new Commonwealth a reputation as a 'social laboratory'. Scholars have seen these policies, in retrospect, as a 'national settlement'.[19] While it is true that as a result Labor was further integrated into state organisations, and the opportunities for class collaboration increased, and without denying that the working class felt the impact of nationalist ideas, nonetheless, during this period, labour welcomed these developments as much for their benefits to workers as for their nation-building significance. This burst of state building is better seen as a compact between organised labour and the progressive part of organised capital, analogous perhaps to the social democratic compromises that followed the Second World War in parts of Europe.

What were the main components of the 'settlement'? In 1901 the Immigration Restriction Act gave force to the notorious 'White Australia' policy. This Act excluded new 'non-white' immigrants by forcing them to take a dictation test of fifty words in a European lan-

---

17 Francis G. Castles, 'Australia and Sweden: the Politics of Economic Vulnerability', *Thesis Eleven* 16 (1987), pp. 116–17.
18 McLachlan, *Waiting for the Revolution*, p. 2.
19 P. Beilharz, *Transforming Labor. Labour Tradition and the Labor Decade in Australia* (Melbourne, Cambridge University Press, 1994), pp. 7–10; P. Kelly, *The End of Certainty* (Sydney, Allen and Unwin, 1992), p.2.

guage; other Acts set in train the process of deporting Pacific Islanders who had been indentured to work in the Queensland sugar industry. 'Race' operated as a powerful unifying symbol in the nationalist project, and was therefore supported by all classes and regions, but for labour there were also arguments about the supposed protection of jobs and working conditions. The welfare state was inaugurated with the intro- duction of old age pensions, invalid pensions, and maternity allowances between 1909 and 1912. Here the rationale in terms of citizenship rights also strengthened the nationalist project but of course most recipients of these benefits were workers. However, the core social experiment was known as 'the new protection', an arrangement whereby industries that paid 'fair and reasonable wages' would be entitled to tariff protection. In 1904 the Conciliation and Arbitration Act established the Arbitration Court, 'a new province for law and order', but also a guarantee to trade unions that they were legitimate players in economic disputes. In 1907, in his famous 'Harvester judgement', the new president of the court, Mr Justice Higgins, defined a minimum wage – sufficient for an unskilled labourer, his wife and three children to live in frugal comfort – and before long this standard was in use in other wage decisions. Although a subsequent ruling by the High Court that the new protection Acts were invalid meant that the state could not enforce the arrangement, in prac- tice both sides kept to the bargain. 'Laborist commonsense' about employment dictated that Labor would continue to support high tariffs, while import replacement manufacturers had an interest in ensuring that working-class consumers could afford their products. In wages, as in jobs, welfare and immigration, the idea of a 'fair and reasonable' outcome in disputes between classes sums up the intent of the several parts of the early twentieth-century 'settlement'. Australia developed 'a wage-earners' welfare state', based on the strength of organised labour in the market place, rather than a universal model of welfare that might have integrated workers as citizens.[20]

These developments occurred as a result of federal government action. Commentators who focus on nation building are inclined to neglect what the state governments were doing at the same time, but for the analysis of labour and state building this level of government is sig- nificant. Not only was Labor electorally more successful at this level but it was also understood that state power could best be used on behalf of the working class by state governments. In New South Wales and Queensland in the 1910s the establishment of state enterprises went far

20 Francis G. Castles, *The Working Class and Welfare* (Sydney, Allen and Unwin, 1985), p. 102.

beyond the public utility or infrastructural models that had justified government ownership of such services as railways and schools since the middle of the previous century. Labour governments in these states embarked on a wide range of state enterprises, including mines, a fishing fleet, pastoral stations, butcher's shops, bakeries, brickworks and hotels. They were justified in various ways – as revenue raisers, as services to consumers, and as challenges to capital. They were also seen as a basis for economic development, but they were not, and cannot be, seen as evidence of a nation building project in the labour movement. The hostility they elicited from the national bourgeoisie in the 1920s and 1930s is proof of that. Subsequent conservative governments closed them down without a thought for the national interest.

War and the nation state

By the 1910s state building had become a deeply ambiguous project for Labor. Use of the state for democratic ends (for example to control prices and monopolies) was blocked by conservative forces in the federal and state parliaments which were deeply hostile to the post-federation settlement. Further, state power itself came to be seen as problematic by Labor intellectuals. The turning point occurred in the First World War, when the potential of nationalism to hold the line against Labor's advance became apparent. Gerhard Fischer has recently stressed the efflorescence of imperial loyalty during the war, and has denied that there was any breakthrough to an independent Australian identity at this time, but the truth is that war-inspired patriotism could insert itself into a variety of nationalisms, including Labor's democratic nationalism, if only because they were complex and incoherent mixtures of collective loyalties. In 1914 the war was overwhelmingly popular with all classes, and even anti-imperialist intellectuals were likely to enlist.[21] It was not simply the case that moderate Labor men succumbed to imperial jingoism while militants remained uncorrupted. There were, of course, Labor imperialists – William Morris Hughes, Labor's wartime Prime Minister being simply the most prominent – but it should be remembered that Hughes endeared himself to Australians of all classes because he stood up to the British government at the end of the war. Hughes and other proponents of conscription were expelled from the Labor Party in 1916 but the split in the party did not revolve around two

---

21 I am thinking here of Esmonde Higgins. Gerhard Fischer, '"Negative Integration" and an Australian Road to Modernity: Interpreting the Australian Home-front Experience in World War I', *Australian Historical Studies* 26:104 (1995), pp. 475 f.

different versions of nationalism. Rising inflation and unemployment accompanied the war, but even before 1914 the party was in trouble with the trade unions. Conscription was, thus, the lightning rod that attracted the labour movement's various class-based disappointments at the ineffectiveness of Labour governments in the states and federally since 1910.

More pertinently, the war was a state and nation-building moment of a peculiar kind. Hughes, after negotiations with his conservative opponents, formed and led a 'Win the War' or National Party government from early 1917. The war required economic controls, and Hughes with his Labor background did not hesitate to impose them. But now of course his intent was not Labor's. The federal government organised businessmen into the war effort. It exercised surveillance over intellectual radicals and trade union militants. Members of 'unlawful associations' – chiefly the Industrial Workers of the World – were jailed and some were deported. The press was censored and the War Precautions Act was used to intimidate and punish those who were seen as obstructing the war effort – even parliamentarians. Finally, the unsuccessful attempts to introduce conscription by referendums in 1916 and 1917 indicated the lengths to which Hughes would go to enlarge the powers of the state.

This use of the state was a revelation to Labor intellectuals. Their assumption that state organisations were neutral and that state power could be wielded to benefit Labor instead of employers now had to be supplemented by the possibility that democracies such as Britain and Australia could become 'servile states', societies in which the overweening power of the state reduced its functional groups, its civil society, to the status of servility. Gordon Childe, a prominent Labor intellectual, discovered 'Prussian Australianism' in this possibility.[22] It was also clear from the wartime propaganda that nationalism was the best cover for the encroaching state. Labor intellectuals were thus confronted with a new meaning for nationalism: as oppressive state worship. This development, rather than the loyalties associated with the war, was the catalyst for the reconsideration of nationalism in Labor ranks in the 1920s and 1930s.

The war altered the configuration of state and nation. Before the war there was a degree of separation between them. State building had

---

22 T. H. Irving. ' "On the work of Labour Governments": Gordon Childe's Plans for Volume Two of *How Labour Governs*', in P. Gathercole, T.H. Irving and G. Melleuish (eds), *Childe and Australia. Archaeology, Politics and Ideas* (Brisbane, University of Queensland Press, 1995), p. 86.

meant the labourist and social liberal programme of the 'post-federation settlement'; nationalism was about the openness of identity, and the good society. From the 1880s labour intellectuals had taken the moral high ground on nationalism; in their eyes the labour movement spoke for the typical Australian and embodied his dreams of a society that would rise above the evils of the Old World. After the war the main conservative party is called 'National', and its leader had demonstrated a darker side of the active state. Moreover, the experience of war meant that the dream of national perfection is streaked with the blood of sacrifice. In fact, in nationalist discourse the rituals and myths that emerge to honour the war dead provide a new transcendent element. An integralist form of national identity begins to take shape, positively encouraged by the state. For the labour movement there is a double crisis. As nationalists they have been outflanked; as state builders they have been politically blocked and intellectually neutralised.

There were two responses in the 1920s and 1930s. The Labor leadership and the moderate wing of the labour movement reacted by turning inwards. With the labour movement weakened by the split over conscription, Labor's conservative opponents in the National government unleashed a campaign of state repression to deal with working-class unrest. Overseas-born 'agitators' were deported, the importation of 'seditious' literature was banned, and the government was given the power to suppress strikes affecting Australia's trade and commerce. At the same time the post-war recession made organising in the working class more difficult. The triumphant conservatives seized the opportunity to label all Labor activity as part of the international Communist conspiracy against the British Empire. In this situation, trade union and Labor Party leaders, in order to differentiate themselves from the Communists, were forced to play down the legacy of anti-imperialism from their radical nationalist past. Instead, Labor opted for an alliance with the national bourgeoisie, exploiting the tension between Australian manufacturing capital and British financial, pastoral and commercial capital.[23] The logic of this depleted national vision pointed to isolationism. At its most positive it recalled the position of Hughes at the 1919 Peace Congress, that 'Australia should not allow the statesmen of any country to determine her course of action'. As international crises became more threatening, the negativity of Labor's

---

23 P. Cochrane, *Industrialization and Dependence. Australia's Road to Economic Development* (Brisbane, University of Queensland Press, 1980), p. 107; M. Dunn, *Australia and the Empire. From 1788 to the Present* (Sydney, Fontana/Collins, 1984), pp. 113–14.

isolationism became more insistent. In 1935 the federal ALP caucus resolved that:

The attitude of the Australian Labor Party is clear and unequivocal. It wants no war on foreign fields for economic treasure. It wants Australia to be kept free of the entanglements leading to a repetition of the horrors of 1914–18. Therefore, the Australian Labor Party . . . today says '*non-participation*'.[24]

The left and radical nationalism

Meanwhile the intellectuals and organisations of the revolutionary left had retrieved the banner of radical nationalism. This occurred against the background of the 'revolt against politicalism' among the militants of the trade union movement. Self-identified as 'industrialists', they led a wave of strikes, most notably a general strike in New South Wales in 1917. Their agitation was not so much against the Labor Party as its class-collaborationist leadership. In this context, nationalism was more clearly connected with anti-capitalist politics. A socialist intellectual during the war argued that 'A belief in Australian nationalism implies a desire to destroy the present economic system, if only to make it national.' There was, however, another dynamic at work. By 1925, now a Communist Party leader, the same intellectual was arguing that Australia could not escape the coming international crisis of capitalism. He was therefore critical of the Labor Party for fostering 'all kinds of romantic notions about Australia as a world apart, which may expect to reach social salvation by isolating itself from the rest of the world'.[25] This internationalist dynamic was promoted, of course, by the Communist Party, which had been formed in 1921, but it built upon the legacy of Australian anti-imperialism, especially among workers of Irish extraction. With just a few hundred activists, the Australian branch of the Communist International was tiny, but the strength of internationalism among Australian workers was considerable in the 1920s and 1930s. The Labor Council of New South Wales affiliated to the Red International of Labour Unions at its first Congress in Moscow in 1921, and the Pan-Pacific Trade Union Secretariat was an Australian innovation, supported by the Australian Council of Trade Unions until 1931.[26]

The Labor intellectuals who were drawn to the Communist movement found themselves more deeply immersed than their Labor col-

---

24 Federal ALP Caucus Minutes, extracted in B. McKinlay, *Australia Labor History in Documents* II, *The Labor Party* (Melbourne, Collins–Dove, 1979), pp. 106–07.
25 E. M. Higgins, 'Australia the Superior', *Communist* 2, February 1925.
26 F. Farrell, 'Explaining Communist History', *Labour History* 32 (1977), pp. 5–6.

leagues in questions of national peculiarities precisely because of their internationalism.[27] One dimension of this was the provincialist fear that Communists in Britain would assume a paternalistic role in relation to them. In fact, because of their cultural heritage and in some cases earlier experience, Australian left intellectuals naturally followed British developments closely, as did their conservative counterparts. They relied on British left publications, especially Rajani Palme Dutt's *Labour Monthly*, to compensate for their own underdeveloped left intellectual sphere. Nonetheless, it was an irritating dependence. In Communist circles, complaints about the indifference of the British party to Australian needs were common, drawing as they could at this time on a just emerging, broader tradition of post-colonial resentment of the insensitivity of metropolitan patrons. That there was some justification for the resentment can be seen in Dutt's comment to his wife: 'Australia is an artificial closed box where nothing ever happens or will happen.'[28] Of course, this was a common attitude among Comintern operatives, who were resolutely Eurocentric, despite a series of contradictory attempts to deal with 'the Eastern Question' at congresses between 1919 and 1928.

The Communist Party was well placed in the 1930s to attract workers and intellectuals radicalised by the events of that decade. In Australia any kind of radicalisation – left or right – had to confront the issue of the country's relationship with the centres of world power, capitalist or Communist, especially in this decade. A new generation of novelists, poets and historians emerged who posed the questions of national character and national independence with greater sharpness. As the Labor Party retreated into 'Australia first' isolationism it was an easy mark for these critics, who referred sarcastically to the way the party 'never tired of referring to the "concrete achievements of Australia in the social sphere" '. Such an approach, they felt, ignored the struggle for freedom, which was exemplified by what was happening in Manchuria, in Abyssinia and in Europe – events that required intervention by democratic forces, according to the Communist Party. 'Freedom' was also, these intellectuals discovered, a way to organise their account of

27 This section is based on my 'Labour Intellectuals and Empire: Gordon Childe and Esmonde Higgins (to 1930)', presented to the 'Labour and Empire' conference at the International Institute for Social History, Amsterdam, May 1996.

28 Dutt to Salme, late February 1924, transcript kindly supplied by Kevin Morgan from his notes from the Communist Party archives in Britain. On relations between the Australian and British Communist parties see E. Higgins, 'To the Colonial Committee, CPGB', Australian Archives, ACT, CRS A6126, item 67, Australian Security Intelligence file on H. B. Higgins.

Australian history and culture. By the end of the 1930s, in the work of Vance and Nettie Palmer, Brian Fitzpatrick, Katherine Susannah Prichard and others, the foundations had been laid for two related tra-ditions, of literary nationalism and radical nationalist history. The con-nection between the two was a common focus on the working class as the bearer of nationalism. For the literary nationalists the bush worker became the typical Australian, freed from the class-bound customs of the Old World by frontier life; for the historical nationalists the labour move-ment was the working class's attempt to reshape society in more egalitar-ian, democratic and socialist ways by struggling against a pro-British ruling class. Many of these intellectuals joined, or were drawn in to the orbit of, Communist cultural movements.[29]

Militant workers followed a similar trajectory. The Great Depression was disastrous for the labour movement. It was ushered in by a series of industrial defeats for the unions, and Labor governments were unable to resist ruling-class pressure, especially from the City of London, for cuts in wages and government expenditure. With the Labor Party and the labourist leaders of the unions discredited by their fail-ures, it was the Communist Party that benefited most when a revival of militancy occurred among the unemployed and the trade unionists in the mid-1930s. Its membership increased, and its industrial cadres suc-cessfully colonised key unions in the mining, maritime, transport and manufacturing industries. At the same time, Communist-led anti-impe-rialist and peace movements attracted middle-class intellectuals. Workers and intellectuals were brought together by campaigns that used industrial muscle for anti-imperialist and anti-fascist ends, as in the *Dalfram* dispute on the Port Kembla wharves, when unionists refused to load pig iron for Japan in 1938.[30] This gave a distinctly 'radical nation-alist' edge to the revival of left politics in the labour movement in the 1930s.

Labour actors; nationalist dynamics

As with many other issues in Australian labour history, in order to say something sensible about the working class and nationalism one has

29 For useful surveys of these developments see the essays in C. Wallace-Crabbe (ed.), *The Australian Nationalists, Modern Critical Essays* (Melbourne, Oxford University Press, 1971) and Andrew Wells, 'The old Left Intelligentsia 1930–60' in B. Head and J. Walter (eds), *Intellectual Movements and Australian Society* (Melbourne, Oxford University Press, 1988).

30 A. Davidson, *The Communist Party of Australia. A Short History* (Stanford, Cal., Hoover Institution Press, 1969), pp. 55–93.

first to brush away the cobwebs of labourist myth.[31] When labourist scholarship contemplates the connected histories of Labor and nation it dissolves the class identity of Labor into populist statements about the instinctive nationalism of the people. It asserts that labourism was 'part of the national myth'. Since labourism is the natural expression of working-class interests, it must follow that the working class was nationalist. As a recent scholar puts it, the working-class ethos and the national ethos merged. Arguing in this way avoids questions about how the working class is formed and the meaning of labour demands and national sentiments to different parts of the employed population. Indeed, the result of this kind of argument is to dissolve the working class into the surrounding society – in the approved labourist fashion.[32]

Most of the scholarship that purports to tell us about the hold of nationalism as a set of ideas on the working class is actually about Labor organisations and intellectuals. Thus Noel McLachlan's argument about the 'radical nationalism' of the working class in the 1880s and 1890s is based on the Labour press and the Labor Party. It would be possible, however, to discuss the economic and ideological pressures on the working class as data for the development of Labor practices of state and nation building, and thus to infer how a nationalist knowledge might have been created among workers. There are, however, no studies dedicated to showing how labour organisations and intellectuals operated as class builders, let alone as nation builders. Studies of ethnicity and nationalism focus almost entirely on middle-class sources, and they produce an intellectual history rather than a history of practices. It would be interesting, for example, to know how Irish national organisations interacted with labour organisations in the formative period, and to ask whether this had any bearing on Labor's attitude to federation. Labour historians like to point to the Irish Catholic contribution to the Labor Party, especially after the split of 1916, but it may be wrong to assume that workers of Irish descent were more nationalist than other workers. Andrew Parkin's survey of ethnic politics in Australia concludes

31 T. Irving, 'Labourism: a Political Genealogy', *Labour History* 66 (1994), pp. 1–13.
32 John Dalton, 'An Interpretative Survey: the Queensland Labour Movement', in D. J. Murphy, R. B. Joyce and C. A. Hughes (eds), *Prelude to Power. The Rise of the Labour Party in Queensland 1885–1915* (Brisbane, University of Queensland Press, 1970), p. 24. Drawing on this tradition is the analysis in D. W. Lovell, 'Australian Socialism to 1917: a Study of the Relations between Socialism and Nationalism', *Australian Journal of Politics and History,* special issue, 40 (1994), pp. 144–59. For a critique see J. Murphy, 'Populism and Democracy: a Reading of Australian Radical Nationalism', *Thesis Eleven* 16 (1987), pp. 85–99.

that the politics of class cleavage was always dominant over the politics of ethnic cleavage.[33]

Let us assume that the more non-unionised, internally divided and politically leaderless a wage-earning population is the more likely it is to respond to national than to class appeals. On that assumption it would not be difficult to conclude that Australian workers would be able to resist the economic, political and cultural pressures from nationalist forces. In 1890–91, with about 21–3 per cent of the work force unionised, the key colonies of New South Wales and Victoria were the most unionised in the world. More important than this statistic, however, was the extent to which the principle of organisation had been accepted among all sections of the work force. Not just tradesmen but unskilled transport, mining and bush workers; not just 'proletarians' but 'middle-class workers' in shops and offices tried their hand at organising themselves. Wages were more 'solidaristic' – that is, the differential between skilled and unskilled wages was less – than in Britain, thus undercutting the potential for a volatile underclass to develop.[34] The existence of tiny populations from Asia (about 1·5 per cent in New South Wales and Victoria in 1881) and the Pacific Islands (about 2 per cent in Queensland in 1891) made for much unjustified fear of racial contamination but provided no basis for a general assault on working conditions. The population was in fact overwhelmingly British in origin. Among them was the Irish component of between a quarter and a third of the population in 1900, and most of them were working-class.[35] Here indeed was a sizeable ethnic minority, with a distinct communal life and religion (three-quarters were Roman Catholic) that was largely working-class. It provided recruits for movements that despised 'the master race' (the English) and opposed British domination of Ireland. Their impact on Australian national practices, however, was felt via the labour movement, whose collectivist orientation was attractive to the Catholic value system.[36] The

33 A. Parkin, 'Ethnic Politics: a Comparative Study of Two Immigrant Societies, Australia and the United States', *Journal of Commonwealth and Comparative Politics* 15:1 (1977), p. 32. C. Hamilton, 'Irish Catholics of New South Wales and the Labor Party 1890–1910', *Historical Studies Australia and New Zealand* 8:31 (1958), pp. 254–67, studies contemporary press attitudes and election results. There was pervasive racism among Anglo-Celtic workers, but instances of organised opposition on the grounds of race or ethnicity, such as strikes against Chinese seamen in 1878 and 1885, or the riots against Italian gold miners in 1919, were comparatively rare. See G. Cresciani, 'Italian Migrants in Australia 1900–22', *Labor History* 43 (1982), p. 43.
34 G. Patmore, *Australian Labour History* (Melbourne, Longman Cheshire, 1991), pp. 54–62.
35 O. MacDonagh, *The Sharing of the Green. A Modern Irish History for Australians* (Sydney, Allen and Unwin, 1996), p. xi.
36 Parkin, 'Ethnic Politics', pp. 26–7.

nationalism of the Australian bourgeoisie made little headway among the Irish Australians. In fact workers in general were located in a class situation that immunised them from bourgeois nationalist appeals.

One of the central contributors to the study of Labor and nationalism, Russel Ward, argued in *The Australian Legend* that 'the rapid growth of the trade union movement, especially in the new industrial and bush unions, helped to spread the national ethos through the community and the cities'.[37] The evidence of nationalist symbols and attitudes in labour organisations is clear. The elaborate banners that unions commissioned in imitation of those carried in Labour processions in the 'old country' replaced or supplemented the rose, shamrock and thistle with the wattle, kangaroo and emu.[38] However, Ward's belief that there was a single national ethos, derived from the experience of the pastoral worker, is no longer accepted. Accordingly we must ask what function national sentiment played in the labour movement. The crucial point is that these attitudes were put to work to build cross-class alliances. In fact the evidence that trade unions were adept at playing the nationalist card is very strong. At the Inter-colonial Trade Union Congresses in the 1880s and 1890s delegates framed their 'class' demands with resolutions about immigration, racial purity and democracy, all of which drew on nationalist rhetoric. At other times, the frame invoked was socialist and racist, especially in Queensland. That these were nationalist framing efforts in which the term 'nation' was absent or subordinate to other terms only underlines how important it is to distinguish Labor state building from the bourgeois nationalist project. The general point is that cross-class politics in the labour movement were to do with establishing its legitimacy in the liberal political system before they were to do with establishing the nationalist credentials of the movement. Certainly, a class-collaborationist labour movement should not be mistaken for a nationalist working-class constituency driving the unions and the party in a nationalist direction.

One of the most influential ideas in recent discussions of nationalism is that the nation is an 'invented community' whose horizontal and fraternal bonds prevail over the vertical tensions of inequality and exploitation.[39] In some situations, however, the national community will have different meanings in parts of the population on different sides of

37 R. Ward, 'The Australian Legend Revisited', *Historical Studies* 18:71 (1978), p. 189. Ward's book was published in 1958.
38 A. Stephen and A. Reeves, *Badges of Labour, Banners of Pride. Aspects of Working Class Celebration* (Sydney, Allen and Unwin, n.d. [probably 1986]).
39 B. Anderson, *Imagined Communities. Reflections on the Origins and Spread of Nationalism* (London, Verso, revised edn 1991), pp. 6–7.

a vertical divide. Such was the case in Australia. The ethnocentric Britishness, 'the crimson thread of kinship' that was just as much a labour as a conservative approach to the nation, nonetheless was articulated differently in the labour movement. Douglas Cole has identified an 'indigenous Australian ethnic consciousness' whose positive expression conceived of Australia as 'free from class distinctions, overbearing aristocracy, sweated pauperism, and oppressive militarism'.[40] 'Australian' ethnocentrism, in other words, placed its emphasis on the democratic agency of the people. This was not, of course, how conservatives understood the benefits of being part of the British race.

A similar point can be made about Labor racism. It was intertwined with radical egalitarianism because the egalitarian impulse allowed dominance over a subject race only by denying its humanity.[41] It was also associated with the rational cast of non-Marxist socialism, as Graeme Osborne has shown in his study of the Victorian Socialist Party. Beginning as an internationalist party in 1905, by the latter part of the First World War the VSP had become both rationalist and nationalist. Contemporary scientific thought at the climactic moment of formal imperialism accepted the notion of racial difference and inequality.[42] It was also rational to be democratic. Recent discussions of Labor nationalism have rediscovered the British chauvinism and racism that flowed from Australia's place in the imperial system, but in the process they have let go of the 'novel theory of democracy' that flowed from Labor's place in the class structure.[43] We should ask not only what Labor 'thought' but what it did – how it took part in the construction of the national state. Labor's state-building activity was a nationalist practice, but it was democratic rather than integralist.

40 D. Cole, ' "The Crimson Thread of Kinship": Ethnic Ideas in Australia 1870–1914', *Historical Studies* 14:56 (1971), p. 518.
41 Parkin, 'Ethnic Politics', p. 25.
42 G. Osborne, 'A Socialist Dilemma: Racism and Internationalism in the Victorian Socialist Party, 1905–21', in A. Curthoys and A. Markus (eds), *Who are our enemies?* (Sydney, Hale and Iremonger, 1978), pp. 126–7.
43 I am thinking here of H. McQueen, *A New Britannia – An Argument concerning the Social Origins of Australian Radicalism and Nationalism* (Ringwood, Penguin Books, 1970).

Treading the diverse paths of modernity: Labour, ethnicity and nationalism in South Africa, 1870–1946

The relationship between organised labour, ethnicity and nationalism in South Africa during this period was shaped fundamentally by the migrant labour process, itself largely formed by the late nineteenth-century discovery of gold and diamonds which sparked off South Africa's own industrial revolution. Although migrant labour was a feature of many industrialising societies, the longevity of the process in South Africa – lasting into the 1990s – makes it somewhat unique. Indeed, South Africa provided a veritable laboratory of differing con-sciousnesses in the period in question, due largely to the longevity of migrancy. This allowed African identities, often rural in nature, the crucial space needed in which to reformulate themselves in the wake of colonial capitalism. The existence of these identities, and the attempt by nationalist culture brokers to capture them for their own political pro-jects at specific historical junctures, provides a rich field for exploring the changing consciousnesses and identities of Africans and Afrikaners. These groups, for various political, ideological and economic reasons, experienced very different rates of proletarianisation. Rural Africans remained largely a migrant labour work force throughout this period, whereas previously rurally based Afrikaners were incorporated perma-nently into urban areas at a much quicker pace. The differing rate of incorporation into the capitalist economy between these groups was a significant shaping factor in terms of nascent working-class conscious-ness.[1] The legacy of the South African war, marked opposition to British imperialism, and the poverty caused by rapid but narrow industrialisa-tion were also significant factors in shaping the identities of Afrikaners who had only recently entered the urban milieu. These issues also affected the development of Afrikaner-organised labour movements.

Unlike European economies in this period, the South African economy was skewed towards agriculture and primary extractive indus-

---

1 See B. Bozzoli, 'Marxism, Feminism and Southern African Studies', *Journal of Southern African Studies* 9:2 (1983), pp. 139–71.

tries, especially mining. Census returns between 1904 and 1946 divided the population in terms of four main 'racial' groups: 'White', 'Coloured', 'Asian' and 'African'. In this period whites varied approximately between 21 per cent and 22 per cent of the total population. Africans varied approximately between 67 per cent and 69 per cent. The percentage of fully urbanised whites in 1911 was 51·6, compared with 12·6 for Africans. In 1936 the figures were 65·2 and 17·3 respectively. Hence the largest sector of the population remained predominantly rural during this period, owing largely to the implementation of the migrant labour process and segregationist policies. This ensured that African workers on the mines received far lower wages than their white counterparts. Migrant labour gave capitalists a work force without the full costs of supporting African workers and their families in town, mine management arguing that the shortfall in wages could be made up through subsistence production in the rural areas. For example, in 1911 white workers on the gold mines received an average wage of R660, compared with R57 for African workers. In 1931 the average wages were R753 and R66 respectively. The ratio of whites to blacks in mine employment was 1:7·75 in 1910; by 1924 the ratio had changed to 1:9·83.[2] However, this meant that there was a potential for conflict between management and white workers, who wished to protect their higher-status jobs, which did not always accord with mine management's desire for cheap labour. This was especially the case with recently proletarianised Afrikaner workers. The particular structure of the labour force, and the fact that Africans, unlike fully proletarianised Afrikaners, retained a tenuous hold on rural identities owing to the very existence of the migrant labour process, were central elements affecting the development of African and Afrikaner nationalism during these years. They were also important influences in terms of the particular shape organised labour movements took, and the relationship these had with the two main forms of nationalism that existed.

This chapter explores these issues, and in doing so demonstrates the intricate, fluid relationships between both African and Afrikaner nationalisms and the growth of working-class consciousnesses, within a context of institutionalised racism.[3] It is divided into four main sections.

2 These statistics have been drawn from the following sources: appendix one, table one, in W. Beinart, *Twentieth Century South Africa* (Oxford, Oxford University Press, 1994), p. 261; M. Lipton, *Capitalism and Apartheid* (Totowa, N.J., Rowman and Allanheld, 1985), pp. 401–10; R. Davies, *Capital, State and White Labour in South Africa 1900–60* (Atlantic Highlands, N.J., Rowman and Littlefield, 1979), table 5, p. 70.

3 The various forms of black African and Afrikaner consciousnesses were not the only ethnicised identities which underwent reformulation in this period. Indian,

The first explores the complex relationship between African nationalism, trade unionism, nascent class consciousness and rural ethnic identifications among black Africans in late nineteenth- and early twentieth-century South Africa. The second section examines similar issues set within the specific context of migrant labour and the mine compounds. This is followed by an analysis of the connections between black African male youth associations and developing class and nationalist identities. These are shown to be related to the changes in rural consciousness initiated by South Africa's particular socio-economic development. The final section surveys the connections between British imperialism and the development of Afrikaner class and nationalist identities, set within a process of rapid proletarianisation.

African nationalism, trade unionism and ethnic mobilisation over land, *c.* 1870–1930

The discovery of gold and diamonds in the late nineteenth century, the 1899–1902 South African War, and the 1910 Act of Union were all significant landmarks in the formation of nationalist, and more explicitly ethnic, forms of identity in South Africa. They were also crucial factors in forging the relationship between nationalist and organised labour movements. These events initiated the formation of both the ANC in 1912 and the Afrikaner Nationalist Party in 1914, which, in a sense, represented the same political phenomenon. Their members originated respectively from the black and white professional intelligentsias of the time, all were men, and both aimed to mobilise a wider support base in order to overcome their exclusion from power as a result of British hegemony.[4] There were, however, fundamental differences between the two: the former promoted non-racial, inclusive ideals, while the latter gradually developed an inward-looking, exclusive, racist ideology. Additionally, the early ANC was not strongly anti-imperialist, unlike the Nationalist Party. The former represented civic, as compared with the other's ethnic, nationalism.

'Coloured' and other identities also experienced considerable change. However, African and Afrikaner identities receive particular attention, as they produced the two main forms of nationalism promoted in the first half of the twentieth century. For examples of Indian and 'Coloured' ethnic identity reformulation see S. Marks and S. Trapido (eds), *The Politics of Race, Class and Nationalism in Twentieth Century South Africa* (London, Longman, 1987), and L. Vail, *The Creation of Tribalism in Southern Africa* (London, James Currey, 1989).

4 See, for example, S. Marks and S. Trapido, 'The Politics of Race, Class and Nationalism', in *id., The Politics of Race, Class and Nationalism*, pp. 1–70. This work discusses both forms of nationalism in a comparative format.

The ANC had particular problems in relating to more rurally based, local identities in this period. It was only in the late nineteenth century that the last of the African chiefdoms, in what was to become South Africa, were finally conquered or otherwise subsumed by the forces of British imperialism. Many rural Africans still centred their identities around the institution of the chieftaincy, and were primarily interested in retaining access to land which was being rapidly expropriated by both Briton and Boer. The chieftaincy often provided a focus of resistance to land expropriation in the late nineteenth and early twentieth centuries, and this led to many rural Africans identifying themselves with mobilised, rurally based, ethnic particularisms. This did not easily resonate with African nationalists' concerns regarding political equality, and a broadly inclusive form of national identity. In fact, especially during the 1920s, other organisations, such as the Industrial and Commercial Workers' Union (henceforth the ICU) were far more successful in terms of popular mobilisation, owing to their greater readiness to incorporate these more local grievances within a broader political objective.

The small, mission-educated elite that made up the bulk of the ANC were partly forged in the colonial world and sought, unlike the majority of rurally based Africans, a place in the colonial order. Their origins were rooted in a time of mid-nineteenth-century Victorian liberalism, centred in the Cape region, which to a certain extent aimed at incorporating educated blacks within colonial society. However, by the late nineteenth century the 'incorporative elements of Victorian liberalism were being jettisoned in British and colonial thinking, replaced by the loose amalgam of ideas sometimes called Social Darwinism'.[5] Racial ideas and policies hardened as confidence in the mid-Victorian 'civilising mission' began to wane. White fears regarding black urbanisation and proletarianisation lent themselves to policies of segregation. Furthermore, these policies originated more from the machinations of British imperialists and segregationist ideologues than from Afrikaners. African chiefs, who in the mid-nineteenth century and before were regarded as a threat to British imperial and colonising interests, gradually came to be perceived as bastions against an organised black working class. Ironically chiefs were often the central pivot around which rural African peoples forged their identities. Thus policies of segregation met the needs of various interest groups. These included chiefs who wished to maintain their political importance and status, mine management and various white segregationist ideologues. They also included small groups of elite-educated Africans, who selectively supported, and rein-

5 Beinart, *Twentieth Century South Africa*, p. 68.

vented, the remnants of pre-colonial African political and cultural structures in order to protect their own vested interests. This often seemed
to be in blatant contradiction of their professed nationalist orientations.

Perhaps the best illustration of this change in British imperial
policy, and its effects on rural African peoples' consciousnesses,
occurred in 1920s Natal, itself a very 'British' region. Here the legacy of
the nineteenth-century Zulu kingdom, a rural populace which could still
be mobilised behind the Zulu paramountcy,[6] white fears regarding the
possibility of a black organised working class, the labour requirements
of – largely mining – capital, and the activities of the ICU, all combined
to forge a plethora of nascent class and ethnic identities. The example
of Natal also provides a striking illustration of the relationship between
the elite Zulu intelligentsia and the Zulu royal house, which further illus-
trates the complex interplay between rural ethnic particularism, class
consciousness and African nationalism in this period.

John Dube, a Zulu *kholwa* (elite, mission-educated Zulu) and first
president of the South African Native National Congress, graphically
demonstrated the rejection of pre-colonial forms of culture and custom
in an early published tract, arguing that it was Britain's imperial 'duty'
to help the Zulu 'rise' to British levels of 'civilisation'.[7] He made similar
appeals in his inaugural presidential address. However many *kholwa*,
including Dube himself, were pushing for the restoration of the Zulu
monarchy and a return to selective custom and 'tradition' by the late
1920s, in seemingly complete contrast to their earlier professed beliefs.
This considerable change in attitude towards the Zulu paramountcy was
due largely to *kholwa* class interest. The growth in support for the ICU,
and the consequent radicalisation of agricultural labourers, some of
whom were employed by this early African elite, challenged their class
status.[8] This was already under threat from such legislation as the 1913

---

6 The paramount chief of Zululand. This institution was dismantled by the British in
the late nineteenth century, but retained a powerful pull on the consciousness of
rural Zulu people. See J. Guy, *The Destruction of the Zulu Kingdom* (London,
Longman, 1979).

7 J. Dube, *The Zulu's Appeal for Light and England's Duty* (London, Unwin, 1908), p. 5.
The pamphlet is littered throughout with these forms of subservient appeal, and
demonstrates the strong link with Britain and Enlightenment thought among the
elite African intelligentsia of the time. However, Dube's appeals should also be
read partly as a shrewd way of raising funds for his Ohlange industrial school, set
up in the early part of the century. The pamphlet was specifically aimed at philan-
thropic bodies such as the Aborigines' Protection Society.

8 S. Marks, 'Natal, the Zulu Royal Family and the Ideology of Segregation', *Journal
of Southern African Studies* 4:2 (1978), pp. 180–201, and N. Cope, 'The Zulu Petty-
Bourgeoisie and Zulu Nationalism in the 1920s: Origins of Inkatha', *Journal of
Southern African Studies* 16:3 (1990), pp. 431–51.

Land Act, which aimed at increasing segregation, enlarging 'native reserves'[9] and making it illegal for Africans to purchase or lease land from Europeans anywhere in South Africa outside the reserves. The Act in some respects was a response to the prosperity gained by some *kholwa* and other black African agricultural entrepreneurs in the late nineteenth and early twentieth centuries. Hence the restoration of the paramountcy served diverse interests, which nevertheless could buttress white domination.

White ideologues such as George Heaton Nicholls, a prominent Zululand MP, perceived the need to encourage this restoration in order to avoid the formation of a radicalised African proletariat, and what they perceived as the possibility of a 'class war'. Nicholls advocated the restoration of Solomon ka Dinuzulu, heir to the Zulu throne, in order to divert Zulu people's consciousness from assuming a more radical dimension. Dube, and others like him, did likewise in order to maintain their own privileged status, which was under dual threat from the activities of the ICU and from government legislation.[10] This unlikely alliance led to the formation of the first Inkatha movement in 1922–23, which supported the restoration and promoted 'traditional' Zulu custom.

However, political machinations, class self-interest and colonial manipulation of identities had to be based on a solid foundation, reflecting the experience and consciousness of the mass of largely rural Zulu people. People are socialised into pre-existing identities and ethnic mobilisation has to be rooted in the real experiences of ordinary people. Although the uneven incursion of a capitalist economy and colonial domination had fractured Zulu society, many facets of pre-colonial Zulu morality and values remained. The role of the king had played an integral part in unifying pre-colonial Zulu society since the early nineteenth century. It would also be incorrect to assume that there was an inevitable rift between the mission-educated *kholwa* elite and the old elite of chiefs. Many *kholwa* came from, or married into, chiefly families, and their own consciousnesses were inevitably partially shaped by these experiences.

9 'Native Reserves' were demarcated by the colonial administration for the African rural populace, and involved a degree of land alienation unrivalled in any other sub-Saharan African context. See Beinart, *Twentieth Century South Africa*, chapter 1, for an incisive overview.
10 The Zulu monarchy had previously been seen as a threat by the British colonial power, posing the possibility of unifying the Zulu against white rule. The ill fated Bambatha rebellion of 1906, the last time in this period that black Africans attempted to resist colonial rule by armed force, reinforced this largely paranoid fear. See S. Marks, *Reluctant Rebellion. The 1906–08 Disturbances in Natal* (London, Oxford University Press, 1970). Furthermore, Dube and others like him had earlier in the century been perceived by the Natal government as dangerous radicals.

It was perhaps inevitable, then, that people should have turned to the royal family as well as the ICU at a time of social and economic crisis. The Zulu royal family had been a central factor in defining pre-colonial Zulu ethnic identity, and the fact that full proletarianisation was being delayed through the migrant labour process meant that these loyalties remained the prime focus for many people. The ravages of the 1897 rinderpest epidemic, the 1903 drought, colonially imposed taxes, enforced migrant labour, and the appropriation of land by white settlers, together with the implementation of segregation, meant that people readily looked back to the past for security and an answer to the pressing question of increasing impoverishment. Many early African Nationalists did not fully take into account these localised experiences, and therefore did not attract large-scale support. However, the ICU did manage to penetrate rural areas.

The ICU was launched in 1919 in the Cape Town docks. It spread rapidly throughout South Africa, and beyond, in the mid-1920s, thanks in no small part to its eclecticism and willingness to take up a wide range of issues both urban and rural in nature. As such it overtook the ANC in terms of a wider mass support. The influence of the ICU was strongest in the rural areas undergoing rapid transition towards capitalist agriculture, such as the eastern Transvaal. However, it also attracted considerable support in Umvoti district, Natal, where African labour tenants were coming under increasing pressure in terms both of eviction and increased work for white farmers. These farm labourers were still steeped in the traditions, experience and values of precolonial times, even though some had lived on white holdings for decades. As such the institution of the chieftaincy was a prime shaping factor in terms of how they identified themselves. The success of the ICU in this area was directly related to its ability to articulate these identities with resistance against land expropriation and demands for higher wages and better conditions of work. People still perceived the land as divided into the chiefdoms of pre-colonial times, and therefore had a powerful sense of 'Zulu-ness' strongly embedded in the land. As Bradford states, it was 'by meshing such nationalist aspirations with the class concerns of rural blacks undergoing proletarianization that the ICU achieved mass support in Umvoti'.[11] This version of Zulu identity was in direct contrast to that of culture brokers such as Dube, who

11 H. Bradford, 'Lynch Law and Labourers: the ICU in Umvoti 1927–28', in W. Beinart, P. Delius and S. Trapido (eds), *Putting a Plough to the Ground. Accumulation and Dispossession in Rural South Africa 1850–1930* (Johannesburg, Ravan Press, 1986), p. 443. Here Bradford is referring to Zulu ethnic nationalism rather than the 'civic' nationalism promoted by the ANC.

sought to use the symbolism of the Zulu monarchy in order to avoid the radicalisation of rural people and to protect their own threatened nascent class interests.

The period from the late nineteenth century to 1930 was a time of proliferating, contested, ethnicised identities, often centred around resistance to white land expropriation, and articulated through reformulated versions of pre-colonial consciousnesses and experiences.[12] To refer to just one example, Zulu identity was reformulated by elite African culture brokers, white segregationist ideologues and more radical movements such as the ICU, each with its own different and contesting agenda. The mass of the Zulu people could only be mobilised when these wider, competing, political objectives were made to resonate with their own concrete experiences and concerns. The Zulu paramountcy was a central pivot around which these forces strove to embed their political messages in rural people's consciousnesses, and as such the liberal 'gradualism' of the ANC found little purchase in rural areas. However, these contested forms of identities were also forged in the mine workplaces themselves, and further added to the complex compound of identities with which African nationalist and labour movements had to contend.

Migrant labour, moral dignity and class consciousness on the mine compounds, *c.* late nineteenth century to 1946

There is a substantial overlap between rural ethnic mobilisation over land and the beginning of the migrant labour system. Migrant labour became increasingly widespread after the discovery of diamonds and gold in the late nineteenth century, but it existed before the mineral revolution. For example, southern Mozambican migrant workers were employed on the Natal sugar plantations from the mid-nineteenth century. Migrant labourers remained very much part of the rural economy, which suited the cheap labour requirements of the plantations, and later the mining compounds, as well as the patriarchal structure of African rural society. Nevertheless, the ethnicised identities formed on the mine compounds did contain elements specific to those locations, which had considerable repercussions in terms of developing

12 For other examples of the mobilisation of rural ethnicised identities in order to resist land expropriation see, for example, the following: W. Beinart and C. Bundy (eds), *Hidden Struggles in Rural South Africa* (London, James Currey, 1987); P. Delius, 'The Ndzundza Ndebele', in P. Bonner, I. Hofmeyer, D. James and T. Lodge (eds), *Holding their Ground. Class, Locality and Culture in Nineteenth and Twentieth Century South Africa* (Johannesburg, Ravan Press, 1989), pp. 40–60.

class consciousness and the ability of organised labour and nationalist movements to mobilise workers.

Identities on the mine compounds reflected reworkings of male identities within a specific workplace context. Workers were often separated in ethnically segregated housing, according to mine management's perceptions of what entailed specific ethnic identities, although work teams could be ethnically mixed. These imposed forms of identification were often accepted by the African workers themselves. Ethnic identities were also based upon putative physical and mental characteristics which made a specific ethnicised group more amenable to a particular type of job. Mine management invariably encouraged these ethnicised categorisations, often in a somewhat primordialist manner. For example, Sotho workers were stereotyped as particularly suited to the arduous job of shaft sinking, owing to their mountainous origins, which were argued to foster endurance. Similarly, Bhaca workers developed a monopoly of night soil removal and latrine cleaning, Mpondo invariably gained employment as drillers, and 'Shangaans' and Zulus often became mine police. Ethnic stereotyping benefited management by facilitating control of the work force. Dividing workers into discrete groups according to management's concept of 'tribes' meant that workers were divided among themselves, and any potential organised hostility towards management was thus more easily diverted. Mine workers accepted these ethnicised stereotypes as they could sometimes entail a qualified means of protection, higher wages and some sort of status in a context of severe labour oppression.[13]

However, it is important not to conceive of these constructions purely in terms of reductionist materialism. As illustrated, ethnicised identities were reformulated in the late nineteenth and early twentieth centuries in order to resist colonial expropriation of land. People's consciousness was rooted in the institution of the chieftaincy and the rural homestead, and migrant labourers on the mines still strongly identified with the customs and socialisation processes inherent in these rural communities. Chiefs often initially supported the concept of migrant labour, as it gave them access to money with which to purchase guns and defend political independence. But by the end of the nineteenth century they

13 For comprehensive studies of ethnic identifications on the mine workplace see, for example, the following: J. Guy and M. Thabane, 'Technology, Ethnicity and Ideology: Basotho Miners and Shaft Sinking on the South African Gold Mines', *Journal of Southern African Studies* 14:2, (1988), pp. 257–78; P. Harries, *Work, Culture and Identity: Migrant Labourers in Mozambique and South Africa c. 1860–1910* (London, James Currey, 1994); D. Moodie, *Going for Gold: Men, Mines and Migration* (Berkeley, Cal., University of California Press, 1994).

had begun to lose control of the labour supply. Nevertheless, men were still tied to the rural economy. Tactics such as bridewealth inflation[14] initially ensured that village elders and fathers controlled access to their sons' wages and discouraged them from breaking with their rural links. Patriarchal rural hierarchies also kept women entrenched in the countryside, another reason for men to return home. Additionally, patriarchal ideologies, forged in a rural environment, meant that men often wished to promote their rural connections. Wages in the mines were also relatively high in the nineteenth century, although this was to alter with the onset of more systematic segregation. Nevertheless the black urban population did continue to increase in this period, despite these ideological obstacles.

The very masculine constructions of ethnicised identities on the mines were rooted in African male concepts of self-worth and integrity, centred on the upkeep of the rural *umzi* (homestead). Songs and stories reflected this accommodation of migrant labour into male concepts of integrity. Migrant cultures 'came alive in such narratives as quests, epics of resistance to proletarianization built into the very self-formation of black mineworkers'.[15] Male migrant workers often used networks of 'homefriends' – miners from their communities already working on the mines – in order to facilitate employment, and workers tended to keep to these groups when they joined the mines, furthering ethnic group solidarities. As explored below, male African rural socialisation processes also influenced this form of ethnicised identification in the workplace, and this could influence ethnicised conflict among workers. As the twentieth century progressed, migrant labourer identities seem to have shifted from the institution of the chieftaincy (although it still remained an important focal point) to that of a broader, more cultural form. However, as ethnic groups often define themselves in contrast to an 'ethnic other', this produced ethnic tensions which could spill over into so-called 'faction fights' as workers struggled to gain a monopoly over scarce resources. This was exacerbated by mine management manipulation of ethnic categories, and could preclude effective worker organisation.

It was with these reformulated ethnic identities that African Nationalist and organised labour movements had to work. Black mine workers did stage a major strike in 1920 for higher wages, which

---

14 Bridewealth was paid by the husband's family to the wife's, often in the form of cattle. By inflating the price of bridewealth, fathers attempted to ensure that their sons kept investing their wages at home.
15 Moodie, *Going for Gold*, p. 30.

attracted considerable support. However, the strike itself was organised not along union lines but through the migrant associations and home-friend networks already existing among the mineworkers themselves. The strike came at a time of considerable unrest as the ANC was briefly drawn into a more radical working-class politics. The strike was unsuccessful, but it did encourage mine owners to ease the job colour bar, which in turn helped precipitate the 1922 white Rand Revolt (see below). The ANC was to turn back to a more 'gradualist' approach soon after, and was partially supplanted by the ICU in terms of popular support.

African national protest remained insignificant in the 1930s. The ANC remained a somewhat self-enclosed elitist organisation, and the ICU dissolved amid internal dissension and fragmentation. There was a second brief period in the late 1920s when the ANC radicalised under the leadership of Josiah Gumede. Gumede's visit to Moscow, and his attendance at a meeting in Brussels of the Comintern-sponsored League against Imperialism, resulted in his returning to South Africa enthusiastic about the Soviet Union. At the same time, the South African Communist Party (CPSA) was tentatively turning its attention to the rural areas as a potential source of revolution. In 1928 the Comintern was seeking anti-imperialist alliances, and this led it to push the CPSA into rural organisation. This resulted in the birth of the latter's 'Native Republic' policy. Based on the theoretical premise of the Lenin/Roy theses of 1920, the CPSA was to work with 'bourgeois democratic' movements such as the ANC in order to pursue that end. In effect, they were advocating allying with other organisations in order to radicalise a national liberation movement. Previously the CPSA had aimed solely at radicalising the white working class, arguing that black Africans were not part of the proletariat and therefore not ready to embark on revolutionary change. The 'Native Republic' policy, and the move towards allying with 'bourgeois' organisations, led the CPSA to attempt to work with the ICU.

However, these alliances soon soured. The more 'gradualist' wing of the ANC succeeded in replacing Gumede with the right-wing Seme in 1930, and the ICU was bitterly divided over whether to co-operate with the Communists. Many members found it difficult to ally with (mainly white) CPSA members in an environment of institutionalised racism. A rift also appeared in the ICU between a right-wing group urging cautious moderation and a more radical group made up largely of CPSA members. Kadalie successfully expelled CPSA members in 1926. In addition the ICU itself was collapsing from within, owing to internal dissension and corruption, and the CPSA was split over the 'Native Republic' policy. Many members considered it overemphasised racial matters at the expense of class-based analysis and action. The tenets of orthodox Marxism, and the conviction that the white working class needed to be 'won over' to Communism, meant that the party was deeply split over whether black rural unrest was theoretically compatible with a proletarian revolution. Many leaders were heavily involved in trade union work and perceived it as a more fruitful area for socialist revolution. The 'Native Republic' policy was eventually dropped in the early 1930s, when the Comintern advocated 'Russia first' policies and the concept of a united front. This, combined with internal wrangling and purges, meant the party remained seriously weakened throughout the 1930s. Communist attempts at organising rural areas were not pursued again until after the Second World War.[16] The splits and dissensions demonstrate the complexity of the relationship between African nationalism, socialism, organised labour and rural Africans. There were attempts to forge alliances across these organisations, but they foundered largely owing to the 'gradualism' of the ANC, the internal dissensions and anti-Communist feeling in the ICU and the split among the CPSA with regard to mobilising rural Africans.

However, manufacturing industries became far more prominent after the depression of the early 1930s, and the Second World War entailed a shortage of labour. This provoked the state partially to relax the pass laws – which aimed at reducing black urbanisation through oppressive legislative measures – in order to fill vacancies with black workers, and more blacks subsequently entered the towns. Unions began to build up their bases. Between 1936 and 1945 at least twenty-seven unions for black workers were organised in Natal. In the Western Cape the black South African Railways and Harbour Workers' Union was formed in 1936, and the Food and Canning Workers' Union in 1941. Communist Party members were often involved in organising these unions. The outbreak of war in 1939 opened up further opportunities for unions to grow, as the war economy entailed local substitution of previously imported products, and the demand for labour increased markedly to meet the requirements of a war economy.[17] A series of strikes was

16 See C. Bundy, 'Land and Liberation: Popular Rural Protest and the National Liberation Movements in South Africa 1920–60', in Marks and Trapido, *The Politics of Race, Class and Nationalism*, pp. 250–92, and J. and R. Simons, *Class and Colour in South Africa 1850–1950* (London, James Currey, 1983), chapter 17. Also H. Bradford, *A Taste of Freedom. The ICU in Rural South Africa 1924–30* (London, Yale University Press, 1987), especially chapter 4.
17 J. Baskin, *Striking Back. A History of Cosatu* (Johannesburg, Ravan Press, 1991), chapter 1.

called throughout the 1940s, culminating in the 1946 mineworkers' strike, and wages for black workers increased significantly. However, the spread of militant action was dampened by the policies of the ANC and the CPSA towards the war. The ANC tended to support Britain in its fight against Germany, and the CPSA supported the war effort after the German invasion of the Soviet Union. Both therefore discouraged strike action, arguing it should only be used as a last resort.

The 1946 strike reflected the importance of migrant worker organisations and networks as well as union organisation. The participants in the strike demonstrated the importance of the rural connection and changing forms of political consciousness in facilitating widespread and organised action. The strike itself again depended heavily upon the informal 'homefriend' and other migrant labour networks. It was headed by the African Mineworkers' Union (AMWU), formed at the beginning of 1942. The ANC was involved in its genesis, the Transvaal branch of Congress having called a conference in 1941 in order to discuss the formation of a mineworkers' union. The CPSA also established strong connections with the AMWU, as it did with other unions in the service and small industry sector when the economy picked up after the depression. However, in the case of the AMWU, this led to conflict with the ANC (see below). The union faced considerable problems at the time in terms of mobilising workers. Dunbar Moodie argues that most mines had evolved a form of 'moral economy', whereby migrant workers' local complaints were addressed by mine management, thus precluding a wider form of resistance.[18] Small, localised demonstrations did erupt from time to time but, before the arrival of the AMWU, wider mobilisation of the work force did not occur.

The AMWU deliberately aimed at addressing the various grievances of the mineworkers from 1944. Interestingly, the core support for the newly formed union among mineworkers came from *tshipa* (literally 'absconders from home'), who had purposely broken from their rural ties and were living as proletarianised urbanites in the mine compounds and townships. Many of the migrant workers, who kept up their rural connections and therefore still identified more readily with rural–ethnic particularisms and kinship networks, were not even aware of the existence of the AMWU, and yet many still participated in the strike. Not enough is known about the connections between the union's call for a strike and migrant workers taking up the call. However, it seems probable that one connection was provided by the *izibonda*, voluntary leaders who were elected for each mine compound dormitory by the workers themselves.

18 Moodie, *Going For Gold*.

Being unpaid, they could not be manipulated by mine management, and had the workers' interests at heart. They were also an integral part of the mine 'moral economies', with mine management taking their complaints about individual cases of abuse, bad food or other forms of ill-treatment seriously. Ironically, this precluded wider, more organised forms of resistance until the 1946 strike. These men probably provided the connection between the AMWU's call for a strike and the positive response of many migrant workers who were not members of the union.

The strike itself marked the end of worker militancy in this period. Migrant workers remained a fragmented force, and the end of the Second World War meant that the shortage of workers (which blacks had filled) ended. Unions had failed to gain enough influence among migrant workers, and state repression took its toll. However, rural people were available to be mobilised on a wider basis at times throughout this period, and rural youth organisations could be an important element of this mobilisation, as explored in the following section.

Male youth associations, national identity and nascent class formation: changing rural consciousness, c. 1920–46.

Youth associations often represented an important arena for rural male socialisation in pre-colonial southern African communities. It was through these associations that patriarchal control was established and the moral values of the community were entrenched. However, the gradual penetration of migrant labour, and the permeation of mission-led education, entailed increasing debate among many young men regarding the value of these socialisation processes, which did not adequately reflect their life experiences. Many therefore broke away from traditionalist youth groups and established their own informal youth organisations. These could become involved in violent acts and criminal activity, but also contained a moral code which, ironically, reflected many of the values inherent in more traditionalist groupings. Furthermore, they often contained elements of a fluid, processual ethnic identity. These groups operated in urban, rural and mine compound contexts in the first few decades of the twentieth century.[19] William Beinart argues that 'in a system which relentlessly criminalised workers

19 There is a considerable literature on the growth of these male associations, their connections with rural forms of ethnicity and their availability for wider political mobilisation. See for example the following: W. Beinart, 'Worker Consciousness, Ethnic Particularism and Nationalism: the Experiences of a South African Migrant', in Marks and Trapido, *The Politics of Race, Class and Nationalism*, pp.

and the poor, and in the absence of sustained union organisation, they seem to have been central vehicles of "self-organisation".[20]

Although they were difficult to capture for political purposes, there were attempts by some political organisations to mobilise these associations against the state. For example, between 1929 and 1930 the Durban branch of the ICU managed to mobilise Zulu male youth associations known as *amalaita*, which had also been involved in crime.[21] It is difficult to assess to what extent these associations represented specifically working-class organisations as well as reformulated forms of rural identity. Many participated in violent crime, and were feared by many rural, compound and urban residents. However, especially in urban areas during the 1930s, the repressive state system led many Africans to participate in crime in order to survive, and the strongly anti-authoritarian nature of these associations did seem to represent a working-class consciousness of sorts, although infused with rural identifications and a strongly masculinist culture. They were available for mobilisation, and perhaps if the organised labour and nationalist movements had made more strenuous attempts to forge alliances with them the former could have gained a wider range of organised support.

The somewhat gradualist, elitist approach of the ANC leadership during the 1930s and 1940s precluded this possibility until the end of the Second World War. As illustrated above, the AMWU also found it difficult to mobilise among migrant workers. At the time of the 1946 strike the then president of the ANC, Dr A. Xuma, was very reticent in supporting the cause of the AMWU, owing to its socialist tendencies, and he also opposed strike action. This was partly due to the fact that J. B. Marks, a Moscow-trained Communist, had taken over the presidency of the AMWU in 1942, which resulted in the union becoming independent of the Transvaal African Congress. Many individual Communists worked hard to support the strike, and this rankled with the more conservative

286–309; W. Beinart, 'The Origins of the Indlavini', in P. Spiegel and P. McAllister (eds), *Tradition and Transition in Southern Africa* (Johannesburg, Witwatersrand University Press, 1991), pp. 103–24; C. Van Onselen, *Studies in the Social and Economic History of the Witwatersrand*, 2 vols (London, Longman, 1982); J. Guy and M. Thabane, 'The Ma-Rashea: a Participant's Perspective', in B. Bozzoli (ed.), *Class, Community and Conflict. South African Perspectives* (Johannesburg, Ravan Press, 1987), pp. 436–58; P. La Hausse, '"The Cows of Nongoloza": Youth, Crime and Amalaita Gangs in Durban 1900–36', *Journal of Southern African Studies* 16:1 (1990), pp. 79–111; P. Bonner, 'Family, Crime and Political Consciousness on the East Rand 1939–55', *Journal of Southern African Studies* 14:3 (1988), pp. 393–420.

20 W. Beinart, 'Political and Collective Violence in Southern African Historiography', *Journal of Southern African Studies* 18:3 (1992), pp. 393–420.

21 La Hausse, '"The Cows of Nongoloza"', pp. 105–10.

members of the ANC. The 'gradualism' and elitism of the ANC at the time did not resonate with concepts situating the African worker at the centre of the struggle against the state. However, a vigorous Congress Youth League was growing at the time, including people such as Nelson Mandela and Oliver Tambo, which sought to forge closer relations between the union and the ANC, as well as taking rural issues more seriously. Nevertheless, rural concerns did not become central to the ANC agenda until after apartheid was established in 1948. The difficulties faced by the AMWU in contacting migrant workers meant that it was the *izibonda* and other forms of male migrant labour associations which formed the essential organising force behind the strike, which otherwise might have collapsed before it got off the ground. However, without effective leadership, it eventually crumbled, and the 1946 strike marked the end rather than the beginning of a period of militant unionism.

British imperialism, class consciousness and the growth of Afrikaner nationalism, *c.* 1899–1948

Twentieth-century Afrikaner nationalism, like many other nationalisms, was based on older foundations of language, ethnic ties and religious affiliation. It grew out of the uneven development of capitalism and the changes wrought by the late nineteenth-century mineral discoveries, which provoked further British imperial interventions. Cattle diseases such as rinderpest, the growth of capitalist agriculture, the South African War of 1899–1902 fought against the British and the subsequent rapid urbanisation of formerly rural Afrikaners led to a process of assimilation during the early twentieth century in which poorer Afrikaners merged with other peoples, ethnic boundaries breaking down and becoming more fluid.

This alarmed the more radical among the Afrikaner intelligentsia, who sought to promote a more exclusivist Afrikaner identity in order to protect their own interests, as set against the economic and political hegemony of the English-speaking population. English had established itself as the language of commerce and government in the nineteenth century, and Britons gained the greatest advantage from the late nineteenth-century mineral discoveries. Attempts were made at the time to codify the Afrikaans language, which, while largely Dutch, had diverse origins, including Malay, Portuguese, Khoisan and elements of German, French, English and Southern Nguni languages.[22] Thus a great diversity

22 I. Hofmeyer, 'Building a Nation from Words: Afrikaans Language, Literature and Ethnic Identity 1902–24', in Marks and Trapido, *The Politics of Race, Class and Nationalism*, pp. 95–123.

of dialects had existed among the parochial and dispersed rural Afrikaner communities of the early nineteenth century. The codification of Afrikaans, and attempts to purge it of former slave and African influences, was a deliberate attempt by the displaced Afrikaner intelligentsia to forge a more coherent white Afrikaner identity, in direct competition with the High Dutch spoken by the small upper class which had developed from the original Dutch immigrants. It was also an attempt to combat the policy of social, political and economic Anglicisation pursued by the British High Commissioner Alfred Milner in the years immediately after the war.

However, the coming to power of the Liberal Party in Britain in 1906, which aimed at lessening direct British rule in South Africa, ameliorated the situation in the short term. The 1910 Act of Union united the Boer republics of the Transvaal and the Orange Free State with the British colonies of the Cape and Natal. The two Boer generals, Louis Botha and Jan Smuts, emerged as the leaders of the South Africa Party that formed the first government. Both had a respected war record, and this facilitated their attempts at taking Afrikaners in a new political direction. Botha and Smuts pursued a broad vision of a South African identity that merged both Afrikaans and English-speaking peoples, whilst excluding blacks. However, the rapid proletarianisation of previously rural Afrikaners, and the poverty which attended this process, soon provided the catalyst for opposition to this version of white South African identity.

Afrikaner families, unlike many African ones, entered the urban economy together, and therefore retained fewer of their rural ties. Afrikaner men initially worked as transport riders, or set up small brickmaking works and transport businesses. However, these opportunities fell away with the introduction of trams, railways and factory-produced bricks. The police, the state-run railway system and the mines provided the main avenues of employment thereafter, but the latter two brought Afrikaners into more direct competition with black workers. Afrikaner men working on the mines sought to protect their superior status and wages *vis-à-vis* blacks. This could provoke conflict with mine management and the state, owing to the peculiarities of the mining, especially gold-mining, industries, which favoured cheap labour. Gold mining required huge capital investment, and mine companies knew they could reduce costs by limiting the number of whites employed and taking on black workers at a much lower rate of pay. White workers went on strike in 1907 and 1913, the second strike specifically concerning the right to establish trade union organisations and to protect and enhance white interests. The latter strike caused widespread riots in Johannesburg, and was brutally suppressed by Botha and Smuts, who brought in imperial

troops to quell the rioters. The harsh treatment meted out to the striking miners meant that deep grievances towards the government were
harboured by English-speaking and Afrikaner miners, and poor
Afrikaners in general. Anti-British feeling also came to a head at the
beginning of the First World War when the Union government came out
in support of the British Empire. Several generals who had participated
in the South African War against the British rebelled against the government, and gained their support largely from poorer whites. The rebellion was crushed, but it demonstrated the intensity of anti-imperial
feeling among some Afrikaners, and provided further ammunition for
a more exclusive, Afrikaner ethnic nationalism. However, it would be
wrong to see a direct connection between the rebellion and the 1913
strike. In fact the 1913 strike was put down by rural Afrikaner comman-
dos led by two men who later led the rebellion itself.[23]

Nevertheless, the groundwork of an exclusivist Afrikaner nationalism, which appealed to the needs of poor, proletarianised Afrikaners,
had been laid. General J. B. M Hertzog split away from the South Africa
Party in 1914 to form the Nationalist Party, which sought more tenuous
links with the British Empire. This combined with the work of the above-
mentioned ethnic culture brokers, who were attempting to forge a more
exclusive Afrikaner nationalism than the broad white South African
identity that remained the vision of Botha and Smuts. The latter were
perceived by many of the more radical Afrikaner intelligentsia as in
league with the interests of big capital, and this resonated with the grievances of poor working-class Afrikaners. Therefore the attempt to forge
a more exclusive Afrikaner identity began to gain more purchase. The
Dutch Reformed Church, to which many Afrikaners belonged, facilitated the creation of this ethnicised consciousness by promoting the
idea of Afrikaners as a people with a 'sacred destiny'. These concepts
were easily incorporated into the work of culture brokers busy constructing a 'sacred history' which saw Afrikaners as a 'chosen people' destined
to inherit the land. This did not mean that all Afrikaners were strictly
religious. But the message of the Church did gain purchase with people
in definite need of a concrete identity in uncertain times.[24]

23 D. Yudelman, *The Emergence of Modern South Africa. State, Capital and the Incorporation
    of Organised Labour on the South African Gold Fields 1902–39* (London, Greenwood
    Press, 1983), pp. 83–4.
24 Many studies provide detailed analyses of the rise of twentieth-century Afrikaner
    consciousness and nationalism. See, for example, the following: D. Moodie, *The
    Rise of Afrikanerdom. Power, Apartheid and the Afrikaner Civil Religion* (London,
    Routledge, 1975); H. Giliomee, 'The Beginnings of Afrikaner Ethnic
    Consciousness 1850–1915', in Vail, *The Creation of Tribalism*, pp. 21–54.; I.
    Hofmeyer, 'Building a Nation from Words', pp. 95–123.

This corresponded with the increasing Afrikanerisation of the white mining work force, especially during the period 1914–21.[25] Skilled artisanal mineworkers, who tended to be immigrant English-speakers, were gradually replaced by semi-skilled Afrikaner workers. This was in part an attempt by the state to ameliorate Afrikaner unemployment and partly mine management's wish to replace skilled artisans working with unskilled labour by white supervisors supervising black labour. British and Australian miners had brought a radical socialist strain to the miners' unions in the first two decades of the twentieth century. They were also an important element of support for the South African Labour Party, formed in 1909. Part of the reason for the Afrikanerisation of the work force, apart from state pressure to reduce Afrikaner unemployment, was that Afrikaners were considered to be generally more docile and less likely to participate in trade union activity. This latter assumption was to be proved quickly wrong. The interplay between socialism, British jingoistic nationalism and Afrikaner republicanism in the years 1914–21 lucidly demonstrates the complex relationship between nationalism and organised labour movements. The radical socialism displayed by English-speaking miners in the 1913 strike did not stop them from flocking to enlist in the army during the First World War – despite the fact that British troops had been used ruthlessly to suppress the strike. By contrast, many Afrikaner members of the working class, only a generation away from the effects of the 1899–1902 war, harboured strong republican ideals and did not generally support the British war effort.

The division between Afrikaner republicanism and English-speaking jingoism was a serious blow to the Labour Party, which was aiming at uniting a white working class. The division split the white working class politically and allowed the Nationalist Party to gain purchase in urban constituencies. The change in the structure of white jobs united Anglophone and Afrikaner workers in terms of industrial action, but there was no political coherence. It soon became clear that the Afrikaner miner was a threat to the state, owing to his nationalist republican radicalism rather than his working-class radicalism. English-speaking mineworkers were largely members of craft-based trade unions. Afrikaner workers were largely excluded, and the latter were thus more available for mobilisation by ethnic culture brokers. The Afrikanerisation of the work force, together with deskilling, meant that craft-based unionism was replaced by more general industrial unions. Afrikaner workers were able to use these as vehicles to pursue their republican aims.

There was a distinct nationalistic and revolutionary strain among

25 This paragraph draws heavily on Yudelman, *The Emergence of Modern South Africa.*

these Afrikaner miners, many of them fervently in support of the restoration of an independent Boer republic. High inflation immediately
after the First World War, and consequent attempts by mine management to reduce white mine employment, resulted in the 1922 Rand
Revolt, when white, largely Afrikaner, mineworkers struck. The strike
itself turned into a revolt, and for a time a workers' government seemed
possible. The notorious slogan of the strikers displayed the mixture of
republicanism, racism and working-class revolutionary thought behind
their actions: 'Workers of the world unite and fight for a white South
Africa.' However, Smuts – in sole charge of the South African Party with
the recent death of Botha – suppressed the revolt with even greater ruth-
lessness than before. Nevertheless, the revolt perhaps marked the death
knell of Smuts and his party. He had become increasingly unpopular
with working-class whites, especially Afrikaners, owing to his policy of
lessening the gap between black and white workers' wages on the mines,
in conjunction with mine management, and his general reluctance to
intervene in defending white privileges at a time of considerable poverty
for many Afrikaners. Whites increasingly had to compete with blacks for
jobs on the mines and elsewhere, and this ensured the support of many
Afrikaners for the more exclusivist, ethnic version of Afrikaner political
identity promoted by Hertzog. Afrikaner ethnic nationalism and
Afrikaner working-class interests began to unite.

Hertzog's Nationalist Party formed a pact with the largely English-
speaking Labour Party in 1924, which defeated Smuts's government. A
more exclusivist Afrikaner identity was established, and institutionalised
racism and segregation hardened through the period of Hertzog's
office. With the Afrikanerisation of the bureaucracy, and other state-run
enterprises, the defeat of the 1922 revolt became less significant. Job
protection for Afrikaners became widespread and the 'colour bar' was
strengthened. Elements of organised labour merged with Afrikaner
nationalist tendencies. The Labour Party was largely instrumental in
initiating the racist 'civilised labour policy', which aimed at reserving
jobs exclusively for whites, and the Nationalist Party was happy to leave
the organisation of white workers to the former. However, it is important
to recognise that this policy was never fully implemented, owing to the
need for cheap black labour. The Labour Party had also declined in significance since the First World War, and never again enjoyed the support
it had beforehand.[26] It is also important to acknowledge that there were
examples of non-racial trade unionism among the newly formed industrial trade unions during the mid- to late 1920s and 1930s. These

26 Yudelman, *The Emergence of Modern South Africa*, chapter 7.

included the Garment Workers' Union (see below) and the Furniture Workers' Industrial Union. Socialists such as Bill Andrews also kept alive a tradition of socialism which pursued non-racial policies, and the CPSA was an important driving force behind many of the unions formed in this period. As Shula Marks and Stanley Trapido state, 'until the 1940s if not the 1950s Afrikaner class consciousness stood as a formidable obstacle to the simple capture of the Afrikaner working class by the apostles of nationalism'.[27] It was only by playing on the racist attitudes and insecurities of the Afrikaner working class, often developed independently of Afrikaner nationalism, and the promotion of 'white only' job provision, that Afrikaner ethnic entrepreneurs began to gain considerable purchase on Afrikaner popular consciousness and control of the Afrikaner-dominated trade unions in these decades.[28] This is not to suggest that Afrikaner-dominated trade unions before the late 1940s did not promote racism, but they often did so independently of Afrikaner nationalists.[29]

The rise of the Nationalist Party owed much to the work of ethnic culture brokers who sought to reconstruct an Afrikaner identity in the wake of the South African War and the dislocating effects of rapid industrialisation and uneven capitalist expansion. Together with the Dutch Reformed Church, this Afrikaner intelligentsia sought to make Afrikaans an official language of South Africa, and this was achieved in 1925. Furthermore, during the first few decades of the twentieth century, these groups sought to Afrikanerise every facet of social, economic and political life. Education had to reflect the reconstructed history of Afrikanerdom and the 'sacred destiny' of the Afrikaner people. Popular magazines, articles and newspapers sought to repackage virtually every facet of life as specifically Afrikaans. Afrikaner ethnic entrepreneurs were literally seeking 'to build a nation from words'.[30] This was possible because of the introduction of compulsory education for whites.

However, the 1929 Wall Street Crash and the onset of worldwide economic depression again brought Afrikaner political identity into crisis. Hertzog's mismanagement of the economy in the wake of the depression, especially his refusal to abandon the gold standard until the end of 1932, meant his popularity waned. This resulted in the 1934

27 Marks and Trapido, 'The Politics of Race, Class and Nationalism', in *The Politics of Race, Class and Nationalism*, pp. 16–7.
28 J. Lewis, *Industrialisation and Trade Union Organisation in South Africa 1924–55* (Cambridge, Cambridge University Press, 1984), chapter 5.
29 Lewis, *Industrialisation and Trade Union Organisation*.
30 Phrase taken from I. Hofmeyr, 'Building a Nation from Words'.

'fusion' of Smuts's South Africa Party with Hertzog's Nationalist Party in order to form the United Party. The economy was gradually turned round, and Smuts became Prime Minister from 1939 to 1948 owing to Hertzog's resignation over whether to support Britain against Germany in the Second World War.[31] Nevertheless, the war was a major element in Smuts's downfall and the rise of apartheid. Old Afrikaner anti-imperialist sentiments were rekindled, and combined with white fears of blacks taking 'white' jobs. Consequently strong, organised political opposition against Smuts and his United Party took root.

In fact Afrikaner identity had already fractured again before the war. The 'fusion' coalition between the parties of Smuts and Hertzog had already provoked a further split among Afrikaner nationalist politicians. D. F. Malan split away to form the Gesuiwerde (purified) Nationalist Party in 1934, the party that would introduce the policy of apartheid when it came to power in 1948. The growth of support for Malan's party needs some explanation, as the growth in manufacturing industry during the 1930s had opened up new opportunities for the Afrikaner working class, especially in such fields as clothing, textiles and food processing. Many Afrikaners had joined English-speaking-dominated trade unions, some of which attempted to forge links with black workers. Nevertheless, the influx of black workers into urban areas, which accelerated in the 1930s as the increasing inability of 'Native Reserves' to provide a sustainable living became increasingly apparent, kindled working-class Afrikaner fears of being swamped by a proletarianised black work force. Wealthier rural Afrikaner farmers also railed against the movement of blacks to urban areas, as the wages they paid their own black workers could not compete with the manufacturing sector. Consequently there was a drift of black agricultural workers from white farms to the cities. Afrikaner culture brokers worked hard to fan the flames of exclusivist Afrikaner ethnic nationalism. The Broederbond, a secret all-male organisation formed in 1919, endeavoured to encourage the growth of a Christian nationalist ideology that sought to elevate Afrikaner identity. Capitalism was not being resisted wholesale, only the control of the capitalist system by non-Afrikaners. These ethnic nationalists sought to incorporate trade unions within this ideology, and gradually their ideas filtered down to the Afrikaner working class.

However, this is not to suggest that Afrikaners converted wholesale to this form of ethnic nationalism, with its concepts of an elect people

---

31 For a compact analysis of the gradual recovery of the South African economy from the depression see Beinart, *Twentieth Century South Africa*, chapter 5.

with a sacred history. 'Cultural entrepreneurs [might] spice their speeches with such notions but for an audience it was enough to be told that they were a separate people with particular interests that could best be promoted through mobilisation.'[32] It was only with the entry into the Second World War, and the subsequent resurrection of anti-British feeling, that the concept really began to take hold. The fact that many blacks had taken jobs vacated by whites during the war exacerbated tensions when Afrikaner workers returned home in 1945. Additionally, Smuts had relaxed some of the influx legislation in order to encourage some blacks into urban areas and keep the wartime economy buoyant. He also seemed to recognise the need for a more non-racial urban work force in order for the economy to work more efficiently in general. The combined onslaught of the Nationalist Party and organisations such as the Broederbond which promoted an exclusivist Afrikaner identity eroded just enough of the United Party's support in the 1948 election for the Nationalist Party to gain power and the era of apartheid to begin.

Nevertheless, the gaining of power by Malan's ethnic nationalists, and the subversion of socialism and organised Afrikaner labour, was never a foregone conclusion. Afrikaner working-class women, who often entered the urban economy slightly before their menfolk, became very active in socialist-oriented trade unionism during the 1930s. Male Afrikaner culture brokers sought to construct an idealised picture of Afrikaner womanhood during the first few decades of the twentieth century. They addressed women primarily as mothers or spouses, and Afrikaner women were portrayed as *volksmoeders* – 'Mothers of the Nation' – the domestic cultural bedrock on which male-dominated Afrikaner nationalist identity was to be built.[33] One of the main reasons for the construction of this gendered ideology was the increasing independence of parental control gained by young women entering the

32 H. Giliomee, 'The Growth of Afrikaner Identity', in W. Beinart and S. Dubow (eds), *Segregation and Apartheid in Twentieth Century South Africa* (London, Routledge, 1995), p. 198.

33 See, for example, the following: J. Butler, 'Afrikaner Women and the Creation of Ethnicity in a Small South African Town 1902–50', in Vail, *The Creation of Tribalism*, pp. 55–81; I. Hofmeyer, 'Building a Nation from Words'. African traditionalists, concerned about the increasing independence of young women in urban areas, and the breakdown of pre-colonial social controls, also sought to reformulate precolonial identities in order to reinforce a crisis-ridden patriarchy. See, for example, S. Marks, 'Patriotism, Patriarchy and Purity: Natal and the Politics of Zulu Ethnic Consciousness', in Vail, *The Creation of Tribalism*, pp. 215–40; However, African women could defend rural tradition in earlier periods if it could be utilised in resisting colonial land expropriation. See, for example, W. Beinart, '*Amafelandawonye* (The Diehards): Popular Protest and Women's Movements in Herschel District in the 1920s', in Beinart and Bundy, *Hidden Struggles*, pp. 222–64.

urban economy. The patriarchal authority of husbands and fathers was being challenged, and fears over the sexual conduct of young Afrikaner women, and the possibility of so-called 'miscegenation' in less segregated urban working-class areas, lent growing support to this ideological construction from Afrikaner working-class and professional males alike. However, this ideology was sometimes reformulated by working-class Afrikaner women in order to accommodate their different experience in an industrial environment.

For example, Afrikaner women working as garment workers on the Rand sought to retain their Afrikaner identity whilst becoming integrated into a proletarianised work force. Many Afrikaner women employed in this industry became members of the Garment Workers' Union, one of the most militant unions during the inter-war years. Afrikaner women had entered the industry in the 1920s, when mass factory production was initiated. Previously it had been dominated by male European-trained craftsmen. Women were taken on as semi-skilled operatives, displacing white men and deskilling the jobs they had held. This met the needs of mass capitalist production, providing a cheaper labour force, but did not sit easily with the reconstructed patriarchal form that Afrikaner ethnicised identity had taken. The union was formed in response to a rift between these women workers and the skilled male workers, and was able to forge a socialist consciousness among the former which partially transcended Afrikaner nationalist ideology by absorbing and celebrating cultural facets of Afrikaner identity whilst working for better wages and working conditions for women workers. The union also sought to forge a multi-racial membership, and had early successes. However, with the expansion of the industry during and after the Second World War, and the subsequent increase in first 'Coloured' and then African women in the work force, the union was forced to introduce separate branches for African, 'Coloured' and white members. Nevertheless, the Garment Workers' Union's work in the 1930s had demonstrated that cultural identity could sit with a socialist consciousness, if somewhat uneasily. Perhaps, however, the non-racialism of the union was possible only when there was little competition for jobs from African and 'Coloured' workers.

Conclusion

Both African and Afrikaner nationalism were shaped by the particular development of South Africa's economy during this period. The reliance on agriculture and primary extractive industries, and the development of the migrant labour process, entailed a particular relationship between nationalism and labour peculiar to South Africa. The legacy of British imperialism, the still vibrant remnants of rural African chief-doms, and the anti-imperialist grievances harboured by the newly pro-letarianised Afrikaner working class, all contributed to the formation of two distinct forms of nationalism, civic and ethnic, although the distinc-tion was blurred and never uncontested. Labour movements were shaped fundamentally by the legacy of British segregationist policy and imperialism, and it was with this legacy that nationalist movements had to work.

It has been argued that conflicts over identity often stem 'from the hurt felt when an outsider has the power to define identity in ways which deny the individual's own expert knowledge, composed as it is of core experiences, desires and yearnings and strategic plans for life'.[34] This certainly resonates with the experience of Africans and Afrikaners during the period. The more rapid proletarianisation of the Afrikaner working class, and the subsequent impoverishment and unemployment it faced in an economy firmly under English-speaking hegemony, meant that its very concept of itself as Afrikaner was threatened. Parochial rural identities were not relevant in the urban milieu, and Afrikaner identity was thus available for reformulation by a variety of different interest groups. Trade union, Socialist and Communist organisations all attempted to gain purchase within the new Afrikaner working class, and the 1922 Rand Revolt did seem for a time to herald the era of a workers' government. However, Afrikaner participants in the revolt mobilised as much around radical republicanism as around concepts of working-class revolution. Mining capital's need for a cheap labour force, and Smuts's reliance on mining for the development of the economy, meant that Afrikaners were brought into direct competition with Africans for jobs, and this seriously hindered the possibility of a united working class. The jingoism of English-speaking miners also prevented any political alliance with Afrikaners, reducing the effectiveness of the Labour Party. These factors meant that many working-class Afrikaners were available for ethnic political mobilisation by the small Afrikaner intelligentsia, itself displaced by British commercial dominance. The 1924 Pact Government worked hard to incorporate trade unions and working-class Afrikaners within its ideology of Afrikaner ethnic nationalism, and in some areas succeeded.

Nevertheless, there was room for a redefinition of Afrikaner cultu-ral identity which articulated with a non-racial, working-class identity,

34 F. Wilson and B. Frederiksen, 'Introduction', in F. Wilson and B. Frederiksen (eds), *Ethnicity, Gender and the Subversion of Nationalism* (London, Frank Cass, 1995), p. 2.

especially as manufacturing industry began to assume more importance from the 1930s onwards. The Garment Workers' Union is perhaps the best example. Women members also partially subverted the patriarchal ideology of Afrikaner ethnic entrepreneurs. It was only the onset of the Second World War, the rekindling of old anti-British imperialist feelings and the lapsing of influx controls which allowed blacks to take up many jobs previously reserved for whites that finally paved the way for the rise of the Nationalist Party and the implementation of apartheid.

African nationalism was left with a rather different legacy from British imperialism. The elite intelligentsia who made up the South African Native National Congress (later the ANC) were not anti-imperialist, and many sought to gain a place in the colonial order. Most had benefited from a mission education and the legacy of mid-Victorian liberalism, which had ensured strong ties with Britain. This only began to change with the onset of systematic segregation and the migrant labour system. Both of these owed much to the industrialisation of South Africa and more widely the growth of racist ideologies such as Social Darwinism among British colonial administrators. The fact that many Africans still retained rural roots, and still identified with rural chieftaincies and parochial ethnicities, meant that this small elite group found it difficult to gain widespread support for its nationalist message. Many rural Africans were more concerned with fighting colonial expropriation of land than with abstract concepts of democracy, and this provided the support base for black ethnic culture brokers as exemplified by the first Inkatha movement. The only organisation in the 1920s which gained considerable support from rural South Africans was the ICU, and that was specifically because it addressed the concerns of the mostly rural black populace.

The Communist Party also found it difficult to mobilise support in rural areas during the first two decades of the twentieth century. This was due not least to its particular ideology concerning the importance of a developed proletariat in initiating a working-class revolution. The short spell in the late 1920s when the ANC briefly radicalised and the CPSA began to promote the idea of a 'Native Republic' suggested that a more radical African nationalism was possible which embraced the interests of the rural populace. The CPSA also sought to forge links with the ICU. However, it failed, for the reasons outlined above. Nevertheless the development of manufacturing industry in the 1930s, and the speeding up of African urbanisation, led to the development of more organised African unions, and by the 1940s the ANC Youth League was vigorously arguing for more links with the black rural populace. However, they were not developed until the era of apartheid.

Much of the organised protest on the mines was achieved by black

African migrant labour networks. These were very important in the context of the 1920 black African mineworkers' strike, and an integral part of the 1946 strike. The AMWU's role in the latter strike, although it worked hard to forge links with migrant workers, was hampered by the elitism and 'gradualism' of the ANC at the time, and the difficulty of penetrating the mines. The migrant labour process had led to a prolife-ration of reformulated identities during the 1920s and 1930s among migrant workers, which reflected rural ethnic particularisms and a nascent working-class consciousness. This was evident in male youth organisations, which drew on reworked cultural identities and customs in order to make sense of a more industrial climate. There were some attempts by the ANC and the ICU to work with these associations, but they were difficult to mobilise.

Both Afrikaner and African people were treading diverse paths towards modernity in this period, owing to the uneven penetration of capitalism and, for Africans, the migrant labour process. Identities could harden or soften, and it was not least the legacy of British imperialism which contributed to ethnic exclusivism and institutionalised racism. Organised labour movements working within this complex socio-eco-nomic and cultural milieu were no less ambiguous in terms of promot-ing either a democratic socialism or ethnic exclusivism and institutionalised racism.

Nationalism, ethnicity and the working classes in India, 1870–1947

It is universally acknowledged that the social processes which inform class formation respect neither territorial principles nor national boundaries. Yet the history of the working classes has usually been conceptualised in terms of the nation state. In part, this paradox may be explained by the fact that the idea of the working class as well as the nation state entered political discourse and gained their widest currency at the same time and developed in opposition to each other. In Europe the conflicting histories of the working class and the nation state directed attention to the tensions between them. While socialism was assumed to be the true political expression of working-class movements, scholars and observers of the latter fully recognised that nationalism often constituted a significant obstacle to the emergence of class consciousness. The teleology of working-class history was shaped by the legacy of nineteenth-century socialism. The point of studying the history of the working classes, in this tradition, was to trace the evolution of the labour movement precisely because it was assumed to form the prologue to the rise and triumph of socialism. Historians investigated how far the working class could in each national case achieve its 'historic mission' or, alternatively, seek to explain the factors which prevented its realisation. The play of ethnic and nationalist identities were always liable to impede, certainly to complicate, the formation of class consciousness. While nationalist sentiments, religious solidarities or communal loyalties may not have foreclosed the development of class consciousness, they have often been believed to limit and contain its expression.

In India, however, the teleologies of working-class history and nationalism often moved in parallel directions. The history of Indian nationalism has often been represented as a steady awakening and a rising consciousness, gradually diffused among different social strata in the early twentieth century. In this view, its first stirrings in the 1870s and 1880s found expression in the aspirations of western-educated elites in the Presidency capitals of Bombay, Calcutta and Madras. In its next phase, its appeal extended to a widening circle, encompassing local landed and mercantile elites and often reaching out beyond into the vast hinterland of the subcontinent. Finally, under the inspiration of Gandhian leadership, between 1917 and 1947, the Indian National Congress was able to swing the masses behind its banner and gather up peasants and workers in its embrace. The history of the Congress thus became an account of its increasingly popular appeal and its widening social base until it reached its apogee with its incorporation of the working classes. In this light, as the Congress acquired a mass character, it seemed to represent not so much an obstacle as a potential source of encouragement for the development of working-class politics. In the 1920s and 1930s, for all their suspicion of the Congress as a bourgeois party, the left could scarcely oppose 'the anti-colonial struggle' or consistently regard it as anything less than progressive. In stepping forward as the guardian of working-class interests, the left hoped to push the nationalist movement in an increasingly socialist direction and eventually to assert their hegemony over it. The trajectories of working-class struggles and the nationalist movement appeared less contradictory and more compatible than they had seemed in the West. In India, unlike Europe, the meta-narratives of working-class and nationalist histories were brought closely into relation with each other. This meant simply that historians of India would have to contend with competing teleologies which came to be inextricably intertwined with each other.

The nationalist movement, no less than working-class politics, was riddled with tensions and conflicts shaped by diverse caste, linguistic, religious and regional identities. In the early twentieth century, colonial surveys enumerated nearly 200 distinct languages spoken in India and over 500 dialects.[1] Virtually every known faith was practised in the subcontinent. Since the late nineteenth century, religious tensions and antagonisms, especially between Hindus and Muslims, had begun to acquire increasing prominence in Indian politics. Indeed, communalism came to be regarded as a peculiarly Indian phenomenon.[2] Yet, if these 'communal' tensions acquired the shape of ethnic difference, it was at least in part because of the political context in which they were expressed and within which they were increasingly defined. Similarly, caste differences sometimes exacerbated tensions within the nationalist movement, while they also contributed to the development of working-class sectionalism. The caste system has often been portrayed as the

1 G. A. Grierson, *Linguistic Survey of India*, 11 vols (Calcutta, Office of the Superintendent of Government Printing, India, 1903–28).

2 G. Pandey, *The Construction of Communalism in Colonial North India* (Delhi, Oxford University Press, 1992), pp. 6–9. Used specially in relation to India, 'communalism' has denoted the antagonisms entertained by religious and ethnic groups, taken as real and unified entities, about each other.

characteristic, even defining, feature of Indian tradition. In colonial discourse, it was represented as an integral aspect of Hinduism. Anthropologists who focused upon the caste system as unique to Indian civilisation elaborated its ritual and religious aspects to establish and explain its hegemonic force.[3] But there was another side to this picture, not quite so clearly etched. Caste did not simply encapsulate the moral order which anthropologists imagined for India, it also contributed to the creation and reproduction of the social order. The identification of caste too closely with tradition and religion has served to obscure its role in facilitating the control and deployment of labour, in terms not merely of the product but also of the whole body and being of the labourer. Caste hierarchies were shaped in large part by attempts to define the relationship and share the product between dominant groups and land controllers and between them and their labourers, commonly drawn from low-caste and dalit[4] groups. The control of land and labour influenced the nature of social hierarchies between various village elites and upper castes as well as between them and artisanal and menial castes and dalits. Thus, caste hierarchies in the old, densely settled fertile areas along the banks, or in the deltas, of the great river systems were often more intricate, subtle and finely graded than those in the more egalitarian production regimes of the newly colonised arid tracts.[5] The adaptability and flexibility which anthropologists have often noted about the caste system were fashioned over time, at least in part, by the imperatives of economic change and labour control. The orientalist assumption that Indian society comprised a multitude of separate and distinct cellular communities divided from each other was often belied by the close connections between them. Not only were these so-called 'communities' riven by internal differences but they were also to be found in a continuous process of formation and reconstitution, while the boundaries between them were largely defined by particular historical and political contingencies. The contingent nature of identity meant that neither caste nor religion, neither language nor occupation, could be treated as fixed units or foundational categories of social organisation.

The relationship between the working classes and the nationalist movement has often proved difficult to pin down and specify, not only

3 L. Dumont, *Homo Hierarchicus. The Caste System and its Implications* (London, Weidenfeld and Nicolson, 1970); see also R. Inden, *Imagining India* (Oxford, Blackwell, 1990).

4 Literally 'oppressed groups', signifying 'untouchable' castes.

5 D. Ludden, *Peasant History in South India* (Princeton, N.J., Princeton University Press, 1985).

because it was constantly in flux but also because neither side could be reduced to a single, homogeneous identity or ascribed a uniform character. The hybrid and protean character of the working classes was a consequence of the diverse influences which shaped their formation. The working classes have often been identified with an industrial labour force. But this remains a rather narrow definition. There was little to distinguish factory workers from casual or general labour in most cities and industrial centres. Workers in the factories and mills were often recruited on a casual and daily basis and retained the most tenuous hold on their jobs. Participation in a strike, for instance, or a downturn in trade could result in their dismissal. Workers long employed in a factory or mill could, thus, suddenly and arbitrarily lose their jobs and find themselves in the casual labour market. Similarly, factory workers were recruited largely from smallholding peasant households, predominantly from particular regions and districts, such as the eastern United Provinces and Bihar or the Ratnagiri and Satara districts in western India, which established close links with the industrial centres.[6]

The heterogeneity of the working classes was not simply the product of the pre-capitalist or backward character of the economy; rather, it bears testimony to the diverse and overlapping processes which shaped their formation in the colonial period. Until the mid-nineteenth century the subcontinent was characterised by a relative scarcity of labour and a relative abundance of land. Colonialism transformed a labour market once characterised by mobility, relatively high wages and some measure of independence. It sought to immobilise forest dwellers, itinerants and wandering groups and tied them to the land, while disbanding armies and courts, forcing artisans and various service groups to seek a livelihood from agriculture.[7] Under the weight of colonial policies, a growing proportion of the rural population became dependent upon agriculture for their sustenance. In the nineteenth century the agrarian economy was increasingly shorn of its diversity. Moreover, the apparently insatiable thirst of the colonial state for revenue, which had driven its territorial expansion in the first place, had already increased

---

6 R. Chandavarkar, *The Origins of Industrial Capitalism. Business Strategies and the Working Classes in Bombay 1900–40* (Cambridge, Cambridge University Press, 1994). There is a large case study literature about the migration of labour in India, but few syntheses have been attempted since L. Chakravarty, 'Emergence of a Labour Force in a Dual Economy: British India 1880–1920', *Indian Economic and Social History Review* (henceforth *IESHR*) 15:3 (1978), pp. 249–328, and G. Omvedt, 'Migration in Colonial India: the Articulation of Feudalism and Capitalism by the Colonial State', *Journal of Peasant Studies* 7:2 (1980), pp. 185–244.

7 D. Washbrook, 'Progress and Problems: South Asian Social and Economic History, *c.* 1720–1860', *Modern Asian Studies* (henceforth, *MAS*), 22:1 (1988), pp. 57–96.

the pressure on cultivators to produce crops for sale. While the weight of revenue demand declined in the later nineteenth century, the enterprise of peasant households generated a sufficient export surplus to pay for some of Britain's trade deficits with hard-currency areas.[8] This commercial buoyancy necessarily opened up differences between those peasants who had the luck or the ability to take advantage of the growing market opportunities and those who did not. The effect of commercial expansion and its attendant agrarian buoyancy, together with colonial policies, now seeking to conserve the smallholding base of Indian agriculture, enabled many impoverished households to retain their plots and survive. At the same time a growing proportion of such households found that off-farm earnings, primarily through wage labour, became indispensable to their reproduction.[9]

For smallholding peasants the most common means of securing a supplementary income was through agricultural labour, especially during the harvest, in neighbouring districts and sometimes farther afield in the large cash-cropping tracts. Some scoured the towns for wage-earning opportunities. Having migrated to the towns and factories, workers usually continued to maintain their connections with their village base. They deployed their village, caste and kinship connections to secure jobs, credit and shelter in the industrial setting. Workers often returned to their villages in periods of sickness and unemployment or in their old age, and at regular intervals to help with the harvest, to participate in religious festivals and attend feasts and marriages, thereby renewing their links with the village. Frequently, workers who migrated to the towns and factories were drawn from similar social groups to those who were recruited to the tea plantations, mines and overseas colonies. Workers who sought agricultural employment might after a period of time or in the slack season switch their attention to the towns or back again to the countryside. Peasants from the eastern United Provinces and Bihar who were recruited to the Assam tea gardens had to change trains at Naihati, where, in the late nineteenth century, they sometimes changed direction and went to work in the steadily proliferating jute

8 S. B. Saul, *Studies in British Overseas Trade* (Liverpool, Liverpool University Press, 1960); B. R. Tomlinson, 'India and the British Empire 1880–1935', *IESHR* 12:4 (1975), pp. 339–80.

9 J. Banaji, 'Capitalist Domination and the Small Peasantry: Deccan Districts in the late Nineteenth Century', *Economic and Political Weekly* 12:33–4 (1977), pp. 1375–404; N. Bhattacharya, 'Agricultural Labour and Production: Central and South East Punjab 1870–1940', in K. N. Raj, N. Bhattacharya, S. Guha and S. Padhi (eds), *Essays on the Commercialization of Indian Agriculture* (Delhi, Oxford University Press, 1985), pp. 105–62; S. Guha, *The Agrarian Economy of the Bombay Deccan, 1818–1941* (Delhi, Oxford University Press, 1986).

mills of Bengal.[10] Sometimes workers, having left their villages in search of urban and industrial employment, migrated between industrial centres. Occasionally they moved between industrial centres across very considerable distances.

None of this should lead to the conclusion that rural migrants simply sought casual employment wherever it was to be found. Circuits of migration and pilgrimages of employment brought dispersed and disparate groups of the Indian working classes into relation with each other within the labour force or, more abstractly, within the labour market: the landless poor and rural smallholders, *dalits* and *adivasis*,[11] impoverished artisans and low-caste groups, the urban poor and skilled industrial workers. Less than 10 per cent of the labour force were employed in manufacturing industry in the early twentieth century and the proportion remained unchanged at least until the 1960s.[12] However, the connections through which the working classes were constituted reached across the vast expanses of Indian society. The changes in production relations which underlay this process of proletarianisation suggest that conventionally historians have underestimated the extent to which the working classes formed and existed as a class in an operational sense. Conversely, they have tended to assume too readily the inherent propensity of the working classes to political and ideological unity. The diversity of the working classes makes it difficult to identify the nature of workers' responses to nationalist rhetoric or the images and boundaries of the nation to which they subscribed. But it has also ensured that workers' political responses to the Congress, to the anti-colonial movements of the late nineteenth and twentieth centuries and to the various competing definitions of nation which jostled for political space in this period offers a unique vantage point from which to examine the social roots of Indian nationalism.

There was both a spatial and a geographical context to class formation as well as an economic and industrial dimension, rooted in production relations. The internal tensions and conflicts within this working class related to locality and neighbourhood as well as to the workplace and the economy. Their interplay was vital to the shaping of the working class. Constituted through migration and divided by language and region, caste and religion, occupation and skill, the working classes

10 S. Basu, 'Workers' Politics in Bengal 1890–1929: Mill Towns, Strikes and Nationalist Agitations', unpublished Ph.D. thesis (University of Cambridge, 1994), p. 26.
11 Literally 'original inhabitants', denoting tribals, forest dwellers and those listed as 'scheduled tribes' under the Indian constitution of 1950.
12 J. Krishnamurthy, 'Secular Changes in Occupational Structure of the Indian Union 1901–61', *IESHR* 2:1 (1965), pp. 42–51.

became the site of at least two sources of conflict emanating from locality and neighbourhood. First, they experienced tensions and antagonisms between migrants and those who staked a prior claim to the
territory they inhabited. Thus conflicts emerged between local labour
and migrants from the United Provinces and Bihar, which sometimes
took a communal turn, in the Calcutta jute belt.[13] Similar differences
between *paschimas*, migrants from the west, and the *dehatis*, local back-
woodsmen, coincided with lines of competition for work and wages in
the Jharia coalfields.[14] UP *bhayyas* were treated with derision and hostility by Marathi-speaking workers in Bombay in the early twentieth
century, despite the fact that many who saw themselves as 'sons of the
soil' had themselves come to the city recently, and often temporarily,
from considerable distances.[15] Second, there was a tendency for these
ethnic and communal identities to be more clearly and sharply defined
by the competition for jobs, credit and housing in the towns, both in the
large industrial centres and in the smaller bazaars and district headquarters, bloated by the influx of migrants from the surrounding countryside.[16] Flows of migration could generate rapid changes in the social
composition of the work force and exacerbate tensions and intensify
competition along ethnic lines.

The industrial and economic dimension of labour force formation
also served to open up differences between workers and sometimes reinforced lines of ethnic and communal division. Migration occurred
largely within the framework of village and kinship connections. Around
ties of kinship, village and neighbourhood, workers sought to build their
own networks of support in hard times. It should not surprise us if
workers were to cleave to them in moments of conflict and competition.
The importance of these rural connections also helps to explain why so
many workers strove so hard to maintain them even when their village
holdings were no longer capable of providing substantial material
support. The nature and strength of their rural connections opened up

13 Basu, 'Workers' Politics in Bengal'; D. Chakrabarty, 'Communal Riots and Labour:
    Bengal's Jute Mill Hands in the 1890s', *Past and Present* 91 (1981), pp. 140–69.
14 R. Ghosh, 'A Study of the Labour Movement in Jharia Coal Field 1900–77', unpub-
    lished Ph.D. thesis (University of Calcutta, 1992); D. Simeon, *The Politics of Labour
    under late Colonialism. Workers, Unions and the State in Chota Nagpur 1928–39* (New
    Delhi, Manohar, 1995).
15 W. L. Rowe, 'Caste, Kinship and Association in Urban India', in A. Southall (ed.),
    Urban Anthropology. Cross-cultural Studies of Urbanization (New York, Oxford
    University Press, 1973), pp. 211–49; Chandavarkar, *The Origins of Industrial
    Capitalism*, chapter 4. *Bhayya*, literally 'brother', was used derisively in Bombay to
    describe Hindi-speaking immigrants from north India.
16 Nandini Gooptu, 'The Urban Poor and Militant Hinduism in Early Twentieth
    Century Uttar Pradesh', *MAS* 31:4 (1997), pp. 879–918.

differences among migrant workers. Labour for the tea plantations was recruited under systems of indenture and disciplined with a brutality which set it apart from most other cases, with the exception of coal mining.[17] Coal mining, like tea cultivation, was conducted in a rural setting. In the case of the coalfields of Raniganj and Jharia, the tribals of the neighbouring areas were induced to work by the grant of plots for cultivation in the vicinity of the mines. A substantial number of colliery workers had direct interests in agriculture, concurrent with their employment in the coal-mining industry. Significantly, the worst labour shortages experienced in the coal mines occurred in the harvest season, when workers were drawn away by higher agricultural wages.[18] There was an even more intimate connection between agricultural and industrial work in the seasonal industries, which were concerned primarily with the processing of raw agricultural products and offered employment as soon as the harvest ended. Centres like Bombay, Calcutta and Jamshedpur received a significant proportion of long-distance migrants, who retained close connections with their villages.[19] Some industrial centres of considerable significance, notably Coimbatore, Kanpur or Sholapur, recruited their labour force largely from immediately contiguous districts. Two-thirds of the mill labour force in Ahmedabad were recruited within the district and one-fifth were not only exclusively dependent upon industrial employment but were also permanent residents of the city.[20] The nature of the rural connections of industrial workers varied widely. As the Royal Commission on Labour in India observed, 'with some the contact is close and constant, with others it is slender and spasmodic, and with a few it is more an inspiration than a reality'.[21]

Similarly, methods of labour recruitment and organisation based upon intermediaries, often known as jobbers or sardars, could also serve

17 R. P. Behal and P. P. Mohapatra, ' "Tea and Money versus Human Life": the Rise and Fall of the Indenture System in the Assam Tea Plantations 1840–1908', in E. V. Daniel, H. Bernstein and T. Brass (eds.) *Plantations, Proletarians and Peasants in Colonial Asia* (London, Frank Cass, 1992), pp. 142–72.
18 *Report of the Royal Commission on Labour in India* (henceforth *RCLI*) (London, HMSO, 1931), pp. 115–17.
19 Chandavarkar, *The Origins of Industrial Capitalism*, chapter 4; Samita Sen, 'Women Workers in the Bengal Jute Industry 1890–1940: Migration, Motherhood and Militancy', unpublished Ph.D. thesis (University of Cambridge, 1992); M. D. Morris, 'The Labour Market in India', in W. E. Moore and A. S. Feldman (eds), *Labour Commitment and Social Change in Developing Areas* (New York, Social Science Research Council, 1960), pp. 173–200.
20 *RCLI, Evidence taken in the Bombay Presidency*, I, pt 1, Memorandum of the Government of Bombay, p. 4.
21 *Report of the RCLI*, p. 13.

to sharpen competitive tensions within the work force, sometimes along the lines of kinship, village, caste and religion. It was axiomatic in colonial discourse that Indian society was trapped in a web of tradition characterised by the joint family, the village community and the caste system, from which officials and employers assumed it would be impossible to extricate a supply of labour.[22] On the other hand, they also feared that, once released, labour would prove impossible to discipline and control. Systems of indentured labour and jobber recruitment were believed to be essential under Indian conditions both to prise labour out the institutions which held it captive and to pin it down to the workplace. Officials and employers often claimed that the role of labour intermediaries was necessitated by the peculiarities of the work force: its pre-capitalist mentalities, its peasant character and its cultural heterogeneity. But this claim, like many regarding workers' culture, was sustained by circular reasoning. Thus, for instance, planters were said to value labour contracting as a patriarchal system particularly suited to the social and cultural needs of Indian workers.[23] For the most part, employers valued jobbers more for their managerial and disciplinary functions than for any cultural or social purpose they might serve. The jobber's role was to provide an adequate supply of cheap, pliant labour, often in the face of fluctuating demand. In other words, his task was to restrain the pressure for increased wages, to facilitate the flexible use of casual labour and to contain labour unrest, serve as a bulwark against industrial action and help break strikes when they occurred. Ordinarily, though not exclusively, jobbers recruited and operated along the lines of caste, kinship and village connections. Employers benefited less from their role as a mediators of the cultural heterogeneity of the work force than from the effect they had in exacerbating its sectional and sectarian divisions.[24]

It is scarcely surprising that this pattern of migration and prevailing methods of recruiting and organising labour should have given rise to residential and occupational clusters by caste and village, language and religion. Since migration occurred within the framework of village and kinship connections, job seekers would tend to go to occupations, towns and neighbourhoods in which their acquaintances had already established themselves. Once a nucleus of workers from a given caste or

22 This argument is elaborated in R. Chandavarkar, *Imperial Power and Popular Politics. Class, Resistance and the State in India 1850–1950* (Cambridge, Cambridge University Press, 1998), chapter 1.
23 Omvedt, 'Migration in Colonial India', p. 193.
24 Chandavarkar, *The Origins of Industrial Capitalism*, pp. 99–110, 195–201 and 295–307.

village had formed within an occupation or a neighbourhood, they would attract a stronger flow of their friends and relatives. This was a response to the competitive pressures of an overstocked labour market in which wages were low and conditions of work uncertain. By seeking to monopolise a particular occupation, albeit with varying degrees of success, a group of workers could tighten their hold upon it and perhaps increase their bargaining power in relation to their employers. Moreover, by helping newly arrived migrants to find work, credit and housing, older residents of the urban or industrial setting could extend and renew their village and kinship connections, which were in any case indispensable to their own strategies for survival.

Significantly, when contemporary observers reported the formation of ethnic clusters in patterns of employment or residence, their principles of classification often appeared vague and arbitrary. Thus the Labour Officer of the Bombay Millowners' Association classified some workers according to religion, others according to broad caste categories rather than *jati*[25] groups, and North Indian migrants not according to caste at all but simply as 'bhayyas'.[26] Such confusion about classification in part reflected the fluidity and permeability which marked workers' definition of their own identity. The social connections through which workers operated in the city were not limited to endogamous, intermarrying and inter-dining *jatis* but could also take the form of linguistic, regional, religious or political associations, with each of these shifting and contingent identities cutting across each other. The brotherhood of villagers in the city, which could often include people of various castes and different religions, was an ideal to which city dwellers subscribed sometimes with an enthusiasm not always evident in their villages.[27] Finally, the coherence and strength of caste, kinship and village connections in the cities were often greatest among the most marginalised groups within the working class: either in casual and unskilled occupations or among groups which had only recently entered the labour force and were weakly established within the social nexus of the neighbourhoods. Thus village and kinship connections, caste and religious ties, bonds of language and region drew a particular strength and fresh definition from the social organisation of workplace and neighbourhood.

25 *Jati* refers to endogamous, commensal caste units among Hindus which were in turn notionally located within the four *varna* orders or categories of classical Hindu sociology: *brahman* (priest), *kshatriya* (warrior), *vaishya* (trader) and *sudra* (cultivator).
26 R. G. Gokhale, *The Bombay Cotton Mill Worker* (Bombay, Bombay Millowners' Association, 1957).
27 Chandavarkar, *The Origins of Industrial Capitalism*, especially chapter 4.

Production relations, not simply an autonomous sphere of culture, shaped these diverse and overlapping ethnic identities.

Moreover, political conflicts and competition at the level of the state also heightened the significance of ethnic and communal identities. The political system which the British created in India was the outcome of several conflicting aims: to centralise authority to enable them to deploy Indian resources in their global interests and to win the acquiescence and collaboration of powerful Indian interests by giving away large areas of power and control; to secure their base of collaboration without becoming the prisoner of their allies; and to achieve the broadest representation of Indians which they could tolerate within the institutions of government at every level but to avoid affording permanence to any particular distribution of political resources between castes, religious communities and social groups, variously defined. The official rhetoric of representation, with its claim to provide suitably for each deserving interest, was simply an invitation to Indians to define themselves in its terms and to organise to wrest a larger share of the political rewards on offer. As a result, British rule helped to develop a vocabulary of sectarianism and to create a political language of social and communal interests within which competition of diverse sorts came to be conducted. From the late nineteenth century onwards, numerous political movements formed along caste, linguistic, religious or regional lines. Movements of Muslim separatism, non-Brahminism or the depressed classes focused primarily upon issues of access to education and government jobs, and demanded special electorates and better representation within the political institutions of British rule.[28] Similarly, regional movements emerged around demands for the redrawing of district or even provincial boundaries, on the calculation that a revised political arithmetic would afford its protagonists improved access to political power. Despite their limited aims, such programmes could sometimes extend their appeal to the working classes. For education and government employment opened up avenues of social mobility. The prospect that their progeny and their relatives might secure opportunities for education and a job within government, and, in turn, provide them with help, protection and advancement, could elicit the support of those who, it seemed, stood to gain nothing directly from this charter of demands. The rhetoric of nationalism, like that of class, sought to

---

28 F. C. R. Robinson, *Separatism among Indian Muslims. The Politics of the United Provinces' Muslims 1860–1923* (Cambridge, Cambridge University Press, 1974); D. Washbrook, 'The Development of Caste Organisation in South India 1880 to 1925', in C. J. Baker and D. A. Washbrook, *South India. Political Institutions and Political Change 1880–1940* (New Delhi, Macmillan, 1975), pp. 151–203.

transcend the boundaries described by ethnic identity. However, just as caste and communal identities were sometimes fostered by the very processes of class formation, so the growth of nationalism could serve to inscribe more firmly the cultural divisions it sought to subsume. The Indian National Congress, founded in 1885, claimed to be the representative voice of the nation. But its preliminary task was necessarily to forge the nation it claimed to represent. Those who felt that their needs were unduly neglected by the Congress sometimes challenged its claim to serve the 'true' interests of the nation, deploying the idiom of nationalism but emphasising affinities of religion and caste, language and region.

'Of course, everyone knows that the Congress is not a labour organisation . . .' wrote Jawaharlal Nehru, when he was president of the All-India Trades Union Congress in 1929. 'To expect it to act as a pure labour organisation is a mistake. The National Congress is a large body comprising all manner of people.'[29] The Congress had developed largely as a national forum for significant local interests. Its success in attaching these interests depended upon its ability to offer them the means and opportunities to influence government, especially at the imperial level. It was precisely to fortify its claim to represent the nation as a whole that the Congress had to serve as a forum for 'all manner of people.' For this reason, too, it was constrained to operate behind an inevitably thin facade of unity which it maintained by emphasising only those issues which united its constituents and glossing over those which might divide them. This was always liable to narrow the range of options before the Congress as a movement of opposition to colonial rule. To demonstrate its representative character, it was essential for the Congress to expand and diversify its social base. In part, this depended upon its ability to bring the working classes into the nationalist fold. Yet, as labour registered an increasingly prominent presence in the political arena, it only deepened the contradictions which beset the Congress. By serving the cause of labour, the Congress was always liable to imperil its increasingly intimate links with a variety of commercial interests, including elements of industrial capital.

Thus committed to seeking working-class support without entering into confrontation with capital, the Congress chose to preach class harmony. Until the 1910s the Congress and its leading lights rarely concerned themselves with labour. Indeed, in the late nineteenth century, nationalist leaders were said to be 'indifferent or hostile to the efforts

---

29 J. Nehru to D. B. Kulkarni, 10 September 1929, AICC Papers, File 16 of 1929, pp. 111–13, Nehru Memorial Museum and Library (henceforth, NMML).

being made to ameliorate the conditions of work of the factory workers'.[30] Even Bal Gangadhar Tilak, against whose conviction for sedition in 1908 the Bombay millworkers had launched a general strike, and his extremist allies were found to have been 'insensitive and even opposed to the cause of labour'.[31] It was only after the First World War that the annual conference of the Congress first began to take cognisance of the problems of the working classes.[32] Increasingly, as systems of representation were placed on a wider basis, and the working classes asserted themselves more forcefully in the public arena, politicians and publicists began to show a growing interest in their struggles. Not only the local and secondary level leaders of the Congress but also some of its more prominent national figures occasionally stepped forward to represent labour in industrial disputes: most dramatically Gandhi, in the case of the Ahmedabad millworkers' strike in 1918 and Subhas Chandra Bose in Jamshedpur in the late 1920s.

As the Congress engaged more closely with the working classes, however, its rhetoric sought to subsume the contradictions between exploiter and exploited within its concept of the nation. In treading this path the Congress was by no means unique among nationalist movements. Indeed, its choice flowed naturally from the claim to represent the nation as a whole. However, it demarcated the limits within which the Congress would lead the working classes. Nationalist rhetoric often dwelt upon the common interests of labour and capital. Joseph Baptista, who played a prominent role in the general strike of 1920 in Bombay, addressing the All-India Trade Union Congress in the same year, described workers and capitalists as 'partners and co-workers, and not buyers and sellers of labour. They are all engaged in promoting the well-being of society.'[33] As president of the AITUC in 1920 Lala Lajpat Rai invited labour and capital 'to join hands to develop Indian industries'.[34] Gandhi often used the metaphor of the family in discussing industrial relations and sought to reconcile the conflicting interests of labour and capital within its figurative framework. His ideal, he said, was that labour and capital 'should be a great family living in unity and harmony', with

---

30 Bipan Chandra, *The Rise and Growth of Economic Nationalism in India. Economic Policies of the Indian National Leadership 1880–1905* (New Delhi, People's Publishing House, 1966), p. 330.

31 *Ibid.*

32 V. Bahl, 'Attitude of the Indian National Congress towards the Working Class Struggle in India 1918–47', in K. Kumar (ed.) *Congress and Classes. Nationalism, Workers and Peasants* (New Delhi, Manohar, 1988), p. 3.

33 *AITUC – Fifty Years: Documents*, I, (New Delhi, All-India Trade Union Congress, 1973), p. 12.

34 *Ibid.*, p. 29

the capitalists serving as 'the trustees' for the moral and material 'welfare of the labouring classes'.[35]

The 'higher ideal of partnership' could, taken a step further, prescribe that workers should restrain their demands in the short term in the expectation that their needs would be fully met once independence was achieved. Strikes in Indian-owned industries could, on the contrary, serve to exacerbate foreign domination. During the strike at Tata Iron and Steel Company in 1929 Sir Ibrahim Rahimtoola assured the young business magnate G. D. Birla that Subhas Chandra Bose recognised, even as he intervened on behalf of the Golmuri tinplate workers in Jamshedpur in 1929, that 'if as a result of the strike, the industry is forced into other than Indian hands, it would be highly detrimental to national progress.'[36] One week later, Birla was able to pass the message on to Thakurdas, the leading Bombay capitalist. 'Mr Bose,' he wrote, 'can be relied upon to help Tata Iron and Steel Works whenever necessary.' For 'Mr Bose,' he explained, 'appreciates the necessity of co-operation with reasonable and advanced type of capitalists. . . . His main object in labour matters no doubt is service to the labour but not necessarily inimical to the capitalist.'[37] The 'conciliatory' role of some Congress leaders in industrial disputes often served to alienate workers, who after all bore the risks which a strike entailed. Nor could the Congress expect to consistently attract the working classes by advising them to subordinate their current grievances to a future projection of the national interest. In any case, this was an argument which employers could turn just as readily against trade unions and strikers. Social conflict was, in nationalist rhetoric, often subordinated to political objectives. Nationalism, as I have argued elsewhere, was primarily a discourse of political exclusion, not of social conflict or economic grievance. The social evils of British India were perceived and portrayed as the outcome of the political injustice of foreign, imperial rule. When the Congress advised the postponement of social struggle until the achievement of independence, this was not simply an expression of its determination to subordinate the class interests of the poor to its own long-term political goals. Rather, it reflected its diagnosis of the underlying cause of existing social evils in terms of the larger system of colonial oppression, political coercion and tyrannical power.[38]

Not all Congress publicists who styled themselves as labour leaders

---

35 *Young India*, 20 August 1925; Chandavarkar, *Imperial Power and Popular Politics*, pp. 281–91.
36 Sir Ibrahim Rahimtoola to G. D. Birla, 9 July 1929, Thakurdas Papers, File 42 (II), NMML.
37 Birla to Thakurdas, 16 July 1929, Thakurdas Papers, File 42 (I). NMML.
38 Chandavarkar, *Imperial Power and Popular Politics*, chapter 8.

operated exclusively within the limits demarcated by its rhetoric of class harmony. However, as the Congress acquired a more coherent organisation and its 'high command' exerted tighter control over its members, the publicists who acted in its name found fewer options open to them. In the 1910s and early 1920s a wide range of politicians associated loosely with labour, and an increasing number disclosed a willingness to intervene in labour disputes. According to one calculation, nearly a quarter of trade union office holders in Bengal between 1918 and 1921 were 'nationalists', including 15 per cent who were 'non-cooperators'.[39] Similarly, in the Madras Presidency, 'most of the labour leaders in the immediate post-war period were either supporters or members of . . . the Indian National Congress'.[40] Between 1915 and 1922 the political and ideological character of the Congress seemed both open and fluid. Not surprisingly, perhaps, Congress in its agitational mode provided a refuge for irreconcilables with varied and often conflicting political aspirations.

By the 1930s the relatively flexible relationship between labour and the Congress began to change. As the Congress became less tolerant of divided loyalties within its ranks, it also acquired the opportunity and the power to discriminate between its followers. Few ambitious politicians could now afford to ignore the party's high command and hope to progress within its ranks. As dominant peasants and mercantile elites acquired greater influence within the Congress, so labour leaders, especially the more radical among them, were marginalised within its fold. It became increasingly difficult to reconcile the task of adequately representing workers with the constraints of serving other, more powerful political constituents of the Congress. In the 1920s, labour was only one of a range of political concerns for the publicist, and often a rather marginal concern. More labour leaders emerged in the following decade who were concerned exclusively with labour matters. In the 1930s leading labour became a rather more specialised profession. The growth of socialist and communist organisations within the labour movement was an outcome of this development: in Bengal and Bombay, in Kanpur and Ahmedabad, in Sholapur and Coimbatore.[41] In the 1920s and 1930s communist trade unions, in particular, bore the brunt of the hostility

---

39 S. Gourlay, 'Nationalists, Outsiders and the Labour Movement in Bengal during the Non-cooperation Movement 1919–21', in Kumar (ed.), *Congress and Classes*, p. 39. 'Non-cooperators' referred to those members of the Congress who supported Gandhi and participated in his campaign to refuse cooperation with the colonial government.
40 E. D. Murphy, *Unions in Conflict: A Comparative Study of Four South Indian Textile Centres 1918–39.* (New Delhi, Manohar, 1981), p. 63.
41 Chandavarkar, *Imperial Power and Popular Politics*, chapter 8.

and repression of employers and the state. Nevertheless, they were also the most successful in several centres at mobilising the support of the working classes. Unlike many labour leaders, the communists adopted a stance of unremitting opposition to both employers and the state, sought to allow workers' militancy its head and remained largely immune to the blandishments of collaboration. Few trade unions achieved institutional permanence, least of all those which became the target of repressive action. However the linkages which some of these oppositional and confrontational unions forged through industrial action endured sufficiently to be revived and redeployed in large-scale strikes in the following decade.

In view of the sustained hostility of employers and the state to workers' combinations, it would be misleading to suppose that the formation of trade unions reflected the nature and extent of class consciousness. At the same time, nationalist agitation, which gained the support of the working classes, sometimes served to sharpen caste and communal antagonism. Conversely, conflicts which were portrayed in caste and communal terms sometimes arose from an assertion of class interests. For instance, disputes rooted in the organisation of production in late nineteenth-century Bengal sometimes focused on the refusal of the jute mill owners to grant religious holidays, culminating in strikes and even violence. Such disputes were often given a communal construction, sometimes without cause, by employers and policemen, politicians and the local press.[42] In the mill townships of Bengal managers, as local magistrates, called upon the local police to break strikes and enforce order. The interventions of the police led workers to identify the state with their managers, which in turn informed their support for the *swadeshi*[43] movement in Bengal between 1905 and 1908.[44] However, the *bhadralok*[45] nationalist leaders were badly placed to develop this support. For the most part they stayed aloof during strikes, at best offered themselves as mediators and increasingly alienated their working-class followers.[46]

Workers' politics in Bombay was shaped by a similar pattern of interaction between caste, communal, class and national identities.

42 See Basu, 'Workers' Politics in Bengal', pp. 123–5.
43 Literally 'of one's country'. The *swadeshi* movement focused principally on the boycott of foreign goods as a protest against the partition of Bengal in 1905. See S. Sarkar, *The Swadeshi Movemment in Bengal 1903–08* (New Delhi, People's Publishing House, 1973).
44 Basu, 'Workers' Politics in Bengal', pp. 140–51.
45 'Respectable', gentlefolk of Bengal recruited largely from the literate upper castes.
46 Basu, 'Workers' Politics in Bengal', pp. 140–51; Sarkar, *The Swadeshi Movement.*

Caste and kinship ties, village and neighbourhood connections, which were vital to their social organisation, also shaped workers' combinations. Thus labour organisations in this period often appeared loosely organised around caste.[47] However, when the nationalist leader Bal Gangadhar Tilak was convicted for sedition by the Bombay High Court in 1908 the city's workers took to the streets and the mills were shut down for a week in what could plausibly be seen as a remarkable display of nationalist fervour. Yet several influences, not all of them nationalist, had a bearing on the strike of 1908. First, it occurred at a time when the labour market witnessed considerable disruption. The introduction of electricity to the mills enabled owners to extend the length of the working day when their order books warranted it. The result was intense wage competition, increased mobility of labour between mills and the breakdown of jobber control.[48] Second, the millworkers' support for Tilak also arose from their identification of his political opponents among the 'moderates' in the Congress with the millowners, the municipal administration which they dominated and especially the Governor's court, where they remained influential. Third, the workers had already experienced the colonial state as an intermittently interventionist, sometimes repressive, even brutal, force: during strikes in the individual mills and workshops, the plague epidemic of the late 1890s and 1900s,[49] the demolitions conducted by the City of Bombay Improvement Trust in the first decade of the twentieth century[50] and in the conflicts over the conduct and control of Mohurram.[51]

Between the two world wars this interplay between class, ethnicity and nationalism developed further and often took forms which the protagonists neither intended nor anticipated. By 1917 inflation and scarcities had begun to give rise to increasingly vociferous wage demands, while the expectations of political reform after the war had induced politicians, always aware of the need to widen their constituencies, to pay

---

47 Chandavarkar, *Origins of Industrial Capitalism*, pp. 426–7.
48 *Report of the Indian Factory Labour Commission*, (henceforth *IFLC*), (Simla, Government of India Press, 1908); *IFLC*, II, Evidence, pp. 85, 109, 113, 182; *Annual Reports of the Bombay Millowners's Association*, 1905–07.
49 R. Chandavarkar, 'Plague Panic and Epidemic Politics in India 1896–1914', in P. Slack and T. Ranger (eds.) *Epidemics and Ideas. Essays on the Historical Perception of Pestilence* (Cambridge, Cambridge University Press, 1992), pp. 203–40.
50 Chandavarkar, *The Origins of Industrial Capitalism*, pp. 43–4, 35–44.
51 S. M. Edwardes, *The Bombay City Police 1672–1916. A Historical Sketch* (London, Oxford University Press, 1923), especially, appendix; J. Masselos, 'Power in the Bombay "Moholla" 1904–15: an Initial Exploration into the World of the Indian Urban Muslim', *South Asia* 6 (1976), pp. 75–95. The Mohurram festival mourns the martyrdom of Husain and his followers at Kerbala and is observed over a period of ten days.

closer attention to the discontents of the working classes. Nationalist agitations between 1917 and 1922, as well as the civil disobedience campaigns of the early 1930s, provided a cover for working-class struggle and offered local industrial disputes a wider political focus. The Congress, for its part, was able thereby to convey the impression, sometimes to project the reality, of widespread support. The timing of the major Congress campaigns was not driven by the groundswell of popular political action but rather determined by the imperatives of constitutional reform and imperial policy. Popular participation in these campaigns was rooted in local grievances and social conflicts, which outdated the nationalist agitations and continued long after they had been called off.[52] Not surprisingly, perhaps, there was both chronological and geographical unevenness in the response of the working classes to the Congress. Workers who were drawn readily into the non-cooperation movement in the early 1920s sometimes remained aloof from civil disobedience a decade later; towns which appeared insurrectionary in the early 1930s remained relatively quiescent in the early 1940s. Non-cooperation flourished among various working-class groups in Bengal[53] but civil disobedience drew a more muted response, while labour, it is said, 'remained largely irrelevant to the Congress strategy.'[54] The strikes of 1920–22 in Jamshedpur fed conveniently into the non-cooperation campaign, while civil disobedience failed as workers ignored the *satyagrahis*[55] and achieved record levels of production,[56] but the Quit India campaign of 1942 registered an impressive and dramatic response from the town's industrial workers.[57]

If nationalist agitation provided a cover for industrial action, strikes during the non-cooperation and civil disobedience movements focused largely upon workplace issues. It is not intended to suggest that the working classes were left unaffected by nationalist sentiment. On the

52 A. Seal, 'Imperialism and Nationalism in India', in J. Gallagher, G. Johnson and A. Seal (eds) *Locality, Province and Nation. Indian Politics 1870–1940* (Cambridge, Cambridge University Press, 1973), pp. 1–15. This axiom of the 'Cambridge school' of the 1970s has now become a shibboleth of the 'Subaltern school' in the 1990s.
53 Basu, 'Workers' Politics in Bengal', chapter 5; Gourlay, 'Nationalists, Outsiders and the Labour Movement in Bengal'.
54 T. Sarkar, 'The First Phase of Civil Disobedience in Bengal 1930–31', *Indian Historical Review* 4:1 (1977), p. 94.
55 Those who participated in *satyagrahas*, struggles for truth, or Gandhian passive resistance.
56 V. Bahl, 'TISCO Workers' Struggle 1920–28', *Social Scientist* 10:8 (1982), p. 44, n. 34.
57 *The Transfer of Power 1942–47* II, *Quit India, 30 April–21 September 1942* ed. N. Mansergh (London, HMSO, 1971), especially Documents Nos. 600–2, 612, 636, 650 and 672.

contrary, their experience of confrontation at the workplace could lead them to identify with political programmes directed against the colonial state. As nationalist rhetoric adopted a more explicitly anti-colonial tone, it spoke more immediately to the political experiences of the working classes. However, the growth of the labour movement and the increasing frequency of strikes also served to heighten the social and political contradictions within the Congress. If Congress publicists championed labour's cause, they were likely to invite the opposition of mercantile and propertied elites who now gained increasing influence within the party. As Congress publicists gained power within the political structure of British rule, now increasingly open to Indian politicians, their political influence encouraged employers to seek their help in settling disputes. If they gained the confidence of the employers and the state, and thus acquired a reputation for getting things done for the workers, they could build up a significant following within the mill or the factory. However, industrial action could put their wider political connections at risk. For this reason, the more secure and more extensive their connections, the more likely it was that such publicists would find themselves seeking to restrain workers in moments of confrontation or to negotiate a settlement when they were eager to prolong it, and thus liable to be deserted by their followers.

The Ahmedabad strike of 1918 was an emblematic moment for the relationship between the Congress and the working classes. Not only was the strike one of the first campaigns with which Gandhi announced his presence in Indian politics, but it created the basis for the only direct, organic relationship which the Congress maintained with a trade union. Gandhi was invited to mediate in the wage dispute largely because he had already won the trust of the Ahmedabad millowners. In leading the strike Gandhi showed, not for the first time, his extraordinary political skill as an organiser, communicator and negotiator. His style of leadership was highly personal, open and accessible. As his secretary, Mahadev Desai, put it, Gandhi 'decided to enter into the life of the workers'. His prominent 'advisers' in the strike – Anasuyabehn Sarabhai, Shankarlal Banker and Chhaganlal Gandhi – were detailed to visit the workers' homes and to collect information about them, their families and their conditions of life. These visits served 'the purpose of enabling the advisers to feel the pulse of the entire labour community'.[58] Workers were also encouraged to visit the leaders' homes whenever they wished to discuss the strike or seek help and advice. Indeed, during the dispute Anasuyabehn Sarabhai

---

58 M. Desai, *A Righteous Struggle. A Chronicle of the Ahmedabad Textile Labourers' Fight for Justice* (Ahmedabad, Navjivan Publishing House, 1951), pp. 8–9.

was said to meet workers whenever they visited her, at all hours of the day and night. Few strikes had been conducted in this open manner; nor would they be in the future. Finally, when the strike was on the point of collapse, Gandhi, recognising that its conduct had led workers and their families to the point of starvation, undertook a fast which reflected their own deprivation. In the event, Gandhi's fast served to secure the workers' demands, for neither the millowners nor the state could countenance the political consequences of the Mahatma's death.[59]

In the aftermath of the 1918 strike Gandhi was able to persuade the millowners to accept the arbitration procedures which he had advocated from the earliest stages of the dispute and in 1920 to recognise the Ahmedabad Textile Labour Association as the principal bargaining agent on behalf of the workers. Once the ATLA was thus recognised by the millowners, Gandhi withdrew from active involvement in the union's affairs. Buoyed up by their triumph in 1918, the Ahmedabad workers mounted numerous strikes, often wildcat and spontaneous actions, which occurred without reference to the leaders or the union. Between 1920 and 1922 the non-co-operation and Khilafat movements[60] provided a further spur to industrial action effected by workers against the advice of the Congress leadership.

Similarly, in Bengal, in Madras and on the railways, the nationalist agitations of the early 1920s created an opportunity for workers to press their demands and seek redress for their grievances with a reduced threat of employers' sanctions against them.[61] The strikes and the exodus of the Assam tea plantation workers in 1921 have often been taken to demonstrate the popular roots of non-cooperation. In fact, the grievances of the plantation workers related to wages and working conditions and had been expressed before the non-cooperation campaign was under way.[62] When the plantation workers reached the nearest railway station at Chandpur, the army was called out to prevent them proceeding further. Its brutal intervention provoked a supposedly 'sym-

59 S. Patel, *The Making of Industrial Relations. The Ahmedabad Textile Industry 1918–39*, (Delhi, Oxford University Press, 1987), chapter 3; Desai, *A Righteous Struggle;* E. Erikson, *Gandhi's Truth. On the Origins of Militant Non-violence* (New York, Norton, 1969).
60 The Khilafat movement was launched in 1919 to prevent the British and their allies from undermining the spiritual and temporal authority of the Islamic caliphate in the post-war settlement.
61 Basu, 'Workers Politics', chapter 6; L. Jagga, 'Colonial Railwaymen and British Rule: a Probe into Railway Labour Agitation in India, 1919–22' in B. Chandra (ed.), *The Indian Left. Critical Appraisals* (New Delhi, Vikas, 1983) pp. 120–7; Murphy, *Unions in Conflict*, chapter 4.
62 R. P. Behal, 'Forms of Labour Protest in Assam Valley Tea Plantations 1900–30', *Economic and Political Weekly* 20:4 (1985), pp. PE-21 to PE-22.

pathetic' strike by the employees of the Assam–Bengal Railway, which stirred the imagination, fed the anxieties and encouraged the enthusiasm of contemporaries. On closer scrutiny, however, it does not appear to have been particularly sympathetic. The railwaymen were aggrieved that, while attacking the fleeing tea garden labourers, the troops had been sufficiently indiscriminate to assault them as well. Once the strike began, both railwaymen and steamer crews focused upon their wages and working conditions and the union quickly distanced itself from the nationalist agitation.[63]

During the civil disobedience movement in the early 1930s a similar pattern manifested itself. Local circumstances and the tensions and conflicts generated by them often determined whether the working classes would march behind the Congress banner. However, these tensions were now more debilitating than they had been a decade earlier. As the scale and frequency of strikes grew, employers became increasingly concerned that discipline was at stake and sought to assert their control more vigorously. The Depression provided the opportunity and created an imperative for the managerial offensive. In Bombay city, following the general strikes of 1928 and 1929, and helped by the arrest of the communist leaders of the Girni Kamgar Union for conspiracy to overthrow the King-Emperor[64], this offensive took a particularly determined and ferocious form,[65] but it was also repeated elsewhere, notably for instance in Jamshedpur.[66] The civil disobedience movement strengthened the resolve of the colonial state to assist the disciplinary efforts of capital. Trade unions and workers who had been active in the struggles of the 1920s encountered the sustained hostility of employers and the state and their organisations were weakened and, in some cases, broken. In the early 1920s the Congress leadership had often expressed anxiety about the involvement of the working classes in nationalist agitations.[67] A decade later they paid less attention to labour as a distinct social category. On the other hand, the weakening and collapse of labour organisa-

---

63 Gourlay, 'Nationalists, Outsiders and the Labour Movement in Bengal', pp. 49–53.
64 In all, thirty-two trade unionists, mainly communists, from all over India, were arrested in March 1929, tried for conspiracy at Meerut and sentenced in 1933. This judicial action was directed primarily against the leaders of the Bombay Girni Kamgar Union, in the aftermath of the successful general strike of 1928. The Meerut case ranks among the most prominent political trials of the period.
65 Chandavarkar, *Imperial Power and Popular Politics*, chapters 4 and 5.
66 Simeon, *The Politics of Labour under late Colonialism*, chapter 4
67 See, for instance, Gandhi's comments on labour and nationalist agitation in *Young India*, 16 February 1921, *Collected Works of Mahatma Gandhi* (henceforth, *CWMG*), (New Delhi, Publications Division, Ministry of Information and Broadcasting, 1966) XIX, p. 366.

tion facilitated a freer and more individual association of the working classes with civil disobedience. Paradoxically, however, in the 1930s the Congress showed itself less willing to engage specifically with the grievances and conflicts of the workplace. They refrained from representing labour as such, but sought to incorporate the working classes as citizens within the nationalist fold.

Where the Congress had little influence among the working classes – and where the labour movement was already relatively strong – its attempts to incorporate them often served to divide their ranks. Thus, in Bombay city, the Congress tried to extend its linkages within working-class politics by allying with the local opponents of the communist Girni Kamgar Union and subsequently by manipulating the differences which opened up within the union leadership after the Meerut arrests and the collapse of the general strike of 1929.[68] Significantly the efforts of the Congress to develop a working-class base thus fed the rivalries, deepened the antagonisms and accentuated the sectionalism of the labour movement.

In 1937 the Congress contested elections held under a reformed constitution and formed the government in seven out of eleven provinces. The Congress in power often proved to be as repressive as the preceding colonial regime. As Indian elites gained greater influence over the colonial state, at local and provincial levels, they revealed an increasing concern to discipline labour and maintain order. In Bombay the Congress Ministry passed trade disputes legislation which severely curtailed the freedom of action available to trade unions. In passing this legislation, apparently directed against the Bombay millworkers and the red flag unions, the Congress was motivated in part by the competitive pressure exerted upon the ATLA by the weavers in Ahmedabad, who had formed the communist-led Mill Mazdoor Sangh.[69] When the Bombay millworkers staged a one-day strike in protest against the trade disputes bill in November 1938, the police opened fire and caused a number of deaths. The Congress governments in Madras and Uttar Pradesh showed a similar willingness to open fire upon striking workers.[70] In Bengal, however, where the Krishak Praja Party was in

---

68 Government of Bombay, (henceforth GOB), Home (Special) File 750 (39) – II of 1930. Maharashtra State Archives (henceforth, MSA); Chandavarkar, *Imperial Power and Popular Politics*, pp. 313–14.

69 GOB, Home (Special) Files 550(24) of 1938, 550(25) III A, MSA; All-India Trade Union Congress (henceforth AITUC) Papers, File 59, NMML.

70 Chitra Joshi, 'Hope and Despair: Textile Workers in Kanpur in 1937–38 and 1997', paper presented to the conference on 'Worlds of Industrial Labour', CASA, Amsterdam, December 1997; Murphy, *Unions in Conflict*, chapters 8–10.

power, the Congress high command proved rather more supportive of the general strike in the jute mills and the Congress socialists in the province played a leading role in its organisation.[71]

By its very nature, the Congress had to resist pressures to define the terms on which different social groups might be incorporated within the nation. However, just as the Congress sometimes exacerbated the rivalries within the labour movement, nationalism also developed and sharpened ethnic identities even as it claimed to transcend them. Tilak's attempt to establish the Shivaji festival and to counterpose the Ganpati festival to the observance of Mohurram in the late nineteenth and early twentieth centuries had already revealed that nationalism had a communal colouring.[72] In the 1930s Congress rhetoric in Utaar Pradesh and in Bengal acquired, among some of its protagonists, a distinctly Hindu idiom.[73] Certainly, the Congress campaigns, especially in the 1930s and 1940s, led Muslims, to ask themselves about the rights which they might enjoy in the Ramrajya.[74] Congress agitation, especially the picketing of liquor and cloth shops, could aggravate local conflicts, provoke communal antagonism and sometimes lead to large-scale violence. The boycott of foreign cloth during the civil disobedience movement opened up rifts in the trade between those who controlled the import trade and those who concentrated on the domestic markets. Where many of the large import traders were Muslims, the boycott and the picketing of their shops and markets were infused with communal antagonisms and sometimes provoked violence. Thus the picketing of cloth merchants led to

71 V. B. Karnik, *Strikes in India* (Bombay, Popular Prakashan, 1967), pp. 284–6; see also the contrasting tone of Jawaharlal Nehru's speeches to the Kanpur textile and the Bengal jute strikers in *The Selected Works of Jawarharlal Nehru* (New Delhi, Orient Longman, 1976) VIII, pp. 92–5, 328–34, 351–4 and 321–5. On the role of the Congress Socialists in the jute strike see Tony Cox, 'Rationalisation and Resistance: the Imperial Jute Industries of Dundee and Calcutta', unpublished fellowship dissertation, Trinity College, Cambridge, 1997, chapter 6.

72 R. I. Cashman, *The Myth of the Lokamanya. Tilak and Mass Politics in Maharashtra* (Berkeley and Los Angeles, Cal., University of California Press, 1975), chapters 4 and 5. Shivaji, the seventeenth-century Maratha ruler, became an enduring nationalist hero largely for his martial exploits against the Mughal Empire. The public worship of Ganpati or Ganesha, the elephant-headed god, was developed by Tilak in part to draw Hindus away from participation in the Mohurram festival.

73 G. Pandey, *The Ascendancy of the Congress in the UP 1926–34. A Study in Imperfect Mobilization* (Delhi, Oxford University Press, 1978), chapter 5; J. Chatterji, *Bengal Divided. Hindu Communalism and Partition 1932–47* (Cambridge, Cambridge University Press, 1994); S. Sarkar, 'Identity and Difference: Caste in the Formation of the Ideologies of Nationalism and Hindutva', in *Writing Social History* (Delhi, Oxford University Press, 1997).

74 Ramrajya, or the kingdom of Rama, the divine hero of the Hindu epic, the Ramayana, was used as a metaphor in nationalist rhetoric for the utopia which would follow freedom from British rule.

communal violence in Banaras in 1931[75] and in Bombay in 1932.[76] The attempt by Congress 'volunteers' to enforce a *hartal* in Kanpur on the day of Bhagat Singh's execution led to a ferocious communal riot in 1931.[77]

Since the competition for jobs (as well as housing and credit) could follow lines of caste and communal difference, trade union rivalries, sometimes promoted by the Congress, could also acquire a communal edge. Employers frequently sought to diversify the caste and communal composition of their labour force to extend their control over it.[78] When, during strikes, they tried to recruit workers of a different religious, caste or regional identity from those who had struck, their attempts to manipulate the social composition of the work force could deepen rivalries, provoke violent conflict on the picket lines and lead – as it did in Bombay, for instance, in February and May 1929 and again in May 1932 – to communal riots.[79] Similarly, in the later 1930s, jute millowners and colonial officials in Bengal gratefully encouraged the Muslim League unions formed by Suhrawardy as a bulwark against the communists.[80]

Political developments and public discourse in the final decades of colonial rule increasingly provided a wider focus for ethnic conflict. In a sense, the policies of government and the politics of the provincial Congress sanctioned the increasingly free expression of communal antagonisms in public discourse. Constitutional negotiations about special electorates and communal safeguards, which brought in their train issues about rights and immunities, increasingly informed the way in which Hindus and Muslims perceived each other. The suspension of non-cooperation after the burning of the police station at Chauri

75 Pandey, *The Ascendancy of the Congress*, pp. 129–30 ff.; N. Gooptu, 'The Political Culture of the Urban Poor in North India, 1920–47', unpublished Ph.D. dissertation (Cambridge, University of Cambridge, 1991), chapter 5.

76 GOB, Home (Special) Files 792 of 1932, 793 (1) of 1932 and 793 (1), Parts I–III, of 1932. MSA. *Times of India*, 5 April 1932.

77 *Report of the Commission of Inquiry into the Cawnpore Riots and Resolution of the Government of the United Provinces, Parliamentary Papers, 1930–31* XII, Cmd 3891; Pandey, *The Ascendancy of the Congress*, pp.129–42.

78 For Bengal in the 1890s see Das Gupta, 'Factory Labour in Eastern India', pp. 299–300, 289–303; on Madras, in the early 1920s see E. D. Murphy, 'Class and Community in India: the Madras Labour Union 1918–21', *IESHR* 14:3 (1977), pp. 292–321; on Bombay in the 1920s and 1930s see Chandavarkar, *The Origins of Industrial Capitalism*, chapter 9; on Kanpur in the late 1930s see Chitra Joshi, 'Kanpur Textile Labour: Some Structural features of Formative Years', *Economic and Political Weekly* 16:33–4 (1981), p. 1827.

79 Chandavarkar, *The Origins of Industrial Capitalism*, chapter 9.

80 D. Chakrabarty, *Rethinking Working Class History. Bengal 1890–1940* (Princeton, N.J., Princeton University Press, 1989), pp. 199–203.

Chaura in February 1922 was regarded by many Muslims as a betrayal of – indeed, treachery against – the Khilafat.[81] The refusal of the Congress to countenance communal electorates and constitutional safeguards, for instance in the Nehru Report, was sometimes perceived as a signal that it intended to assert a Hindu hegemony and marginalise Muslim interests.[82] Such suspicions and anxieties were, of course, deepened and consolidated by the recurrent outbreaks of communal violence. By the mid-1940s, under the shadow of the partition of India, communal riots became more frequent and affected more people. Some saw the impending prospect of partition as a betrayal; others invested in the creation of Pakistan their utopian hopes and visionary dreams of the future; most viewed political developments with uncertainty and confusion, anxiety and suspicion. These conditions were liable to tip social tensions into communal violence. Indeed, as the Congress pressed for partition in the end game it created conditions conducive to the uninhibited expression of communal sentiment.[83]

However, there was one important theme of Congress rhetoric which had significant implications for the development of working-class politics. But its consequences were unintended and unforeseen. In the 1920s and 1930s the colonial state was subject to increasingly stringent political criticism. The rhetoric of the Congress became more explicitly anti-colonial. It no longer spoke of the un-Britishness of British rule in India but questioned the morality of the colonial state. It challenged the justice of its laws; it withheld its co-operation from the government; it elevated civil disobedience into an act of heroism. In the domain of working-class politics, its benefits accrued not to conciliatory Congress trade union organisers but to political groups which, seeking to represent labour, were marginalised by employers as well as the state. These publicists, notably communists, were forced by their own marginality in industrial politics, by their exclusion from the workplace, not only to adopt a stance of continuous opposition to the employers and the state but also, through their repeated intervention in the disputes of workplace and neighbourhood, to realise this rhetoric in political action.

Between 1914 and 1947 one of the most significant factors in working-class politics was the growing presence of the state. Attempts to recruit workers for a distant and irrelevant war caused considerable dis-

81 For an excellent study of the events at Chauri Chaura and their implications see S. Amin, *Event, Metaphor, Memory. Chauri Chaura 1922–92* (Berkeley and Los Angeles, Cal., University of California Press, 1995).
82 Mushirul Hasan, *Nationalism and Communal Politics in India 1885–1930* (New Delhi, Manohar, 1991).
83 Chatterji, *Bengal Divided.*

quiet in 1917. The economic dislocations of the war and its immediate aftermath were widely perceived as a failure of government.[84] The tariff, excise and monetary policies of the state impinged directly upon working conditions, employment and wages, and sharpened the lines of antagonism between workers and the state.[85] Large-scale, sometimes industry-wide, strikes – frequently, prolonged and bitter disputes – stoked official anxieties about public order. Strikers were now more closely and sometimes more forcefully policed. The intervention of the state to settle disputes worked more often to defeat their objectives and to negate their demands than to secure them, while trade union legislation passed in the 1930s was perceived within the labour movement as hostile and repressive.

The political experience of the working classes was constituted in relation to the state. The anti-colonial rhetoric of the Congress, by challenging the legitimacy of the state, paid handsome dividends to trade unions and political groups which pursued an active strategy of confrontation. Opposition to the state provided a focus around which a fragmented and sectionalised working class could at times coalesce. In the late 1920s and 1930s, in Bombay and Sholapur, and later in the decade in Coimbatore, Kanpur and Calcutta, communist trade unions gained considerably from their stance of consistent opposition to the state.

In the 1940s, however, this situation was reversed. After 1941 the communists abandoned their oppositional stance altogether. They sought actively to prevent strikes, to encourage greater productivity, even to dissuade workers from participation in nationalist agitations and tried to convince their once enthusiastic followers that they were fighting the people's war.[86] On the other hand, the Congress now appeared to be the only party which was willing to move against the state. Having accepted office in 1937, it had spurned it during the war. The Quit India movement was a far more impressive campaign than civil disobedience had been and it attracted widespread support in Bombay, Ahmedabad and Jamshedpur and more generally, in Gujarat, Uttar Pradesh and Bihar, Bengal and Orissa.[87] Between 1942 and 1945 Congressmen were imprisoned in droves while the communists, standing shoulder to shoulder with the British to fight the people's war, were

---

84 D. Arnold, 'Looting, Grain Riots and Government Policy in South India, 1918', *Past and Present* 84 (1979), p. 145.
85 Chandavarkar, *The Origins of Industrial Capitalism*, chapter 9.
86 The fate of the communists in Bombay during the Second World War can be followed in GOB Home (Special) File 543 (13) – B (4) of 1941–43 and File 543 (13) – B (5) of 1943–45. MSA.
87 G. Pandey (ed.), *The Indian Nation in 1942* (Calcutta, Bagchi, 1988).

ironically able to operate openly and legally. During this period, communist labour leaders entrenched themselves effectively in political institutions, and especially in the trade union movement, but their influence among the working classes began to wane. The people's war was to cast a lengthening shadow over its strategists as well as its foot soldiers. As the prospect of independence drew closer, it brought with it the promise of social renewal and transformation as well. Now that the political aims of *swaraj*[88] were about to be achieved, the social questions which had been subordinated to it would be more explicitly addressed. Between 1945 and 1947 the working classes could more closely identify the Congress with a political programme which appeared most consistently and effectively to encompass their interests. Ironically, at the same time, the objectives of the Congress now focused less on mobilising these aspirations than, increasingly, on curbing them.[89]

The relationship between the working classes and nationalism has conventionally been cast in oppositional terms. Historians, who took it for granted that class consciousness flowed naturally from the proletarian condition, investigated the labour movement as the prelude to the rise of socialism and readily assumed that the working classes had an inherent propensity to unity. When the working classes failed to fulfil their expectations, historians focused upon the impediments to their realisation. Among the most prominent has been the play of national, religious and ethnic identities. The history of the working classes in this perspective appeared to reflect a continuing internal struggle between class and other competing identities. The assumption that class consciousness flowed naturally from the proletarian condition has not precluded the rather pessimistic conclusion that it has readily yielded to identities of race, religion and nationality. But there is no reason to suppose that ethnic and national identities were necessarily or inherently more compelling for workers than the solidarities of class.

In the twentieth century Indian nationalists sometimes characterised 'communalism' as a product of ignorance and superstition, reflecting a rather more primitive vision of politics than their own. Similarly, Marxists have tended to portray class consciousness as an advanced stage of political development which had evolved beyond the primordial claims of religion, race and nationality and remained by comparison both more sophisticated and more vulnerable. Both sets of teleology have limited our understanding of working-class politics. What they have

88 Self-rule.
89 S. Sarkar, 'Popular Movements and National Leadership, 1945–47', *Economic and Political Weekly* 17:14–16 (1982), pp. 677–89.

shared in common is their proclivity for attributing a certain fixity to class, ethnic and national identities. Yet, as this chapter has argued, each of these identities was malleable and contingent upon changing contexts of production and politics. Workers' politics in India was constituted by the interplay between class and caste, region and religion, language and nation. The affinities of caste and community sometimes expressed class interests and were not simply produced by religious belief or an autonomous sphere of cultural practice. Communal difference took shape, in part, through the social organisation of workplace and neighbourhood and it was further elaborated and developed by public discourse, political argument and government policy. Class conflict could exacerbate communal tensions, just as the rhetoric of nationalism sometimes served to inscribe and deepen ethnic divisions. Moreover, class consciousness did not simply arise from production relations but was also shaped by workers' experience of politics and the state. The increasingly vociferous nationalist critique of the colonial state between 1920 and 1947 helped to clarify the lines of opposition which the working classes faced and thus served to define their own sense of mutuality. For much of this period the socialists and especially the communists in the labour movement reaped the political dividends, while the growth of labour militancy exposed the internal contradictions within the Congress, laid bare the limitations of its social vision and served to alienate the working classes. The identities of caste and religion, language and region which divided the nation also served to fragment the working classes. Indeed, the play of competing identities which threatened to undermine nationalism were also those which were actively being produced by the political and economic context which shaped class relations. To conclude from this interplay of the multiple identities of the working classes that they simply coexisted with each other would be rather tame. Certainly these identities were often produced by the same processes. Obviously, they could conflict with each other. The contingent nature of these identities suggests that, if our enquiries focused upon whether nationalism impeded the development of class consciousness or retreated before its rise, they would be misdirected, if simplified. Rather, these overlapping, if conflicting, identities were shaped by political discourses and political programmes which within particular and changing historical contexts provided the working classes with a means of comprehending their immediate situation while also suggesting how they might be realistically transformed.

Select bibliography

1 Between Scylla and Charybdis

Beilharz, P., *Labour's Utopias. Bolshevism, Fabianism, Social Democracy* (London, Routledge, 1992).

Berlanstein, L. R. (ed.), *Rethinking Labor History. Essays on Discourse and Class Analysis* (Urbana, Ill., University of Illinois Press, 1993).

Cummins, I., *Marx, Engels and National Movements* (London, Croom Helm, 1980).

Davis, H. B., *Nationalism and Socialism. Marxist and Labour Theories of Nationalism to 1917* (New York, Monthly Review Press, 1967).

Eley, G., and R. Grigor Suny (eds), *Becoming National. A Reader* (Oxford, Oxford University Press, 1996).

Garscha W. R., and C. Schindler (eds), *Labour Movement and National Identity*, ITH Tagungsberichte 30 (Vienna, ITH, 1994).

Haupt, G., M. Lowy and C. Weill (eds), *Les Marxistes et la question nationale* (Paris, Maspéro, 1974).

Hutchinson, J., and A. D. Smith (eds), *Ethnicity* (Oxford, Oxford University Press, 1996).

Jordan, G., and C. Weedon (eds), *Cultural Politics. Class, Gender, Race and the Postmodern World* (Oxford, Blackwell, 1995).

Marwick, A., *Class. Image and Reality in Britain, France and the United States since 1930*, 2nd edn (London, Macmillan, 1990).

Paluski, J., and M. Walters (eds), *The Death of Class* (London, Sage, 1995).

2 British and German Socialists

A short selection of key secondary works discussing the relationship between Labour, nationalism and ethnicity in Britain and Germany. Note that no works mentioned in the notes to this chapter are separately mentioned here.

Berger, S., *The British Labour Party and the German Social Democrats 1900–31* (Oxford, Oxford University Press, 1994).

Berger, S., 'Nationalism and the Left in Germany', *New Left Review* 206 (1994), pp. 55–70.

Buckland, P. and J. Belchem, (eds), *The Irish in British Labour History* (Liverpool, Institute of Irish Studies, 1993).

Conze, W., and Groh, D., *Die Arbeiterbewegung in der nationalen Bewegung. Die deutsche Sozialdemokratie vor, während und nach der Reichsgründung* (Stuttgart, Klett, 1966).

Field, G., 'Social Patriotism and the British Working Class: Appearance and Disappearance of a Tradition', *International Labor and Working Class History* 42 (1992), pp. 20–39.

Fielding, Steven, *Class and Ethnicity: Irish Catholics in England 1880–1939* (Buckingham, Open University Press, 1993).

Fryer, P., *Staying Power. The History of Black People in Britain* (London, Pluto, 1992).

Kulczycki, J. J., *The Foreign Worker and the German Labor Movement. Xenophobia and Solidarity in the Coal Fields of the Ruhr 1871–1914* (Oxford, Berg, 1994).

Lunn, K. (ed.), *Race and Labour in Twentieth Century Britain* (London, Frank Cass, 1985).

Panayi, P., *Immigration, Ethnicity and Racism in Britain 1815–1945* (Manchester, Manchester University Press, 1994).

Pelling, H., 'British Labour and British Imperialism', in *id.*, *Popular Politics and Society in Late Victorian Britain* (London, Macmillan, 1968), pp. 82–100.

Price, R., *An Imperial War and the British Working Class* (London, Routledge, 1972).

Schröder, H-C., *Sozialismus und Imperialismus. Die Auseinandersetzungen der deutschen Sozialdemokratie mit dem Imperialismusproblem und der 'Weltpolitik' vor 1914* (Hanover, Verlag für Literatur und Zeitgeschehen, 1968).
Taylor, M., 'Patriotism, History and the Left in Twentieth Century Britain', *Historical Journal* 33 (1990), pp. 971–87.
Wehler, H. U., *Sozialdemokratie und Nationalstaat. Nationalitätenfragen in Deutschland 1840–1914* (Göttingen, Vandenhoek und Ruprecht, 1962).

3 Spaniards, Catalans and Basques

Alvarez Junco, J., *El emperador del paralelo. Lerroux y la demogogia populista* (Madrid, Alianza, 1990).
Balfour, S., *The End of Spanish Empire 1898–1923* (Oxford, Clarendon Press, 1997).
Blas, Andrés de, *Tradición republicana y nacionalismo español 1834–1930* (Madrid, Taurus, 1991).
Connelly Ullman, J., *La semana trágica* (Barcelona, Ariel, 1972).
Cuadrat, X., *Anarquismo y socialismo en Cataluña. Los orígenes de la CNT* (Madrid, Revista del Trabajo, 1976).
Culla i Clarà, J. B., *El republicanisme lerrouxista a Catalunya 1901–1923* (Barcelona, Curiel, 1923).
Duarte, A., *El republicanisme català a la fi del segle XIX* (Vic, Eumo, 1987).
Durgan, A., 'Sindicalismo y marxismo en Cataluña: hacia la fundación de la Federación Obrera de Unidad Sindical', *Historia Social* 8 (1990), pp. 29–45.
Ealham, C., 'Anarchism and Illegality in Barcelona 1931–37', *Contemporary European History* 4:2 (1995), pp. 131–51.
Gabriel, P., 'Sindicalismo y sindicatos socialistas en Cataluña: la UGT 1888–1939', *Historia Social* 8 (1990), pp. 47–72.
Graham, H., 'Community, Nation and State in Republican Spain 1931–38', in C. Marolinero and A. Smith (eds), *Nationalism and the Nation in the Iberian Peninsula. Competing and Conflicting Identities* (Oxford, Berg, 1996), pp. 133–48.
Hernández Sandoica, E., and M. Fernanda Mancebo, 'Higiene y sociedad en la guerra de Cuba 1895–1898: notas sobre soldados y proletarios', *Estudios de Historia Social* 5–6 (1978), pp. 361–84.
Mees, L., *Nacionalismo vasco, movimiento obrero y cuestión social* (Bilbao, Fundación Sabino Arana, 1992).
Pablo Fusi, J., *El País Vasco. Pluralismo y nacionalidad* (Madrid, Alianza, 1985).
Serrano, C., *Fin de imperio. España 1895–98* (Madrid, Siglo XXI, 1984).
Smith, A., 'The Nation and the People: Nationalist Mobilization and the Crisis of 1895–98 in Spain', in A. Smith and E. Dávila-Cox (eds), *The Crisis of 1898. Colonial Redistribution and Nationalist Mobilisation* (Basingstoke, Macmillan, 1999), pp. 152–79.
Ucelay da Cal, E., *La Catalunya populista* (Barcelona, Malgrana, 1982).

4 Appropriating the symbols of the *patrie*?

Brubaker, R., *Citizenship and Nationhood in France and Germany*, (Cambridge, Mass., Harvard University Press, 1992).
Cross, G., *Immigrant Workers in Industrial France* (Philadelphia, Temple University Press, 1983).
Gallie, D., *Social Inequality and Class Radicalism in France and Britain* (Cambridge, Cambridge University Press, 1983).
Horne, J., *Labour at War. Britain and France 1914–18* (Oxford, Clarendon Press, 1991).
Jenkins, B., *Nationalism in France. Class and Nation since 1789* (London, Routledge, 1980).
Magraw, R., *A History of the French Working Class*, 2 vols (Oxford, Blackwell, 1992).

Milner, S., *The Dilemmas of Internationalism. French Syndicalism and the International Labour Movement 1900–14*, (Oxford, Berg, 1990).
Tucker, K., *French Revolutionary Syndicalism and the Public Sphere* (Cambridge, Cambridge University Press, 1996).
Weber, E., *Peasants into Frenchmen* (Stanford, Cal., Stanford University Press, 1976).

5 Labour and the national question in Poland

Haustein, U., *Sozialismus und nationale Frage in Polen* (Cologne, Böhlau, 1969).
Himka, J-P., *Socialism in Galicia. The Emergence of Polish Social Democracy and Ukrainian Radicalism 1860–1890*, (Cambridge, Mass., Harvard University Press, 1983).
Kieniewicz, S., *Historia Polski 1795–1918* (Warsaw, PWN, 1983).
Kieniewicz, S., *The Emancipation of the Polish Peasantry*, (Chicago, University of Chicago Press, 1969).
Kieniewicz, S. (ed.), *Polska XIX Wieku. Państwo, społeczeństwo, kultura* (Warszawa, Wiedza Powszechna, 1986).
Leslie, R. F., *Reform and Insurrection in Russian Poland 1856–65* (London, Athlone Press, 1963).
Leslie, R. F. (ed.), *The History of Poland since 1863* (Cambridge, Cambridge University Press, 1980).
Naimark, N. A., *The History of the 'Proletaryat'. The Emergence of Marxism in the Kingdom of Poland* (New York, Columbia University Press, 1981).
Tomicki, J. (ed.), *Polska odrodzona 1918–39. Państwo, społeczeństwo, kultura* (Warsaw, Wiedza Powszechna, 1982).
Tych, F., *Socjalistyczna irredenta* (Kraków, Wydawnictwo Literackie, 1982).
Żarnowski, J., *Społeczeństwo Drugiej Rzeczypospolitej* (Warsaw, PWN, 1973).

6 Stalin's victory over Lenin

Suny, R. G., *The Revenge of the Past. Nationalism, Revolution, and the Collapse of the Soviet Union* (Stanford, Cal., Stanford University Press, 1993).
Ascher, A., *The Revolution of 1905. Russia in Disarray* (Stanford, Cal., Stanford University Press, 1988).
Rawson, D. C., *Russian Rightists and the Revolution of 1905* (Cambridge, Cambridge University Press, 1995).
Rogger, H., 'Was there a Russian fascism? The Union of the Russian People', *Journal of Modern History* 36 (1964), pp. 398–415.
Pipes, R., *The Formation of the Soviet Union* (Cambridge, Mass., Harvard University Press, 1954).
Ezergailis, A., *The 1917 Revolution in Latvia* (Boulder, Colo., Westview Press, 1974).
Ezergailis, A., *The Latvian Impact on the Bolshevik Revolution. The First Phase, September 1917 to April 1918* (Boulder, Colo., Westview Press, 1974).
Hunczak, T., (ed.), *The Ukraine 1917–21. A Study in Revolution*, (Cambridge, Mass., Harvard University Press, 1977).
Adams, A. E., *Bolsheviks in the Ukraine. The Second Campaign 1918–19* (New Haven, Conn., Yale University Press, 1963).
Mace, J., *Communism and the Dilemmas of National Liberation: National Communism in Soviet Ukraine 1918–33*, (Cambridge, Mass., Harvard University Press, 1983).
B. Krawchenko, *Social Change and National Consciousness in Twentieth Century Ukraine* (London, Macmillan, 1985).

7 The working class in the United States

Barrett, J. R., 'Americanization from the Bottom up: Immigration and the Remaking of the Working Class in the United States 1880–1930', *Journal of American History* 79:3 (1992).

Bucki, C., 'Workers and Politics in the Immigrant City in the early Twentieth Century United States', *International Labor and Working Class History* 48 (1995).

Cohen, L., *Making a New Deal. Industrial Workers in Chicago 1919–39* (Cambridge, Cambridge University Press, 1986).

Gerstle, G., *Working Class Americanism. The Politics of Labor in a Textile City 1914–60* (Cambridge, Cambridge University Press, 1989).

Higham, J., *Strangers in the Land. Patterns of American Nativism 1860–1925* (New York, Atheneum, 1963).

Kirk, N., *Labour and Society in Britain and the USA 1780–1939* II, *Challenge and Accommodation 1850–1939* (Aldershot, Scolar Press, 1994).

Lane, A. T., *Solidarity or Survival? American Labor and European Immigration 1830–1924* (London, Greenwood Press, 1987).

Mink, G., *Old Labor and New Immigrants in American Political Development. Union, Party and State 1875–1920* (London, Cornell University Press, 1986).

Montgomery, D., 'Labor and the Republic in Industrial America 1860–1920', *Mouvement Social* 111 (1980).

Montgomery, D., *The Fall of the House of Labor. The Workplace, the State and American Labor Activism 1865–1925* (Cambridge, Cambridge University Press, 1987).

Montgomery, D., 'Labor and the Political Leadership of New Deal America', *International Review of Social History*, 39 (1994).

Roediger, D., 'Race and the Working Class Past in the United States: Multiple Identities and the Future of Labour History', *International Review of Social History*, 38, supplement 1 (1993).

Zieger, R. H., *American Workers, American Unions 1920–85* (Baltimore, Johns Hopkins University Press, 1986).

8 Labour, state and nation building in Australia

Curthoys, Ann, and A. Markus (eds) *Who are our Enemies? Racism and the Working Class in Australia* (Sydney, Hale and Iremonger, 1978).

Cochrane, Peter, *Industrialization and Dependence. Australia's Road to Economic Development* (Brisbane, University of Queensland Press, 1980).

Dunn, Michael, *Australia and the Empire. From 1788 to the Present* (Sydney, Fontana/Collins, 1984).

Fischer, Gerhard, '"Negative Integration" and an Australian Road to Modernity: Interpreting the Australian Home-front Experience in World War I', *Australian Historical Studies* 26:104 (1995), pp. 452–76.

Lovell, David W., 'Australian Socialism to 1917: a Study of the Relations between Socialism and Nationalism', *Australian Journal of Politics and History*, special issue, 40 (1994), pp. 144–59.

MacDonald, Roger, *Reflecting Labor. Images of Myth and Origin over 100 Years* (Canberra, National Library of Australia, 1991).

McLachlan, Noel, *Waiting for the Revolution. A History of Australian Nationalism* (Ringwood, Penguin Books, 1989).

McQueen, Humphrey, *A New Britannia. An Argument concerning the Social Origins of Australian Radicalism and Nationalism* (Ringwood, Penguin Books, 1970).

Osborne, Graeme, 'A Socialist Dilemma: Racism and Internationalism in the Victorian Socialist Party', in Ann Curthoys and A. Markus (eds), *Who are our Enemies?* (Sydney, Hale and Iremonger, 1978), pp. 112–28.

Murphy, John, 'Populism and Democracy: a Reading of Australian Radical Nationalism', *Thesis Eleven* 16 (1987), pp. 85–99.

Parkin, Andrew, 'Ethnic Politics: a Comparative Study of two Immigrant Societies, Australia and the United States', *Journal of Commonwealth and Comparative Politics* 15:1 (1977), pp. 22–38.

Stephen, Ann, and Andrew Reeves, *Badges of Labour, Banners of Pride. Aspects of Working Class Celebration* (Sydney, Allen and Unwin, 1986).

Ward, Russel, *The Australian Legend* (Melbourne, Oxford University Press, 1958).

Wells, Andrew, *Constructing Capitalism. An Economic History of Eastern Australia 1788–1901* (Sydney, Allen and Unwin, 1989).

Wells, Andrew, 'The Old Left Intelligentsia 1930–60' in B. Head and J. Walter (eds), *Intellectual Movements and Australian Society* (Melbourne, Oxford University Press, 1988), pp. 214–34.

White, R., *Inventing Australia. Images and Identity 1688–1980* (Sydney, Allen and Unwin, 1981).

9 Treading the diverse paths of modernity

Bekker, S., *Ethnicity in Focus* (Natal, Indicator South Africa, 1993).

Journal of Southern African Studies, 20:3 (1994), pp. 473–694. Special edition on ethnicity in southern Africa.

Mare, G., *Ethnicity and Politics in South Africa* (London, Zed Books, 1993).

Marks, S., *The Ambiguities of Dependence in South Africa. Class, Nationalism and the State in Twentieth Century Natal* (London, Johns Hopkins University Press, 1986).

Marks, S., and S. Trapido (eds), *The Politics of Race, Class and Nationalism in Twentieth Century South Africa* (London, Longman, 1987).

O'Meara, D., *Volkskapitalisme. Class, Capital and Ideology in the Development of Afrikaner Nationalism 1934–48* (Cambridge, Cambridge University Press, 1983).

Tamarkin, M., *Cecil Rhodes and the Cape Afrikaners. The Imperial Colossus and the Colonial Parish Pump* (London, Frank Cass, 1996).

Vail, L., *The Creation of Tribalism in Southern Africa* (London, James Currey, 1989).

Wilmsen, E., and P. McAllister (eds), *The Politics of Difference. Ethnic Premises in a World of Power* (Chicago, University of Chicago Press, 1996).

Although not solely concerned with the relationship between race, labour, nationalism and ethnicity in South Africa, the following are also useful references:

Beinart, W., and C. Bundy, *Hidden Struggles in Rural South Africa* (London, James Currey, 1987).

Journal of Southern African Studies 18:3 (1992), pp. 455–702. Special edition on political violence in southern Africa.

Van Onselen, C., *Studies in the Social and Economic History of the Witwatersrand*, 2 vols (London, Longman, 1982).

10 Nationalism, ethnicity and the working classes in India

Amin, S., *Event, Metaphor, Memory. Chauri Chaura 1922–92* (Berkeley, Cal., University of California Press, 1995).

Chakrabarty, D., *Rethinking Working Class History. Bengal 1890–1940* (Princeton, N.J., Princeton University Press, 1989).

Chandavarkar, R., *The Origins of Industrial Capitalism. Business Strategies and the Working Classes in Bombay 1900–40* (Cambridge, Cambridge University Press, 1994).

Chandavarkar, R., *Imperial Power and Popular Politics. Class, Resistance and the State in India 1850–1950* (Cambridge, Cambridge University Press, 1998).

Chatterjee, P., *Nationalist Thought and the Colonial World. A Derivative Discourse* (London, Zed Books, 1986).

Chatterji, J., *Bengal Divided. Hindu Communalism and Partition 1932–47* (Cambridge, Cambridge University Press, 1994).

Gallagher, J., G. Johnson and A. Seal (eds), *Locality, Province and Nation. Indian Politics 1870–1940* (Cambridge, Cambridge University Press, 1973).

Hasan, Mushirul, *Nationalism and Communal politics in India 1885–1930* (New Delhi, Manohar, 1991).

Murphy, E. D., *Unions in Conflict. A Comparative Study of Four South Indian Textile Centres 1918–39* (New Delhi, Manohar, 1981).

Newman, R., *Workers and Unions in Bombay 1918–29: A Study of Organization in the Cotton Mills* (Canberra, Australian National University, 1981).

Pandey, G., *The Ascendancy of the Congress in the UP 1926–34. A Study in Imperfect Mobilization* (Delhi, Oxford University Press, 1978).

Pandey, G., *The Construction of Communalism in Colonial North India* (Delhi, Oxford University Press, 1992).

Patel, S., *The Making of Industrial Relations. The Ahmedabad Textile Industry 1918–39*, (Delhi, Oxford University Press, 1987).

Sarkar, S., *Writing Social History* (Delhi, Oxford University Press, 1997).

Simeon, D., *The Politics of Labour under Late Colonialism. Workers, Unions and the State in Chota Nagpur 1928–39* (New Delhi, Manohar, 1995).

Sisson, R., and S. Wolpert (eds), *Congress and Indian Nationalism. The Pre-independence Phase* (Berkeley and Los Angeles, Cal., University of California Press, 1988).

Tomlinson, B. R., *The Indian National Congress and the Raj, 1929–42* (London, Macmillan, 1976).

Index

Act of Union (1910; South Africa) 217, 231
Action Française 106, 108–9, 114
Addison, Paul 43
AFL *see* American Federation of Labor
African National Congress (ANC) 217–19,
    221, 240
  and gradualism 222, 225–6, 229–30, 241
  and Second World War 227, 229
  and trade unions 227, 230
Afrikaner Nationalist Party *see* Nationalist
    Party (Afrikaner)
Afrikaners
  national identity 215–16, 217, 230–8
  and nationalism 9, 230–8
  proletarianisation 25, 216, 217, 231–2,
    238, 239
Afro-Americans, and labour movement
    174–6, 179–80, 184–5, 190
agriculture
  black African 220–1
  capitalist 220, 230
  collective 156, 157–8, 161
  colonial India 245–6, 249
  French 110
Agulhon, Maurice 118
Alberti, Rafael 79
Allard, M. 100
Alliance movement (USA) 176
American Federation of Labor (AFL) 168,
    179, 191
  and conservatism 16, 20, 164, 166, 177,
    182–4, 187, 188, 190
  and immigrants 169–70, 177, 182, 184,
    185
  and racism 176, 177, 185–6
American Indians, and labour movement
    175
anarchism
  and federalism 10, 72–3
  and internationalism 12, 64
  in Spain 66–8, 71–3, 77–8, 81–2, 85–8, 92
anarcho-syndicalism
  and internationalism 12, 20, 41–2, 74
  and the nation state 62, 64, 95
ANC *see* African National Congress
Anderson, Benedict 28
Andrews, Bill 235
Angell, Norman 33

anti-capitalism, in Russia 146
Anti-Socialist Union (Britain) 37
anticlericalism
  in France 7, 97, 112
  in Spain 71
antisemitism
  in Britain 44
  in France 107–9, 117
  in Germany 53
  in Poland 27, 129, 131, 138–43
  racist 22
  in Russia 14, 146, 162
apartheid in South Africa 230, 236, 237, 240
Arana, Sabino 90
Araquistáin, Luis 79
Armenia, and Soviet federation 159
army and socialism
  in Britain 35–6, 62
  in France 7–8, 101–3, 108
  in Germany 7, 34–5, 36, 49, 62
  in Poland 136
  in Russia 158
  in United States 179
assimilation
  and immigration 23, 112, 118, 139, 173,
    178, 181–2, 185
  and Jews 53
Australia
  and Commonwealth of Australia 193–4,
    199–202, 211
  and ethnicity 211–12, 214
  Eureka rebellion 198
  and First World War 7, 194, 205–8
  and immigration 198, 199, 203–4, 213
  and imperialism 205
  and Irish workers 26, 208, 211–13
  and isolationism 207–8, 209
  and labour integration 20, 195, 199–204
  and labour mobilisation 198, 200, 202,
    207
  and labour movement 4, 7, 9, 193–214
  labourism and nationalism 5, 204, 210–14
  and liberal nationalism 5, 7, 195, 197–8,
    205
  and national settlement 202–5, 207
  and 'official' state nationalism 7, 16
  and racism 213, 214
  and radical nationalism 208–10, 211

and state formation 4, 7, 194–5, 199, 211, 213
and transfer of state power 195–9
and 'white Australia' policy 24, 203–4
  see also Labor Party, Australia; trade unionism
Australian Labour Federation (ALF) 198–9
Austria, and neo-nationalism 2
Austro-Hungarian Empire
  and ethnicity 22–3
  and nationalism 5, 10
  and Poland 136–7
  and Social Democracy 14–15
Austro-Marxism 13, 14–15, 17
authoritarianism
  and anti-socialism 36, 63, 99
  socialist opposition to 18–19, 45, 77, 84, 92
autonomy
  cultural 14–15, 41–2, 52, 142–3, 150–1
  national 94, 124, 150
  regional 14, 159, 161, 252
  territorial 134–5, 150–1
Azaña, Manuel 71
Azerbaijan, and Soviet federation 159

Bakunin, Michael 10
Balfour, Sebastian 69
Banker, Shankarlal 260
Baptista, Joseph 254
Barbusse, Henri 104
bargaining, collective 20, 76, 79, 87, 99, 182, 189–90
Barnes, George 48
Barrès, Maurice 103, 105, 107–8
Barrett, James R. 181–2
Basque nationalism 2, 64, 66, 68, 77, 80, 88–91, 92
  and Spanish socialism 79, 84 n.32, 92
Basque Nationalist Party (PNV) 88–90
Bauer, Otto 14–15, 40, 134
Bax, Ernest Belfort 61
Bebel, August 37, 39, 44, 54
Beinart, William 228–9
Belchem, John 23
Belorus/Byelorussia
  and Poland 15, 122, 125, 132, 134
  and Soviet federation 159
Berlin, Ira 170–1
Bernstein, Eduard 17, 53, 60
bhadralok leaders 257
Biétry, Pierre 109, 115

Birla, G. D. 255
Blasco, Ibañez, Vincente 70,73
Blatchford, Robert 31, 35–6, 43, 48
Boer War 61, 217, 230, 232, 235
Bolsheviks
  and nationality 14, 150–2
  revolution 20, 78, 95, 106, 132, 133, 152, 185
  and Soviet federations 152–8, 159–60
  see also Communist Party (Russia)
Bonapartism, populist 106–7
Borotbist party *see* Ukrainian Socialist Revolutionary (SRs) Party
Bose, Subhas Chandra 254, 255
Boston, Ray 170
Botha, Louis 231–2, 234
Boulangism 16, 65, 107–9
bourgeoisie *see* middle classes
Bradford, H. 221
Brailsford, Henry Noel 61
Braun, Otto 44, 48
Britain
  and class and national identity 31–63
  and colonialism 4, 196–8, 230–8
  and First World War 16, 18, 36, 46–8, 63
  inter-war nationalisation 48–51
  and Irish workers 24, 26–7, 54–5, 57–8, 97
  and labour movement
    and employers 37, 61–2
    immigration and ethnic minorities 53, 54–8, 63
    and imperialism 43–4, 60, 61–2, 63, 100
    integration 15–16, 31, 32–9, 46, 47, 57, 62–3
    and judiciary 36, 62
    and liberal nationalism 5, 7
    and militarism 35–6, 43, 46, 61
    and national discourse 42–4
    nationalisation 45–6, 49–51, 63
    and religion 32–3, 38, 62, 97
  and monarchy and imperialism 8, 58–62, 63
  as multinational state 2, 42
  and 'official' state nationalism 8
  parliamentarianism 8, 38
  and working-class Toryism 16, 38, 97, 100
  see also Australia; Conservative Party; imperialism; India; Labour Party (Britain); 'New Labour'; South Africa; trade unionism
British Union of Fascists 57
Broederbond (South Africa) 236–7

Bröger, Karl 46
Bucki, Cecelia 165, 192
Buhle, Paul 186
Bukharin, N. I. 151, 159
Bund
  in Poland 129–30, 142
  in Russia 150

capitalism
  in Australia 193–4, 203, 207, 208
  in Britain 46, 61
  in France 96, 97–8, 100–1, 107–8
  and globalisation 1–2, 194
  in India 253–5, 262
  and the nation state 10, 28–9
  in Poland 124, 125, 141
  in South Africa 215–16, 220–1, 230, 232,
    235–6, 238–9, 241
  in Spain 72, 74, 79
  in USA 165, 167–9, 173, 177, 179–82, 184,
    186, 189
  welfare 188
Caporali, Emile 114
Carpenter, Edward 45, 61
caste system
  and nationalism 243–4, 253
  and working class 247, 250–1, 257–8, 265,
    269
Castles, Frank 203
Catalan Republican Left (ERC) 85–8, 91
Catalan Republican Party (PRC) 84
Catalanism 2, 64, 68, 77, 80–8, 92, 182
  and labour movement 86–7
  and migrant labour 28, 82, 87–8, 91
  and political parties 83–6
  and republicanism 70, 85–6
  and socialism 68, 79, 91
Catholicism
  American Irish 173
  Australian Irish 211–12
  and Basque nationalism 88–91
  British Irish 54
  and Catalanism 80
  and labour movement 24, 32–3, 38, 52, 58,
    97, 99, 109
  and middle class 65, 80
  Polish 128–9, 141
  and republicanism 67, 95, 106–7, 119
  and socialism 54–5, 69, 72
Centre Party (Germany) 38
Cercle Proudhom 109
Childe, Gordon 206

Church and labour movement 7, 32–3, 38,
  62, 65, 97, 108, 146, 232, 235
  see also Catholicism; Protestantism;
    religion
Churchill, Randolph 38
CIO *see* Congress of Industrial Organisations
citizenship
  and class 1, 39, 63, 99, 119, 167, 172, 187,
    192, 263
  and ethnic minorities 52, 53, 174, 191
  and liberal nationalism 4, 165–6, 204
class
  and citizenship 1, 39, 63, 99, 119
  class struggle 12, 20, 40, 48, 68, 88, 115,
    122–3, 125, 157, 185
  construction 29, 165–6, 242, 247–8, 253
  and ethnicity 26, 27, 88, 90–1, 129–30,
    141, 165, 169, 174–6, 185, 212
  and gender 176, 184–5, 190, 191, 237–8,
    240
  and liberal nationalism 4, 91
  and loyalty xii, 2, 6, 11–13, 32, 115
  and patriotism 95, 115
  and postmodernism 29
  and racism 58, 225–6
  and revolution 78–80, 86, 99
  see also identity; middle classes; peasants;
    solidarity; working class
class consciousness *see* identity, national, and
  class
Clemenceau, Georges 99
clientelism 25, 65, 109
CNT (Confederación Nacional del Trabajo;
  Catalonia) 28, 76, 80, 84–8, 91
Cohen, Lizabeth 190
Cole, Douglas 214
colonialism
  and ethnicity 22
  and independence struggles 30
  internal 93
  and liberal nationalism 4, 5
  and militarism 18, 19–20
  and 'official' state nationalism 6, 9
  and racism 24
  and reformism 17
  and republicanism 69–71
  and socialism 18, 60–1, 74, 100
  see also imperialism; India
colonies, white settler
  and ethnicity 22
  and immigration 26
  and independence 30, 196–7

and labour differentiation 27
and labour republicanism 20
and official state nationalism 16–17
see also Australia; South Africa; United
    States
communalism, in India 243, 248, 252–3, 257,
    264–6, 268–9
Communism
    European 19
    in India 256–7, 262–3, 265–9
    and internationalism 12, 19–20
    and nationalism and socialism 1, 11–12,
        13–14
    and 'Popular Front' 19, 77, 80, 109, 111,
        114, 120
    see also Marxism
Communist Party of America 28, 185
Communist Party of Australia 20, 208–10
Communist Party of Catalonia (PSUC) 86,
    88, 91
Communist Party of France (PCF)
    and First World War 104
    and immigration 114, 118
    and imperialism 101
    as New Jacobins 94–5, 99, 109, 119
Communist Party of Germany (KPD) 20, 36,
    41
Communist Party of Great Britain (CPGB)
    44, 209
Communist Party of Russia (RKP) 14, 155,
    158, 159
Communist Party of South Africa (CPSA)
    and labour militancy 229–30, 235
    and 'Native Republic' policy 225–6, 240
    and Second World War 226–7
Communist Party of Spain (PCE), and Civil
    War 76–7, 78, 91
Communist Party of Ukraine (KPU) 154–5,
    157–8, 159, 161–2
Communist Workers' Party of Poland
    (KPRP) 132–4, 137, 138, 142
Communist Workers' and Peasants' Bloc
    (BOC: Catalonia) 86, 91
Comorera, Joan 86
Congress of Industrial Organisations (CIO)
    and immigrants 20, 27
    and the state 189, 191
    and unskilled labour 20, 190
Connolly, James 15
conscription
    in Australia 205–6, 207
    in France 101, 102–3

in Germany 34
in Spain 65
Conservative Party (Britain)
    and the Churches 33
    and labour movement 37, 50, 191
    and parliament 38
    and trade unionism 36
Conservative Party (Germany), and
        parliament 38
Constant, Henri 114–15
corporatism, in Spain 77, 80
Costa, Joaquín 75
culture
    and autonomy 14–15, 41–2
    democratic 73
    ethnic 224, 232–8, 240–1
    and identity 142, 215, 224, 232–8,
        239–40
    labour movement 21, 44–6, 63, 71–3, 76
    popular 46, 101
    working-class 21, 76, 96, 101, 111, 118–19,
        128, 162, 250
Czech lands, and liberal nationalism 4

Darwinism, Social 26, 60, 108, 178, 218,
    240
David, Eduard 33, 47
Déat, Marcel 109
democracy *see* nationalism, democratic;
        Social Democracy
Democratic Party (USA) 174–5
Déroulède, Paul 107, 108
Desai, Mahadev 260
Deutsch, Karl 28
Dicenta, Joaquín 73
discourse
    competing 3, 9, 80, 122
    and labour movement 39–44
    and nationalism 18, 28, 62–3, 74–5, 77,
        207
    racial 52–3
Dmowski, Roman 132, 138
Domann, Peter 60
Doriot, Jacques 101, 109
Drahomanov, Mykhailo 126
Dreyfus affair 99, 102, 120
Drumont, Eduard 108
Dube, John 219–20, 221–2
Dubreuil, Henri 114
Duncker, K. (quoted) 31
Dutch Reformed Church 232, 235
Dutt, Rajani Palme 209

Eastern Europe
  and ethnic nationalism 1
  and Russian nationalism 14
Ebert, Friedrich 60
economics
  agricultural 215
  and immigration 111–16
  and imperialism 100–1
  and labour movement 5, 188–9
  and nationalism xi–xii, 98–9, 105, 107,
    131, 135, 138–9, 166, 199, 200
  and regulation 169, 189
education
  and anti-socialism 32, 33, 38, 62
  and ethnic nationalism 235
  and 'official' state nationalism 6, 7, 21
  secular 96–7, 104, 107
  and socialism 45, 71–2, 76
empire, multinational 4–5, 10, 13–14
  and ethnicity 22–3
  see also Austro-Hungarian Empire; Britain;
    imperialism; Russia
employers
  and anti-socialism 37, 38, 62, 183
  and anti-unionism 77, 92, 168, 174,
    187–90, 200, 257, 260–2, 265–6
  and ethnic minorities 185, 258
  and ethnic nationalism 90
  and immigrant labour 52–3, 112, 115,
    179–80, 181–2, 185
  and independence struggles 254–5
  and paternalism 8, 90, 97, 98–9
Endecja (National Democrats; Poland) 131,
  138–40, 143
Engels, Friedrich 11, 44, 68 n.6, 126
Englander, D. (quoted) 35
Erdmann, Lothar 49
Erfurt Programme, and Social Democracy
  39, 125
essentialism, and nationalism 10, 17, 28, 53
Estonia
  and Poland 133
  and Soviet federation 155
ethnicity
  and class 26, 27, 88, 90–1, 129–30, 165,
    169, 174–6, 185, 212
  construction 29, 164–5, 191
  and ethnic conflict 1, 25, 224, 243, 248,
    252–3, 257, 264–6, 269
  and immigration 22–6, 63, 169–73
  and labour movement 21–8, 149, 164,
    168–76, 185, 190–1

  and racism 22–3, 26, 170, 217
  see also identity; nationalism, ethnic
European Union 1–2
Evans, Richard 36
exceptionalism, United States 164, 166,
  188–91, 192
Exclusion Act of 1882 (USA) 174

Fabian Society (Britain) 61
Falski, Leon 127
fascism
  in France 94, 95, 108–9, 120
  and liberal democracy 18–19, 30, 191
  in Spain 77, 80
  and Union of Russian People 146, 162
Federal Republicans (Spain) 81
federalism 10
  in Poland 125–6, 133–4
  in Soviet Russia 152–8
  in Spain 66, 72–3, 79
  see also Australia
Fédération Républicaine (France) 109, 115
Ferrer, Francisco 73 n.11
Ferry, Jules 96, 100
Fichte, Johann Gottlieb von 3, 40
Fink, Leon 167, 170, 179
First International 39
First World War
  and Australian labour 7, 194, 205–8
  and British labour 16, 18, 36, 46–8
  and French labour 16, 18, 24, 95, 97–8,
    103–6, 113
  and German labour 16, 18, 41, 46–8, 53–4
  and Indian labour 266–7
  and Lenin 151, 155
  and Polish labour 133, 136–7
  and South African labour 232, 233–4
  and Spanish labour 84
  and United States labour 180, 182–3,
    185–7
Fischer, Gerhard 205
Fitzpatrick, Brian 210
Foner, Eric 175
Ford, Henry 181
France
  and Boulangism 16, 65, 107–9
  and democratic nationalism 94
  and ethnic nationalism 95
  and First World War 16, 18, 24, 95, 97–8,
    103–6, 113
  and 'great state' nationalism 13
  and imperialism 100–2, 117, 119

and labour integration 7–8, 16, 97–100, 102, 105
and labour mobilisation 103–4, 106, 111
and militarism 101–4
as nation state 93, 117
and neo-nationalism 2, 108, 111, 117, 120
and 'official' state nationalism 7–8
and radical right populisms 106–10, 113–14, 116–20
and revolutionary traditions 7–8, 94–5
Second Republic 94, 106
Third Republic 5, 7, 18, 93–120
see also immigration; peasants; republicanism; Socialist Party (France); trade unionism
Franco, Francisco 77, 80
Franko, Ivan 126
Frederiksen, B. 239
Friedländer, Otto 49
Fusi, Juan Pablo 75
Fyfe, Hamilton 59

Galdós, Pérez 73
Gandhi, Chhaganlal 260
Gandhi, Mohandas (Mahatma) 254–5, 260–1
Gapon, Fr 145–6
Gaxotte, Pierre 114
Gellner, Ernest 28
gender, and class 176, 184–5, 190, 191, 237–8, 240
General Strike of 1926 (Britain) 37, 39
Georgia
  and revolution of 1905 148
  and Soviet federation 159
Germany
  and class and national identity 31–63
  and First World War 16, 18, 41, 46–8, 53–4, 63, 103–4
  and labour mobilisation 42
  and labour movement 7
    and employers 37, 62
    and immigration and ethnic minorities 51–8, 63
    and imperialism 60–1, 63
    integration 31, 32–9, 46, 47, 56, 62–3, 99
    and judiciary 36, 62
    and monarchy 8, 59–60, 63
    and national discourse 39–42, 44
    nationalisation 44–6, 48–9, 52, 63
    and militarism 18, 34–6, 44–5, 46, 48, 60

and National Socialism 6, 39, 49
and neo-nationalism 2
and parliamentarianism 37–8, 47, 49
and Poland 40, 52, 122, 133
revolution of 1918/19 41, 47, 48, 49, 52
Weimar Republic 18–19, 37–41, 48–9, 52
see also army; Church; republicanism; Social Democratic Party (Germany); trade unionism
Gerstle, Gary 187, 191
Gesuiwerde Nationalist Party (South Africa) 236
ghettoes 56–7, 140
Ghijaldo, Alberto 64
Giliomee, H. 236–7
Glasier, Bruce 55
globalisation
  and capitalism 1–2
  and socialism 10
Gompers, Samuel 170, 177, 182, 183
gradualism 8, 16, 182, 222, 225–6, 229–30, 241
Great Depression
  in Australia 194, 207, 210
  in France 107, 109
  in India 262
  in South Africa 226–7, 235–6
  in Spain 77–9, 87
  in United States 164, 179, 188–9
Greece, independence 4
Griffiths, Dan 33
Griffuelles, Victor 117
Guesde, Jules 13, 74, 111, 114, 115
Gumede, Josiah 225
Gutman, Herbert 165, 170–1

Halévy, Elie 97
Hardie, Keir 46, 55, 58, 61
Haubach, Theodor 49
Henderson, Arthur 47, 49–50
Herbert, Ulrich 54
Herder, Johann Gottfried von 3, 10
Hertzog, J. B. M. 232, 234, 235–6
Higgins, Esmonde 205 n.21
Hinton, James 165
history
  ethnic national 232, 235, 236
  postmodernist 3, 29
  radical nationalist 210
Hobsbawm, Eric v, 13, 28, 29
Hobson, J. A. 43, 61

Hroch, M. 6 n.9
Hughes, William Morris 205, 206, 207
Hyndman, H. M. 43, 61

Ibárruri, Dolores 77
identity, national
    and class 2, 11–14, 29, 242
        in Australia 4, 199–200, 211
        in Britain 51, 54, 62
        in France 97, 119
        in Germany 51, 62
        in India 242, 247–8, 257–8, 268–9
        in Poland 122–32, 136–7
        in South Africa 215, 217, 219–20,
            228–30, 239, 241
        in Spain 64, 91
        in United States 166, 167–8
    construction 28–9, 164–6
    as contingent 3, 29–30, 244–5, 251, 269
    and culture 51, 142, 224, 232–8, 239–41
    and ethnicity 1, 21–2, 25, 28, 242
        in India 248–53, 264, 268, 269
        in Poland 139–40
        in South Africa 28, 217, 219–24, 228,
            230–2, 234–41
        in Spain 91–2
        in United States 165
    fragmentation 3
    and local identity 28, 135–6, 218, 240,
248
    and multiple identities 2, 28–30, 221–2,
        251–2, 269
    rural black African 217–19
    and Social Democracy 1, 17, 28, 42
    and war 103–4, 207
Iglesias, Pablo 75
immigration
    and assimilation 23, 54, 112, 173, 178,
        181–2, 185
    Australia 198, 199, 203–4, 213
    and Basque nationalism 88–9
    and Catalanism 80, 82, 87–8, 91
    and First World War 113, 180
    France 24, 93, 107–9, 110–14, 118
    and Irish workers 24, 26–7, 54–5, 57–8, 97
    and labour movement xii, 22–6, 51–8, 63,
        93–4, 165, 170–6
    opposition to 19, 26, 106, 109
    restriction 23, 51, 55–6, 114, 172, 175, 177,
        180, 182, 184, 187
    United States 24–7, 165, 169–87, 190–1,
        192

Imperial League against Social Democracy
    (Germany) 37
imperialism
    British 43–4, 60, 61–2, 63, 100
        and Australia 196–8, 205
        and South Africa 61, 215, 217–19,
            230–8, 239–41
    and 'civilising mission' 15, 18, 60–1, 100,
        119
    French 19, 100–2, 117
    German 60–1, 63
    internal 138
    and labour movement 7, 21, 31, 43–4,
        138
    and national stereotyping 22
    Polish 15, 122, 132–43
    and rise of nationalism 6
    'social' 98, 100, 133, 137–8
    Soviet 133
    Spanish 69–71, 74, 101
    US 4, 177, 178–9, 183, 185
    see also empire, multinational
indenture systems 204, 249–50
Independent Social Democratic Party
    (Germany; USPD) 41
India 242–69
    class and ethnicity 248–53, 264, 269
    class and nationalism 5, 242–4, 247,
        253–69
    and colonialism xi, 61, 243, 245–7, 252,
        259–60, 266–7, 269
    and labour integration 243, 263–4
    and labour mobilisation 243, 245, 257,
        268
    and migrant labour 25, 246–51
    and non-cooperation and civil
        disobedience 259–67
    partition 266
    Quit India movement 259, 267
    and socialism 9, 243, 264, 269
    see also caste system; communalism; trade
        unionism
Indian National Congress
    and labour movement 9, 243, 247, 253–6,
        258–63, 266, 268–9
    and nationalism 253, 264, 266–7
    in power 9, 263–6
individualism, United States 166, 169, 177–8,
    186
Industrial and Commercial Workers' Union
    (South Africa; ICU) 218, 219–22,
        225–6, 229, 240–1

industrial relations
  Britain 179
  France 104–5
  Germany 37, 39
  India 254–5
  Russia 146
  USA 177, 179, 183, 189–90
  see also militancy, labour; trade unionism
Industrial Workers of the World
  Australia 206
  United States 176, 183, 184–6
industrialisation
  in England 46
  in France 94, 98–9, 110, 115
  in India 247, 249
  in Poland 123–4, 141
  in South Africa 215, 235, 236, 240
  in Spain 80, 88–90
  in Ukraine 149, 162
Inkatha movement (South Africa) 220, 240
intellectuals
  and anti-state nationalism 15
  and ethnicity and nationalism 217, 219,
    230–2, 235, 239–40
  and patriotism 125, 137
  and radical nationalism 208–10, 211
  and socialism 11, 13, 124
  and state building 205, 206–7
  and trade unionism 200
internationalism
  and inter-ethnic solidarity 26, 101
  and labour movement xi, 1, 2, 6, 39, 62,
    64, 91, 114, 119
  and Marxism 1, 17, 39–40, 107, 128
  and patriotism 31, 40–1
  and Social Democracy 1, 17–18, 128
  and socialism 2, 6, 12–14, 19–20, 130, 137,
    185–6, 208–9, 214
Ireland
  and Irish workers *see* Australia; Britain;
    United States
  and socialism and nationalism 15, 42
irredentism 4, 123–32, 135, 137–8
isolationism
  Australian 207–8, 209
  United States 178
Italy, unification 4

Jaurès, Jean 93, 94, 100, 108, 111, 116
Jews
  in England 27, 54
  in France 107–9, 117

  in Germany 53
  in Lithuania 126–7
  in Poland 27, 129–30, 135, 138–43
  in Russia 146–7, 150
  in Ukraine 126–7, 162
  in United States 27
  see also antisemitism
jobbers (India) 249–50, 258
Jones, Gareth Stedman 51
Jones, Maldwyn 170, 172
Jouhaux, Léon J. 98, 105, 119
judiciary, and labour movement 36, 38, 62,
    168, 179, 188

Kanatchikov, S. I. 149
Kautsky, Karl 10–11, 17, 40, 53, 74
Kerensky, A. F. 153
Khilafat movement 261, 266
Kiernan, Viktor 51
Kirk, Neville 3, 5, 191
Knights of Labor (USA) 168–70, 174,
    176
Koestler, Arthur 115
Kohn, Hans 6
Kon, Feliks 130
KPD *see* Communist Party (Germany)
KPRP *see* Communist Workers' Party of
    Poland
KPU *see* Communist Party of Ukraine
Krishak Praja Party (India) 263–4
Ku Klux Klan 187

Labor Party, Australia (ALP)
  and ethnicity 24, 26
  and First World War 205–8
  and national federation 199–202
  and national identity 193–4
  and national settlement 202–5
  and nationalism xi, 16, 193, 194–5, 201–2,
    205–7, 211
  and racism 214
  and radical nationalism 208–9
  and states 204–5, 206, 210
labour market
  and attitudes to nationalism xi
  casual 185, 245–7, 250–1
  and immigrants 110–12
  imperial 198
  and labour shortage 226–8, 245, 249–50,
    258
  oversupply 251
  polarisation 139–41, 142

labour market (*cont.*)
  and racism 173–4
Labour Monthly 209
labour movement
  and antisemitism 22, 27, 44, 53
  and education 7–8, 33, 252
  and ethnicity 21–8, 51–8, 149, 169–76,
    185, 190–1
  integration into nation state *see under*
    individual states
  inter-war 48–51
  and internationalism xi, 1, 2, 6, 39, 91,
    111
  leadership 21, 26, 29, 104, 114, 170,
    255–7, 260–1, 268
  in national discourses 39–44
  and national state xi, 6–7, 15–16, 31, 64,
    128–91, 242
  nationalisation 44–6, 48–51, 52, 58, 63
  and nationalism xi, 4–5, 15–16, 28–30, 91,
    197, 210–14
  and 'official state' nationalism 6–7, 16
  and racism 27–8, 48, 101–2
  segmentation 52–3, 104, 112
  see also Communism; Marxism; militancy,
    labour; mobilisation of labour;
    nationalism; socialism; working
    class
Labour Party (Britain)
  and the Churches 33
  and immigration 54, 55
  and imperialism 61
  and Irish workers 54–5
  and monarchy 58–9, 63
  and nationalisation 49–51
  and nationalism 21, 43–4, 63
  parliamentary party 38
  and support for war 18, 47–8, 63
Labour Party (South Africa), and Afrikaner
    nationalism 24–5, 233, 234, 239
Land Act of 1913 (South Africa) 219–20
Lane, A. T. 169–70, 175
language and nationality 11
  in France 93, 96, 118
  in Germany 56
  in India 243, 247, 251, 269
  in Poland 129, 140
  in South Africa 230–1, 235
  in Ukraine 148, 156, 162
  in USA 181
Largo Caballero, Francisco 76, 79
Lasalle, Ferdinand 40

Latvia
  and Poland 133
  and revolution of 1905 148
  and Soviet federation 152–3, 154–6,
    157–8
Latvian Social Democratic Party (LSD) 150,
    152–3, 155–6, 157
Le Pen, Jean-Marie 111, 116
Leber, Julius 49
Legien, Carl 47
Legitimism, France 106–7
Leipart, Theodor 49
Lenin, V. I.
  and Australian Labor Party 193, 194
  and national identity 13–14, 84, 143,
    153–8, 162–3, 225
  and Stalin 14, 150–2, 154, 158–60, 161
Lensch, Paul 47
Lerrouxism (Spain) 70–1, 81–3, 88
Lewis, John L. 190, 191
liberal democracies
  and opposition to fascism 18–19, 30, 77
  and white settler colonies 196–7
Liberal Party (Britain) 33, 38, 54, 231
liberalism
  distrust 77
  and exclusion 5–6, 14
  and inclusion 218, 240
  see also nationalism, liberal
Liebknecht, Wilhelm 39, 60
Limanowski, Bolesław 124–5, 126
List, Friedrich 11
Lithuania
  and Poland 15, 122, 125–7, 134
  and Soviet federation 155, 159
Lithuanian Social Democracy (LSD) 126
Lliga Regionalista (Catalonia) 81, 83
localism, and national identity 129, 135–6,
    199
Lombroso, Cesare 116
Louis Napoleon 106–7
Louis, Paul 100
loyalty, class/national
  in Australia 205, 206
  in Britain 32, 44
  in France 94, 104, 115
  in Germany 32, 41, 44, 49
  in South Africa 221
  in United States 178, 180–1
  see also patriotism; solidarity
loyalty, class/national xii, 2, 6, 11–13
Lüdtke, Alf 42

Luxemburg, Rosa
  and internationalism 12–13, 128
  and Jews 53
  and territorial autonomy 135

MacDonald, James Ramsay 17, 48, 49–50, 61
McLachlan, Noel 203, 211
Majority Social Democratic Party (Germany; MSPD) 48
Malan, D. F. 236, 237
managerialism, USA 177
Mandela, Nelson 230
Marks, J. B. 229
Marks, Shula 235
Martin, Kingsley 58
Marx, Karl, and Poland 126
Marxism
  Austro-Marxism 14, 17
  and black working class 226
  and colonialism 17
  and economic determinism 59
  and internationalism 1, 17, 39–40, 107, 128
  and the nation state 10–12, 13, 15, 39–40, 62
  and nationalism 40, 68, 110, 268
Mayer, Gustav 47
Mazzini, Guiseppe 3–4
Mensheviks, and nationality 150–1, 152
Merrheim, Adolphe E. 98
Michels, Robert 53
middle classes
  in Australia 205, 207, 210
  and Basque nationalism 89
  and Catalan nationalism 82–3, 85
  and the Church 65, 97
  and First World War 47
  and imperialism 21
  and labour movement 7, 9, 37, 38, 109
  and nationalism 6, 12–13, 15, 121, 146, 155, 161
  in Poland 121, 124–5, 141
  and Spanish republicanism 66–7, 69, 70–1, 74, 83, 85–6
  see also intellectuals
Mierendorff, Carlo 49
militancy, labour
  in Australia 206, 207, 208, 210
  in Britain 35, 56
  in Catalonia 87
  in France 93, 95, 97–8, 104–5, 108, 112–13, 119

in Germany 52, 56
in India 254–5, 257–64, 267, 269
in Poland 127
in South Africa 226–30, 231–2, 234, 238, 241
in Spain 19, 70, 78–80, 85–6
in USA 168, 180, 183–4, 186–7, 190
militarism
  Britain 35–6, 43, 46, 61
  and colonialism 18, 19–20
  France 101–4
  Germany 18, 34–6, 44–5, 46, 48, 60
  Spain 65, 70–1
Millerand, Alexandre 98
Milner, Alfred 231
minorities, ethnic
  in Britain 53, 54–8, 63
  in Germany 13, 51–2, 63
  in multinational states 2, 22, 25, 51–8
  in Poland 122, 125–7, 132, 134–7, 138–43
  in Russia 147, 159–60
  in USA 175, 179–80
  in the workplace xi, 139–42
Mintz, Jerome B. 72
Mishkinsky, M. 142
mobilisation of labour 6–8
  see also under individual states
mobility, social 46, 54, 57, 96, 170, 245, 252, 258
monarchy
  Britain 8, 58–9, 63
  France 106–7, 109, 114
  Germany 8, 59–60, 63
  Spain 65, 67, 71, 75
Montgomery, David 167–8, 170–2, 173–4, 176, 177, 179–80, 186–7
Moodie, D. 224, 227
Motte, Eugène 115
Mühsam, Erich 49
Murphy, Richard 57

Nairn, Tom 42
Napoleon I 106
nation state
  and centralisation 118
  construction 28–9
  democratisation 62–3
  and exclusivism 5–6, 14, 59, 62, 184
  'historic'/'non-historic' 11, 126
  and labour integration *see under individual states*

nation state (*cont.*)
  and labour movement xi, 6–7, 15–16, 31,
      40–1, 43, 64, 68, 247
  and liberalism *see* nationalism, liberal
  and Marxism 10–12, 13, 15, 39–40, 62
  and nation building 6, 10–11, 14, 39,
      195–205, 206, 211, 213–14
  and statism 65–6, 132–43
  and war 205–8
  see also loyalty; working class
National Democrats (Endecja; Poland) 131,
    138–40, 143
National Industrial Recovery Act of 1933
    (USA) 189–90
National Labor Union (USA) 168–9, 176
National Labour Party (Britain) 50–1
National Socialism
  and racial nationalism 6, 30, 39, 53–4
  and Social Democratic Party 49
National Workers' Party (NPR; Poland) 137
nationalism
  African 216, 217–22, 240–1
  Afrikaner 25, 230–8, 239–40
  anti-state 15, 81
  civic 17–18, 197, 217, 239
  and class 242–5
  construction 28–9, 164–6, 191, 211
  cultural 1, 15
  democratic 20, 42, 63, 94, 195, 197–8, 205
  economic 11
  ethnic 1, 6, 18, 22
    in Australia 211
    in Britain 42, 56–7
    in France 95, 117
    in Germany 56, 63
    in South Africa 217, 230–8, 239–40
    in Spain 80–91
    in United States 187
  'great state' 13–15, 162
  integral 7, 17–19, 30, 143, 207, 214
  irredentist 4, 6 n.9, 123–32, 135, 137–8
  Jacobin 93–120
  and labour movement xi, 4–5, 15–16,
      28–30, 197, 242–3
  left-wing 30
  liberal 3–5, 6, 10–11, 13–18, 28–30
    in Germany 40
    in Spain 64–6, 68, 73–7, 84, 91–2
  literary 210
  and Marxism 40
  New 2, 108, 111, 117, 120
  'official' state 5–9, 16, 18, 30, 52, 183

  oppositional 44–62
  'oppressed state' 14–15
  political 56, 196–7
  populist xii, 8–9, 65, 113–14, 116–20, 122,
      145–7
  'producerist' 175
  racial 6, 30, 39, 131, 138, 143–4, 204
  radical 20, 191, 195, 207, 208–10, 211,
      233, 240
  revival 1–3
  statist 65–6, 132–43, 144
    see also identity; patriotism; socialism
Nationalist Party (Afrikaner) 217, 232–7, 240
nativism, United States 173, 175, 185
Nazism *see* National Socialism
Negrín, Juan 64, 77
Nehru, Jawaharlal 253
neo-corporatism 98
New Deal (USA) 9, 189–90
'New Labour' (Britain), and Social
    Democracy 2
Nicholls, George Heaton 220
Nin, Andreu 84
Noske, Gustav 60–1

Olssen, Erik 185
Osborne, Graeme 214

Painter, Nell 174
Palmer, Vance & Nettie 210
Paris Conference (1892) 125–7
Parkin, Andrew 211–12
parliament
  and cross-party cooperation xi, 38–9, 47,
      50, 131
  and labour movement 8, 32, 37–8, 62, 77,
      107, 199–200
  and monarchy 59
  and Social Democracy 16, 49, 59
  and socialism 125
Parti Populaire Français (PPF) 109
Parti Social Français (PSF) 109
parties, political, and cooperation xi, 9,
    38–9, 47, 50, 74–6, 129–31
Pataud, Emile 108
paternalism
  employer 8, 90, 97, 98–9
  social 106–7, 209
patriarchy
  in India 250
  in rural South Africa 224, 228
  in urban South Africa 237–8, 240

patriotism
  and anarchism 72–3
  and class 95, 115, 128–9, 137
  and colonial wars 66–7
  and education 33
  and First World War 47, 103–4, 183, 186, 205
  local 129, 136
  and nationalism xii, 18–19, 31–2, 40–1, 51, 94, 116, 138
  radical 43–4, 62–3, 167, 191
  and republicanism 69, 70, 75, 96–7, 103–4, 118
  social 43, 122, 124–30
  and Social Democracy 31–2, 40–1, 49, 62
  and socialism 31–2, 40, 43–4, 47, 94, 124–5
  working-class 94–5, 103–4, 109, 114, 128–9, 138, 165–6
PCE *see* Communist Party of Spain (PCE)
PCF *see* Communist Party of France (PCF)
peasants
  France 93, 110, 111
  India 245–6, 256
  Latvia 156, 158
  Poland 121, 123–5, 129, 135–6, 141
  Russia 146–7, 148, 157–8
  Spain 72, 87
  Ukraine 126, 157, 158, 161, 162
Perl, Feliks 134
Piłsudski, Józef 5, 128, 130, 132, 133, 134, 136–8
POF (Parti Ouvrier Français) 13, 111
Poland 121–44
  and antisemitism 27
  and class solidarity 13, 121, 123–32
  and ethnicity 23, 27
  and First World War 133, 136–7
  as 'gentry nation' 121, 123
  independence 5, 15, 122, 123–5, 127, 131, 132–3, 135, 137
  and irredentism socialism 4, 123–32
  and labour integration 138, 143
  and labour mobilisation 21, 121, 123, 137
  and liberal nationalism 4, 5, 15, 121–2
  and 'little imperialism' 15, 122, 132–43
  as multinational state 122, 124, 134–6
  as nation state 121–2, 125, 132–43
  and 'non-historic' nations 126
  as 'people's nation' 121–2, 128, 132, 137, 143–4
  as 'propertied nation' 121, 144

  as racist nation 121, 122, 138–43, 144
  revolution 1905-07 128, 131
  Second Republic 132–43
  as statist nation 122, 132–43, 144
  see also Communist Workers' Party of Poland; PPS-Left; PPS-Right; SDKPiL; Socialist Party (Poland); statism; trade unionism
Poletaev, N. G. 149
Polish Communist Party (KPP) 132
Polish United Workers' Party (PZPR) 143
Polish-Lithuanian Social Democratic Party 150
politics
  of class 78, 200
  and ethnicity 25
  of identity 3, 28–30, 235–6
  and non-working-class parties xi, 252
  and religious difference 23–4
'Popular Front' alliances 19, 77, 80, 109, 111, 114, 120
populism
  Bonapartist 106–7
  Communist 19, 162
  demagogic (Conservative) 38
  and nationalist culture xii, 8–9, 65, 90, 122, 211
  and republicanism 5, 70
  right xi, 106–10, 113–14, 116–20, 145–7, 149
Populist movement (USA) 176
postmodernism, and identity 3, 29
PPS-Former Revolutionary Faction 138
PPS-Left (Lewica) 130, 132, 141–2
PPS-Opposition 134
PPS-Right (Frakja Rewolucyjna) 122, 128, 130–1, 132–3
Predkaln, A. I. 149
Prichard, Katherine Susannah 210
Prieto, Indalecio 75–6, 77, 84 n.32
Primo de Rivera, Miguel 76, 85
Próchnik, Adam 134
progress
  economic 167
  and nationalism and socialism 10, 74, 81, 84
proletarianisation
  of Afrikaners 215, 216, 217, 231–2, 238, 239
  of black Africans 215, 218, 220–1, 224, 227, 236
  in India 247, 268

proletarianisation (*cont.*)
  of Jews 108, 127, 139–40
  in USA 168, 172, 184
proletariat and revolution 11–12, 14, 20, 84,
    226
  in Poland 124, 127
  in Spain 74–5, 78–80, 91
Proletaryat (Polish Marxist party) 124
propaganda
  class 128, 130
  nationalist 18, 21, 103, 130, 132, 141,
    206
  racial 138, 139, 140
Prost, Antoine 118
protectionism, in Australia 203, 204
Protestantism, and labour movement 7,
    23–4, 32, 97, 117
PSF *see* Parti Social Français
PSOE *see* Spanish Socialist Workers' Party
PSUC *see* Communist Party of Catalonia

race
  and criminality 116
  and nationalism 6, 9, 21, 203
  see also segregation
racialism, and Basque nationalism 90
racism
  anti-Slav 54
  and antisemitism 22, 27, 108
  biological 108
  class 58
  and ethnicity 22–4, 26–8, 51–8, 170, 217
  and First World War 48, 113
  institutionalised xii, 24–5, 27–8, 216, 225,
    234–5, 240–1
  and nationalism 6, 30, 131, 138, 143–4
  settler 17
  and socialism 17, 51–8, 63, 185
  and unemployment xi–xii, 113–14
  working-class 28, 51–8, 63, 101–2, 110–13,
    173–4, 176–7, 184, 187, 192, 213,
    234
Rahimtoola, Sir Ibrahim 255
Rai, Lala Lajpat 254
Rakovskii, Khristian 156, 158 n.23, 160
Ranger, Terence 28
Realism, Socialist, in Spain 78–9
reformism 16–21
  in Britain 8, 38, 43
  in Catalonia 83, 87, 92
  in France 95–6, 99–101, 104–5, 119
  in Germany 8, 40–1, 48–9, 59–60

and gradualism 8, 16, 182
and labour movement xi, 7, 16–20, 28,
    36–7, 38, 43
and liberal nationalism 4, 32
and middle class 85–6, 99–100
and 'official' state nationalism 8
in Poland 125
in Spain 71, 73–8, 84, 92
regenerationism 75
regionalism 1, 13
Rehbein, Franz 34
religion
  and class 54–5, 97, 247, 257, 269
  and ethnicity 22, 23–4, 54–5, 135–6,
    243–4, 264–6
  see also Church
Republican Party (USA) 174, 179
republicanism, labour 4–5, 8, 20–1
  in Britain 58
  and ethnicity 25–6
  in France 5, 7–8, 19, 94–120
  in Germany 49, 59–60
  radical 95, 167–77, 191, 239
  in South Africa 233–4, 239
  in Spain 5, 16–17, 19, 66–9, 70–1, 74–9,
    80–3, 85–6, 92, 115
  in USA 4–5, 8, 20, 164, 167–77, 191
Robert, J-L. 104–5
Rocker, Rudolf 41–2
Roediger, David 165
Roosevelt, Franklin D. 189
Rothstein, Theodore 61
royalism *see* monarchy
Russia 145–63
  and Civil War 158, 159, 161
  and First World War 151, 155
  and labour mobilisation 8–9, 147–9
  and labour movement
    and ethnicity 149
    integration 14, 145
  and militarism 19–20
  as multinational state 1, 145
  and national communism 160–3
  and overthrow of empire 8, 13–14, 145,
    147–8, 152
  and Poland 15, 122, 125–31, 132–3,
    138–9
  and populist nationalism 145–7, 162
  revolution of 1905 145–6, 147–9
  and Social Democracy 147–52
  see also Bolsheviks; Lenin, V. I.; Soviet
    Union; Stalin, Josef; trade unionism

Russian Social Democratic Labour Party
(RSDLP) 128
and ethnicity 149
and nationality 149–50, 152–3
and revolution of 195 147–8
Russian Socialist Revolutionary (SR) Party
153–4
Ruthenia, and Poland 126

Sabiani, Simon 109
Salmerón, Nicolás 71
Samuel, Raphael 3, 44
Sanacja government (Poland) 135, 142–3
Sarabhai, Anasuyabehn 260–1
sardars (jobbers; India) 249–50, 258
Scheidemann, P. 31, 37, 59
Scotland, and nationalism 2, 42, 43
SDKPiL
and ethnicity 23, 129–30, 142
and internationalism 130
and territorial autonomy 134–5
and working-class solidarity 13, 122, 128
see also Communist Workers' Party of
Poland
Second International
and internationalism 12, 39–40, 94
and socialism 2 n.1, 16, 68, 73–4, 79, 133
Second World War
in India 267–8
in South Africa 226–8, 229, 236–8, 240
segregation
in Britain 57–8
in France 113
in South Africa 25, 27, 216, 218, 220–2,
223–4, 234, 239–40
in United States 176, 178
Seguí, Salvador 84, 85, 86
self-determination
and Leninism 14, 150–1, 153–4, 159, 163
and Luxemburg 13
Sellier, Henri 105
Seme, P. 225
Sender, Ramón J. 79
SFIO *see* Socialist Party (France)
Shumskii, O. 160–1
Singh, Bhagat 265
Skoropadsky, P.P. 157
Skrypnik, Mykola 161
Smuts, Jan 231–2, 234, 236–7, 239
Snowden, Philip 47, 48, 50, 61
Social Democracy
and gradualism 16

and internationalism 1, 17–18
and left-wing nationalism 30
and liberal nationalism 13, 193
and national identity 1, 17, 28, 42
and patriotism 31–2, 40–1, 49
and reformism 16, 17
spread 2
Social Democracy of the Kingdom of
Poland and Lithuania (SDKPiL) *see*
SDKPiL
Social Democratic Party (Austro-Hungary),
and ethnicity 22–3
Social Democratic Party (Germany)
and antisemitism 53
and Erfurt Programme 39, 125
and ethnic minorities 51–2, 58, 63, 152
foundation 39–40
and France 94
and imperialism 60–1
and internationalism 39–42, 62
and the judiciary 36
and Marxism 39–40, 59
and militarism 7, 34–5, 44–5, 49
and monarchy 59–60, 63
and nationalism 21, 49
and Nazism 49
parliamentary party 37, 38
and racism 54
and republicanism 49, 59–60
and skilled labour 20
and the state 7, 8, 13, 16, 32–3, 40–1,
48–9, 62
and support for war 18, 47–8, 63
socialisation, and South African youth
associations 224, 228–30, 241
socialism
and colonialism 18
and education 33
and ethnicity 22–3, 26, 235, 237–8
evolutionary 125
and internationalism 1, 2, 6, 12–14, 17–18,
19–20, 185–6, 214
and liberal nationalism 5, 10, 13, 91
and the nation state 10–11, 40–1, 43,
242
national 107
and nationalism 1–2, 9–21, 49, 94, 122,
124–5, 129–30, 233, 242–3
and patriotism 31–2, 40, 43–4, 47, 94,
124–5
and racism 17, 51–8, 63, 185, 235
and war 18, 39–41, 46–7, 63

socialism (*cont.*)
  see also Communism; Marxism; reformism;
    Social Democracy; *and individual*
    Socialist Parties
Socialist Party (France; SFIO)
  and immigration 114, 115
  and imperialism 101
  and internationalism 94, 111
  and nationalism 16, 21, 94, 98, 109, 119
  and reformism 2, 95–6
  and support for war 18, 95, 105
Socialist Party (Italy) 111
Socialist Party (Poland; PPS)
  and antisemitism 130, 132, 138, 141–3
  and Communist Party 133
  and ethnicity 23, 52, 129–31, 142
  and internationalism 13, 124, 128
  and liberal nationalism 5, 122
  and 'little Entente' states 133–5
  and national integration 138
  and national liberation 15, 52, 124, 126–7
  and state-centrism 134–7, 142
  see also PPS-Left; PPS-Right
Socialist Party (Spain) *see* Spanish Socialist
    Workers' Party
Socialist Party (USA) 176, 184–6
Socialist Union of Catalonia (USC) 84
Solidaritat Catalana campaign 82–3
solidarity
  class 12–13, 52, 55–7, 68, 91, 111, 121,
    126–31, 140–1, 172–3, 185–6, 200
  ethnic 26, 224
  national 46, 48, 98, 108, 121, 123, 130–1
  and race 55–7, 101, 174
Sota, Ramón de la 90
South Africa 215–41
  and Afrikaner identity 215–16, 217, 230–8
  and chieftaincy 28, 218–22, 223–4, 239,
    240
  and First World War 232, 233–4
  and institutionalised racism xi, 9, 24–5,
    27–8, 216, 217, 225, 234–5, 240–1
  and labour integration 27–8, 215, 233, 239
  and liberal nationalism 5
  and migrant labour 25, 27–8, 215–17, 221,
    222–8, 230, 237, 238–41
  and mobilisation
    industrial labour 222–8, 230–8, 239, 241
    rural labour 217–22, 226, 228–30, 240
  and 'Native Republic' policy 225–6
  and Rand Revolt 225, 234, 239
  see also Boer War; trade unionism

South Africa Party 231–2, 234, 236
Soviet Union
  and federation 152–8, 160–1
  and 'great state' nationalism 14, 162
  and labour integration 14
  and Poland 132–4, 136–7
  and South Africa 225, 227
Soviet-Polish War (1920/21) 21, 132, 134,
    137, 138
Spain
  Civil War 76–7, 80, 88, 91–2
  and colonial wars 19, 66–71, 74, 101
  and fascism 77, 80
  and 'great state' nationalism 13
  and labour mobilisation 8–9, 65, 74, 77, 91
  and labour movement
    and ethnicity 80–91
    integration 70, 75–8, 81, 92
    and nationalism 16–17, 69–80
  and liberal nationalism 8–9, 64–6, 68,
    73–7, 84, 91–2
  and migrant labour 80, 82, 87–8
  and militarism 65, 70–1
  and monarchy 65, 67, 71, 75
  as multinational state 2, 64
  as nation state 64, 68, 91–2
  and Popular Front 80
  and proletarian revolution 74–5, 78–80,
    91
  Restoration 8, 64–9, 77
  Second Republic 18–19, 71, 75–8, 85–7,
    89–90, 92
  see also anarchism; Basque nationalism;
    Catalanism; middle classes;
    republicanism; Spanish Socialist
    Workers' Party; trade unionism
Spanish Socialist Workers' Party (PSOE)
  and Basque nationalism 89–90
  and Catalan nationalism 81, 84, 91
  and Civil War 76–7, 91–2
  and colonial wars 68–9, 71
  and internationalism 73–4
  and nationalism 13, 21, 64, 77
  and reformism 71, 73–8, 84, 92
  and republicans 74–9, 85, 92
  and socialist culture 72–3, 76, 81
  and youth movement 78–9
Spanish-American war 1898 19, 66–7, 69, 178
SPD *see* Social Democratic Party (Germany)
Stalin, Josef
  and Lenin 158–60, 161
  and nationality 14, 30, 150–2, 154, 161–3

Stampfer, Friedrich 47, 49
state
  and ethnicity 23
  and labour movement xi, 6–7, 15–16,
    188–91, 195, 197, 199
  multinational 1, 2, 42, 145
  see also nation state; welfare state
statism *see* Poland, as statist nation
stereotypes
  ethnic/racial 16, 22, 25, 88, 108, 138
  and immigrant/migrant labour 23, 25, 52,
    56, 173, 223
Sternhell, Z. 107–8
Stolypin, Peter 147
strikes *see* militancy, labour
Stuchka, P. 152–3, 155–6
suffrage
  in Australia 195, 197
  in France 95, 106, 110, 119
  in Spain 9, 65
  in USA 167, 176
Sutcliffe, J. T. 199
swadeshi movement, Bengal 257
symbolism, national 9, 19, 21
  in Australia 213
  in France 95, 119–20
  in Germany 49
  in Poland 129
  in Spain 91
syndicalism
  in Britain 38
  in France 85, 96, 97–8, 103–6, 108–9, 110,
    117, 119
  in Spain 84, 86
  in USA 182–3, 185

Tabili, Laura 53
Tambo, Oliver 230
Tawney, R. H. 43
Third International, and Societ federations
  154
Thomas, Albert 119
Thomas, J. H. ('Jimmy') 50, 59, 61
Thompson, E. P. 29, 117
Tilak, Bal Gangadhar 254, 258, 264
Tillett, Ben 55
trade unionism
  Australian 197–200, 202, 204, 206–7, 208,
    210, 212–13
  Basque 89–90
  British 36–7, 39, 53, 55–6, 58, 61, 179, 188
  Catalan 84–8

and Catholicism 33, 89
  French 19, 94, 97–9, 101, 103, 105, 108–9,
    111, 113–15, 119
  German 37, 39, 49, 52–3, 56, 117
  and immigrants 27
  Indian 256–7, 260–3, 265–8
  Polish 127, 129–32, 137–8, 139
  and racism 26, 52–3, 234
  Russian 145–6
  South African 24, 217, 218–21, 225–30,
    231, 233–40
  Spanish 19, 71, 74, 76, 77, 78–9, 82, 92
  United States 5, 16, 20, 27, 168–70, 174–6,
    179, 182–8, 189–90
  see also Bund
Trapido, Stanley 235

Ukraine
  and Poland 15, 122, 125–6, 132, 134–5
  and revolution of 1905 147, 148–9
  and Soviet Russia 153–5, 156–8, 159–62
Ukrainian Socialist Revolutionary (SRs)
    Party 153–4, 157, 158, 160–1
Ulmanis, Karlis 156
unemployment
  and labour militancy 79–80, 188–9, 210
  and nationalism xi–xii, 79, 87, 113–14,
    206, 233
Union of the Russian People (URP) 8–9,
    145–7, 149, 162
United Party of South Africa 236–7
United States 164–92
  Antidraft Riots (1863) 174
  and Civil War 167–8
  and class identity 166, 167–8
  and ethnicity 169, 174–6, 185, 187, 190–1
  and exceptionalism 164, 166, 188–91, 192
  and First World War 164, 180–1, 182–3,
    185–7
  and immigrant workers 20, 24–7, 165,
    169–87, 190–1, 192
  and imperialism 177, 178–9, 183, 185
  and Irish workers 24, 27, 173, 175
  and labour integration 27, 189–90
  and labour mobilisation 175–6
  and labour radicalism 188–91
  and labour republicanism 4–5, 8, 20, 164,
    167–77, 191
  and liberal nationalism 4, 166
  and 'official state' nationalism 16, 183
  and racism 28, 170, 173–4, 176–7, 184,
    185, 187, 192

United States (*cont.*)
  and radical nationalism 191
  and working-class conservatism 20, 177–88
  see also Afro-Americans; American
      Federation of Labor; Congress of
      Industrial Organisations;
      Spanish–American war; trade
      unionism
urbanisation
  in Australia 203
  in South Africa 25, 216, 226, 230–1, 240
URP *see* Union of the Russian People
USC (Catalonia) 86
utopia, in socialism and nationalism 11, 94

Vaillant-Couturier, Paul 94
Valois, George 109
Van der Linden, Marcel 8
Victorian Socialist Party 214
Vincent, Stephen 118

Wagner Act of 1935 (USA) 190
Wales, and nationalism 2, 42, 43
war
  and the nation state 205–8
  and socialism 18, 39–41, 46–7, 63
Ward, Russel 213
Waryński, Ludwik 124, 127
Webb, Sidney & Beatrice 17
welfare state
  in Australia 201, 204
  in Britain and Germany 32, 36–7, 39, 41,
      62, 99
  and ethnicity 23
  in France 97–9, 116, 119
  and reformism 20
  in USA 8, 188
Wels, Otto 49
Wendel, François 115
Western Europe, regionalism and
      globalisation 1–2
Wheatley, John 54
Wilentz, Sean 168
Wilhelm II, Kaiser 59
Wilson, F. 239
Wilson, Havelock 53
Wilson, Woodrow 182–3
Winnig, August 35

women
  and trade unionism 170, 175–6, 184–5,
      190, 237–8, 240
  and worker chauvinism 105–6, 117
working class
  and Catholicism 32–3, 58
  and conservatism 177–88
  construction 164–6
  differentiation 20–1, 27, 79, 139–40, 165,
      176, 184, 212, 267
  and ethnic nationalism 232
  and immigration 26, 63, 107, 170–2,
      179–80
  and imperialism 21, 69–71, 138
  and internationalism 13
  and labourism 211
  and liberal nationalism 5, 7, 10
  marginalisation 4, 20, 21, 65, 99, 251
  and militarism 18, 34–5, 44–5
  and monarchy 58–60, 63
  and the nation state 5–6, 14, 40–1, 50–1,
      162, 242–5, 247, 266–7
  and neo-nationalism 2
  and patriotism 94–6, 103–4, 109, 128
  and radical nationalism 210
  and socialism 12, 242–3
  see also class; culture; First World War;
      identity; labour movement;
      proletarianisation; proletariat; racism;
      socialism; solidarity
workplace
  and citizenship rights 191
  and class consciousness 222–8, 230–8,
      259–60, 269
  and nationalism xi, 222, 231, 233, 266
  and segregation 57–8

xenophobia
  and immigration 23, 93, 110–14
  working-class 52, 53–7, 105, 118
Xuma, A. 229

Yearley, Clifton K. 170
Yvetot, Georges 117

Zeligowski, Lucjan 134
Zionism, socialist 53, 131, 143
Zubatov, S. 145